gap
years
for
GROWN
UPS

Susan Griffith

VACATION WORK
PUBLICATIONS

DISCLAIMER

The opinions expressed in the case studies set in this style of box are entirely those of the featured organisation.

While every effort has been made to ensure that the information contained in this book was accurate at the time of going to press, some details are bound to change within the lifetime of this edition. If you do take a gap year or come across something which might be of interest to readers of the next edition, please write to Susan Griffith c/o Crimson Publishing, Westminster House, Kew Road, Richmond, Surrey TW9 2ND, or email her at info@crimsonpublishing.co.uk. Substantial contributions will be rewarded with a free copy of the next edition, or any other Crimson title (see inside back cover).

Gap Years for Grown-ups
This fourth edition first published in Great Britain 2011 by Vacation Work, an imprint of Crimson Publishing, Westminster House, Kew Road, Richmond, Surrey TW9 2ND

© Crimson Publishing 2011

The right of Susan Griffith to be identified as the author of this work has been asserted by her in accordance with the Copyright, Designs and Patents Act, 1988.

First published 2004. Revised in 2006 and 2008.

A catalogue record for this book is available from the British Library.

ISBN 978 1 85458 634 6

Typeset by Refinecatch Ltd, Bungay, Suffolk
Printed and bound in the UK by Ashford Colour Press, Gosport, Hants

GAP YEAR THAILAND
**'I developed skills that I never knew I was capable of...
I went to Thailand seeking an experience that would
enrich my career. What I got was so much more than that.'**

To get a broad experience I chose to be placed in two schools, helping teach English, particularly spoken English; that was perfect for my requirements and helped me get more out of the venture.

It was certainly the challenge that I had been hoping for! I always believe you learn the most when you're out of your comfort zone and getting your teeth into a challenge. Looking back, my time in Thailand made me realise that I developed skills I never knew I was capable of and this has aided my confidence and belief of what I can achieve at home.

In addition to the rewarding work-based programme, my time outside the classroom was equally compelling. The teachers in both the schools I taught at were wonderful to me. So kind and so friendly and really interested in what my life was like in the UK. In fact, during a national holiday the teachers took me to Koh Samet island. It was great to feel included as part of the team as ten of us stayed on the island to see the 'fire-dancers' on the beach at night and to take an early morning swim in the ocean. I'm no stranger to travelling, but however much I love the 'backpacker' lifestyle, my time spent teaching in Thailand was just so much more rewarding.

Now I'm back home, it's not the end of the experience. Not only do I have all the precious memories, gifts and photos but I've made friends on the other side of the world and I have those new-found skills that I can use every day. A big thank you to the Gap Year Thailand team for helping to make this trip a reality!

Kimberley White

CONTENTS

GAP YEARS FOR GROWN-UPS

CONTENTS

PREFACE

The present economic crisis is bound to be a factor in anyone's decision to take time out. In the corporate world, many companies have been handing out unpaid leave while business is slow, and more and more employers are introducing a sabbatical policy. Redundancy is often a prompt for people going off travelling or volunteering abroad. Far more people now work from home and on contract, and if the gaps between contracts get longer during a recession, this is the obvious time for them to carry through a long-held wish to take a break from 'real life'.

Even though dashing off to a distant corner of the world on a gap year might seem irresponsible in these troubled times, it could be exactly the right approach to the problem of job stasis and defeated morale. Joining a project, improving a language or taking an unpaid internship abroad can pep up a CV in lots of ways.

The cost may be far less than you imagine, especially if you are in a position to rent out a property at home. In a remarkable way, the cost of travel has been coming down in real terms for at least two decades. To give one tiny example: just this week I booked a coach trip from Montreal to Toronto for CAN$17. For fun I looked up the price in an old guidebook on my shelf from 1997 in which the price quoted for the same journey was CAN$66. The explosion of no-frills airlines and the intense competition among travel providers around the globe have together resulted in a welcome democratisation of travel. Some books and documentaries about gap years have been guilty of focusing on individuals, couples or families with seemingly unlimited means. But in writing the first and subsequent three editions of *Gap Years for Grown-ups*, I have been drawn to the stories of ordinary wage-earners who have managed to take some months away from their jobs to do something amazing. This book contains their inspirational stories.

Last year saw the film *Eat Pray Love* bring one woman's fantasy gap year to the big screen. Although most people's extended travels do not involve that much pizza, meditation or love, the film (based on a true account by Elizabeth Gilbert) captured a strand of 21st century longing that this book tries to address more realistically.

No longer is it the unique privilege of the young to be able to contemplate taking time off to travel in search of adventure. The rising popularity among enterprising and energetic grown-ups from all backgrounds of temporarily leaving it all behind, has prompted a corresponding increase in the number of programmes and schemes offered by specialist companies. The path leading to exciting and memorable gap year experiences, whether teaching in Vietnam, learning to tango in Buenos Aires, or monitoring the health of reefs in Madagascar, may be smoother than you think.

This book aims to canvas the possibilities as comprehensively as possible, and covers a wealth of both mainstream and obscure options. An adventure abroad can equip you to return to your workaday life with a smile on your face and a song in your heart. In addition to providing practical and realistic advice about where and how to spend your gap year, these 390 pages aim to spark the imagination of anyone trying to decide whether or not to take time out.

Susan Griffith
Cambridge
April 2011

ACKNOWLEDGEMENTS

This fourth edition of *Gap Years for Grown-ups* owes a substantial debt to all the kind folk (some of them personal friends – thank you Ambrose and Leah) who have told me how they finally came to bite the bullet and head off into the unknown. I never get tired of meeting and hearing from those intrepid (and sometimes not-so-intrepid) grown-ups who have set the workaday world to one side long enough to explore places and test dreams.

This new revised edition would not have been possible without the help and inspiration of grown-ups from all walks of life, whose stories I have gathered since the last edition was published in 2008. My enthusiastic informants include an auxiliary nurse, a senior vice-president of a private bank, a freelance editor, and a barman. All have generously shared their experiences and insights, which have been distilled into the pages that follow.

I would like to thank Miranda Crowhurst for her constructive input into Part 8: Taking the Family. I am also grateful to the many directors and PR staff of the specialist year out organisations who patiently rooted round in their client files to put me in touch with grown-ups who have had some amazing experiences on their various gap years.

DRAMATIS PERSONAE

All of these individuals, couples, and families have generously shared their memories, insights, and pearls of travelling and volunteering wisdom over the past few years since the last edition of this book was researched and published in 2008. Case studies of these and other enterprising grown-ups are dotted throughout the book.

Hannah Adcock is a freelance writer and events organiser from Edinburgh. After organising the third annual West Port Book Festival in June 2010, Hannah and her husband Andrew were free to go travelling. They divided their time between trekking in Ladakh (where they had to make a sudden escape because of the devastating floods) and a scuba diving course on an idyllic island in Indonesia. Their next destination was Cairo to study Arabic and then Dahab on the Red Sea as a cheap and sunny place to live while freelance editing, at least until February 2011, when the uprising that overthrew Mubarak resulted in the temporary closing down of internet access. At last report, they had returned, working wilh clients who don't mind if she is 'in Edinburgh, Cairo or on the moon, provided I have internet'.

Christine and Mike Benson first thought of travelling round the world for their honeymoon but the cost of the wedding soon quashed that hope. Undaunted, they worked, saved, and planned and set off in January 2010 for an amazing ten-month trip round the world, on which they tried to stick to a budget of $60 a day. Despite the name of their blog (www.checking offeverywhere.com), many countries remain to be visited.

Annalisa Winge Bicknell is 43, half-British and half-Norwegian, and was enjoying a high-flying international career in finance when she negotiated unpaid leave. She joined a series of environmental projects through Earthwatch in France, China, Mongolia, and arctic Canada, before returning to London to find that because of the recession her employers no longer had a suitable job for her. Undaunted, she has filled her life since with a series of satisfying ventures including a stint of volunteering in the Earthwatch office in Boston, MA.

Anna Bisson was reeling from a dreadful discovery. Her husband of 33 years was living a parallel life with a 23-year-old Thai partner who was also expecting his baby. She picked herself up and joined a volunteering scheme at an orphanage in Mexico, where for the first time in her life she was free to make her own choices and join in the social life of the other volunteers without deferring to her spouse.

Sara Buck gave herself an unusual 50th birthday present, from which her friends benefitted as well. She and four friends stuffed their luggage with wax crayons, colouring books, and chilli flakes and headed for Kenya. They gave the crayons and colouring books to the children in the project arranged through Adventure Alternative, and they used the chilli to flavour the local food. Although she realises that their input in helping to build schools was a drop in the ocean, she thought it did demonstrate to local people what was possible with teamwork. Kenya is now under her skin and she intends to return.

Laura Clarke was enjoying a glamorous job with a leading restaurant group in London but was always hankering after the Alps. On a ski holiday she met Mike, who had been made redundant from his job in logistics and was now working the season in a ski resort. They fell in love and Laura happily ditched the commute to move to La Rosière in France, where she and Mike (now her husband) run a successful catered chalet company, SnowCrazy Ltd, and a chalet host cookery course.

Nicole and Shane Collins were running a national wholesale distribution company in Queensland when they, like so many parents, wanted to spend more time with their children before adolescence. Their first thought was to travel all around Australia in a caravan, but their caravan lost its wheels and gained a keel. Shane had sailed for many years and Nicole was happy to try to catch up by taking an RYA competent crew and day skipper course before they set off on their yacht *Grace* to sail from Sweden to New Zealand with Neisha (9), Jack (7) and Jessica (7).

Cath Cooper was the driving force in the South African gap year she and her husband Steve planned. They spent seven glorious months in South Africa, part travelling, part volunteering, before completing their year out to backpack around Australia and New Zealand. Returning to their home near Doncaster and the depths of the recession, they were both lucky to find work before Cath embarked on an entirely new direction: to retrain as an occupational therapist.

Barbara Darragh first went to Thailand to volunteer just after the tsunami. Knowing that she wanted to return for a longer period, she enlisted in a course in Chiang Mai to qualify as a teacher of English as a foreign language. She offered her new-found expertise to a local school and stayed on for six months, making lots of Thai friends and loving the job.

Julie Fairweather works as a health care assistant in a busy Accident and Emergency Department in Dundee. As her 40th birthday loomed, she began to long for an extended trip to Africa, thinking it was now or never. Through Amanzi Travel, she fulfilled a childhood dream of working with cheetahs and other wildlife at a rescue centre in Namibia.

Sue Wrenn Fenton lives in a village near Inverness with her husband and dog. Like all parents, she took a keen interest when her daughter Mairi was planning her gap year travels to Fiji and India, and asked if she could join her on the final leg. Together they volunteered at an orphanage in Kathmandu before trekking in Annapurna, and visiting Chitwan National Park. All of these experiences served to strengthen the mother–daughter bond, and completely justified the horrendous backlog of work Sue returned to at the environmental magazine she edits on a self-employed basis.

Minna Graber had fallen under the spell of Romania when she celebrated the New Year there many years ago, and wanted to find a way to return. Through a specialist volunteer teacher placement charity, SOL (www.sol.org.uk), she left her music teaching job in the East End of London to teach English in a top school in Bucharest. As well as enjoying her job because the students are a delight to teach, she has a very nice lifestyle despite earning a meagre wage. She takes private lessons in Romanian, goes to the best concerts, attends martial arts classes, sings in a choir, and goes mountain climbing with the local club.

Ricky Grice was a self-employed IT and management consultant in London, whose business was very successful throughout his 20s, but seemed to have hit the doldrums in 2009/10. He decided to head off to the tropical coastal city of Mombasa in east Africa, to use his IT skills in a charity that uses theatre to deliver life-saving information about HIV/AIDS in the most under-served areas in Kenya.

Jenny Hickman from Australia received a generous redundancy package after working for ten years in a stressful and unrewarding job. In her 50s, she felt that she both needed and deserved a break from the 'real world'. A friend who had recently been travelling in Africa told her about an interesting education project in Uganda. Jenny emailed Soft Power Education who replied the next day, and she went with the flow, signing up herself and her 17-year-old nephew to spend some weeks attached to the project. She found it all so enjoyable and inter-esting that she took a TEFL course back at home in preparation for returning to Uganda the next year for a stay of nearly five months.

Barry Irvine was bored with his telecoms job at the same time that his marriage was collaps-ing. He stuck a tentative toe into the world of travelling by spending six weeks volunteering at a lion sanctuary in Zimbabwe, which he enjoyed so much that when he returned home to Amsterdam in October, he couldn't really imagine going back to work. He spent the next year travelling the length and breadth of the Americas, and at the time of writing is planning to spend months exploring Asia and the Antipodes.

Bradwell Jackson gave up his job as a youth counsellor in the United States to work and travel the world at whim. So far he has taught English in Mexico, Mauritania, China, and plans to move on possibly to Taiwan in 2011.

Peter Kenyon took long service leave from his real job as Professor of Economic Policy at Curtin University of Technology in Perth, Australia, to pursue a long-held dream of working in the kitchen at the Loose Box, one of Perth's premier fine dining restaurants. His cooking career continued when he cooked for an International Classical Music Festival in Tuscany two years running.

Ann Knight is a 63-year-old grandmother who works as a teaching assistant at a special school, and rides horses as her main hobby. Instead of taking her usual riding holiday in the summer of 2010, she joined a programme through Amanzi to volunteer at a wildlife rescue centre in Namibia.

Lisa Lubin is an Emmy award-winning television writer/producer with more than 15 years' experience. Three years ago she quit her job to take a sabbatical, which turned into more than three years of travelling and working her way around the world. She wrote an entertaining blog (www.LLworldtour.com), and is now putting together a portfolio career largely based on her travels.

Kath McGuire decided to go travelling when she was 33 and joined a volunteer teaching programme in Sri Lanka through VESL (Volunteers for Educational Support and Learning). After spending all of 2009 in the subcontinent, she returned home to England to do some part-time maths teaching and streamlining spreadsheets and databases in offices in order to save enough to return – this time travelling overland via Poland, Russia, Kazakhstan, China, Tibet, Nepal, and India.

Ann McLeod from Grantown-on-Spey worked from 8am till 4pm every day assisting at a church-run orphanage and school in Ghana. She looked after a group of toddlers in a daycare situation: feeding them, changing them (with just a bucket of cold water!), playing with them, singing nursery rhymes and teaching simple counting games. She greatly enjoyed it though had to admit it was tiring, and made her realise that perhaps at 55 she was a little old for this type of work.

Ambrose Marsh and **Leah Norgrove** from Victoria, Canada, had been great travellers in their youth. With their sons Griffin (13) and Simon (10), they took a whole year away. Since they are both doctors, they were in the fortunate position of being able to work constructively at a hospital in Tanzania, trying to train local staff to carry on work in palliative care. Meanwhile, the boys attended a local primary school in Muheza for six months and learned some Swahili. Leaving Africa, they were reunited with their bicycles – including a tandem which they shipped to Istanbul – and spent the spring months pedalling nearly 4000km from Thrace to Tallinn, crossing 13 countries.

Jerry Melinn left school at 16, got a business degree at 46, took early retirement at 56 and then decided, with the approval of his family, to teach English in Greece. He gained a TEFL certificate in Corinth, and quite easily got a job at a flourishing private English language institute in Athens. His wife considers his Athens flat (provided by the school) to be her holiday home and spends a lot of time there. In fact, Jerry reckons he spends more time with his wife now than when he was living at home and working in the telecommunications industry.

Steph Morrison volunteered with Gap Year Thailand in 2010/11, which caters to career-breakers as well as gap year students. Realising that some prospective volunteers would worry about the initial financial outlay to join a volunteer scheme, she wrote to say that it is possible to earn some pocket money by doing some supplementary English teaching. After only three weeks in Thailand, Steph had several private students who wanted tutoring.

Chris Morvan had made a comfortable living from freelance writing for two decades, until the recession saw business fall away. Discouraged by the gloomy employment picture in the UK, he moved to the country of his new partner: Venezuela. Even before he had finished an online TEFL course, he had been offered three teaching jobs in Caracas.

Mark Nash worked as a bicycle courier by day and a restaurant barman by night to save enough to join a group of 11, who took six months off from their respective jobs to cycle from Cambridge to Kenya (www.downrightkenya.org). Together they raised more than £60,000 to help build a new school in rural Kenya through the British charity Harambee Schools Kenya. Mark is home now, working as manager at the courier company, teaching kids on the government's Bikeability scheme, and planning to return to Kenya soon to check out progress on the new school.

Kate Nelson demonstrates the old proverb 'Physician heal thyself'. After a stressful corporate career, she trained as a life coach and set up a business on the side, specialising in helping people to plan their career breaks and return to work afterwards. She decided the time had come to treat herself to her own career break and went off volunteering and travelling in South Africa, where she met a man and stayed on. Together they set up a guest farm and adventure trails business. Kate says that they might even be in a position to welcome others taking a career break.

Alexandra Neuman, 50, took a blank exercise book, labelled it 'My Year of Living in Italy', decorated the cover with beautiful Italian scenes and began planning her gap year from journalism, alongside her husband John, also about 50. While maintaining their mortgage in Sydney, they moved to Bergamo – an old hilltop town about an hour out of Milan. After 11 months they re-alised that one year was just not long enough, so they re-evaluated their finances to see if they could stay longer, which meant Alex needed to find work. The only work available in addition to her freelance writing was teaching English, and she soon landed a job with a local language school.

Peter Ngufor is a 34-year-old computer programmer from London who worked on the South African Wild Coast Schools Computer Literacy project through Kaya Volunteers in summer 2010. He found it thoroughly refreshing to spend time with such different people: both the in-ternational volunteers from all walks of life, and the locals in Chintsa (a small beautiful town on the coast near East London) who were very friendly and made Peter feel like part of the com-munity. Going outside for a 15-minute break between lessons and seeing giraffes, zebras, and ostriches wandering past was a completely surreal experience for him. He is already saving for a return visit and hoping to persuade his company to donate a satellite computer to the project.

Helen Norton wanted to change the direction of her career and move away from A&E nursing into aid agency work. She decided a good way to further her ambition was to volunteer as a medic on a Raleigh expedition. While strengthening her CV she had some amazingly memo-rable moments, such as when they walked through a cloud of butterflies and all the different colours lit up the forest. Everybody froze to enjoy this *Avatar* moment.

Kate Owen took voluntary redundancy after working in a law firm that specialised in litigation and advocacy. She wanted to return to Raleigh, this time as a volunteer expedition manager. She came to see that when you are trekking through the jungle with a dozen other people, feel-ing cold, wet, hungry, and aching, you have to find a way to meet your objective, in the same way as when you are leading a due diligence exercise and 12 hours before exchange the other side drops 300 documents on you.

Reza Pakravan, once a professional basketball player in his native Iran, works as a market security and rating analyst in London's insurance industry. Last year he took a mini-gap in Madagascar working for NGO Azafady in a school building project. He found it liberating to live in a tent, eat rice and beans every day, and be part of an amazing project. He then decided that his gaps from work would be more productive for the charity if he spent them fundraising. So far he has raised nearly £40,000 for Azafady by cycling across the Nepalese Himalayas, and he is now training hard for a record-breaking cycle ride across the Sahara in 2011, with a fundraising target of £20,000.

Dev Parikh was struggling with a small law practice in Indianapolis and was generally fed up with life. He took himself off to Costa Rica to study Spanish with a view to helping Spanish clients at home. When the school where he was studying asked him to stay and teach, he gladly accepted and is still in Costa Rica, about to get married and have a child.

Fiona Passey had just obtained her MBA and had a high-level banking job before deciding to spend three months teaching in India with VESL. Her husband was totally supportive and is determined to accompany her next time.

Mark Perriton was managing director of a successful company in East Anglia and knew that he wanted to be a long way away from his office to celebrate his 50th birthday. A keen sportsman and cyclist, he decided to follow his ambition to take a year out to cycle round the world – starting in Alaska in September 2010. His younger son joined him for part of the ride through British Columbia, his brother joined him in Chile, and his supportive wife met up with him in Auckland for Christmas.

Deanne (Dini) Peterson was stuck in a rut, including with her vacations, which had always been family-oriented and/or resort style, with room service, umbrella drinks, amusement parks, cruise ships, and guided tours. When her two sons outgrew the family holiday, Dini decided to mount a revolt against having turned 40 and go off to volunteer at a Street Kids Project in Knysna, join a marine conservation project in Cape Town and go on a safari in Africa, all organised through Travellers Worldwide. Working with orphans and street kids, diving with great white sharks, sky-diving, and zip-lining through jungles have given her a new lease of life.

Rosie Prebble retired at 60 from her job as a learning support assistant in a comprehensive school, never having flown in her life before. Idly Googling one day, the image of Romanian orphans popped into her head from the television reports after the fall of Ceausescu, and before she knew it she had booked a volunteer placement through Projects Abroad.

David Rutter did not want to slide into a comfortable retirement from teaching, and became a volunteer project manager on a Raleigh expedition in India, which changed his views about many things. He learned many improvised building 'tricks' from the Indian masons, who built a superb building with very few tools. He learned that the age difference didn't matter to young people on the expedition, and he saw clearly that people were happiest when they had done something they hadn't expected to be able to do.

Phil Tomkins qualified as a primary teacher late in life, but did not get on with the profession nor with the politics and climate of his native England all that well. In his early 40s he obtained an English teaching certificate in Corinth and is now teaching enthusiastic students on the little Cycladic island of Kea.

Madeleine Wheare had recently resigned from a very time-consuming and poorly paid semi-volunteer job that had kept her at home in Oxfordshire for six consecutive years between September and April. She wanted to have a chance to use her talents to be useful to society, as well as wanting to be somewhere warm during the winter months. She stumbled across Global Volunteer Projects on the web, and they seemed to have a credible presence in India – which is where she wanted to go. Just before Christmas she set off to volunteer with a Catholic charity working with impoverished fishing communities in the coastal region of Trivandrum, South India.

INTRODUCTION

The concept of the gap year is firmly embedded in the consciousness of school leavers, and increasingly with grown-ups too. The market is booming, as evidenced by the student travel agency STA launching a sister agency Bridge the World for the over 50s in 2010. Statistics in this area are fiendishly difficult to establish but, according to research published in a report 'Adult Gap Years (International)', produced by the market analyst company Mintel, an estimated 90,000 working-age Britons take career breaks every year – compared with 230,000 young people, and 200,000 retirees aged 55+.

The astronomical increases to student fees announced in 2010 will undoubtedly discourage some school leavers, at least in the next year, from taking a year out, in order to get into higher education before the fees increase. But the number of grown-up gap years being taken continues to escalate. Part of the explanation is not a particularly happy one: some of these gap years have arisen in the wake of redundancy – voluntary or otherwise. The mess in which the British economy finds itself has had a massive impact on employment. A report published last year by www.employeebenefits.co.uk maintained that 2% of all UK workers had been offered a semi-paid sabbatical, while 6% had been offered an unpaid sabbatical since the recession began. In the modern era of flexible employment practices, many bosses struggling to survive the recession turned to sabbaticals instead of redundancies as a way to cut costs, while keeping their skilled workers on hand for a time when the economy looks up. Similarly, self-employed people have seen contracts cancelled and clients withdrawing business in these fiscally trying times.

What better time to consider taking an extended period of time to travel, volunteer, or pursue other interests? Of course the old motivations are still present in abundance: wanderlust, the need to escape from stress and burn-out, interest in volunteering in less privileged parts of the world, fear of turning middle-aged before one's time, and so on. It seems that more and more people in the working world are taking off on shorter and longer gap years.The concept of a break is central to the natural world. We spend a third of our lives sleeping at night to rejuvenate ourselves for the day, so why then should it be considered self-indulgent or lazy to take a chunk of time out of our working lives to pursue a different agenda? When work becomes onerous, stressful or dull, and begins to swamp other interests, it might be time to reclaim our lives by taking a break.

GAP YEARS FOR GROWN-UPS
A gap year can embrace anything from a period of rest and relaxation to an opportunity for reassessing goals and reconnecting with our real values. For some, it is simply a case of itchy feet; for others it is a chance to test an alternative vocation or spend time with loved ones. Taking stock periodically allows us to look beyond the details to the bigger picture. The sound of the ticking clock can be silenced when pursuing adventures, and worries about work, children, and everything else that have become second nature can be left behind. The stories of the individuals who have

shared their experiences during the research for this book illustrate how liberating and important a gap year can be.

The gap year between leaving school and attending higher education is now a well-established transition between childhood dependence and adult maturity. A new trend is for the parents of these teenagers and their contemporaries to follow suit. A desire to trek in distant mountain ranges, volunteer in an African village, or take a cookery course in Italy is not unique to youth.

In response to the sometimes overwhelming demands of our jobs and the news that we may be expected to work until well past the current retirement age, the notion of a career break is becoming more attractive. One more week dealing with an awkward line manager or waking in the night with your head spinning with office tasks and politics may force your hand. Setting a boundary between the personal and the professional is essential for maintaining good mental health.

In these difficult economic times, an increasing number of working people and professionals are having a gap year thrust upon them. Everyone knows someone who has been made redundant since the recession or who is in fear of redundancy, and with massive cuts to the public sector ahead, the numbers will only increase. In these troubled times, the idea of flitting off to a distant corner of the world on a gap year might sound irresponsible. On the contrary, it could be exactly the right approach to riding out the recession and coping with the disillusionment engendered by the banking crisis. The *Independent* published an article in July 2010 called 'Why an extended break can be a good career move'. Joining a project or taking an unpaid internship abroad on a gap year can pep up a CV in lots of ways – perhaps in improving your facility in a foreign language, or in providing opportunities to develop new practical skills, eg in fields like teaching, building, and conservation. It can also be wonderful for morale. **Chris Morvan** had been a professional writer for 20 years – journalism, advertising, PR, etc – but when the recession hit a couple of years ago his work dried up. This is how he coped:

I'm not actually on a gap year, but sometimes it feels like it. I'm living in Venezuela, baking in the streets of Caracas, and swimming in the Caribbean Sea even in the cooler months here, rather than shivering in the UK. I applied for literally hundreds of jobs by the miracle of the internet and got nowhere. I put it down mainly to my age – I'm in my 50s and that's not a fashionable age. Then I met a Venezuelan woman through a dating website and we got married. With no prospects in the UK we examined my options and decided on taking an online course in Teaching English as a Foreign Language (TEFL). There are lots to choose from and I went for a 100-hour course with one-to-one tuition. This consisted of 20 hours of 'grammar awareness', 60 hours about the science of teaching, and smaller modules on teaching large classes, young people, with limited resources etc. In the meantime I moved to Venezuela, applied for three part-time jobs with agencies and got them all. This was even before I finished the course, but they don't bother about formalities like that out here. I found that I loved teaching. Most of my classes are one-to-one with adults in their offices, so it's early mornings, lunchtimes, and late afternoons. You can get gigs with schools, teaching bigger classes and younger people if you want. The money is not great, to say the least, but it's a new career in which I am in demand, and that makes a change from ungrateful old UK. The course cost me a couple of hundred quid, but it was money well spent. If you have a good command of English, doing this can open doors for you.

The stories in this book establish that taking a gap year can be a choice for everyone, not just people with authority and wealth, or those who want to drop out. Now that institutions like finance companies, health authorities, and the telecoms industry recognise the value of breaks for their employees (between 25% and 40% of employers in these sectors offer unpaid sabbaticals as a staff perk), they are establishing the principle that time out from work is more than just an eccentric and nostalgic hankering for freedom from responsibility. The idea is gradually gaining legitimacy in the corporate world. Government too is pushing the concept of a work/life balance so that family life will not be sacrificed on the altar of Mammon. When people step back and do the calculations, they often conclude that the balance needs to be shifted a little bit more in favour of life.

Gap years have become part of the zeitgeist, the spirit of the age we live in. Julia Roberts ate, prayed, and loved her way through a glorious gap year in one of the hit films of 2010, based on the real gap year of Elizabeth Gilbert. Every week it is possible to find references in the media to adventurous grown-ups taking off as individuals, couples, or families, from the famous ('Emma Thompson plans gap year with daughter, ten') to the ordinary ('Didcot teacher, 57, uses redundancy money to take a gap year in South America'). A prime illustration of media interest in this kind of thing was the airing on Channel 4 in autumn 2010 of a documentary series *My Family's Crazy Gap Year*, and a couple of years before that BBC2 broadcast a mainstream observational documentary series *Grown-up Gappers*, which featured eight individuals who had temporarily packed in their everyday lives to explore the world.

As the number of people pioneering this choice increases, and in a society where the span of a working life is stretching well beyond 40 years, taking breaks may eventually become routine.

Trawling the internet will lead you to the 'blogs' of any number of heroes, eccentrics, and ordinary folk who have thrown over safe secure jobs to do something fresh and inspiring. A typical catchphrase is attached to the blog of a Canadian couple: 'Sold the house, got rid of the crap, traveling the globe with no exact plans.'

A large expanse of time can be the ideal opportunity to stretch yourself or to act on a long-held ambition, whether it be to navigate the Amazon, help to rescue orangutans in Borneo, or perform music. Striving for different experiences is a way of feeling that we have done something with our lives, and it could be something as simple as exploring a temple complex or a mountain range seen on a television documentary. This trend also complements another recent travel phenomenon: the growing interest in ethical or responsible travel.

Often there's a larger purpose to a gap year, which some view as an almost spiritual search for meaning beyond material satisfaction. In the developed world, work has undoubtedly brought great material comforts, and technological progress has also suppressed the threat of hunger and mitigated the worst effects of disease. But you may find that you have to look elsewhere for happiness.

Try not to view a gap year as a self-indulgence, but simply a period to regain your balance. More ambitiously, it can be a rite of passage, like learning to swim again – that moment in childhood of heading out of your depth in the water to learn that instead of sinking, you float. Women in particular can blossom when freed from the habit of always trying to ensure that everything runs smoothly for husband, children, parents, and boss. Some accounts of taking time out resemble mythological journeys of self-discovery. **Deborah Howell** eloquently captures the awe-inspiring benefits of a personal odyssey:

In terms of what I actually 'did' during my year out, the answer is everything! I visited monuments and art galleries. I climbed glaciers and went white water rafting. I met hill tribe people and holy men. I swam with dolphins and sharks. I spent an entire day trying to send a parcel in India. I lay on beaches and sailed around desert islands. I climbed pyramids and temples. In Australia, I was awed by the giant Ayers Rock, panned for opals in an underground town and was offered and declined the chance to get involved in smuggling. I walked away from Las Vegas a winner and flew through the Grand Canyon. I sang karaoke with the locals in China and listened to the voice of Peter Ustinov guide me round the Forbidden City. I played with children in the Vietnamese jungle amidst the ruins of shot down helicopters. I slept in palaces and in squalid, depressing places. I sat on buses and trains for hours and relaxed on deserted, white sandy beaches. I snorkelled with exotic fish and found a scorpion snuggled in my shorts! I missed friends and family and met some wonderful people. I fell in love with some countries and cultures and hated others. Like I say: I did everything.

Philip Larkin's lines from the poem 'Toads', from a volume aptly called *The Poetry of Departures*, describe the feeling of being entrapped by work, and are nothing short of arresting:

Why should I let the toad work
Squat on my life?
Can't I use my wit as a pitchfork
And drive the brute off?

Six days of the week it soils
With its sickening poison –
Just for paying a few bills!
That's out of proportion.

. . .

Ah, were I courageous enough
To shout Stuff *your pension!*
But I know, all too well, that's the stuff
That dreams are made on

The stories told in this book are made on just those dreams.

PART 1

TAKING THE PLUNGE

MY GROWN-UP GAP YEAR: CATH COOPER

It took Cath Cooper and husband Steve from near Doncaster many years of pondering the idea before they finally took the plunge.

After almost 20 years of dreaming I eventually took the plunge, packed in a job I loved, persuaded Steve to pack in a job he didn't love, and set off for a grown-up gap year. I first came across 'Work Your Way Around the World' in 1991 when I was 17. I applied for a couple of jobs in France (snail mail was the only option at the time) but nothing came of it. The following year I met Steve and travelling dreams were put on a back burner whilst money was spent on our wedding and a house deposit. In 2003 I came across the new edition of the book, but it took a couple more years researching and persuading before we made the decision to go.

We knew that we wanted to start in South Africa, and found the South African organisation AVIVA (www.aviva-sa.com). We booked a three-month project with the option of staying longer, then started sorting out visas (complicated if you want to stay more than three months), booking flights, and arranging to put normal life on hold. When we arrived in South Africa we expected to train for a month as field guides, followed by mentoring local guides and assisting with their English language skills. We did the training, but as with many best-laid plans, there were no local guides to mentor. After some negotiation with a local school and the business sponsor, we set up an after-school sports project. It wasn't as planned, and I never dreamt of teaching kids to play cricket! But it was the best experience of our lives. We were just outside Kruger National Park and on our last day in the area we managed to take a group of 60 children on their first ever safari.

In all we spent seven months in South Africa, part travelling and part volunteering. We found flying to be the easiest option, and fairly cheap to cover long distances using Itime airlines (www.Itime.aero). For travelling in South Africa, we used a booklet from the organisation Coast to Coast (www.coastingafrica.com) as our bible for finding hostel accommodation. It also had useful information on transport, attractions, and some little-known volunteering opportunities. One of the highlights of our time there was Bulungula Lodge (www.bulungula.com) in the Eastern Cape. It's not easy to get to but well worth the effort. A beautiful, peaceful place with volunteer opportunities available for those who want them.

We then decided we could just about afford three more months split between New Zealand and Australia. As recommended in 'Gap Year for Grown-Ups', we used hostels and were surprised by how many offered double rooms of a good standard at very low prices, many with en-suite bathrooms for a small supplement.

Unfortunately, by the time we came home the recession was hitting and finding jobs was difficult. I also made the decision to change from a career in administration to study Occupational Therapy. Luckily we both found some work. I have just completed an Access to Higher Education Diploma and started my three-year degree course in September 2010. It was a struggle when we returned home since we had used savings to self-fund our trip but neither of us would change a thing. My experience not only provided me with a chance to work out what I want to do as a future career, but it was a big help in getting accepted into university.

WHAT IS A GAP YEAR?

In the first place, a gap year need not be literally 12 months long. Mini-gaps lasting a couple of months can be invigorating and bring with them all the benefits extolled throughout this book. But the expression 'gap quarter-year' is unlikely to catch on (just as the new coinage 'quarter-life crisis' is not likely to achieve common currency).

The term 'gap year' must remain a loose one, but essentially, it means changing the regular pattern of your working life over a period that is longer than just a regular holiday. A short gap 'year' might last six weeks, though the premise of this book is that you will have three, six or 12 months of freedom from professional and domestic obligations: a miraculous period of time in which to pursue dreams and create memories.

In academia and the teaching profession, the notion of a sabbatical is established by tradition. A sabbatical leave of absence from duties allows a teacher or lecturer to recharge, refresh their knowledge of a subject, conduct original research, or go abroad. Whereas sabbaticals that are earned with loyal service are normally paid, gap years or career breaks tend to be thought of as self-granted and unpaid. But sabbaticals are a version of gap years, and the expression 'career sabbatical' is often used by companies that permit them. In business, the concept of an earned break is becoming more common as an incentive for staying on with the same employer. Typically, after a fixed period of time, the employee is allowed to take up to a specified number of weeks off – normally without pay but without loss of benefits, like pension contributions. Even in companies where there is no formal policy of granting career breaks, employees are negotiating unpaid gap years on a discretionary basis: a concept which is gaining wider acceptance.

More and more companies are introducing a sabbatical policy. For example, in the summer of 2009, Sony UK began offering year-long (unpaid) sabbaticals as part of its flexible working agenda, and Penguin Books grants up to six-month breaks to staff after three years of service. All of these companies want to retain good employees. In fact, most companies on the *Sunday Times'* list of Top 100 Best Companies to Work For offer some kind of sabbatical provision.

The recession saw some major employers offering semi-paid sabbaticals to staff, to avoid having to make them redundant during the economic downturn. For example, at the beginning of 2009, Vauxhall offered the 2,200 production workers at its Ellesmere Port factory a sabbatical of up to nine months on half-pay – a move that was widely welcomed as an imaginative response to the crisis. (Incredibly, only 15 employees took up the offer.) Other firms stipulate that time off must be used for personal development; for example, in addition to its offer of unpaid six-month sabbaticals, Avis makes awards available for personal development (study, volunteering) that need not be directly connected to the employee's role in the company. A gap year may take place as a pause from a specific job to which you fully intend to return. Alternatively, it can encompass leaving one job to further your education or taking the opportunity to experience an extended period of travel before returning home to look for new employment. In either case your professional life is put on hold.

Going abroad is not an essential component since career breaks at home are perfectly feasible. For some it might simply mean stepping off the treadmill to slow down (or whatever metaphor you wish to use), or spend more time with children, immerse yourself in a hobby, or do full-time voluntary work. You don't even need to leave the country to take a challenging journey. A gap year is more disruptive than a holiday, but that is precisely its appeal. It demands a level of radical change in your normal routine.

A gap year provides a chance to re-connect with former interests and old friends, or to acquire new interests and new friends beyond the boundaries of work. Emotionally, your activities during a break may reawaken old loves, introduce new interests, and act to inspire your efforts back in the workplace.

A gap year involves six stages:

- **The Dream.** This might be associated with a specific ambition (eg, to see the world), or just a longing to get out of your present rut.
- **The Determination.** Achieving the confidence to go ahead and do it.
- **Persuading the Boss (or delegating your business).** Employers are increasingly aware that it is in their interests to grant unpaid leave.
- **The Practicalities.** Organising your life, partner, family, mortgage, finances, and so on, must be given careful consideration.
- **The Break Itself.** What you can do with a stint away from work.
- **Re-entry.** What differences can a gap year make when it comes to an end?

PURSUING A DREAM

Grown-up gap years are for people who don't want to end up saying, 'I could have' or, 'I should have' instead of, 'I did'. The decision is never easy. Some experience a 'Road to Damascus' revelation when suddenly they feel a compulsion to pursue a specific dream or escape an unsatisfactory situation. Others take years of toying with the idea, taking a few tentative steps before they finally discover the wherewithal to carry through the idea. **Phil Tomkins**, a 45-year-old Englishman who spent 2010/11 teaching on a tiny Greek island, describes the thought processes that galvanised him into action:

> *I think it comes down to the fact that we are only on this planet for a finger-snap of time, and if you have any kind of urge for a bit of adventure, then my advice would be to go for it! And even if it goes all horribly wrong, you can look people in the eyes and say, 'Well, at least I gave it a try'. You can work 9–5 in an office or factory all day, come home, switch on the Idiot Lantern and sit there watching Michael Palin travelling the world – or you can be bold, seize the day, and do something amazing. One thing I can guarantee: when we are lying on our deathbed many years from now, we will not be saying to ourselves 'Oh, I wish I'd spent more time at that dead-end job and had a little less adventure in my life!'*

There seems to be no end to the original and energetic ways to spend two, four, six, or 12 scintillating months, found by working people of all ages. Once you have squared taking a break from work, either by sorting something out with your employer or working out the financial implications of not earning for a time, it all gets much easier. After you have explained to your friends and family that you have decided to take a chunk of time off work (they will either be envious or disapproving), and once you have booked your flight, enrolled in a course, contacted some voluntary organisations, put a specific project in motion, or embarked on whatever you want to do with your gap year, the rest seems to look after itself.

WHO CAN TAKE A GAP YEAR?

Anyone who has uttered the words, 'How I'd love to be a …' or, 'I'd give anything to see…' is a possible candidate for achieving their dream on a career break. People sometimes hide behind an assumption that something they dream of doing is impossible because of the pressures of work and home life. While airing your fantasies, your family or friends might be tempted to say, 'Why don't you just go ahead and do it?' – whatever it is, such as write a play, build a harpsichord, renovate a bothy, climb Kilimanjaro with your children, work for Mother Teresa's charity in Calcutta, or even explore your genealogy. When **Laura Clarke** chucked in her senior position with one of London's top restaurant companies in order to work in the Alps, her friends all said, 'About time too'. Apparently it was all she'd talked about for years.

Taking a year off is a luxury: a product of a wealthy society. If you suggested the concept to, say, a Nepali porter, Brazilian taxi driver or Polish farmer, they would think you were speaking Martian. But in the privileged west, people from many backgrounds, not just an elite few, have the freedom to exercise the choice to withdraw temporarily from work. This is a freedom that should be cherished and not squandered.

The thesis of this book is that ordinary people can entertain extraordinary ambitions and do extraordinary things. An eye-catching ad campaign was run by VSO (Voluntary Service Overseas) a while back to persuade ordinary working people to consider a stint of voluntary work. A flyer read: 'The tanned, toned, blonde Australian Ironman Champion who normally hands out these flyers is in Liverpool helping to build a youth centre for disabled children.' Another one was displayed prominently on a truck: 'This truck should have been towed away but the driver is away in Peru rescuing llamas by four-wheel drive.' People on ordinary wages have managed to save enough money to fund trips to far corners of the world to do amazing things.

When you are wondering whether you are the right sort to take a break from work, do not imagine that your circumstances are peculiarly disadvantageous. Since the last edition of this book, I have heard from:

- A physiotherapist, who lived with a local family while using her professional skills at a centre for disabled children in Mexico.
- Childhood sweethearts who saved up for several years after their wedding to fund ten months of round-the-world travels and adventure.
- A teaching assistant in her 60s, who volunteered on a game reserve in Namibia.
- A Canadian family of four, who divided their ten-month sabbatical between working and living in Muheza in Tanzania, and cycling from Turkey to Estonia.
- A managing director of an office design company, who decided to take a year out to cycle around the world, and celebrated his 50th birthday in Chile just before this edition went to press.
- The self-employed editor of a Scottish environmental magazine, who joined her gap-yearing daughter volunteering at an orphanage in Kathmandu.
- A wife and mother, whose family came to appreciate her domestic labours while she was away in Africa diving with great white sharks and volunteering with street children.
- A management consultant who volunteered for a charity in Mombasa, which he enjoyed so much that he is staying on in Kenya to invest in small local businesses.
- A woman who, when she discovered that her husband of 33 years had set up with a 23-year-old Thai woman, took herself off to Mexico to volunteer with disabled children for nearly four months.
- A television writer and producer in her mid 30s, who gave up her glamorous-sounding job to travel for the better part of three years, picking up odd jobs along the way.
- A lawyer, who came to realise that many of the skills acquired as a project manager on a Raleigh expedition were transferable to a city legal job, including retaining a sense of humour in adversity.

THE DETERMINATION TO
REALISE YOUR DREAM

Deciding to take a period of time off work and then deciding how to spend it may not be as momentous as some other life decisions – like choosing a life partner, having babies, choosing or changing careers – but it is as individual. It certainly takes guts, and that is an essential ingredient in achieving a break from your career. The hardest step is simply fixing on your departure date. No book or even trusted adviser can make the decision for you. All that outsiders can do are set out the possibilities and see if any of them take your fancy enough to pursue. Do as much research as possible, let the ideas swill around in your head, and see what floats up.

There is no doubt that it is far easier to stay on the funicular of employment that chugs along its tracks to the goal of retirement, than diverting off course. After all, that is exactly what the majority of working people still do. For many people in work, the decision to treat oneself to a sabbatical is a difficult and complex one. The first question to ask yourself is: does the idea have a strong appeal? Do you get a buzz if you close your eyes and imagine yourself trekking through a Costa Rican rainforest, or teaching in a Tanzanian village school, or studying in an Italian language class? The next question is: do you have the energy to make the dream an actuality?

REASONS TO BE TEMPTED

We all fantasise about taking extended time off from work, but acting on this fantasy is a daunting prospect. What are the practical implications for our careers, families, and daily responsibilities? Much depends on the complexity of our lives and to what extent we rely on the structures and routines we have built to provide personal security, self-esteem, professional achievement, and financial stability. Younger people in their late twenties and early thirties with fewer commitments are better placed to take an extended break. However, individuals in their 40s and 50s will be more likely to have a degree of financial security and better professional qualifications, which may allow a smoother return to professional life.

Sometimes we just need to step back from work to put our lives in perspective or re-evaluate our goals – professional or otherwise. People sometimes feel that their lives have become too detached from simple pleasures and the rhythms of nature. Even if the gap year you choose does not specifically focus on the natural world, exposure to beautiful landscapes is often a byproduct of travel and volunteering in distant lands, as **David Mackintosh** commented about his MondoChallenge placement teaching in Kalimpong in West Bengal:

> *I had gone from a bustling office (Conservative Party HQ), with people screaming of political scandal and urgent deadlines, to the calm tranquillity of the Himalayas with snow-topped Kanchenjunga in the background and no mobile reception for days!*

Perhaps you have simply become miserable in your job and want a complete change. Increasingly, people are being forced into a 'career break' just as resting actors are. The financial collapse and damage to the British and US economies have resulted in thousands of redundancies with more to come. At a deep level some people are dissatisfied with their lives – not necessarily because of their job but for reasons unrelated to work. Perhaps your relationship is foundering and it is time to break free for a while. Perhaps you are single and are longing for a shake-up in your social life. Perhaps your children have recently left home and you and your partner are looking for a new activity to fill the emptiness at home. Perhaps you have come into an inheritance on the death of a relative or found yourself with a windfall. Perhaps you are grieving at the loss of a loved one or for a marriage that has ended. Illness or accidents might have reminded you of the shortness of life and the necessity of filling it with variety and excitement. Your personal circumstances may have altered for any number of reasons, making it possible in practical terms to consider a break from work.

Provided you can delegate or shed your responsibilities (see Part 2: Nuts and Bolts), ask yourself 'why *shouldn't* I take a gap year?' In all probability you have worked very hard and earned the right to step back temporarily from the demands of your job, to concentrate on yourself for a change and to establish what you really value in your life.

TRIGGERS AND MOTIVES

Most of us sail along on our normal work-a-day and domestic course more or less contentedly. But then something happens that throws us off-course and makes us wonder where the meaning lies in our ordinary routines. Why do we have to spend hours every day on crowded tube trains or in boring meetings or placating irate bosses? When was the last time we gasped with amazement at some new sight or laughed out loud at some absurdity?

Sometimes we have no choice in the matter. Women are lucky in this respect as many have a career break thrust upon them when a baby is born. Few experiences in life so radically change daily routines as the birth of a child. People who are made redundant and are forced to take a career break are less lucky, but even this can have a positive outcome. Understandably, people can be thrown into total consternation by redundancy but with luck and determination, this will only last 48 hours. If you have marketable skills you may find that it will mark a liberation, as it does for those who treat themselves to an exciting break with their redundancy money and then come home to make their way as a freelancer, thereby achieving a more balanced lifestyle. After enjoying the 'experience of a lifetime' in Uganda, Australian **Jenny Hickman** wanted to express her thanks to the people who made it all possible, including: 'my ex-employer in the finance industry, for making my stressful job of ten years redundant'.

Sometimes there is an identifiable event or circumstance that prompts a desire to do something a bit mad. It is not unusual for career breaks to follow in the wake of a failed romance, as one 30-year-old gapper described it: 'The main catalyst for going was that I had just had my heart well and truly trampled over, and I felt that by far the best way was to go abroad to feel good about life once again'.

But often it is the culmination of a background urge long suppressed: to do something self-less, to pursue a sport, to swim with dolphins, or visit the Pyramids before you die – whatever it is. The worst thing about doing the same thing for years on end is how it makes time speed up. Because there is so little to delineate one day from another, the days all collapse in on one another and get compacted, as if by a computer programme trying to make more space. But if you do something completely different, suddenly each day and each week stretches to accommodate the range of new experiences.

The impulse to organise a gap year can come from many directions. You may find yourself thinking (obsessively) that if you don't grab the opportunity now you never will. You may have come to the realisation that you desperately need de-stressing or simply have been inspired by the travel tales of a sibling, friend, or television presenter.

All those who *do* it, rather than merely talk about it or dream about it, arrive at a point of no psychological return. For **Polly Botsford**, a lawyer who had just turned 30, there was an underlying conviction that *something* was needed to shake up her life. For her it felt a bit like the need to change her bedroom around or try a new hairdresser. She thinks that if she had been younger, she might have been satisfied with a change of job. But once you are entrenched in a career, you cannot nonchalantly walk out of one job and into another. So the solution is to have an extended holiday from your job – which is what she did when she went to work for a small charity in Cambodia.

BURN-OUT

No matter how glamorous and interesting a job may be, it usually has the capacity to lead to boredom or burn-out at some level. No matter how hard you work, you can sometimes never clear the backlog, which can lead to a feeling of defeat and profound weariness. And it is this problem that a gap year can address. American TV documentary-maker **Holly Morris** has a vivid expression for what she felt in a nine-to-five job: 'Rigor mortis of the soul'. Her solution was to take a sabbatical in Sumatra to rethink her position. On her return she went part-time as an editor, spending the other half freelancing and working on an idea for a TV series about strong adventurous women around the world. She simply created a more flexible life for herself, which allowed her to make a pilot programme in Cuba. She then sold it to PBS and went on to make a TV series called *Adventure Divas*.

Ricky Grice had sat behind a desk for ten years as a UK-based self-employed IT and management consultant, working mainly for the big clearing banks. He needed a change, both in work and social culture. When the income from his consultancy dropped to zero, he decided to go abroad to do something entirely different. Whereas most people might gravitate to a destination with which they were already familiar, Ricky set his sights on East Africa because, although he had travelled widely with work, he had never been to this part of the world and thought the time had come to remedy his ignorance. Rather than just backpack around, he decided to work as a volunteer in order to get to know the region and its people in more depth.

MY GROWN-UP GAP YEAR: BARRY IRVINE

Barry Irvine's gap 'year' started in August 2009, when he was nearly 37, and is still going strong. He had reached a point in his life where he felt his personal happiness was diminishing with the monotony of the day-to-day grind, so he quit his job to do something completely different. Since making that decision he has collected an amazing range of experiences, from climbing Mt Kilimanjaro to studying Spanish in Quito, and even touring Patagonia. From hesitant beginnings as someone who was reluctant to travel alone, he has blossomed into an adventurous

solo traveller. Not surprising for someone who had worked in the communications industry, Barry has recorded all his travels on his blog www.bazzastravels.wordpress.com.

My wife and I were going through a rough patch in our marriage (we have since divorced) and it became obvious that we needed some time apart to work things out. I was also generally dissatisfied with my job in the mobile telecoms sector, and found it unchallenging. I decided that I wanted to travel but was a bit afraid of travelling on my own - so I decided that volunteer work with animals would be ideal. After discovering that the waiting list was too long to work with the orangutans at Sepilok in Borneo, I opted for working with lions in Zimbabwe - arranged through Travellers Worldwide.

My initial break was only for six weeks and I was quite sure that I could get my contract back after my time away if I wanted to. As it happened I had such a good time that I couldn't imagine rejoining the workstream, and so I continued my travels.

I've had many highlights during my trip and I can list some of my favourite moments: going on my first lion walk at the lion breeding project in Gweru, Zimbabwe; bungee jumping at Victoria Falls; white-water rafting down the Zambezi; reaching the summit of Mt Kilimanjaro; the breathtaking scenery of Patagonia; seeing the moai (rock carvings of humans) in Easter Island; seeing Machu Picchu for the first time; the Nazca lines; sandboarding in Huacachina; the Galapagos islands; the lost city trek in Colombia; interacting with sloths in Costa Rica; volcano boarding in Leon, Nicaragua; and swimming in the cenotes (open water pools) outside Merida in Mexico. Some of my best moments have been when I had no particular expectations.

I'm still technically travelling because I'm just waiting for my rucksack to be fixed before setting off again. I'm now heading east to Cambodia, Vietnam, and Laos before probably heading to Japan, South Korea, India, Australia, and New Zealand. I'm not actually sure exactly how much I've spent and I'm a bit scared to work it all out, but I do feel that you can't really put a price on all the different activities that I've enjoyed over the past year and a bit. So it is definitely justifiable. I also think it was the perfect medicine for what would otherwise have been a tough emotional breakup.

EXCESS AND AFFLUENCE

You have only to read a newspaper or watch the television news about the plight of earthquake victims and the cholera epidemic in Haiti, or the AIDS crisis in Africa, or the feelings of hope-lessness among Palestinians, to realise the extent to which citizens of Britain, North America, and other developed countries are extraordinarily privileged even to be able to contemplate a grown-up gap year. Such a concept would be entirely alien to the vast majority of the inhabit-ants of the globe, for whom it is an unrelenting daily struggle to obtain basic necessities.

Undoubtedly many of us have never been better off or had more opportunities at our dis-posal. Some might even consider themselves members (reluctant or otherwise) of the 'have-it-all generation'. With apologies to Harold Bloom's famous study of poetry called *The Anxiety of Influence*, the anxiety of *affluence* is (fortunately) not uncommon in our culture. The disparity between what we have and what millions of others lack through no fault of their own can be overwhelming at times. It is an awareness of our amazing good fortune to be born when and where we have been, that prompts some people to withdraw temporarily from the good life and try to bring good to others. Many people want to reverse the cash-rich, time-poor equation. **Reza Pakravan** knows how lucky he has been: 'I have been working in the financial industry for a few years and had a very comfortable life. To let off steam and give something back for all that I have, I decided to participate in a voluntary scheme in Africa'.

It is no doubt the case that a disincentive to many people in taking a gap year is the loss of income that will ensue, if only temporarily. Depending on your predisposition and background, you may find it easy or well-nigh impossible to come to the view that it is probably not essential for you to earn as much as you do. **Phil Tomkins** has altered his priorities over the years and after trying several vocations at home in Britain (primary school teacher, pub landlord), he retrained as a teacher of English as a foreign language and is now happily ensconced on a Greek island:

> *Regarding finances, I long ago reconciled myself to the fact that I would never be a millionaire (certainly not from teaching!) and for some time have been re-adjusting what I want out of life. Peace and contentment, for me, far outweigh the benefits of the rat race and I am happy to live in comfortable 'poverty' on a sunny Greek island doing a job I enjoy, rather than working my fingers to the bone chasing the almighty dollar, and giving whoever is the current architect of our doom a big, fat slice of it. To measure one's successes solely in pounds, shillings, and pence is a sure way to depression, disappointment, and stress. Friends and family have all been very enthusiastic and supportive of me 'doing a Shirley Valentine' – and not a little jealous that even now, at the end of November, I'm still to be found at the beach most days.*

SENSORY OVERLOAD

The choice of goods in the shops, types of coffee in cafés, programmes in the media, training courses and possible career paths, travel destinations, information on the internet: all of these are almost infinite. Many people feel oppressed by the sheer quantity of choice available to us in the 21st century. A famous psychology experiment called 'The Jam Experiment' showed that nearly a third of shoppers presented with a tasting of six jams bought one, whereas most shoppers given a choice of 30 jams bought nothing. It concluded that when you have fewer choices, you go after what you choose with enthusiasm and tend to be more contented with your choice. The simple life has huge appeal, and one way of achieving this is to put one's job on hold for a while, put one's possessions in storage, and remove oneself from the busy crowded world of the materialistic west.

Paradoxically, in the midst of all this profusion of possessions and experiences, we have less time to absorb and reflect on the experiences open to us and often lack the ability to turn them into something of quality. An extended period spent away from the workaday treadmill and the crowded shop shelves can help to make that possible.

Ironically, having to make few choices can be liberating, as **Lisa Lubin** found. Upon returning to Chicago from her three years of travelling, she was confronted with a daunting selection of toothpaste:

Once I settled on a brand, I had to study each package for the various differences – gel, paste, tartar control, whitening, whitening with baking soda, all natural, all chemical, 4 out of 5 dentists recommend it, with fluoride, with crystals, for sensitive gums, for gums of steel, plaque control, minty fresh, orangey goodness, or a swirly combination of everything. Aaaaaaaahhhhhhh-hhh…my brain hurt. Do we really need all this? It was so much easier in Vietnam when I'd go into a tiny shop and buy Colgate toothpaste – because that was the only choice. No unnecessary decisions. No extra brain power wasted. And clean teeth to boot.

DIVORCE

If, as the statisticians tell us, 43% of marriages end in divorce, there are a lot of shell-shocked and lonely people out there. The trauma of divorce can sometimes best be assuaged by taking an exciting career break. Women especially can benefit if they have been confined in a marriage where they had little independence, as **Anne Bisson** was:

I decided to take a break after hearing that after 33 years of marriage my husband has set up home and was having a baby by a 23-year-old Thai girl. My family and friends all said it would be good for me. Through Global Volunteer Projects, I arranged to work in an orphanage for mentally and physically disabled children in Guadalajara, Mexico. Global Volunteers are a great company and very helpful. My team leader in Mexico helped me settle in, gave me lots of confidence, and was always there if I needed help. A highlight of the experience was finding out about myself and gaining confidence, as I had never left my husband's side. So not having to ask for anyone's permission was enlightening, but also very scary. I was not accustomed to thinking or doing things for myself and had always had to consider my husband in anything I did: even just spending money on food, let alone going out and joining groups. For instance, I had never once in my life had a girlie night out. And here I was in the thick of all this.

I am now back at home in Jersey near where my daughter lives. After the break, I found that I got bored, and craved a night out. I wanted more friends and became very lonely. But I am now finding work as a carer with Down Syndrome children. When I left for Mexico, I just wanted to do good and get away. Now I am using my experience to find a job in a related field.

Any newly-divorced readers who want to fantasise about a shiny new future should wallow in the schmaltz of the 2010 hit film *Eat Pray Love*, in which Julia Roberts goes off in search of her true self by indulging first her sensuous side in Italy, and then questing for spirituality in India.

BEREAVEMENT AND DEPRESSION

Who is to say how any of us would react to grief? But some people find it helpful to get away. Not many will be tempted to follow in the footsteps of 57-year-old writer and adventurer Rosie Swale Pope who, after her husband died of cancer, set off to run around the world, raising money in memory of the man she loved. Her incredible journey is recorded in her book *Just a Little Run Around the World: 5 Years, 3 Packs of Wolves and 53 Pairs of Shoes*.

Carol Peden, a consultant anaesthetist just into her 40s, lost her husband unexpectedly. For a while she just wanted to be in a familiar place, but after selling the family house, moving five times, suing two sets of lawyers, and trying to keep a demanding career going, she was exhausted and wanted a break. She was granted six months of unpaid leave provided she could find a suitable replacement to cover her absence. **Tina Freeman** is another woman in her middle years who coped with a tragic loss by going abroad, in her case to a village project in the mountains of Tanzania:

> *My motivation was wanting to do something rewarding and meaningful during a terrible period of grief. I'd always wanted to teach abroad, and was going through a difficult time after losing my son, so it gave me something positive to focus on and look forward to. My placement was a particularly amazing experience considering the 'place' I was in my life when I went. The people who have to deal with poverty and child mortality and death in general every day were so joyous, welcoming and fun – it was such a shock. At first I was coy about disclosing my trauma, but the project leader encouraged me to share the details as this might encourage others in my position.*

Psychological troubles might also propel some people into taking a period off work. Anyone who is truly depressed is unlikely to be able to summon the energy and initiative necessary to plan a constructive gap year, but many people who feel worn down by their jobs and lives contemplate alternatives that will rescue them from their gloomy state of mind. **Caroline Kippen** is one for whom this worked splendidly:

> *I decided to take a gap year because I was finding life quite disheartening and depressing! I made my decision in the depths of winter, when the UK has to be one of the most depressing places to be. I guess I was suffering from a severe case of SAD and decided to pro-actively do something to change my situation. I was also dissatisfied with my job (in customer services for a mortgage endowment company), so I decided that the best thing would be to take a break and then start a new career after that. I guess I went away to decide what I wanted to do next – I kind of had the idea of teaching because it is easy to fall into, but luckily my gap year led me away!*
>
> *Firstly, I went on a two month round-the-world trip and was a real tourist seeing places I had always wanted to see and having incredible fun – that has now all blended into one and I have difficulty distinguishing one place from the next. The other part was volunteering in Africa.*

I chose an organisation called SPW [now Restless Development – Ed] which runs health education programmes in Africa. Teaching about HIV/AIDS seemed so much more important than teaching maths and the rewards have been great. I have so many skills now and my life has meaning and order to it! The drawbacks are that I can never go into another mundane boring job because I will always compare it to my experience, and it means that I have to constantly challenge myself in new ways – but maybe that isn't a bad thing!

In more than a few cases, the death of an elderly parent is a trigger for someone to decide to take a gap year, especially if they have been heavily responsible for the care of their parents and unable to get away. The death of **Sarah Spiller's** father marked a turning point in her life. Planning a volunteer trip abroad provided a distraction not only to Sarah but also to her mother, who was enthusiastic on Sarah's behalf. Because Sarah had inherited some money from her father, she didn't need to worry about the financing of the trip. Her husband was also supportive of her idea to go away and do something different. She settled on Sri Lanka, which had bewitched her on a previous visit, and a turtle protection scheme through Projects Abroad, where she helped escort the turtles safely to their breeding ground, worked in a hatchery for turtle eggs, and helped show visiting parties of Sri Lankan children round so as to instill the conservation message in them.

Similarly, teacher **Nigel Hollington** (then age 50) was spurred to action by the death of his father, which freed him from some of his filial responsibilities. His mother was well looked after in sheltered accommodation but, at her age, he was reluctant to go away for long periods of time at a stretch. So he decided to divide up the year out he had been granted by his headteacher into chunks, do a variety of things, and come home in between.

Siamak Tannazi was 29 when she decided to apply to her boss at BT for a six-month break, partly because she had been in a serious motorbike accident and partly because then the Tsunami happened, which made her think about all the charities in the Indian sub-continent dependent on foreign volunteers. **Neil Munro** had suffered a serious betrayal by his brother, which made Neil fall apart and feel the need to get out of Scotland. Any number of unexpected events can bring you up short and make stepping out of your routine seem a necessity.

MY GROWN-UP GAP YEAR: DEV PARIKH

Looking for a gap in the market, lawyer Dev Parikh decided to learn Spanish in Costa Rica in order to be able to serve Hispanic clients at home in Indiana. But the experience drew him away from the US altogether.

I had a small law firm, specialising in appellate work. By the time I turned 40 I had already lost friends and colleagues, and I felt myself rotting inside. Beginning in October 2008, I studied Spanish for eight weeks in

Heredia Costa Rica. Indianapolis, where I lived, has a growing Spanish speaking community and I convinced myself that I could do well helping Spanish speaking clients with their legal problems. Upon announcing that I intended to take a break from my career, a number of acquaintances tried to dissuade me from leaving, arguing that I was too old, too incapable of change, and too weighed down by responsibility. Over time, I have come to believe that these naysayers were superimposing their own complexes and insecurities on me - they were afraid or felt trapped, hence I was irresponsible in leaving.

During the eight weeks that I was in Costa Rica, I grew quite attached to the families with whom I was staying, and to Costa Rica in general. And I made enormous strides in speaking the language. As the time drew near for my return flight, I knew that I was not ready to return. When I arrived at the airport in Indianapolis, I felt more than a little sick. About a year later I decided to take the plunge again, and returned to Costa Rica.

Looking at the carnage wrought by the economic crisis, starting with the collapse of Lehman Brothers in 2007, I guessed that even more retirees would cash out on their declining assets and flee to Latin American countries, particularly those with reputations for stability and with a large American presence like Costa Rica. Of course, these retirees bring their own legal issues with them, and I thought that a bilingual American lawyer might do well. Some interesting opportunities have presented themselves. I have participated in conferences in which I have sagely opined on the American legal system, and been treated like a kind of rock star. Gringos command great respect in these parts.

These are sporadic gigs, and I still look for the elusive legal job that shimmers just beyond the horizon. It is a hard road, but I am not the only trailblazer here. Other American professionals, including lawyers, are on the lookout, and they tell me to be patient. However, adopting this Zen-like attitude and adapting to the maddeningly slow pace of Costa Rican society has proven difficult. Many, many things have happened to me since I came here, some very good (I am about to get married and have a child on the way), and others not so good.

PROJECTS ABROAD PRO

The volunteer
Name: *Barry Brown*
Age: *55*
Qualification: *Certificate of Proficiency in Bowen Technique with the European School of Bowen Studies*

The project partner
Mr Rajesh Manadhar is the managing director of the Life Development Centre in Kathmandu. He has years of experience caring for people with mental and physical issues and was perfectly placed to provide guidance for Barry when he arrived in Nepal. Rajesh and his wife founded the centre with the aim of caring for and rehabilitating children and youths suffering from mental problems. Over the years this has been expanded to include adults and they normally work with around 30 patients. Rajesh was very interested in Barry's knowledge of the Bowen Technique and together they were able to work out a system whereby his time was spent most efficiently. In this way he was able to focus on the patients that would most benefit from his expertise and both Barry and Rajesh were very pleased with the results.

Role of the volunteer
Barry's role on the physiotherapy project included the following:

- *reading up on patient case notes provided by former volunteers*
- *providing treatment for all patients using the Bowen Technique*
- *consulting with existing staff to get feedback from them and the patients*
- *updating case notes, writing evaluations and preparing documentation for future volunteers and carers.*

Benefits to the community
Rajesh's work over the years and Barry's added help have combined to provide the following benefits to the local community in and around the placement.

- *The centre has grown to provide treatment for patients from the local area aged between 8 and 36 who would otherwise be left in poverty with no access to the care they need.*
- *New premises have now been built which allow the staff to work in a much more suitable environment and provide the best possible care for their patients.*
- *Patients who had behavioural problems exhibited noticeable improvement thanks to Barry's treatment.*
- *There is now a much greater appreciation of the Bowen Technique and the foundation has been laid for more volunteers to join the project and provide much needed treatment.*

THE DANGER AGE

Alongside the pressures to become a property owner, society (often in the guise of a parent) seems to expect people who have been earning a salary for a few years to 'settle down', find a spouse, and reproduce. This might engender panic that it is time to have your last fling with youth. You may therefore derive great pleasure in announcing to all and sundry that in fact you have decided to leave your job for a while to sail across the Atlantic, do marine conservation in the Philippines, or ride your bicycle through Chile. That will teach them to pin their assumptions on you! On a more serious note, you will want to avoid causing unnecessary anxiety to ageing parents. However, you cannot please all of the people all of the time and if a mother is anxious that her daughter has hit thirty without making her a grandmother, this is not a sufficient reason to stay on the straight and (very) narrow.

Although it is possible to have a gap year after parenthood (see Part 8: Taking the Family), the commitment-free gap year is the paradigm. **Jennie Sanders** at age 26 took nine months off from her job with PricewaterhouseCoopers to do a Yachtmaster sailing course:

I will probably spend a lot of the years to come sitting at a desk. To be able to take some time out while I had no commitments such as a family or a mortgage, meant that it was an ideal time to seize the opportunity. I wouldn't say that I came back 'a changed person', but it was a fantastic experience and all I have missed out on is a few months sitting in an office! There were other people on our course who had borrowed from friends, given up jobs completely, sold their businesses, and left family at home to come on the course, and I don't think anyone regretted taking the time out to do something completely different.

PROPERTY LADDER PRESSURES

After starting a job most people are happy to rent property for a few years, but soon the knowledge that hundreds of pounds a month are disappearing into a black hole begins to worry them. Family and friends suddenly seem to be in cahoots with the local estate agent to pressurise full-time earners into getting onto the property ladder at any cost. It has become easier of late to resist this pressure now that house and flat prices are barely rising, and in some places even falling.

Rob Evans came late to the joys of travel but had greatly enjoyed a one-month backpacking trip round Peru with friends in his late 20s, so he began to toy with the idea of taking leave from work to travel. On the same day that his landlord had told him that he wanted to reclaim the flat, he attended a party to welcome back some other travellers he had met in South America, and a couple of choices started to crystallise:

On one hand, I could make my belated first step onto London's property ladder and scour the suburbs for a grotty flat. On the other, I could blow the money I'd been saving for a deposit on doing the thing I'd been threatening to do, and disappear to foreign climes for some time. Given that I was at a party with a large number of people who had been travelling themselves, there was probably only one way this decision was ever going to go.

There will be time enough for locating a grotty flat in the suburbs.

FREEDOM FROM RESPONSIBILITIES

The last child goes off to university or off to a job and all of a sudden, people in their 40s and 50s have a lot more freedom. As their children progressed through adolescence, parents may have been taking their first tentative steps to rediscovering the joys of child-free travel: an anniversary weekend in Barcelona or Prague, or a week in a country cottage in Ireland. But now they are at liberty to plan something more ambitious without having to take any account of their children's propensity to travel sickness, or their dislike of hotels without swimming pools, or of remote villages with no nightlife.

This sudden lifting of parental obligations is often more keenly felt by mothers than fathers. Whether busy career women or not, mothers frequently bear the burden of anxiety on their children's behalf. Not that this vanishes once the children leave home for further education or employment, but many women find that for the first time in many years they have an urge to think about themselves and what they would like. This may not come easily at first and it may take time before they can dust off an old pre-motherhood dream or two, but according to lots of volunteer-sending agencies, the single biggest demographic group among their volunteers is women in their 50s.

Yet men are not immune to post-parenthood restlessness either. **Jerry Melinn** waited until his four children were grown up and he was offered an attractive early redundancy package, before he arranged a gap year in Greece. First he obtained a TEFL certificate in Corinth and then got a job in Athens where his wife visits him frequently.

SIGNIFICANT BIRTHDAYS

Midlife crises are a bit like failing eyesight and greying hair; they can strike at any point between the ages of about 40 and 60. But ad hoc research for this book revealed that the half-century seems to act frequently as a prompt to appraising the direction and priorities of one's life. People coming up to the age of 50 often begin to panic that they have embarked on the gentle slope to retirement. They want something to wake them up, in the hope that it will extend their lives.

Mark Perriton celebrated his 50th birthday in November 2010 in the depths of South America, part way through a one-year round-the-world cycling expedition. To reassure his friends and family, he labelled his blog 'Not a midlife crisis!' (www.markperrlton.com). Another keen cyclist is **Ambrose Marsh**, a Canadian physician. As his 50th birthday approached, his wife Leah asked him what he would most like to do. He thought about it for a while and decided that he would like to do a cycling trip in an interesting part of the world. She cheerfully agreed to look after their two young children while he did a long distance trip from Madrid. He sent round an email to his address book, inviting friends to join him on his 'Birthday-boy-designed perfect celebration', and gathered together a congenial crew to accompany him.

Forty is also a landmark between youth and … non-youth (after all, 41 is far too young to count as 'middle-aged'). **Deanne Peterson** from the USA embarked on a journey to Southern Africa because she was 'in revolt against my recently turning 40':

As a business owner, wife, and mother of two teenage boys, a month-long journey to Africa seemed like something far beyond my reality. My vacation experiences prior to this were always family-oriented and/or resort style, including room service, umbrella drinks, amusement parks, cruise ships, and guided tours. I wanted to see and do as much as I could and experience as much of South Africa as possible. It was a wonderful growing experience for the entire family. For six weeks my two teenage sons and husband did all their own cooking, cleaning and laundry. I felt VERY appreciated when I got home!

Sometimes attending a school or college reunion can instantly reinforce your suspicion that doing the same thing for years on end is not good for you, and this realisation may catapult you into a frenzy of planning on how to make your life take a different course, if only temporarily. After 20 years as an insurance executive, **Marcelle Salerno** signed up for various exotic volunteer roles – including a dive project in the Seychelles – and concludes: 'After all this, if nothing else, I'm more interesting at cocktail parties.'

Time stretches when you are doing something outside your routine: for example, it always seems that you pack much more into a week's holiday than a week spent at home. You can test this hypothesis over two weekends. In the first, do the usual stuff: hoover the sitting room, go to the supermarket, read a magazine, maybe go to the pub, sleep in, read the Sunday paper, and watch television. Then at 7.45 on Monday morning, ask yourself, 'How long ago was Friday?' and the answer will be, 'It seems no time at all'. The following weekend, leave work a little early to catch a train to Bradford/Wales/Brussels; check in to a B&B/pension/hostel and spend the weekend exploring the local landscapes/cafés/museums. Then ask yourself the same question at the same time on Monday morning and the answer is guaranteed to be different. The second weekend will inevitably be more memorable, more rewarding and 'longer'. The same applies even more forcefully to the decade between our 50th and 60th birthdays. A recent coinage of 'denture venturers' for this age group might bring on a premature midlife crisis in some. A less depressing label (at least for the parents) is 'SKI-ers' (Spending the Kids' Inheritance).

Sara Buck gave herself an unusual 50th birthday present. She took four friends with her to placements at the Ulamba Children's Orphanage in Western Kenya, arranged through the charity Moving Mountains endorsed by Adventure Alternative (see Directory entry): 'I'm thinking about Kenya even more now than when I was there. It really gets under your skin and I even miss the smells! Our trip was much tougher than anticipated on all fronts but an amazing experience none of us will forget.' Even if you don't plump for such an ambitious trip to commemorate turning fifty, you might think of a gap year-cum-party. For her 50th, Jakki from Yorkshire found herself between jobs (in management of a housing association), and decided to rent a large villa with swimming pool in Andalucia for an extended period, to which she invited all her friends and family to spend time whenever they could. This seemed to be a good place to be when the invitation to attend the mammogram clinic dropped through her letterbox at home and also meant that she couldn't succumb to the temptation of going to Glastonbury alongside all those other wrinkly professionals.

It is not unknown for spouses in middle life (generally the female of the species) to think longingly of packing their life partner off for a period of time. Usually the idea goes no further than giving hubby a copy of this book for Christmas (hint hint), so I will not be taking up a friend's suggestion that I write a book for disgruntled middle-aged couples called *A Gap Year Apart*.

MY GROWN-UP GAP YEAR: JULIE FAIRWEATHER

Auxiliary nurse Julie Fairweather from Dundee had always been fascinated by African wildlife, but had never been near the continent. All that changed when she decided to treat herself to a mini-sabbatical, volunteering at a wildlife reserve in Namibia through Amanzi Travel.

My 40th birthday was approaching and I had decided I wanted to make a dream a reality. I had always loved watching documentaries about Africa - the people, the animals, the wildlife - but especially the cheetah. When I told my colleagues about my ideas and plans, they thought this was brilliant. One of my colleagues suggested volunteering as a way to get up close and even work with animals. I had not even considered this, but I started to Google 'Volunteer projects in Africa', and was amazed at all the websites that came up. The more I looked into volunteering, the more I thought that this would be so much more rewarding and fulfilling - knowing I could actually go out and help animals and communities, rather than booking a safari trip and sitting on the back of a Land Rover taking pictures. I got very excited at this prospect.

When I was looking for volunteer projects I found Amanzi Travel, which was offering volunteer work at a wildlife sanctuary with lions, baboons, caracals, wild dogs, and also cheetahs. When they offered a chance to get up close and work with tame cheetahs, I knew instantly that this was the place for me. The owner of Amanzi Travel put me at ease by offering to organise my flights, insurance, everything, as this was a bit daunting for me as I had never travelled alone abroad.

When I told my family and friends I would be going out to work with animals in Africa, they thought this was an amazing thing to do and gave me lots of encouragement. I found out that the Bushmen children at a local school loved getting little things like pencils and books; when I mentioned this to family and friends, I could not believe the response I got. Every day I went into work, there was someone else handing me a packet of stickers, books, balloons, pens, and pencils for the children for me to take out. It was brilliant and very encouraging for me. When I arrived at the sanctuary in Africa, the children were adorable, and over the moon with the gifts.

When I arrived at Na'ankuse Lodge & Wildlife Sanctuary near Windhoek, the people were so friendly and helped me with whatever I was nervous about. I had the best experience taking Samira, the tame cheetah, out for a walk in the wild - something I never thought I would ever get to do in my lifetime. Looking after baby baboons and taking them for walks was great also. At night they got scared, so we put nappies on them and took them into bed with us. How many people can say they have done that or will ever get the chance to do that?

I loved learning about the tracking of animals out in the wild and got the chance to go out with the researchers and look for cheetah tracks. We also got to collar wild cheetahs that were in danger of getting shot by farmers. We caught them, collared them, and released them into a safer environment. I got so emotional watching a cheetah head for freedom, and we did the same for a hyena too.

I think helping to build the new school for the Bushmen children has to be a very high point in my time out there. The other volunteers and I helped make bricks and cement for this: a very physical job but we all had great fun. When I saw the finished school with all the children sitting at their desks, I cried with joy knowing I had helped.

After my time was up and it was time to return home, it was quite sad to leave everybody and all the animals. They have very little so I paid for the sanctuary to get a new radio antenna to help them with tracking their animals with collars on. I also sponsored an animal and I get feedback to let me know how they are all doing, which is great.

Until you have been to a developing country, you don't seem to realise how lucky we are. The Bushmen live a very simple life and you don't even hear them complaining. When I got home, every time I had a hot shower, I was thankful. Every time I got in my car, I was thankful. Every time I put on my washing machine, I was thankful. I must admit it felt weird being home, and back at work I was pretty down for a while but eventually things got back to normal. My mum was especially proud of me because she never thought in a million years I would ever go to a strange country on my own or even get the chance. I am so glad I took the chance and did something quite remarkable and rewarding. There is no amount of money can give you that in this life.

RETIREMENT

If a change is as good as a rest, then **Ed McFadd** and **Eva Hagen** have the right idea. As soon as they hit retirement, they left home to do something completely different: Ed went from California to Montreal in the dead of winter to take a French course after rediscovering his long dormant love of the language; and Eva signed up for a conservation/farming project on a homestead in Australia, having harboured a life-long dream to live and work there.

With an increasing number of early retired people expressing an interest in volunteering abroad, some organisations have developed programmes specially for the older volunteer. One such group is MondoChallenge, which caters very well to people who have retired and are looking for something worthwhile and reasonably challenging to do with their time. Charities like this, and like people and places, are aware that over 50s have a huge amount to offer, not least life experience, and have a wider variety of skills that can be put to good use.

Rosie Prebble's experience is typical of many others:

At the age of 60, I felt that it was the right time to leave my job of learning support assistant in a comprehensive school, which I had been doing for ten years. I wasn't sure how I would spend my retirement and had no plans. Romania had always been in my heart since the fall of communism, when we saw the horrific pictures of the orphanages on our televisions. I never imagined I'd go there. In fact I had never been on a plane before. One day I was idly on my computer and decided to look up volunteering in Romania. That's when I decided I wanted to go. I am a widow and have two grown-up children who live close by, so I was in a position to do something that I really wanted to do.

I looked at several voluntary organisations and I warmed to Projects Abroad. I went to an open day in London and learnt first-hand about the projects. I booked up for a care project and chose to work for six weeks in a hospital and six weeks in a foster home. I didn't feel, at my age, that I should get sponsorship to fund my trip. It was something that I knew I wanted to do for myself so was happy to fund it myself. It was just amazing that when I received my work pension, the lump sum was the exact amount I needed to pay for the trip.

Some older volunteers might be deterred from joining an organised project for fear that all the other participants will be young things. Among the lessons learned by retiree **David Rutter** when he project managed an expedition in India with Raleigh was that, 'The only member of the expedition who was preoccupied with age was me! ... and that it didn't matter'. **Dini Peterson** didn't mind in the slightest mixing with young people almost the age of her teenage sons. Sharing adventures with these young folk in South Africa changed her mind about something:

Many of my travelling companions were recent high school graduates and, as a mother, I couldn't have imagined sending my 18-year-old son on a trip like this before seeing it for myself. Now without a doubt I will be planning a volunteer experience with Travellers Worldwide for both of my sons after their graduations. My dream is for my sons and me to have an experience like this together.

OVERCOMING RELUCTANCE

You will almost certainly be assailed by doubts at various points, such as in the early stages when you are wondering whether or not to go for it, as well as at the moment that you show your boarding pass at the departure gate. In between, possibly at your farewell party in the pub, you will suffer some pre-departure blues as you contemplate leaving behind the comfortable routines of home and work. But these separation anxieties are usually much worse in anticipation than in retrospect.

No one can avoid confronting the question: 'What if it all goes horribly wrong?' In the research for this book, I couldn't find anyone who said that they wished they had avoided the hassle of taking off and stayed quietly at home – including those whose gap years included a bout of homesickness, or malaria and a finished relationship. Mark Twain is often quoted in this context: 'Twenty years from now you will be more disappointed by the things you didn't do than by the ones you did. So throw off the bowlines. Sail away from the safe harbour. Catch the trade winds in your sails. Explore. Dream. Discover.'

Fixing the actual date of departure is one of the biggest challenges you will encounter. **Christine and Mike Benson**, who went round the world in 313 days, make it sound straightforward – though of course the decision was made after years of weighing up the pros and cons: 'One day, amidst all the research, we told ourselves that if we didn't decide on a date, we never would. It was then decided that we would leave on 14th January 2010. We bought our tickets in late October, and quit our jobs in the first week of January. Then we left!'

Antoine de Sainte-Exupery's adage '*Fais de ta vie un rêve et de ce rêve une réalité*' ('Make of your life a dream and of this dream a reality') is easy to say. If you are serious about this project, try to make your waffly intentions concrete by writing them down in a designated notebook or in a file on your computer labelled 'Learn Spanish in Guatemala', or 'Annapurna Circuit', or whatever your ambition. Once the decision has been made, obstacles fall away – or at least become manageable.

Four major obstacles to taking a gap year can be readily identified.

■ *It never occurs to people; they do not think outside the box.*
■ *Their spouse/partner is not enthusiastic.*
■ *They worry that they will slip down the career ladder, and when they return will have to start at the bottom again or won't find a job.*
■ *They can't afford it; too many financial commitments.*

RELATIONSHIP ISSUES

Being in a relationship with someone who is not keen or is not at liberty to join you in your adventures can be an understandable disincentive. 'Telegamy' (a neologism for marriage over a distance) is invariably problematic over an extended period. It is impossible to generalise, or even for the individuals involved to know what the right course of action should be. Frequent writing, emailing and phoning alleviates some of the anxiety. Compromise is one answer: for example, to organise a break that might be shorter than otherwise, or plan to rendezvous with your partner part way through the gap year. Part way through his cycling gap year, Mark Perriton paused on his 50th birthday to reflect on his life, and counted among his many blessings a 'strong respectful relationship' with his wife, who allows him to do this round-the-world trip and who was joining him for Christmas in Auckland.

But there is no guarantee of a fairy tale ending. **Nikki McClements**, whose gap year with her daughter was featured in the Channel 4 series about family gap years, realised that calling home had begun to feel like a chore and she found herself procrastinating about calling her boyfriend of 18 months. At first she assumed that it was simply because she didn't want her mind to be dragged back to what she had left. But after a time, she had to face the question of whether she really wanted to go back to her old life and relationship, and to what was on the horizon: marriage to Jamie and more children.

In an ideal world you will have a partner who is just as keen as you are to take a big break, but you may be anxious that this will place too much of a strain on your relationship. Before **Ness Aalten-Voogd** and her husband **Stefan** left to go round the world in their late 30s, they noticed that their families were running a number of books on whether they would still be talking to each other after having been together 24/7/365. **Marie Purdy** and her partner **Howard** used her redundancy money to go round-the-world in five months. Things were harmonious between them most of the time, but Marie experienced flashes of homesickness for the company of women. On such a trip you spend far more time with your partner than you do in the normal routines; if you have spent the whole day with someone, there's not much to say in the evening. One solution is occasionally to go your separate ways during the day to pursue individual interests, and then have something to say to each other when you next meet.

SHAKING OUT THE COBWEBS

You don't have to hate your job to want a change, but we all become stale when we conform to the same routine day in, day out. You can liven yourself up by small things: take an evening class in botanical drawing, or Spanish; join a jazz club or a choir; become involved in Amnesty International or any cause close to your heart; choose unusual destinations for your annual holidays. But these will not alter the fundamentals of your life.

When the home routines begin to pall and you find yourself craving a challenge or an opportunity to expose yourself to risk, it is time to give some thought to bringing about a change. As they say, you'll be a long time dead. Few books (with the notable exception of *Diary of a Nobody*) have been written to catalogue everyday working life. But hundreds have been written by people who have had adventures when away from their offices and factories. The titles of some of these evince how precious time away from routines can be, like Libby Purves's *One Summer's Grace*, about sailing around the perimeter of the British Isles with her husband and two pre-school children.

MY GROWN-UP GAP YEAR:
DEANNE (DINI) PETERSON

After raising a family and building up a business in the northern Michigan town of Ishpeming, Dini decided to cut loose.

I decided to take my big trip to Africa on my 40th birthday. My family thought I was absolutely CRAZY to be going on an adventure like this, but were very supportive once they realised my mind was made up! I own my own business so it took about two months of preparations, getting people trained in and hired to take over for me while I was gone. I had internet and telephone access in most of the places so was able to stay in almost constant contact with people at home and work.

I live in the USA and searched several organisations before I chose to go with the British company Travellers Worldwide, because most agencies I found in the USA were religious-based. My trip was split into two projects and a week-long safari trip in the middle. I spent the first leg of my journey working on a boat that did diving trips with great white sharks. I chose this because of all the volunteering projects offered through Travellers, this seemed to me to be the most terrifying, exhilarating, and most out-of-my-comfort zone, crazy thing to do. It did not disappoint! There isn't a more intense feeling then being in the water and looking a 13-foot great white shark in the eye.

The second part of my journey was spent in travelling from Cape Town to the Addo elephant reserve, with five people from four countries. During that week we travelled up the R44 mountain pass, through mountains, and along the coast. I was in awe for most of the ride. The scenery was breathtaking; the wildlife amazing. We went whale-watching, bungee jumping, zip-lined through the forest, explored ancient caves, and shopped. We visited a brewery and vineyard, soaked in a natural hot spring, rode ostriches and elephants, petted a lion, and went skydiving. It can only be described as a six-day adrenaline rush. In the evenings we sat around campfires and ate delicious local foods and reminisced about the day.

The third part of the trip was spent working with street kids in Knysna, South Africa. I got to see the more tragic side of Africa, the part we hear about in America. It really was heartbreaking to see children living in such horrid conditions, but it felt good to know that I was able to help them, if even in just a small way.

It was a wonderful, growing experience for the entire family. For six weeks my two teenage sons and husband did all their own cooking, cleaning and laundry. I felt VERY appreciated when I got home! It's been a year since my return home, but as I write this I can still remember vividly the taste of the saltwater, and the feeling of the water moving around me from the sheer force of the animal swimming past us underwater. I stay in touch with many people I met in Africa and rarely a day goes by that I don't think about something I did, or someone I met or experienced from that trip. My dream is for my teenage sons and me to have an experience like this together.

HOW WILL A BREAK AFFECT MY CAREER?

The principal concern about taking a gap year is its potential effects on your professional life. Getting out of the swim and losing touch understandably frightens a lot of people. It's indisputable that single people in their twenties will probably feel less wedded to their jobs and their employers than those in their forties with responsibilities at a more senior level, and certainly far less bound than individuals who have spent years building up their own businesses.

As a founder of his own successful business, **Humphrey Walters** is an eloquent advocate of sabbaticals for their value in the modern economy, and is quick to refute the obvious doubts that will arise:

> *I thought if you slogged your guts out and became indispensable and then went away, your business would go down the drain or your career would suffer. That's absolute rubbish. Quite the reverse. If you do not keep yourself in a learning environment you get left behind, because your ability to acquire knowledge is diminished massively. It's essential that everyone should take a break no more than half way through his or her career. It could be going back to university. Just engineer a break.*

The emphasis these days on lifelong learning is underpinned by an appreciation that the nature of work has become flexible, and this meshes nicely with the idea of a gap year. In the modern economy, we are less tied to a career in one field or to employment with one company for the duration of our working lives.

IMPROVING CAREER PROSPECTS

Improving career prospects is not or should not be the major motivation for taking a gap year. The break should be self-fulfilling as a unique opportunity to regain the child-like ability just to have fun, and not to measure everything in terms of success and failure. At the same time, it allows you to step back and examine your life and lifestyle and to enrich and broaden interests and experiences. However, many people do end up deriving concrete career advantages from their career breaks.

Onlookers may doubt the value of a break and may view it as merely a self-indulgent opportunity to ease off the pressure of working life. But a career break can also be an empowering move in the contemporary workplace: a chance to use your own time to equip yourself with experiences and skills that complement your formal professional training. It can be interpreted positively by employers as a sign of self-sufficiency and initiative. If you can re-invent yourself once (as a builder of village schools, carer of oil-soaked birds, round-the-world adventurer), you can do it again, and this confidence and flexibility can be highly valued by employers.

Gap years can also propel you into a different field of work. For example, the leading youth charity Raleigh accepts volunteer managers of all ages and backgrounds, many of whom find that the experience alters their future course. Examples include a 50-year-old accountant who changed roles and started doing lots of charity fundraising as a result of her time in Namibia; another accountant who volunteered as a project manager in Malaysia and is now working for a regeneration charity in Kabul; a keen amateur photographer volunteering in Malaysia who is now trying to set up his own travel photography business; and a graphic designer who took on a logistics role to learn new skills and is now re-training to become a mountain leader. Demanding experiences outside the normal workplace will make a beneficial contribution to anyone's career, which can be particularly useful in cases where the individual is unsure about the next career step.

Even rather frivolous ways of spending a career break have proved professionally beneficial, as in the case of **Michael Tunison** from Michigan:

> *Newspaper work was exactly what I thought I was leaving behind by globetrotting. I'd temporarily sacrificed (I believed) my career as a journalist, and the last place I thought I'd be working was at a daily paper in Mexico. But things never work out as planned and before I knew it I was the managing editor's assistant, and a month or so later the managing editor of the paper's weekend editions. How ironic. By taking a step my newspaper friends believed to be an irresponsible career move, I was soon years ahead of where I'd have been following the old safe route back home.*

EMPLOYERS' ATTITUDES

An independent survey of employees for Direct Line Travel Insurance found that around a quarter of respondents work for a company where sabbaticals are a staff perk. Among those in the public sector, finance, and insurance industries, that proportion rose to 40%, followed by IT and telecoms at 36%.

More and more large companies have introduced formal schemes for employees, some of which have grown naturally out of their maternity leave policy. For example, the BBC has been operating a career break scheme for many years; originally it was designed for staff with caring responsibilities, extended to covering further education breaks, and more recently expanded to cover personal projects – including travel. Marks and Spencer grants career breaks for up to nine months (unpaid); the John Lewis Partnership offers 26 weeks of paid leave after 25 years of service; Asda allows long-standing employees over 50 to take off three months unpaid (referred to as 'Benidorm Leave'); and even McDonald's gives four weeks paid leave after ten years of service.

Companies are having to respond to a growing expectation in the workforce of flexibility in working patterns. Recent research demonstrates that 50% of Generation Y workers (those born since 1982) and 45% of Generation X (born between 1964 and 1981) believe that sabbaticals are important, whereas the figure for Baby Boomers is only 29%. Career break schemes are offered by Lloyds TSB, Tesco, American Express, Littlewoods, Prudential, BT and the NHS. Many companies that have signed up to support the Work-Life Balance campaign offer career breaks alongside flexible working hours. Smaller companies can afford to be more flexible and agree to sabbaticals on a case-by-case basis, though they may have more trouble covering for an absent worker. One of the most attractive examples around is offered by the famous map and travel bookshop, Stanfords in Covent Garden, which keeps open jobs for staff who have worked there for at least one year while they travel for up to three months. When they get back they do a presentation to the rest of the staff about their experiences. Danone, producer of yoghurts, ranks very high on good companies to work for; employees are given up to 12 weeks of paid and unpaid leave plus £1,000 to fulfil their volunteering ambitions (a programme partnered with *i-to-i*).

A vocal campaign is being waged in the US media and online to increase the availability of sabbaticals. In fact, grown-up gap years enjoy a much higher profile than school-leavers' gap years in North America. The website www.yoursabbatical.com offers guidelines on how to campaign for a sabbatical in your company. It also publishes a list of companies with a sabbatical policy, which include everything from the four- to seven-week breaks available at the Random House Publishing Group; to periods of up to 24 weeks off granted by Deloitte, General Mills and others; or the three years by the United States Navy. Breaks can range from several weeks, to the five years of unpaid leave that the Foreign & Commonwealth Office offers to staff who can return to a job at the same level.

Very few companies offer semi-paid leave, but the crucial feature of a formal company scheme is that employment and pension rights are guaranteed. Back in the UK, The Royal Mail Group operates a number of career break schemes; the HR department can explain the eligibility requirements. Permission is granted by the line manager and pension contributions cease during the break. The guidelines stress the importance of maintaining regular contact with the organisation and it makes a point of communicating developments in the company to the employee on a sabbatical. These employees are also required to work a minimum of two weeks every year of the break. The right to return to the former division or business unit on the former grade is guaranteed and retraining is offered if the employee is given a different job.

If you have been promised your old job back, it is prudent to maintain contact with your boss to reassure them that you are still on course to return as planned. There is always an anxiety that out of sight means out of mind. **Annalisa Winge Bicknell** was a high-flying head of international sales at a private bank in London, where the job involved a lot of responsibility, long hours, high profile, and lots of travel. After 18 years of working hard, she decided to take a break:

> *I tried to negotiate a break from my employer, and initially when I started my sabbatical they voiced their support and wish for me to return to Northern Trust after the six-month sabbatical. However, when I wished to return as planned in early November 08, they told me that due to the recession they no longer had a suitable job to give me. This was quite a shock, as no redundancy package was provided to me either since I had taken the sabbatical. My timing was just unlucky because my return from the sabbatical was at the start of a scary recession. However, I have filled my life with other extremely satisfying things, first in the US and now in Oslo, which I wouldn't have been able to do otherwise. If one looks for it, there is generally a silver lining in most things.*

TAKING CHARGE
OF YOUR CAREER

No one anymore can count on having a job for life. In the past it was the norm for individuals to be offered a tight and reliable career structure, but the recession has made the job situation precarious for many. Yet in these times when it is more an employer's market, the good companies continue to offer flexibility and other perks. The prediction is for the contemporary sabbatical to evolve and become an important perk among the list of benefits designed to attract and retain good staff. Managing your own career has become important because your employer no longer looks after your interests as a matter of course. Downsizing is commonplace; final pension schemes are becoming a thing of the past. This new approach stresses the importance of self-motivation, personal responsibility, and a willingness to take risks. Employment practices at the BBC illustrate this shift: where once it encouraged lifelong loyalty, employees are now hired on short-term contracts.

CONSIDERATIONS FOR
THE SELF-EMPLOYED

The sharp rise in the number of people working freelance from home, many in front of computer screens all day, means that more people than ever have the freedom to opt out of work at intervals. Every so often it dawns on a freelance worker that he or she has barely stepped outside the house for days at a stretch, and he or she will think with longing of the cheerful swirl and hubbub of the outside world. That might be the time for a freelancer to step back and answer the question of whether it is really necessary to earn X number of pounds or dollars 52 weeks a year.

The self-employed can make their own decisions about taking time out from work without recourse to a line manager, but they may have clients who depend on them. In an ideal world you could pass the business on to a reliable contact, but at least you should give plenty of warning to customers about your intention to withdraw temporarily. Experienced freelancers who are paid sporadically often become adept at careful budgeting. With luck, they might be able to work extra hard for a limited period in order to accumulate enough savings to fund a career break. The downside is that they have no guarantee of work and benefits when they return.

When self-employed consultant **Ricky Grice** decided to give up the battle to keep his once-successful business going after the recession struck, he found everything fell easily into place:

I received tremendous amounts of encouragement from everybody I knew, who said they would do the same if they had the money/freedom/guts. The total time available to volunteer was limited only by savings, which would have lasted years in East Africa. When I met the founder of the charity 2Way Development, I had a gut feeling that this was the one to choose. They vet each charity with which they are affiliated, so I knew the quality was going to be high. My placement was as an IT specialist with a charity in Mombasa: Sponsored Arts For Education. The highlights were spending time in SAFE's Maasai office, and getting to make lots of Kenyan friends. I settled in more quickly than I expected, and had so much fun that I am staying and setting up business in Kenya.

However, the drawbacks for the self-employed should not be dismissed too readily. Anxiety occasionally clouded **Mike Benson's** ten-month gap year travels with his wife **Christine**. He had worked freelance in the film industry and then for Apple computers, and he couldn't help worrying about what job situation he would return to in November 2010 at the end of their amazing trip:

By leaving the film industry, I was essentially giving up the building blocks of my career and stepping aside while other talent moved right in. Not knowing how this would affect me in the future was a constant worry on the road because as I travelled, my clients would have to find other people to do work for them. If those other people formed more stable relationships with my clients then my network would break down and I'd have to start all over again.

How he and his wife Christine fare in their post-gap year re-entry to the US employment scene can be followed on their blog www.checkingoffeverywhere.com.

PERSUADING THE BOSS

It is surprising how many forward-thinking companies are at least willing to consider granting a sabbatical to a valued worker. When you bite the bullet and finally ask to have a word with your boss, he or she will probably be quite relieved when you do not announce that you have accepted a better job offer elsewhere, but merely want six months' unpaid leave to broaden your horizons. You should give some careful thought to how you can put as positive a spin as possible on what you intend to do so that your employer will be persuaded that the gap year will benefit the company as much as it will you. **Siamak Tannazi's** request to her boss was mentioned earlier. Together with citing her personal reasons for wanting to volunteer in Kerala, she described why the timing of her requested break might be beneficial. It was at a time when BT was preparing for a radical network transformation and Tan (as she is known) wanted to take her break before the change really kicked in. She pointed out to her boss that the other members of her team were happy to provide cover and were willing to support her in her efforts. In the end her boss granted three months' special leave and that turned out to be about right for her. It turned out that the pitch she made was more than empty rhetoric:

As things in India are prone to change ALL the time, you automatically become accustomed to thinking on the spot and expecting the unexpected. For example, half-way through the school term in India, I had to help choose the English teacher out of a selection of applicants in an interview. This task was laid upon me at two minutes' notice. It was a situation that I don't have experience in or ever expected to be placed in, yet it seemed to happen all the time whilst I was in India. This has helped me in BT, as I do actually try to look at the bigger picture when I'm working. So changes happening at the moment don't unsettle me as much as they did before I left for India.

Of course it is much easier to arrange a sabbatical from some jobs than others. The word sabbatical means literally one in seven, and a break (roughly) every seven terms or seven years is built into academic life. Sabbaticals are routinely granted in higher education to allow lecturers to pursue their research, which is as important a part of their job as teaching. Traditionally in the Civil Service, career breaks of up to five years have been offered to established employees – especially if they can argue that a break will enhance their ability to contribute in the workplace. With the depressing expectation that a third of a million public sector workers in the UK will lose their jobs by 2015, the perpetuation of the sabbatical perk cannot be guaranteed.

Big companies spend thousands on team-building exercises and leadership courses for middle managers, which in many cases are aiming for the same benefits as can be gained by a gap year project. The potential benefits of a volunteer expedition include recharged batteries, new skills outside your traditional skills set, improvement of communication and teamwork skills, a new found respect for community values, an appreciation for what privileges we often take for granted, incentives to advance your career, and an enhanced CV.

No longer does a gap on a CV suggest to an employer that a candidate took time out to 'find themselves'. Increasingly nowadays, employers encourage people to take time out, recognising the importance of motivating key staff and encouraging creativity in the workplace. As businesses become globally focussed, an understanding of cultures different from our own is considered a huge asset. Not only that, but you become interesting. How many interviews are conducted which the candidates can barely be distinguished from one another? Everybody looks the same, everybody has the same qualifications, and everybody has the same experience. How many built an orphanage, taught in a school in Africa, or climbed a 10,000ft mountain? Employers are looking for evidence of experience beyond the workplace: for the ability to be innovative and creative.

Everybody's circumstances are different. Many people reading this will feel discouraged, assuming that their present employer would not be prepared to consider granting a leave of absence. For example in manufacturing, construction, banking, and industry generally, companies have been down-sizing and might jump at the chance to get rid of one more employee if they stepped out of the usual groove.

When requesting unpaid leave, marshall as many reasons as you can to persuade your employer to keep the job open for you. Your employer might surprise you and allow you to take a break. If they don't, maybe they were the wrong kind of employer for you in the first place. Individuals will have to decide in advance whether they are sufficiently confident of their skills and experience to walk away from a job if an employer refuses to grant a sabbatical.

Your chances of success when asking an employer for leave are greater if your contribution is highly valued or is in some way difficult to replace. Timing can be critical here – though again success is not guaranteed, as **Paul Carroll** found out:

I started by challenging the two-week maximum single holiday period permitted without CEO approval in the software testing company where I had been working. Upon completion of a major new project for our largest client, I requested a one-month holiday for trekking around the Himalayas. This was rejected. I then did the same six months later upon completion of the second phase for this client. Again, this was rejected. The third time was four months later and the CEO personally took me aside to explain that if he agreed to my request, others would also want a month or more. Although two of the three directors felt flexibility was needed, the CEO (who is responsible to the investors) didn't believe the company could risk key members being away for longer than a fortnight at a time.

So Paul had to reconsider his options, and decided to quit altogether. This left him with six months to join a VentureCo expedition and to travel independently round South America. On his return his old employer offered him a consultancy role, but he has chosen to change his lifestyle considerably instead, exchanging the work-hard, play-hard London lifestyle for a more relaxed travelling consultant's job based near the Peak District. Although he still works quite hard, he now feels he is mobile, in control of his career, and a lot happier with life in general because he is able to achieve his personal goals outside of the working week.

Some companies offer the possibility of sabbaticals, but may not want to advertise or promote it too loudly. In other organisations a formal policy may actually be in place, but is little known or quietly neglected for fear of encouraging a flood of applicants at the same time. Check with the HR department to see whether your company or organisation has established a specific policy on sabbaticals. Even if your employer doesn't have a formal policy, employees should make a case for an unpaid break and its value to the company in the long run. The process should be advantageous to each party and may have the further benefit of allowing colleagues the opportunity to learn new skills.

The more people who take a career break, the more the concept will be taken for granted. According to an article in 2008 called 'Accountants and Sabbaticals', in the journal of the Association of Chartered Certified Accountants, the majority of accountancy firms include sabbaticals as part of their employee benefits package. This is because corporate clients are finding it increasingly difficult to retain talented individuals in financial roles. Rather than face losing the member of staff permanently, they are willing to lose them temporarily.

TAKING THE INITIATIVE

In all but a handful of cases, it is necessary to be proactive about making a grown-up gap year happen. Imagination and determination will be required, so you must be strongly committed to the idea before setting out.

Ceri Evans, a senior sexual health counsellor in the NHS, happened to spot a pamphlet in the human resources office about a scheme which allowed staff with at least two years service to take up to two years' unpaid leave. The policy had not been advertised, nor were applications actively encouraged. It seems that it was primarily intended for staff who needed to travel or care for sick relatives and it included the proviso that paid work was not allowed during the break. She later learned that a colleague's application to the scheme had previously been declined because she had wanted to study at university. Undeterred, Ceri decided to use her initiative to make her plan viable.

Ceri had decided to take a complete break from her work in the HIV field but needed to make the case that she wanted to go to Spain to study treatments there. In reality it was not very practical because she didn't speak Spanish, and her primary concern was to spend a year in Barcelona living with her partner who was working there.

As the manager of her department, Ceri needed to persuade her boss that her absence wouldn't be too disruptive, and so she took the initiative to find a replacement. She found a colleague working in another clinic who wanted the experience afforded by her absence and who wouldn't require any extra salary. She also reassured her employers that she fully intended to resume her job on return, being conscious that there was a prevailing anxiety about losing trained staff. However, be cautious about making promises you suspect you may not be able to keep. Dishonesty and maltreatment of employers will only engender distrust of employees who come after you with a request for a chance to take time away from work.

PERSONAL CONSULTATIONS

Trawling through books and websites may not be enough for some people, who seek personal reassurance and expert advice. Several one-person businesses offer private consultations to anyone considering taking a grown-up gap year. **Tessa Mills** took her own adventurous gap year (see her case history at the end of this book), which inspired her to set up the Career Break Guru. Prospective clients can book an individual or group workshop or consultation for fees ranging from £55 to £190.

Similarly, Gillian Woodward in her 60s did a solo round-the-world trip visiting 32 countries over three years, and now works as a travel mentor – providing travel counselling to anyone who wishes to talk through a planned journey.

- ■ *The Career Break Guru*, Fairbank Studios, 65 Lots Road, Chelsea, London SW10 0RN (020 7193 8352 / 07973 822598; tessa@careerbreakguru.com; www.careerbreakguru. com). Advisory business established in 2007/8. Advisory sessions range from Getting Started (£55), to Getting Going with intensive coaching (£190), when client-specific research is carried out.
- ■ *TravelMentor*, Gillian Woodward (020 7221 4587/07906 099535; gillian.woodward@ talk21.com; www.nottinghillcounselling.co.uk). £55–£75 for a one-hour session.
- ■ *Three Month Visa Coaching and Consulting*, San Francisco (www.threemonthvisa. com). Tara Russell is a 'Life Sabbatical & Long-Term Travel Coach', who works with clients who dream of taking time off to travel, live, work, study, or volunteer abroad. In addition to her work coaching clients one-to-one, she is co-founder of the Meet, Plan, Go! Movement – whose aim is to empower Americans to realise their career break and long-term travel dreams.

CAREER BREAK CHECKLISTS

Working Families is a UK-based campaigning charity working towards a healthy work/life balance. It publishes a fact sheet entitled 'Breaks from Work', which can be read online (www.workingfamilies.org.uk/asp/family_zone/factsheets/Breaks_from_Work.doc). Its guidance on the subject of negotiating a career break includes some of the following:

NEGOTIATING A BREAK

If you want to negotiate leave with an employer without a formal sabbatical scheme, consider the following:

- *What will my employment rights be while on the break?*
- *Will my job be guaranteed on return?*
- *How much responsibility will I have for putting replacement personnel in place?*
- *Can I do some work experience while on the break?*
- *Can I take part in training courses or undertake assignments?*
- *What contact can I have with my employer, in order to keep in touch with changes at work?*
- *When do I want to return to work?*
- *What other benefits can I keep (eg membership of the social club)?*

ESTABLISHING YOUR VALUE

Before approaching an employer, thoroughly identify the skills he or she needs most and think about the following:

- *Your real value to your employer: ie how much has your employer invested in your recruitment, training and development?*
- *The skills shortages in your profession or area of work.*
- *Your employer's future developments and planned growth.*
- *What costs will your employer incur in replacing your skills, experience, and knowledge?*
- *The value of employment breaks to improving employee relations, recruitment, retention, and public image.*

WHAT CAN BE ACHIEVED?

Perhaps you've always dreamed of farming alpacas, playing the harmonium, joining a circus, or sailing through the Bermuda Triangle. Alternatively, you might want to stay at home to look after a newborn child, or learn to paint, or write a guide to pubs in your region. You might simply need an extended break from a demanding job or want to assess the direction of your career. Grown-ups will have their own reasons for wanting to take a gap year. The only activity that is prohibited is to sit around doing nothing.

A gap year abroad is bound to extend your horizons and make you a more enlightened global citizen. One 40-year-old American career breaker, **Dini Peterson**, had done months of preparatory reading and web-browsing, and assumed she was relatively well informed before she arrived in South Africa to do some conservation and community volunteering:

> *I was wrong. I learned more about the people, the cultures, and the customs of South Africa in my six weeks there than anyone could have learned from a lifetime of reading about it. I met people from all over the world, and in living with volunteers from around the globe, I also learned about their countries and cultures. Traveling as a volunteer gives you opportunities to see things from a completely different perspective.*

It is important to strike a good balance between slavishly following a predetermined programme, and starting off with no idea of what you're hoping to achieve. Sometimes, a gap year can lead you in unexpected directions and unpredictability is part of the adventure. **David Rutter's** experiences in India challenged his long-held views about many things:

> *I held fairly strong (left wing) political views before Raleigh, but I now realise that they were based on a rather narrow UK-based viewpoint. I still consider myself to be a socialist, but I find it more difficult to reach a clear conclusion on any issue, because my experience in India has revealed so many complex, extra international factors. I will not now settle into a quiet passive retirement, but will work to raise awareness of the Millennium Development Goals, and (finance permitting) probably go on another expedition soon. I recently became a grandparent and I will try to help my granddaughter to become a responsible international citizen. I know that sounds a bit formal, but there are so many small ways to work towards it.*

Taking a career break affords a unique opportunity to experience an aspect of life that would otherwise be inaccessible to you in the course of your professional life. For some, taking a career break has had a profound effect on their values in life and on their futures.

PART 2

NUTS AND BOLTS:
PREPARING TO TAKE OFF

HOW TO AFFORD A GAP YEAR
THE FINANCIAL IMPLICATIONS
ACCOMMODATION MATTERS

HOW TO AFFORD
A GAP YEAR

Having made a commitment to negotiate a sabbatical or even resolved to leave your job altogether, the next step is to clarify your position financially and personally. Everything can fall into place with the right preparations. How are you going to finance your leave? What are the implications for long term financial security? How can you look after the house if you are going to be away for many months or even a year or more? Will your mortgage lender permit you to rent out your house to tenants? What can be done with the dog, cat, or goldfish if you plan to be away from home? These are some of the many considerations any individual, couple or family needs to consider before stepping away from their work and regular income.

All the exciting talk of renewal and rejuvenation during a gap year must be balanced with an unflinching look at the down side, and organising the logistics of a long stay abroad will take scores of hours. A family spending a year's sabbatical in Paris estimated that even eight months into their stay, one of them was having to spend at least an hour a day on what they termed 'administration'. The **Marsh–Norgrove family** from British Columbia who divided their family year off between Tanzania, Turkey, and a cycle trip to the Baltic, decided that it would be a good idea to take two years off: one to prepare for the Great Adventure and one to do it.

FUNDING

Funding is the biggest stumbling block for most dreamers. Saving enough to finance months off work, even if sticking to a rigorous budget, is a major undertaking. Sometimes the kinds of glamorous gap year featured in newspapers or television programmes are accessible only to the mega-rich, like in several of the episodes of *My Family's Crazy Gap Year* on Channel 4 in 2010. But plenty of ordinary folk scrimp and save – including one of the families featured on the documentary, Nikki McClements, a 29-year-old youth worker in Ivybridge, Devon, who wanted to expose her 9-year-old daughter Beth to the less fortunate. On a shoestring, they volunteered in a South African township, taught English in a northern Thai village, and travelled in Indonesia.

Everyone's circumstances and responsibilities will vary. Being younger with fewer financial obligations is naturally going to be an advantage, but you are probably likely to have fewer savings and no income-generating property to finance the break. As this book illustrates, people take gap years at different points in their lives depending on what their priorities are.

It is crucial to recognise that taking a gap year is probably easier in practical terms than you imagine. It may sound glib to claim that there are ways round most potential obstacles, but others who have gone before have found solutions. The most obvious way to increase savings is to cut out the luxuries like eating out, and to work more hours – which was the simple solution of **Julie Fairweather**, a 39-year-old health care assistant at a Dundee hospital who wanted to volunteer with cheetahs in Namibia through Amanzi Travel:

When I booked the trip I knew it would be a lot of money for me, but I was determined to do it. I had to work a lot of extra hours, and my colleagues knew this so were always offering extra shifts if they became available, but also told me that I can't work myself into the ground. I did notice that you could get sponsors to help pay for the trip but I thought that because it was my dream I didn't want someone else paying for it, so I worked and worked to pay for the whole trip myself. The total cost including flights (£635), malaria tablets and rabies injections (about £200), insurance, etc, came to not too much short of £3,000. But it also gave me great satisfaction knowing I had paid for it all myself. I feel that the price was totally reasonable but I will look into getting some sponsors the next time to help me.

Inevitably, funding a period of time in your life without a salary is going to be expensive, especially if this time includes extensive travel or voluntary work abroad. It would be misleading to gloss over the considerable costs involved, although you have to bear in mind that the cost of living in a developing country might end up being less than it would be if you just stayed at home.

Normally the expression 'burning your bridges' means cutting yourself off and destroying your means of escape. But in the context of taking a major step like deciding to rent out your house to finance some serious travels or volunteer projects, it can mean exactly the opposite. Paradoxically, you might have to burn your bridges (give up your job, move out of your house) to catch a boat to freedom and adventure. This is exactly what long-time careers teacher **Nigel Hollington** did. After negotiating with his headteacher, who promised to keep a teaching job open for him in his Hertfordshire comprehensive, Nigel's first step was to rent out his house – which would force him into action. Nigel had no fixed ideas of what he wanted to do or where he wanted to go, though he knew he wanted to fill the year with constructive things and not just bum around. By November, only a few weeks before he had to give up his house, he still had nothing fixed up and began to take a closer interest in the literature that passed through his hands in the careers room at school. He had an open mind about destinations and was soon signed up for a ten-week conservation project in Zambia. He calculated that his average monthly spending at home left not much change from £1,000, so he reckoned he would be breaking about even by joining this project.

Tempted as you might be by the idea of a gap year, you might be deterred by the assumption that a period of time without a salary would be out of the question in your circumstances. But before you put the idea out of your head or procrastinate yet again, you should be aware that there are many ways of keeping the cost down. If you intend to do something charitable during your break, you can fundraise to support a good cause (and you). It might then mean you could concentrate your energies on finding paid work abroad, even if it was only pocket money. This might involve taking a job in a bar or using your fluency in English to teach the language (see Part 6: Working and Living Abroad, for more details).

Beth Buffam fell in love with Vietnam on a six-month gap year, but when she returned home to the US she found jobs in her profession (computer troubleshooter) in short supply. She then began teaching English as a second language, a skill she took back to Hanoi a few years later, where she was able to save $800 a month to cover the mortgage. Beth's breakdown of her monthly expenses on top of the free accommodation provided by the school are remarkable: $30 for food, $50 for local transport, $50 for gifts and occasional expenses, and $20 for school expenses – proving that gap years need not break the bank. When she told her brother that with the air ticket her total expenditure was less than $2,000, he replied, 'Wow, I spend that much in one day when my family travels'.

If you don't have enough in savings, you could consider increasing your mortgage. If you are in rented accommodation, think how much you would save if you gave it up and maybe moved in with your boyfriend (as **Jane O'Beirne** did in anticipation of their six-month round-the-world trip), or even into your mother's attic (as **Paul Edmunds** did after renting out his house to a young couple in order to pay for his trip to Africa). While planning a 12-month round-the-world trip with her boyfriend, a 20-something woman from Oxford found it tougher to get to the point of departure than she anticipated. Her attempt to rent a studio in London for her art practice while still saving money for travelling was a failure, so she returned home to Oxford where her parents took her in. She comments in her blog at hj153.wordpress.com/author/hj153:

Leaving London was a big deal and coming home, despite its comforts and practicality, felt like a failure. I've worried that going travelling is somehow a cop out; running away from having to get stuck in and make some decisions. Perhaps unsurprisingly, after spending six months at home doing menial administration and clerical work, which drove me utterly to distraction, absolutely nothing looks as scary as having to do something dull every day.

If you can't afford the agency fees, consider finding a low-cost grassroots volunteer project on your own. As experienced and adventurous travellers, **Deby and Peter Hardy** (aged 49 and 53) decided to go to Nicaragua and see what turned up:

We never organised anything before we went, as we wanted to see things for ourselves before we committed. When we visited the old colonial city of Granada, we loved it and knew that was where we would work. We went out the second night there to find a restaurant, and stumbled across a place which Deby said we must go into. It turned out to be the opening night of a restaurant run by ex-street kids and supervised by an American. We were introduced to another American who was involved in a project to refurbish a school/workshop for learning disability and physically disabled artisans. We agreed to work for them there and then, and they even sorted out accommodation for us in a volunteer house! Of course we had to pay rent for the volunteer house which was £125 per month – slightly expensive for Nicaragua, but good accommodation.

If you have a young child in full-time childcare, think of saving that huge expense every month. If you gave up smoking, drinking, the gym, whatever other vice, think how much richer you would be after six or 12 months. If you are a property owner, imagine renting it out for a sum that would cover the monthly mortgage payments with some to spare for your spending money. Some people are lucky enough to benefit from a windfall. The **Whitlock family**, who took a year out to go round the world, made theirs stretch as far as possible:

My grandmother died about a year and a half before we left. She left me £25,000 in her will, and this prompted us to plan the trip. At first we couldn't believe it. It seemed such a lot of money, but really, given the fact that a decent, large family car can cost that much in itself, we couldn't work out how best to spend it. We wanted it to change our lives for the better in some way. The plans for the trip began as dream-talk, but grew and grew, until it would have been a let-down (not least to Gran's memory) not to have gone ahead with it... Some colleagues thought it was rather a reckless thing to do, but most of their concerns seemed to centre on our policy of selling/ chucking away all of our possessions. Frankly, to me, that was the least traumatic thing of all.

DOS AND DON'TS WHEN TAKING A CAREER BREAK

According to Anthony Lunch, who set up the non-profit volunteer-sending agency MondoChallenge, the following practical considerations will help to ensure a smooth and rewarding gap year.

Plan early

- Research your destination thoroughly before you go, and buy a good guidebook and maps. Also look at the advice given by the Foreign & Commonwealth Office (www.fco.gov.uk).
- Be aware of the laws, customs and dress code for the country. Your guidebook should provide all this information.
- If you wish to return to your job on your return, contact your employer as early as possible about the opportunities for taking a sabbatical. Your company may offer paid or unpaid sabbaticals. Emphasise the positive benefits your career break will bring to your company: for example you will return to work more motivated and energised, having learned new skills and gained more confidence.
- Online banking is a great way to manage your finances while you are away. But many internet cafés are slow and access may not always be easy, so don't leave important transactions until the last minute. Set up standing orders for key items (eg household utilities, credit card minimum payments).
- Calculate how much money you will need for your trip and make sure you have some extra. Find out if you can use a credit or debit card to withdraw money at your destination. It's best to have a combination of credit/debit card, travellers' cheques, sterling and some US dollars.
- Visit your doctor for advice on vaccinations and medication needed.
- Contact the relevant embassy or consulate for advice on obtaining a visa; many have online forms. Often visas can be obtained on arrival, although having one in your passport ahead of time can be comforting. If you plan to visit lots of countries, make sure your passport has plenty of blank pages, or get a new one well before you leave.
- Shop around for travel insurance and make sure you are covered for everything you intend to do, eg white water rafting.
- Make photocopies of your passport (including visa pages), insurance details and plane tickets. Leave copies with family/friends and take copies with you.
- Make sure your family or friends at home are aware of your travel itinerary.
- If you intend to use your mobile phone, contact your operator to check whether you will have coverage. If not, you will need to take it into a shop to have the phone 'unlocked'. Warn friends not to call your UK mobile while you are away; you will be paying for all incoming calls from abroad (see below for alternatives).
- Take a good international plug adaptor (or two).
- If you are volunteering through an organisation, ask for the contact details of the most recent volunteers on your project. They will be able to give you the best advice about what to expect on the project.
- If you are planning to take a laptop, make sure you install and become familiar with Skype so that you can keep in touch free of charge with family and friends who also use Skype. It can also be used to dial landlines at very reduced rates.

On arrival

- Register your details and itinerary on the FCO's LOCATE service (www.fco.gov.uk/locate) in countries where embassy officials may need to track you down in the event of an emergency.
- If you are volunteering with an organisation ensure that local managers are aware of your plans, eg if you decide to go away for the weekend.
- Keep photocopies of important documents (passport, insurance info, plane tickets) in separate bags from the original copies.
- Take advice from your local manager about your personal safety and where best to keep your valuables.
- Keep your valuables out of sight. Combination locks are useful for your bags.
- Ensure you respect local customs in regard to dress code, personal relationships, smoking, and drinking alcohol. It is important for you, the organisation you are with, and the other volunteers that you do not cause offence.
- If you are staying in one country for an extended period, consider getting either a cheap local mobile phone or a local sim card for your UK mobile. Don't forget to alert friends back home to the new number. Local texts and calls tend to be very cheap and incoming calls from abroad are free, which avoids the massive charges when using your UK mobile. Even better, ensure your UK contacts have the special access codes available for low cost dialling to your country (try Telediscount or JustCall).

MY GROWN-UP GAP YEAR: MARIE PURDY

Upon being made redundant after a restructuring at Cambridge County Council, Marie (who is Irish) and her partner Howard travelled round the world over five months.

With the extra redundancy money and rental money from a home she inherited from her mother in Ireland, Marie and her partner Howard decided to take a long trip to Australia and New Zealand. When Marie began to do the research with a travel agency, she discovered that for only a couple of hundred pounds more they could buy a Star Alliance round-the-world ticket. Because they did not want to be pinned down to a fixed timetable, they paid a premium so that dates could be changed without penalty: a facility they made use of several times.

Marie tried to anticipate all the logistical problems. She pre-booked accommodation in their stopover destinations (Vienna, Dubai, and Singapore) and

Perth. She rented the Dublin house out through an agent. She made sure her mobile phone was unlocked so that she could buy Australian and New Zealand sim cards. She redirected her mail in both Ireland and England to friends who reported to her anything that looked important.

In Australia they did a huge amount of motoring, first from Perth to the southwest corner, then from Cairns all the way to the Blue Mountains, Sydney, and Melbourne (4,000km in five weeks). In general they would stay in hotels or motels if they were staying in a place for just one night, but tried to find self-catering accommodation if they were staying for longer. Marie admits she is an anxious person and thinks she took her responsibility to choose the perfect places to stay too seriously.

Their week in Cairns was a highlight. They stayed in a lovely place, visited the coral reef, took the Skyrail to Kuranda, visited a bird sanctuary, and so on. This was late November, so out of season - ie, not the school holidays - so travel was very easy. They did a sailing trip in the Whitsunday Islands, and stopped at Surfer's Paradise. They were a bit sniffy about the idea, but it was great fun in the quiet season. The beaches were gorgeous and the theme parks good fun. The key to a successful trip is building in lots of variety, and this coast of Southern Queensland offered something different.

They continued their journey in New Zealand (six weeks), Fiji and the Cook Islands, (where Marie suffered from the heat) and on to Vancouver which they both loved. They had to time their stay in the USA carefully because the only affordable insurance policy they could find to cover Howard (who has had major heart surgery) was for a maximum of 21 days. They spent this whole time in Montana, where old friends (the wife is from the Blackfeet tribe) run a restaurant in Glacier National Park.

Marie concludes that five months is perhaps a little too long for travelling from place to place, and thinks that three months would be ideal. She thinks that the key is to visit fewer places and stay longer. The endless need to make decisions (where to go, where to stay, where to eat) becomes wearing.

But they have further plans to travel, perhaps to South America, and with this in mind, Marie obtained a CELTA certificate to qualify her to teach English if the opportunity arises.

THE FINANCIAL IMPLICATIONS

Taking a career break will have substantial implications for your personal finances. Whatever the purpose of your career break, it means that your financial affairs will be undergoing a period of flux that requires some planning. If you own your home, you are likely to have a mortgage to maintain. Other financial concerns may include a pension, insurance policies, standing orders and direct debits from your bank account to cover regular household costs like the utilities, or personal activities like club memberships, charitable donations, and journal subscriptions. This might be the moment to cash in those premium bonds your grandparents bought for you as a child, or some shares that have risen in value.

Other ways to raise revenue include selling assets like cars or a valuable painting you once inherited but never really liked. A sensible option for homeowners who wish to travel is to make use of the empty property to generate income (see page 61 for a detailed section later in this chapter). This may be possible even if you are not going away for your career break; you could think about taking in a lodger to defray expenses. If you live in a town that has English language schools, contact them to see if they are looking for rooms for their foreign language students. You can increase your income by as much as £100 a week if you're prepared to have halting conversations in English over breakfast.

MANAGING YOUR AFFAIRS

If you are planning to be away for some time, it is useful to set up direct debit arrangements on the television licence, the water rates, and all the other bills that might arrive in your absence. Find out how much flexibility is built in to your mortgage and pension since the regulations allow some leeway (see below).

Naturally, you'll need to leave enough money in the relevant accounts to cover expenses, plus an extra stash for unforeseen emergencies like a tree falling on your roof, a flood in the basement, or a defaulting tenant. And you won't want to return without some in reserve, as **Kath McGuire** who at age 33 took off to volunteer and travel in Sri Lanka explains: 'I had to ensure I had enough money before I left to fund the trip and to fund my first few months back again, so that I wouldn't have to stress about getting work instantly.'

Make an audit of all your additional regular expenses and decide which ones to pay and which to cancel. Unless you have very few ties, shifting your life for a career break will take some military-style planning to ensure your departure is smooth. Note that some organisations like private insurers and gyms might allow members to suspend payments until they return home, without losing the initial joining fee.

It cannot be denied that clearing the financial decks can involve a certain amount of tedium and drudgery. But a personal dream to accomplish a goal outside a career should not be set aside just because some of the preparations might be considered tiresome. Sometimes the hardest things to organise are not financial at all, as **Sue Fenton** from Inverness discovered when she prepared for her 50-something gap in Nepal:

I was self-employed, so it was relatively easy to escape for three months, but as I edit and publish a monthly magazine it meant an extremely heavy backlog of work when I returned. My long-suffering husband was left with the dog-sitting, and everyone was very supportive of my decision to go. The hardest part to organise was getting people to stand in for my voluntary commitments – the community minibus, lunch club for the old folk, etc.

When the list of obligations is drawn up, the task may seem somewhat overwhelming. But if you leave plenty of time and tackle one at a time you will soon have dealt with them all and be able to chime in with the breezy departure of Sir Cedric (from Roy Gerrard's charming children's stories):

There was rushing and fussing and bustling and packing,
and cancelling the milk the last day.
Then the cat was put out and they all gave a shout
For at last they were off on their way.

MONEY MATTERS

One of many advantages of the internet is the ability to use online banking. All the major banks and building societies offer their websites with encryption to account holders, whereby you can access your personal account and check your balance, make financial transactions and payments, and set up direct debits. Furthermore, online banks like Smile (www.smile.co.uk) and Egg (new.egg.com) give favourable rates of interest. However, technological and human errors are likely at some point to delay payment of bills and cause aggravation, usually while you're crossing Mali or Mexico.

Paul Edmunds knew that he did not have enough savings to cover his six-month break – the first three months of which he spent travelling and volunteering in Africa. He had no intention of returning to the workplace he had left after more than 20 years (Gatwick Airport) and was prepared to take a cut in income, even after he returned to work in a freelance consultant capacity. He therefore went in to talk to his bank manager, who arranged an overdraft for him so that he avoided paying expensive interest charges.

Consider consulting a financial adviser if you don't already use one, to help you prepare a financial strategy for your career break so that the time away from paid work can have minimal impact on your long-term financial security. Arguably, the most important aspect of taking a gap year from any corporate employment is to research how a break will affect your benefits. Companies often offer a pension, private health insurance, life assurance, and income protection for their employees. Will these be affected by a break? If you're taking a sabbatical as an employee with a job being held open for you, it's important to understand whether these in-house benefits will be affected. In all probability your company benefits will not be diminished during your absence, particularly if the company has a formal sabbatical scheme, though you'll certainly have to hand back the company car. Typically a career break of more than 12 months may require you to resign from your current position with the promise of a job at the same level being available to you on your return, and this can affect your entitlement to important benefits such as redundancy payments.

HOW WILL MY PLANS AFFECT MY MORTGAGE?

For homeowners, a mortgage is likely to be the greatest financial obligation during their working lives. Maintaining monthly payments is a crucial feature of financial planning. The good news is that mortgage policies are becoming increasingly flexible, precisely because the banks and building societies recognise that the working population needs greater choices to reflect greater competition and changes in the nature of employment.

Many of the leading mortgage companies now offer flexible mortgages, allowing suspension of payments for a few months – colloquially known as a 'payment holiday'. Specific options vary according to each policy and you will need to check with your mortgage lender. More than two-thirds of lenders have signed up to a scheme that allows people to take a holiday of up to two years from making mortgage interest payments, though this is primarily for people in financial difficulty. Mortgage holidays increase overall costs so should not be taken lightly.

Mortgage specialist David Hollingworth, of London and Country Mortgages Ltd (www.lcplc. co.uk), recommends thinking about this question a long way in advance to give you a chance to change your mortgage before taking a gap year:

It's important to look at the small print of your agreement and to be very upfront with your lender about your plans. Try to contact the lender as soon as you have made a decision to take a break, or least before you actually leave work.

Your mortgage conditions must count as the major financial factor in evaluating whether you can afford to suspend your regular salary. A logical and simple solution is to find a paying tenant for the duration of your absence (see page 61: Renting Out Your Property). Remember though that if you decide to rent out the property the payments may increase depending on your mortgage rate.

If in the past few years you have taken out a flexible mortgage, it might give you the opportunity to take back capital you have put in above the mandatory interest payments. For example, if every year you pay in an extra thousand pounds to decrease the total loan, you might be able to take some of that money back in cash. Every policy will offer different benefits and detailed enquiries will have to be made before reaching any decisions about altering the terms of your mortgage. Setting up an offset mortgage which will allow you to take money out of your mortgage account without penalty can be the best course of action.

Another option for raising capital is by taking advantage of your home's increased value to extend your mortgage. If for instance you have a £100,000 loan, you may after five years of ownership be able to increase that loan to £120,000, which would cover any mortgage payments during a break and provide cash for travel or educational expenses in the time off work. Most lenders will allow you to increase the mortgage up to 75% of the current market value.

But don't just renegotiate the mortgage with your current lender: now might be the right time to shop around and switch your mortgage, to take advantage of a lower rate or a more flexible policy to assist your gap year finances. Visit a broker and take advantage of the various deals available in the mortgage marketplace. Each borrower will have unique requirements and the challenge is to find a policy that suits you during your career break, but which will also accommodate any foreseeable career plans after your return.

Paul Edmunds had problems with his mortgage lender, Abbey National, who were reluctant to allow him to continue paying a low rate of interest under his flexible mortgage arrangement if he was sub-letting to tenants while he went to Africa. Although he persuaded the building society to let him keep paying at the low interest rate for a limited time, they told him that after a certain period they would double the rate. With hindsight, he wishes that he had given three months' notice and moved his mortgage to a different kind of account or to a different building society before his gap year started.

Unfortunately, flexibility may not apply to older mortgage policies. Certainly endowment mortgage payments must be maintained regardless of circumstances. Effectively, you are locked into regular payments until the policy matures. The only alternative is to close the policy, but this will incur heavy penalties. Endowments are best left until they mature because, at least in theory, the fund proportionately gains most value during the final years. Similarly, traditional repayment mortgages will require that you maintain regular contributions. Remember that life assurance payments must be kept up, especially if they are attached to a mortgage.

PENSIONS

Pension funding is another important feature of any plan to take a gap year from employment. With the introduction of stakeholder pensions, it is possible for anyone whether in employment or not to get tax relief on pension contributions up to the amount of his or her earnings.

Charles Bailey of Jelf Financial Planning Ltd (www.jelfgroup.com) has helped several clients prepare for a gap year or career break. He advises anyone contemplating a substantial break to investigate how the employer's final salary pension scheme might be affected. Ask the HR department during any negotiations if a long absence from contributions will reduce the total number of years' service with the company, which is used to calculate the pension when you retire or leave the company. The worst situation is if your employer treats you as having left the scheme, or if so many final salary schemes are being abolished that it disappears in your absence. But ideally there will be no break in benefits, especially regarding pensions.

Other individuals may work freelance or for companies that are too small to offer pension schemes. In this case you'll probably be contributing to a private money purchase scheme. Once again, you'll need to check whether there are any penalties if you wish to suspend contributions until you return to regular employment. Many pension companies have introduced flexible pensions with provisions for 'premium holidays': a period each year when you might want to halt contributions without paying a penalty. If your pension predates this change, you will probably have to maintain payments or face some extra charges.

If taking a break of a year or more, some employers expect you to officially resign while promising to re-employ you on your return. Make sure that benefits that have been accrued are merely frozen temporarily rather than suspended.

NATIONAL INSURANCE

Another factor to consider is the possible effect of a break on your state pension. Projections for the state pension are dispiriting and all but a few have stopped relying on it to provide for retirement. Nevertheless, it's still a benefit you're contributing to through compulsory National Insurance contributions. If you fail to make National Insurance contributions while you are out of the UK, you will forfeit entitlement to benefits on your return. You can decide to pay voluntary contributions at regular intervals or in a lump sum in order to retain your rights to certain benefits.

The normal projected figure is calculated to represent contributions from 90% of your working life. A career break will have implications, although it is likely to be marginal, but you will need to check first to see how the state pension will be altered by any suspension of National Insurance contributions. If you are out of the country for an extended period, you are not obliged to continue paying National Insurance contributions; however, you might choose to make voluntary contributions all the same if you want to maintain your rights to a state pension and other benefits (though this won't entitle you to sickness or unemployment benefit). Voluntary (Class 3) contributions currently stand at £12.05 per week (2011). Check HM Revenue & Customs' website for further information (www.hmrc.gov.uk/nic), or if you are self-employed and want to pay Class 2 NICs, ring 0845 915 4655.

As in many important choices in life, these decisions all depend on individual preferences and priorities. Achieving a balance between the imperatives of living a full life right now and making sacrifices for retirement should be the aim. One source of valuable information on pension allowances, stakeholder pensions, and the state pension, is the government's public service portal www.direct.gov.uk. The site enables you to access bodies that regulate taxation and personal finance.

RED TAPE IN THE EU

If you are a national of the European Economic Area and will be living or working in another member state, you will be covered by European Social Security regulations. The online information 'Social security insurance, benefits and healthcare rights in the European Economic Area' can be accessed at www.dwp.gov.uk/international/social-security-agreements. The document *Social Security Coordination: Work, study, travel, retire anywhere in Europe* can be consulted on the European Union website (ec.europa.eu/social-security-coordination).

TAXATION

Taxation is probably the most complex area of personal finance to be affected by any prolonged absence from the UK. As anyone faintly familiar with taxation knows, there's a professional industry dedicated to helping the individual navigate the murky waters of tax. It must be expected that your taxation will be different if you take a gap from full-time employment, since your earnings are likely to drop substantially. Because tax calculations are based on previous earnings, it may be that after your break you will be eligible for a rebate.

Calculating your liability for tax when working or living outside your home country is notoriously complicated so, if possible, check your position with an accountant or financial planner. Everything depends on whether you fall into the category of 'resident', 'ordinarily resident' or 'domiciled' in the UK. Career breakers are normally considered domiciled in the UK even if they are away for more than a year. Formerly it was possible to claim a 'foreign earnings deduction' (ie pay no tax) if you were out of the country for a full 365 days. However, the legislation has changed so that you are eligible for this only if you have been out of the country for a complete tax year (6 April to 5 April), though you are allowed to spend up to 62 days (ie one-sixth) of the tax year back in England without it affecting your tax position. Anyone who is present in the UK for more than 182 days during a particular tax year will be treated as resident, with no exceptions. HM Revenue & Customs has overhauled the system, and as of April 2009, the document HMRC6 'Residence, Domicile and the Remittance Basis' replaced the old IR20 'Residents and Non-Residents: Liability to Tax in the UK'. Any profit from rented property is subject to income tax.

If you decide to stay for a prolonged period of time in another country you will need to check out the requirements for establishing residency. For example, any person who spends more than 183 days a year in Spain is considered a resident and is liable to pay Spanish tax, though Spain has a double taxation treaty with the UK. Almost all countries have double taxation agreements with Britain so it is most unlikely that you will be taxed twice, but it is a wise precaution to keep all receipts and financial documents in case problems arise.

The financial planning company the Fry Group (01903 231545; www.thefrygroup.co.uk) specialises in advising UK expatriates, and can offer expert tax advice on questions of residency. Also, the big five accountancy firms in the UK all have international offices across the world, giving you the advantage of drawing on both UK and foreign expertise: Accenture (www.accenture.com), Deloitte (www.deloitte.com), Ernst & Young (www.ey.com), KPMG (www.kpmg.co.uk), and PricewaterhouseCoopers (www.pwcglobal.com).

BANKING

Advice on how to carry your money while travelling and how to transfer funds in an emergency is included later in Part 3. One way of getting money which will not inconvenience the folks back home works best for those who know in advance where they will be when their funds will run low. Before setting off, find out if it is possible to open an account at a large bank in your destination city, which may have a branch in London. Most won't allow you to open a chequing account, so instant overdrafts are not a possibility, but knowing you have a fund safely stashed away in Sydney, San Francisco, or Singapore is a great morale booster. It can also assist with other red tape problems like obtaining a reference to be a tenant. For example, to open an account at Australia's Commonwealth Bank before leaving home, see www.commbankuk.co.uk

Bank-to-bank transfers usually incur a charge of at least £20. A cheaper way to do it is to use a currency transfer specialist like Moneycorp (0800 910 1604; www.moneycorp.com), which gives a better exchange rate than banks and charges lower fees. After setting up an account and speaking to a dealer on the phone, you make a verbal contract (which is recorded) to fix the exchange rate, and then transfer money to a bank account abroad. The usual minimum transaction fee is £2,000.

If you are planning to spend your sabbatical away from home, you should prepare the ground with your bank. If you are asking family or friends to conduct business on your behalf while you're away, it might make it easier to arrange power of attorney so that your signature is not required. Even something as simple as cancelling a lost or stolen credit card can be tricky for a third party to do. **Stef and Ness Aalten-Voogd**, who used their redundancy money to go around the world for 12 months, nominated Ness's sister Caroline to act as Power of Attorney; although she claimed she did very little for them, it was reassuring to the wanderers to know that there was an anchor of stability at home.

And while you're at it, update or draw up a will. If you die intestate, the government takes an automatic 40% of your estate in inheritance tax and lawyers will get much of the rest as they apportion your wealth according to fixed rules. DIY will-writing kits are readily available, though you may feel happier paying for the services of a professional will writer (not legally trained) or a solicitor.

FUNDRAISING IDEAS

Once you have resolved to meet a particular target, say £2,500, it is surprising how single-mindedly you can pursue it. The ingenuity adult gappers have demonstrated in organising money-making events, etc is impressive: for example, the guy who got everybody he knew to sponsor him to stay up a tree for a week. You may choose to shave your head, jump out of an aeroplane, organise a fancy dress pub crawl, or a thousand other ways to raise money. Publicise your plans and your need of funds wherever you can. Register with JustGiving.com, one of the easiest ways for your supporters to donate money online. Also consider setting up a Facebook group and urging your 542 Facebook friends to support you. Local papers and radio stations might also be prepared to feature your planned expedition, which may prompt a few local readers/listeners to support you. Ask family and friends to give cash instead of birthday and Christmas presents. Consider possibilities for organising a fundraising event like a concert or a ceilidh, a quiz night, wine tasting, or auction of promises. (If you have ever been active in your children's school, you may have previous experience of some of these.)

Target organisations and companies with which you have some links, such as your old school or college, to ask for sponsorship. Local businesses are usually inundated with requests for donations and raffle prizes and are unlikely to give cash, but some might donate some useful items of equipment. Keep track of all the individuals and businesses who have helped you, and be sure to send them a thank you note later on describing the success of your fundraising trip.

Sarah Elengorn's most lucrative event, held a few weeks before her departure for Mexico to work with street kids, was a netball tournament organised through her club at home in Middlesex (which gave her use of the premises free of charge). Twelve teams paid £40 to enter and the event had a Mexican theme with a bar, raffle, etc. Sarah had been hoping to raise £500 but instead made £800.

Wendy Burridge, who went to Uganda with Madventurer, also organised two raffles: one in her hometown and another for brokers on the London art market with whom she had dealings through her job in art insurance. The raffles generated support from many companies who donated excellent prizes, like a £100 hamper, a gym membership, and an evening of drinks.

As the support grew so did her fundraising ambitions. She wrote to every Premiership football team asking for signed photographs and had fantastic support from Liverpool, the FA, Everton, Tottenham, and Arsenal. The raffle raised nearly £1,000.

If you want to go down the route of applying to trusts and charitable bodies, consult a library copy of the *Directory of Grant Making Trusts* (new edition published each April), or contact the Association of Charitable Foundations (www.acf.org.uk), which can offer advice on how to approach grant-giving trusts. Also check the National Charities Database on www.charitiesdirect.com. Local service clubs like Rotary, Lions Club, and Round Table might be willing to consider a well presented application for support, especially if you offer to give a presentation on your return. However, not many are willing to support individuals and so you may meet mostly with rejections. (One enterprising fund-raiser got his friends and family to sponsor him for every rejection.) If you are going through a registered charity, always include the charity number in your letter of request since this may be needed by their accountant.

The Winston Churchill Memorial Trust (www.wcmt.org.uk) awards about 100 four-to-12 week travelling fellowships to UK citizens of any age or background who wish to undertake a specific project or study related to their personal interests, job, or community. The deadline for applications falls in October. Past winners are listed on the website with their diverse topics of study; for example a man in his 50s who was funded to go to the USA to examine the role of volunteers in botanical gardens, and a 42-year-old who embarked on a Congo River expedition.

ACCOMMODATION MATTERS

Younger individuals may decide to break their careers before taking on the large financial commitment of a mortgage. Going away for you may simply involve giving up rented accommodation, and the only major logistical hurdle is finding a place to store your possessions. Disposing of furniture is difficult, but even if your worldly goods consist only of clothes, books, CDs, photographs, and letters, you'll have to find a place for them. It will be a time of shedding superfluous possessions (think of car boot sales, eBay, and so on) and will feel like a symbolic counterpart to putting work to one side as you prepare to head off into the unknown. With luck you'll find a willing parent or friends with spare space in a garage or attic for your clobber. Otherwise you will have to shop around for the cheapest storage facilities; a sample price for storing the contents of a one-bedroom flat might be £125 a month, and £200 for the contents of a three-bedroom house.

Homeowners will have to solve the problem of what to do with their abode if they're taking a sabbatical abroad. The process of making the necessary arrangements to rent out a property – or in a more radical move, to sell it – will take many months, so it is essential to plan a long way in advance.

Five solutions can be considered: leaving the property unoccupied; finding a friend to stay in it rent-free but keeping an eye on it; finding a tenant, either independently or through a letting agency; registering with a house-swapping agency; or using the services of a housesitting agency. The latter is so expensive as to be of interest mainly to the seriously wealthy (see below). Not everyone is comfortable with the idea of strangers living in their house, whether paying tenants or house-swappers, so in the end it will be a personal decision, but be assured that tens of thousands of people have been delighted with the ease with which it can be accomplished.

RENTING OUT YOUR PROPERTY

Assuming you are a property owner, your house or flat is probably your greatest financial asset. It is also your home, a place of emotional and physical security which you will not want to hand over to strangers lightly. However, if you want to spend all or part of your gap year travelling or living overseas, renting out your home can go a long way to covering your costs and is usually worth the bother. Renting to tenants also neatly solves the problem of security and makes use of the home to provide a revenue stream at a time when you may not be drawing an income. If you are lucky you will find a tenant through the 'mates network' (which can be accessed very simply through your email address book), as **Mike Bleazard** did when he wanted to leave home for six months. Mike was very happy to rent his flat to the colleague of a friend at somewhat below the market rate for Cambridge: £800 a month, including all the bills apart from council tax and telephone. This worked out easier all round, because it meant that Mike didn't have to worry about meter readings or disconnections when he left and returned.

During the 1960s and 1970s the problem of sitting tenants who refused to leave at the end of the rental period became notorious. The Housing Act of 1988 and a subsequent amendment have virtually solved this abuse, ensuring that a contract between landlord and tenant explicitly sets out terms for the rental – for example, the prohibition of pets – and makes the time limit legally binding.

Try to avoid switching to a buy-to-let mortgage (as some lenders may try to impose on you), which is almost always more expensive and will force you to pay all the costs of remortgaging (legal fees, valuations, etc). Make sure your lender knows that you will be returning to occupy the property within a specified period. They should give you a 'permission to let' for which there may be a fee (usually under £100), but will allow you to carry on with the same mortgage terms.

Above all, it is essential to notify both your mortgage lender and your insurance company that you intend to rent out your home before agreeing to any tenancy. Any changes to the normal habitation must be cleared first. Most insurance companies are amenable to making provision for your time abroad but they may want to reassess risk if there is a change of occupancy. **Mike Bleazard** was glad that he had topped up his contents insurance before renting out his flat, making sure the policy would cover tenants, because the flat was burgled while he was on his gap year.

If you put many valuable items like furniture or artwork into storage for the duration of a tenancy, this might actually lower the cost of contents insurance. Your insurer will prefer and occasionally even insist that you use a registered agency or at least delegate responsibility for keeping a regular check on the property to a trustworthy person close by.

When notifying the mortgage lender, you need to know whether you have a 'residential mortgage rate' and, if so, whether you can retain these preferable terms while you're renting the property instead of becoming liable for the more expensive 'standard variable rate'. Normally you will be permitted to maintain your mortgage status if you sign a form stating that you are renting to a private individual on an 'Assured Shorthold Tenancy'. With hindsight, **Paul Edmunds** realises that he made an error in accepting his tenants' suggestion of paying six months' rent in a lump sum at the beginning of their tenancy. This meant that he had to declare the rental income for tax purposes in that tax year, whereas if their payments had been staggered or paid later in the next tax year when his income was much lower, he would have had to pay considerably less tax.

Anyone who rents out property for longer than six months is required to register as a non-resident landlord (NRL) with the Inland Revenue. Otherwise the letting agent will be obliged to hold back 20% of the rental income as tax.

Publications that may be worth consulting are *Renting and Letting* (Which? Guides, 2008) and *Renting Out Your Property for Dummies* (John Wiley and Sons Ltd, 2006), which tackles all the common problems that arise between landlord and tenant, and explains how the law operates to help avoid most of them.

USING A RENTAL AGENCY

Putting your home into the hands of professionals often imparts peace of mind, even if it cuts into your financial gain. Most agencies charge a fee of at least 10% of the rent plus VAT. The

Association of Residential Letting Agents, or ARLA (www.arla.co.uk), advises – and of course it is in their members' interests to do so – that you use a professional agency to manage the tenancy while you are away. Homeowners often find comfort in knowing that any problems that arise over money or maintenance can be delegated to an impartial intermediary. Also, agency fees are an allowable expense that can be offset against tax.

A letting agency will screen potential tenants according to particular criteria to ensure that you let your home to responsible people. They may, for example, have regular company customers who rent property on behalf of company employees, diminishing the likelihood of any disputes over unpaid rent. A company let is safer because the company in question becomes legally responsible for any transgressions by the tenant.

Letting agencies are increasingly experienced at working with private homes being placed on the rental market for a set period of time. Short lets are possible to arrange if you are intending to be away for less than six months. Even if renting out your home is a novelty and feels rather risky, there is plenty of professional help available to make it a viable proposition, allowing you to benefit from the property's intrinsic value while maintaining all your legal rights to possession.

If you are using an agency, find out if it is one of the 3,500 offices of ARLA members and therefore obliged to follow a professional code of conduct. These registered agents are bonded, which ensures that any misuse of your rental income or of the tenant's deposits is guaranteed by the Association's special fund. If there are any financial irregularities you can go straight to ARLA for compensation. Links to member agencies can be found on the ARLA website, and most questions should be answered in the 'Information for Landlords' section.

RENTING INDEPENDENTLY

Of course, it is possible to take the independent course and organise the rental yourself and thereby save a substantial sum of money. Managing your own rental will be more difficult if you plan on being abroad; however, with the rise of the internet it is easier to locate suitable tenants and with advances in communications it is possible to keep tabs on a tenant via email.

The tried and tested method of finding a tenant is to advertise in the local newspaper or to target a magazine or website read by the kind of people you want as tenants (ramblers, stamp collectors, vegetarians, alumnae of your old university, etc). Even people who do not happen to live in prime tourist locations can often rent out their houses to people who have come to work at the local hospital, or been transferred by their employer and are renting for a time while they look around to buy. A 57-year-old kitchen fitter from the small Midlands town of Measham, who was planning a long break in New Zealand, recognised that there was not much of a rental market in his town, though he discovered that the local council was looking for properties to rent out for a minimum of a year. The rent was low but they guaranteed to find tenants.

Always ask prospective tenants to supply references from their current employer, bank, and previous landlord, and follow them up because dodgy tenants have been known to fabricate references. Holding one month's rent as a deposit is standard practice. This can be used to pay outstanding bills at the end of the tenancy and to cover any potential damage, and then the difference is returned. Depending on the nature and duration of the tenancy, you can consider putting the utilities in the tenant's name (which is a major hassle) and asking them to pay the council tax. Together, you and your tenant should also draw up an inventory of all the items in the property, which you should both sign in front of a witness. You will want to ask a neighbour (preferably a nosy one) to contact you in the event of problems, especially in an emergency like theft or fire.

The following practical steps should be considered when renting out your house independently and going away for an extended period:

- Notify your mortgage lender that you intend to let the property. They will want you to sign a form stating that you are renting to a private individual on an Assured Shorthold Tenancy.
- Remember: you will be liable for tax on the rental income minus the mortgage payments, letting fees, and other expenses.
- Agree a method of rent payment with the tenant, possibly asking for evidence that a standing order into your account has been set up, or asking for a set of post-dated cheques which you (or a trusted proxy) can pay into your account.
- Read the utility meters at the last minute before departure. If they are not accessible, request that the electricity and gas supplier take interim readings.
- Telephone the phone company for an interim reading. You can leave a cheque made payable to the phone company to cover your share of monthly or quarterly calls and leave the tenant in charge of paying the phone bill.
- Put away valuables such as computers and paintings, plus any items you would be heartbroken about if damaged. It may be that you can store such items in the smallest room, which can be declared off-limits (assuming this has been agreed with the tenant beforehand).
- Prepare a file with all relevant instruction manuals, guarantees, or insurance cover for appliances.
- If tenants are new to the area, a few tips on local shops, services, pubs and restaurants, doctor's surgeries, etc, would be appreciated.
- Ask a friend or neighbour to keep an eye on the property and ask them to contact you by phone or email if anything seems amiss.
- Assuming you are expecting any valuable post, obtain a Mail Redirection application form from any post office; the current fees within the UK are £7.64 for one month, £16.82 for three, £25.96 for six and £38.99 for 12; fees for forwarding mail abroad are nearly triple. These fees apply per surname.
- Cancel subscriptions to newspapers, book clubs, the cleaner, window washing services, etc, after ascertaining that the tenant does not want to retain them.
- To satisfy health and safety regulations, you should make sure that furnishings show labels that prove they qualify under the Furniture and Furnishings (Fire & Safety) Regulations (amended 1993).
- Gas appliances must meet the Gas Safety regulations, so make sure you have a valid safety certificate supplied within the previous 12 months by a Gas Safe-registered engineer.

MANAGING TENANTS

Philip Hardie *was due a sabbatical term and decided to take it away from Cambridge. His twin sons were in their last year of primary school and this seemed like a good opportunity for a change. Although Australia is not the first destination to spring to mind when classicists plan a sabbatical, he had several friends in the department at the University of Sydney who assured him that the welcome would be warm and the library resources adequate for the book he wanted to research.*

The family's first thought was to arrange a house swap for their four-month trip, since there is plenty of sabbatical traffic in the other direction: Sydney to Cambridge. However, matching dates was going to present problems and it seemed simpler to rent out the family house in central Cambridge and find a place to rent in Sydney. Universities often have an accommodation office that caters to visiting academics and Cambridge is no exception. The rather grandly titled Society for Visiting Scholars tries to match accommodation requests from abroad with furnished houses and flats for rent. They are simply an introduction service rather than an agent and charge no commission, though they welcome donations if their services are appreciated. Usefully, the office gives its clients a template of a letting contract.

The family house was registered early in the year for a September departure, with an expectation that expressions of interest would roll in. By July, the family had had just one enquiry that had come to nothing, and the university office could guarantee nothing. Realising that departure was less than eight weeks away, Philip began to panic and discovered a local website for Cambridge accommodation on which he posted (free of charge) brief house details. Within 48 hours he had had three replies: one coincidentally from Sydney, and two others from people already in Cambridge and therefore available to come to view the property. One took it for precisely the dates it would be empty. The family appreciated the chance to meet the tenant in the flesh, especially when they discovered that she was the daughter of a family friend of a neighbour. References (one work, one personal, one bank) were requested and produced, an Assured Shorthold Tenancy Agreement was signed in the presence of witnesses and all went ahead smoothly.

On the family's return, they found their house not only in one piece but mostly unchanged from when they had left it. Inevitably a few dishes had been broken, a saucepan ruined, a lampshade torn, and a wall gouged (the tenant had a two-year-old daughter), but they felt that this was fair wear and tear from tenants paying enough rent to cover all their rental expenses in Sydney.

As for organising the paying of bills, the Hardies had continued to pay the electricity and gas bills by standing order. On their return they read both meters themselves then calculated the number of units used over the whole rental period and added the pro-rated standing charge. The telephone bills had been slightly more problematic. Rather than change the billing name, the bills were forwarded to the owners (since they had organised all mail to be forwarded by the post office). After marvelling at how high their tenants' phone bills were, they sent them on to the tenant and trusted her to pay them. If for some reason she had not paid them, she was the one who would have suffered the inconvenience of having the service cut off. As soon as they returned home, they contacted the telephone company for an interim reading and were told the amount still owing was a sizeable sum. This amount, together with the total amount owed for utilities, came in at about £50 less than the deposit of a month's rent, so there was no need to extract extra money from the tenants after they had gone.

Not every story ends so happily. A couple from Canada were pleased when a 33-year-old 'musician' wanted to rent their lovely log-cabin style home on Vancouver Island for the asking price. When they finalised the arrangement, he said, 'You will leave the house clean won't you? I am a bit of neat freak', which was music to their ears. The rent would go a long way to funding their ten-month gap year working in Africa and then travelling in Europe. On the way home they discussed which friends they wanted to see first, what they wanted to eat, and how they might reorganise the rooms in their home, never for one minute suspecting that they would find, 'Chaos, a mess, damage to house, negligence to our property amounting to $10,000'. The tenant had drunk all the whisky and 12 bottles of fine wine stored in the basement. He claimed the house had just been burgled and that several computers had been stolen. He had burned all the carefully stored hand-chopped wood intended to keep the family warm through the winter after their return. This hint at excessive heat and structural problems in the house made them suspicious. They quickly concluded that he had used their house as a 'grow op' (ie a marijuana farm), a suspicion confirmed when they found a discarded packet of 'Big Bud' – a fertilizer used in hydroponics. They turned to the police, who told them that convictions are rare unless you catch the guilty party in the room with growing plants. The distraught owners kicked themselves for having been so trusting that they had taken no damage deposit. Fortunately the tenant did not vanish and, without admitting liability, did end up paying for most of the damage. With hindsight the owners realised that they should have arranged for a trusted friend to make regular appointments to visit the property every few weeks.

HOUSE SWAPPING

Another option to explore is swapping your home and sometimes your car with an individual, couple, or family in a city or country you want to visit. Exchanging houses with a homeowner abroad will not only save accommodation costs: it immediately takes you off the tourist trail and sets you down in a real neighbourhood. The two main requirements are that you be willing to spend at least a few weeks in one place and that you have a decent house in a potentially desirable location. You also have to be someone who can plan ahead, since most swaps are arranged six months in advance. And of course you must be prepared to bring your housekeeping up to an acceptable standard.

Many home exchange agencies are in the business of trying to match up compatible swappers. Swaps are usually arranged for short holiday breaks of up to about a month in the summer (especially popular with school teachers), but longer ones are possible too. The great advantage of a home swap is that this is not a commercial transaction, so the costs are minimal. The more desirable your home location is, the easier it will be to attract interested swappers. People who live in central London, Sydney, or New York, or in a Cotswold village or near a Californian beach will certainly have an advantage. But families and individuals might be looking not just for historic or culturally interesting destinations, but for a specific university town or a home with easy access to the countryside. Even if you don't live in a popular destination, it is worth registering since you might just happen to find someone who is looking for a property just like yours in your particular area of the country. You can even exchange a caravan in rural Bulgaria for a salubrious house in Islington, as **Lucy Irvine** did in 2010. Lucy Irvine is the free spirit made famous by the film *Castaway* (1986), based on her experience of answering a newspaper advertisement in 1980 to join an older man living on a deserted island near Papua New Guinea.

It is easy to register online with a house swap agency (listed below). You simply complete a questionnaire describing your home and its location, and pay the registration fee. Most agencies have stopped distributing printed directories because of the enormous cost and operate totally in cyberspace, which has brought the cost of annual membership down in most cases. Once you have subscribed, you can search the company's listings and make direct contact with the owners of properties that interest you. The vast bulk of this communication now happens by email, but the final stage is an exchange of formal letters of agreement.

Green Theme International (www.gti-home-exchange.com) is one of the pioneering companies in this field and has an environmental motivation. By encouraging house swaps it is hoping to limit the demand for package destinations and the appeal of second homes. The founder, Kathy Botterill, says success in finding a suitable match is often due to good luck, particularly if you have your heart set on a particular destination. The modest fee for a one-year online listing is £25. A quick perusal of their listings will reveal properties, eg in rural New Zealand, available for swaps of three to six months. Green Theme belongs to First Home Exchange Alliance, which includes Home Base Holidays, Guardian Home Exchange, and Invented City (USA).

Other agencies include Homelink International (www.homelink.org.uk), which is one of the largest agencies with thousands of properties worldwide on its website; the annual membership fee is £115. The longest established company is Intervac (www.intervac-homeexchange.com), whose list includes properties in 50 countries, and who has emailable contacts in many countries of the world. California-based HomeExchange.com has a purported 137,000 listings in 137 countries ($120 membership). The larger organisations can arrange travel insurance specifically tailored for home swaps, covering such problems as cancellation owing to illness, marital collapse, etc. A free house swap website is www.digsville.com.

If you are taking the children, you will obviously check whether the house you're going to live in is safe or suitable for them. Likewise, if a family with children is coming to stay in your home try to check if it meets safety standards. If possible, swap with another family or couple who mirror your lives to some extent – for example, if they have children of a similar age.

It's a wise precaution to notify your insurance company too. Check to see if your home contents and building insurance covers any potential damage; legally, people on a house swap are classified as guests, not tenants. It is also sensible to put into storage your most valuable possessions to avoid accidental damage or breakage. If a car is included in the swap the guests will need to be added to the policy and details given of their driving licences.

LEAVING YOUR PROPERTY EMPTY

Careful preparations should be made to ensure that an empty home is cared for and protected in your absence. Assuming you have decided against renting or lending it out to a lodger or student, can you arrange for a neighbour, relative, or friend to make regular visits? How important is it for the garden to be cared for in your absence, if only to have the grass mown so it looks occupied? Preventing burglary and guarding against burst pipes in winter are real considerations.

Naturally, friends or relatives may not be able or willing to commit the same amount of time or apply the same degree of professional expertise as an agency. Appointing a friend as agent can strain good relations if anything goes wrong, and a bottle of wine and box of chocolates are probably not enough compensation for the anxiety the job may have caused them.

CARS

If you own a vehicle that you do not intend to sell, you can either take it off the road for the duration of your absence, or lend it to a friend/tenant. Motor insurance in the UK is less flexible than in many countries (like the USA and Australia) since it covers named drivers rather than the vehicle. It can be expensive adding one or more names to the car insurance for an extended period, an expense which should be passed on to the borrower. If you have a no-claims bonus, try to find out if it can be protected in the event of another driver having an accident.

If you are taking your car off the road, you will obviously want to store it in a safe place: perhaps a friend's unused garage or driveway. Some homeowners prefer to leave their vehicle in their own drive to disguise the fact the property is empty.

If a vehicle is off the road for more than a calendar month, it is possible to reclaim the unused months of road tax by declaring SORN (Statutory Off Road Notification). Simply ask at a post office for form V11 and send it to the Driver and Vehicle Licensing Agency in Swansea (0870 850 4444). Alternatively, apply online at www.taxdisc.direct.gov.uk.

PETS

Taking a gap year abroad will pose a special challenge for pet owners. Most pets are well-loved friends, especially for children. Your dog or cat is virtually a member of the family and it will be very hard to imagine leaving them behind. The Passport For Pets scheme is now well established and allows you to take a dog or cat (or rodent, rabbit, reptile, or ornamental tropical fish) abroad to a number of approved countries, without subjecting the animal to six months quarantine when you return.

If you plan to take a dog or cat abroad, give yourself plenty of time to make the necessary preparations to comply with the regulations of the pet passport scheme. A dog or a cat will need to be vaccinated against rabies and have a microchip implanted by the local vet which gives the animal a unique number, procedures which will run to several hundred pounds. Essentially, you have to prove that an animal is clear of rabies for the six months following the blood test after the vaccination. See the government website www.direct.gov.uk for more details.

On some journeys, like a walking pilgrimage over the Pyrenees to Santiago de Compostela in Spain, it might be wholly appropriate to take your dog for company. You'll never be far from shops or veterinary care in Europe. On other trips, like driving across Africa, it would be completely impractical. If you are renting or swapping your house, you can hold out for a tenant who is willing to take on the care of your animal. An alternative would be to find a foster family: perhaps a good friend or a relative willing to take on the care.

HOUSESITTING

Ideally you might hear of someone via the grapevine who is looking for temporary accommodation and who would be willing to look after your house, pet, and garden in exchange for a rent-free stay. Graduate colleges and teaching hospitals are just two places with a mobile population and potential housesitters. If you do not know the person beforehand, ask for references just as you would of a rent-paying tenant.

You might also want to investigate other possibilities. A journal called *The Caretaker Gazette* (www.caretaker.org) published in the USA has, since 1983, been listing properties that need live-in caretakers and housesitters. An annual online subscription costs $29.95 and an advert for a housesitter costs $0.65 a word. A UK equivalent is HouseCarers.com, which maintains a housesitting database; annual membership costs £30.

A solution of last resort is to hire a housesitter, who will take care of the pets and provide a range of light domestic support like simple cleaning and gardening, all for a substantial fee. Effectively you'll be hiring an individual or a couple to act as housekeepers. But if you can afford it, and perhaps own a home that requires special care owing to age or an outstanding garden or a menagerie of animals, this might be the only solution. This is certainly not a cheap option and can cost £500 a fortnight plus expenses. In return, the companies will guarantee that the employee will care for your animals according to any instructions you leave. Companies include Animal Aunts (01703 821529; www.animalaunts.co.uk), Home & Pet Care Ltd (016974 78515; www.homeandpetcare.co.uk), and Homesitters (01296 630 730; www.homesitters.co.uk).

STAYING IN PRIVATE HOMES

If you are not in a position to swap your own accommodation for someone else's, you might like to consider a homestay or some variation on that theme. A number of worthy organisations dedicated to promoting world peace and understanding match people interested in hosting foreign travellers with those on the move. Socially it can be a gamble, but financially it is brilliant since expenses are minimal.

The most high-profile online community is the Couchsurfing Project (www.couchsurfing.com), where anyone can register free of charge to access members willing to put up travellers. Like so many internet-based projects, the system depends on users' feedback, which means that you can check on a potential host's profile in advance and be fairly sure that dodgy hosts will be outed straightaway. Couchsurfing is so mainstream that a *Sunday Times* journalist (Fleur Britten) has written a whole book about it called *On the Couch*. Yet another site is www.place2stay.net.

Servas International is an organisation begun by an American Quaker in 1948, which runs a worldwide programme of free hospitality exchanges for travellers, to further world peace and understanding. Normally you don't stay with one host for more than a couple of days. To become a Servas traveller or host in the UK, contact Servas Britain (020 8444 7778; www.servasbritain.u-net.com), who can forward your enquiry to your Area Co-ordinator. Before a traveller can be given a list of hosts (which are drawn up every autumn), he or she must pay a fee of £25 (£35 for couples) and be interviewed by a co-ordinator (rates are less if you are also willing to be a host). Servas US ((707) 825 1714; www.usservas.org) charges a joining fee of US$85 and a refundable deposit of $25 for host lists in up to five countries.

Hospitality exchange organisations can make travel both interesting and cheap. **Bradwell Jackson** had been mulling over the possibility of travelling the world for about a decade, before he finally gave up his drug abuse counselling job in the US to take off for an indeterminate period of time to see the world. On his earlier travels he had discovered the benefits of joining Servas and two other hospitality exchange programmes: Global Freeloaders (www. globalfreeloaders.com) and the Hospitality Club (www.hospitalityclub.org). His first destination was Mexico, where to his amazement he found English teaching work at the first place he happened to enquire in Mexico City:

I really must say right away that Servas is not simply for freeloading in people's homes. However, once you take the plunge and commit to wandering the earth, things just start to fall into place. If you belong to clubs such as Global Freeloaders, Hospitality Club, or any of the other homestay organisations, don't be surprised if the family you stay with invites you for an extended stay. The first such family I stayed with in Mexico invited me to stay for six months. All they asked is that I help with the costs of the food they prepared for me and any hot water I used.

Later Bradwell made use of hospitality exchanges in some unlikely locations. For example, he stayed with a host in Bamako, Mali, who offered to let him stay for two months in exchange for two hours of English lessons a day. His host was a wealthy man who gave Brad all his meals, internet access, laundry, and so on. He commented that, 'Once one lands into a dream situation like this, you are apt to feel a bit guilty, and such hospitality takes time to get used to. Still, I am certainly not complaining'.

Members of the Globetrotters Club are often willing to extend hospitality to other Globetrotters. Annual membership of this travel club costs £15/$29; contact the Globetrotters via their postal address: BCM/Roving, London WC1N 3XX; or on the web at www.globetrotters.co.uk. Members receive a bi-monthly travel newsletter and a list of members, indicating whether or not they encourage other members to stay with them.

Other hospitality clubs and exchanges are worth investigating. Women Welcome Women World Wide (01494 465441; www.womenwelcomewomen.org.uk) enables women of different countries to visit one another. There is no set subscription, but the minimum donation requested is £35 or equivalent, which covers the cost of the membership list and three newsletters in which members may publish announcements. There are currently 2,500 members (aged 16–80+) in 80 countries.

A new web-based accommodation service has recently come out of San Francisco (where else?) called www.airbnb.com, which has a searchable database of privately-owned accommodation that can be rented at very modest prices and where travellers and hosts connect. **Mark Perriton's** one-year cycle trip round the world got off to a smashing start using this service: 'I started my trip by spending a couple of days in New York, where I met a very friendly host via airbnb. Chris really looked after me while I stayed in a great sunny condo in Brooklyn.'

Language courses abroad often arrange for clients to live with local families as paying guests, which is a great way to improve a language in the context of family life. This is commonplace throughout Latin America but can also be arranged in France, Germany, Spain, and so on. And many volunteering programmes include homestay accommodation. Not all grown-ups relish the prospect of becoming a temporary family member. When **Katy Chan** (aged 36) was choosing her programme, she realised it was important to her not to stay with a local family but to be with other volunteers so she could meet new people from different countries and share experiences: 'I felt that staying with a family would isolate me, especially in a country like Costa Rica where there were language barriers.' Forty-something **Paul Edwards** found living with a family in suburban Accra, Ghana during a cricket-coaching placement was not ideal and regretted that he wasn't able to live independently, kind and welcoming as his host family was. He found his situation slightly claustrophobic and he struggled with the Ghanaian diet, yet it was awkward going out to find a more palatable alternative.

FINDING ACCOMMODATION ABROAD

As if it weren't enough trying to work out what to do with your property while you're away, you will have to worry about where you can afford to stay while you're abroad. If you intend to spend your gap year travelling, see Part 7: Travel and Adventure, for some information about where to stay on the road.

Renting a flat or house abroad will be miles cheaper than staying in hotels or other travellers' accommodation, but it is only of interest to people who plan to stay in one place for an extended period. Two of the most useful sites are the free community noticeboards Gumtree and Craigslist; the latter started in San Francisco in 1995 and has spread to 570 cities – from Auckland to Buenos Aires, and Moscow to Cairo. Thousands of landlords post vacancies on these sites.

Property agencies normally charge steep fees and are legalistic about checking the inventory, etc. Numerous online rental agencies offer properties in Europe and worldwide for short or longer-term lets, and their fees tend to be lower and in a few cases non-existent. Try tapping 'self-catering' and your destination into Google.

If you are willing to consider student-style accommodation, it is worth contacting the student housing office or checking noticeboards in student unions, preferably one aimed at graduate students and therefore with notices of accommodation a little more grown-up than undergraduate digs.

One of the main drawbacks of renting is that you will be expected to sign a lease, typically for a minimum of six months, which locks you into staying in one place for longer than you might have chosen. You will probably be required to pay a sizeable bond, usually at least one month's rent, which will be held back if you leave before the lease expires or if you leave the property in less than immaculate condition. Some flat-letting agents will give shorter leases for higher rents. You may be asked to provide a bank reference or evidence of a reliable income.

PART 3

PRACTICAL ADVICE
FOR TRAVELLERS

RED TAPE
WHAT TO TAKE
STAYING IN TOUCH
TRAVEL ARRANGEMENTS
TRAVEL INSURANCE
HEALTH AND SAFETY

TESTING THE WATER

The best advice comes from other people who've done it first. They've learnt the hard way, so talk to your friends, colleagues, and acquaintances who have hit the road or volunteered abroad, and make use of the internet to locate travellers who have gone before. Try searching message boards like Lonely Planet's Thorn Tree or www.travellersconnected. com, an online community site for travellers that is free to use. You can register your profile and contact travellers around the world to seek insider tips, or put you on your way to connecting up with a like-minded companion. Of course you don't always have to act on advice shared on the internet – some of which will be too cautious or too daring for your tastes, may conflict with other reports, and even be downright wrong. Be prepared to cherry pick what makes sense to you.

While travelling, be open to meeting the locals and other travellers because they are a valuable source of information and of course companionship. But the same limitations apply to their advice. You may meet an educated professional in Islamabad who warns you against going up the Karakoram Highway on the grounds that it is populated by bandits. The same day you might meet a hardened traveller who encourages you to wander at will in the hills of the Hunza Valley on that same highway. You will have to choose your own course between these extremes, and try to filter out advice based on prejudice on the one hand or bravado on the other. All the information and contacts in the world are useless unless you make a personal approach to every particular situation. If you have elected for a placement with a local NGO, you will be able to benefit immediately from local advice.

An innovative company named Tripbod (www.tripbod.com) – formerly called Your Safe Planet – provides introductions to trusted locals in your destination who will share their inside travel knowledge and who may also have links to local community-run volunteering projects which are free to join, if that is what you are after. The costs escalate the longer your trip, eg from £50 for a week to £350 for six months.

It is amazing how far the English language can take you in even remote corners of the world. But it is a gesture of respect to learn at least a few local phrases and words. In some cases it may even be essential: for example, in finding the local WC or if you're vegetarian and want to avoid eating meat. At least carry a relevant phrase book or mini-dictionary. **Ambrose Marsh** and family wanted to make a bit of a linguistic effort in the 13 countries they cycled through with their two sons between Turkey and Estonia, and commented wryly, 'We had Lonely Planet phrase books that were virtually useless – but great for pressing flowers.'

Many single women would love to take a gap year travelling but are intimidated by perceived danger. Statistically the chances of serious mishap are negligible, but it still takes courage to organise a solo trip – especially without prior experience. Of course, women should only undertake to travel in a way with which they're comfortable. Travelling in Islamic countries where women are barely seen in public presents special problems. The respected independent travel agency in Bristol, Marco Polo Travel (0117 929 4123; www.marcopolotravel.co.uk/pages/women), offers a one-hour consultancy for up to four women (cost £40) to offer inspiration and build confidence before a major trip.

Thelma and Louise (www.thelmandlouise.com) is an online community of women worldwide which helps members to find travel companions (among other things). Registration is free and enables members to contact other members and use the messageboard. The membership includes women who are interested in gap years and career breaks; members can also post plans to join an expedition or project on the website. Women-on-the-road.com is a site intended to inspire and advise women who want to travel on their own, and another source of possible travelling companions is www.someone2travelwith.com, which operates a bit like a dating agency. Interested parties register the details of their proposed trips on the site and then are matched with other members. When a match is accepted, the fee is £30.

If contemplating an ambitious trip, it might be worth trying a taster trip closer to home or of shorter duration to see if you can enjoy your own company and the delights of choosing an itinerary with reference to no-one but yourself. As mentioned earlier, many suitable companions will be met along the route. Both women and men who remain unconvinced that they could enjoy travelling alone might prefer to travel with an organised expedition (see section on Adventure Travel in Part 7: Travel and Adventure). However, there are no guarantees of finding someone with whom to team up. **Tara Leaver** had easily found congenial company on a summer volunteer project she had joined in the long summer vacation when she was a teacher. She had enjoyed it so much that she decided to use an inheritance to fund a whole year off, starting the following spring with a volunteer project in Costa Rica. In this case, she found that most of the other volunteers on what turned out to be a disorganised and unsatisfactory project were ten years younger than her and she did not find any potential travelling companions among them. She travelled on by herself to Panama, Nicaragua, and Guatemala, where she had some brilliant times but ultimately found it quite lonely. An illness that had dogged her in the past reared its ugly head again and, with no one to look after her, she was forced to cut her gap year short.

RED TAPE

PASSPORTS

A ten-year UK passport costs £77.50 for 32 pages and £90.50 for 48 pages, and should be processed by the Identity and Passport Service within three weeks. The one-week fast track application procedure costs £30–£35 extra and an existing passport can be renewed within one day if it is done in person at a passport office, but only if you have made a prior appointment by ringing 0300 222 0000 and pay the premium fee of £129.50. Passport office addresses are listed on passport application forms available from main post offices, and all relevant information can be found on the website www.ips.gov.uk.

Most countries will want to see that your passport has at least 90 days to run beyond your proposed stay. If your passport is lost or stolen while travelling, contact first the police, then your nearest Consulate. Obtaining replacement travel documents is easier if you have a record of the passport number and its date and place of issue, so keep these in a separate place: preferably a photocopy of the title page, which can be scanned and emailed to yourself.

VISAS

Outside the Schengen Area of Europe, in which border controls have been largely abolished for EU nationals, you can't continue in one direction for very long before you are impeded by border guards demanding to see your papers. Post September 11th, immigration and security checks are tighter than ever before and many countries have imposed visa restrictions, particularly on North Americans. Embassy websites are the best source of information or you can check online information posted by visa agencies. For example, CIBT (www.uk.cibt.com) allows you to search visa requirements and costs for any nationality visiting any country.

Getting visas is a headache anywhere, and most travellers feel happier obtaining them in their home country. Set aside a chunk of your travel budget to cover the costs; to give just a few examples of charges for tourist visas for UK citizens applying in London: £39 for India, £64.50 for China, £11 for Jordan, £38 for Vietnam, and so on. Last-minute applications often incur a higher fee: for example, a Russian visa costs £75 if applied for a week in advance, but £133 for short-notice processing. If you do not want to pin yourself down to entry dates, you may decide to apply for visas as you travel from a neighbouring country, which in many cases is cheaper, though may cause delays and hassle. If you are short of time or live a long way from the embassies in London, private visa agencies will undertake the footwork for you – at a price, in the region of £40–£45 per visa.

If you intend to cross a great many borders, especially on an overland trip through Africa, ensure that you have all the relevant documentation and that your passport contains as many blank pages as frontiers which you intend to cross. Travellers have been turned back purely because the border guard refused to use a page with another stamp on it. **Stefan and Nessa Aalten-Voogd**, who had to cross dozens of borders on their 12-month round-the-world trip, believe that being smartly presented and suitably respectful eased the process and although it is impossible to quantify, they are sure that 'being older than the typical backpacker made a difference when dealing with officials'.

Information about documents needed for working abroad can be found in Part 6: Working and Living Abroad.

MY GROWN-UP GAP YEAR: NIGEL PEGLER

Nigel Pegler wanted to ensure that his contribution to a development project in South Africa would be sustainable. He became involved in a cycle project in the rural village of Mapoch about 40km northwest of Pretoria, after being matched with this project by the British agency people and places.

I was initially interested in volunteering in Madagascar as it is somewhere I would love to visit. But Kate at people and places emailed me about Mapoch, and she suggested that my skills could be very well used on this project. I read the diary of a former volunteer who said that the residents of the village spend nearly a day walking to the doctor and back. At this point I had a bright idea and mentioned to p&p's local partners in South Africa that it would be a great idea to get some bicycles in the village. I am passionate about cycling and know quite a bit about cycle charity projects, so we worked together designing a cycle repair, maintenance and sales project for the village.

The idea of the project was to introduce bicycles into a poor African community, and give the people cheap transport. During the month I was there we turned a grocery shop run by Pastor Peter into a cycle shop, built some bicycles from spares, and renovated some donated bicycles, which we put in the shop for sale. The difference a bicycle can make to a poor South African is amazing: I was told about a district nurse who visited her patients on foot and saw eight patients a day, but after being given a bicycle she can visit 18 patients; as she is paid per visit her income has doubled and more people get treatment. By setting up a cycle shop we have ensured the bicycles will be maintained and we have created employment for the villagers, and they will have cheap transport - which for some of the children will mean they do not have to spend hours each day walking to school.

As I have a holiday entitlement of 27 days a year I was entitled to take a month off work, although taking this amount of time during the summer holidays is not normal for a school caretaker as we often have a lot of building and repair work carried out when the school is closed. I asked the head teacher for the time off and she fully supported me in what I wanted to do. In total, £660 was donated to the project by work colleagues, friends, and even people who I have never met. The money was spent on buying tools, cycle parts and spares, two new bicycles for the villagers, an awning outside the shop for shade, and finally buying parts to build a cycle trailer as a prototype and leaving enough parts to build another one. The amount of money that some people donated stunned me.

Returning to home routines has been bloody impossible, to be honest. Life back in England seemed so pointless even after only a month away. In South Africa I could really help people who needed it: people who have so little but are still happy. The rewards have been immense. I feel empowered to do much more voluntary work, and have a belief in myself and what I can achieve. I have learnt a lot about the culture and customs of South Africans, and have been amazed by their resilience and resourcefulness in the face of adversity.

ACCESSING MONEY ABROAD

Once you are resolved to save for your gap year, set a realistic target and then go for it wholeheartedly. If you are participating in a scheme through a recognised charity, you will be able to fundraise (see the section in Part 4: Doing Something Worthwhile). Estimate how long it will take you to raise the desired amount, set some interim deadlines, and stick to them. If you are lucky enough to be in a position to rent out property while you're away, you will have to make arrangements for transferring the income abroad (covered in the previous chapter).

The cost of a trip varies tremendously, depending on modes of transport chosen, your willingness to sleep and eat modestly, and to deny yourself souvenirs. Grown-ups who are used to splashing out on one or two annual holidays sometimes take time on a gap year to realise that spending patterns have to be different. It is always a good idea to have an emergency fund in reserve, or at least access to money from home, in addition to a return ticket should you run into difficulties. To estimate daily expenses, it might be helpful to know that the average budget of a travelling student is roughly £25–£35 a day, though older, more affluent, gap-year travellers can easily spend much more.

Whatever the size of your travelling fund, you should plan to access your money from three sources: cash, credit cards, and travellers' cheques. Travellers' cheques are falling out of favour and banks able to encash them are not always near to hand, even in Europe, but it is a sensible precaution to keep one or two cheques at the bottom of your luggage for an emergency. They might also be a useful standby if you happen to find yourself stranded in a place without an ATM. The best way to find out where you can change American Express cheques in advance is to log on to www.aetclocator.com, where the contact details of fee-free exchange partners are listed.

The most straightforward way to access money abroad is by using your bank debit card in hole-in-the-wall ATMs. There is usually a minimum fee for a withdrawal, so you should get larger amounts out at one time than you would at home. Read the fine print on those boring leaflets that come with your debit card because it may be that your bank will also gouge you with various loading fees, withdrawal fees, and transaction fees. For example, the Exchange Rate Transaction Fee (ERTF) charges a standard 2.75% for withdrawing foreign currency, plus cash machine withdrawals incur a further percentage more of the sterling transaction (minimum £2, maximum £5). In everyday language this means that a single withdrawal from a hole-in-the-wall usually costs at least £5 in total. The Point of Sale charge is a more reasonable £1.25. If you are going to be abroad for a considerable period and drawing on funds in your home account, it is worth shopping around for the best deal – which is at present offered by the Norwich and Peterborough Building Society. In 2011 it abolished fees on its newly launched Visa debit card (conditions apply). Research can be carried out on www.moneysavingexpert.com.

Travel Money Cards sold by a number of companies including the Post Office are prepaid, reloadable cards that can be used like debit cards at ATMs and most shops, but are not linked to your bank account. You can purchase one online and load it with sterling, euros or US dollars, but be aware that the exchange rate and transaction fees may not be better than the rival methods. A survey of the benefits can be seen at www.cardsmart.co.uk/travel-money-cards, with a comparative list of commission charged by the main providers like Cashplus.

It is always advisable to keep a small amount of cash handy. Sterling is fine for most countries, but US dollars are preferred in much of the world – such as Latin America, Eastern Europe, and Israel. The easiest way to look up the exchange rate of any world currency when planning your travels is to check on the internet, eg www.xe.net/ucc or www.oanda.com. Most banks require a few days' notice to obtain a foreign currency for you. Marks & Spencer's Travel Money offers favourable exchange rates with no commission or handling charges on currency or travellers' cheques. Furthermore, these can be ordered online and posted to your home (for a fee).

Few people think of crediting their Visa, Mastercard, etc account before leaving and then withdrawing cash on the credit card without incurring interest charges (since the money is not actually being borrowed). Even in remote countries like Niger in West Africa, it is possible to draw money on a credit card. The international banking network is limited in Africa and parts of Asia, so some banks and businesses will only accept American Express and/or Visa cards. Check the respective website of your card issuer to see where your card is accepted abroad.

For information on what to do if you need to have money sent to you in an emergency, see the section below on theft.

WHAT TO TAKE

BACKPACKING EQUIPMENT

Outdoor equipment shops carry an enticing range of shiny new products, though if you are operating on a tight budget you should first check out eBay or the small ads in online communities like Gumtree, or scour army surplus and charity shops. Tents are sold very cheaply by Asda (eg, £20–£30) and other discount stores, though they are not built for harsh weather conditions.

For your main luggage, Paul Goodyear of the excellent Nomad Travel Store (www.nomadtravel. co.uk) recommends the new travel sack over the traditional rucksack, which he compares to a tunnel you have to push everything into. By contrast, the 50-litre or 65-litre travel sack can be slung over the shoulder and immediately offers the advantage of making you look less like other backpackers. The travel sack can also be opened at the back for easy access and is designed to be more comfortable for your back during long walks. Another advantage is that it includes a daypack, which can be zipped off to carry essential items like passports and money for a day trip.

Packing for travelling as a backpacker will always entail compromises because you will be limited in the amount of clothing and equipment you can take with you. When you're buying a backpack/rucksack in a shop, try to place a significant weight in it so you can feel how comfortable it might be to carry on your back – otherwise you'll be misled by lifting something usually filled with foam. On **Kath McGuire's** second gap year, in which she spent more than three months travelling overland from England to Colombo via Kazakhstan and Nepal, she fitted everything into a 40-litre bag, but aims to trim even more in future, as she reported from Lhasa, Tibet in August 2010, in her blog (www.kathmcguire.co.uk):

> My bag is only 40 litres, but I've decided next time I want to do it with an even smaller bag. The clothes situation has been fine (two shirts, two T-shirts, two pairs trousers, three sets underwear, fleece, raincoat, and waterproof trousers). I haven't used the waterproof trousers yet, but as I get further south and it gets much wetter, I'm sure I will. I have loads of Ziploc bags and they have been an absolute life-saver. I love them. And they're small and light so I don't mind carrying them either. Fortunately, they're also easy enough to buy (Moscow and Lanzhou). In the essential category also comes antibacterial handwash, tissues, wet wipes, and malaria tablets. I did discard the toilet paper I'd brought because I can use tissues, and they're easier to pack, carry and replenish. I have an issue with other stuff: printouts of bookings, tickets, reservations, information etc, notebook, pen, my Palm (for reading), phone, logic book, phrase book, camera, chargers, head torch, spare batteries etc. I'm not sure how much of this I could consolidate. Perhaps a smart phone is the way to go and just get rid of everything else. I have several just-in-case things: string, spare batteries, first aid kit, etc. The main problem I have with weight and space is food. I could probably fit everything I need (except food) into a 20-litre or 25-litre bag, which could be carried onto a coach or train with me rather than put in the hold. But I still need

water and snacks and, for some train trips, meals. I could stop carrying food and just buy it as I go, but I'm not keen on getting stuck somewhere with no drinking water and no food. There isn't anything that I don't have that I feel I want/need.

All sorts of obscure items can come in handy, though few travellers are likely to follow **Hannah Stevens's** example and remember to pack a nit comb. One tip is to carry dental floss: useful not only for your teeth, but as strong twine for mending backpacks, hanging up laundry, etc. Another important consideration is what you take for sleeping. **Paul Goodyear** recommends a tropical quilt for equatorial areas instead of a sleeping bag. It can be spread out as a bed to sleep on, folded to create a lightweight sleeping bag, or used as a shawl in chilly weather. The other advantage is that it is much lighter to carry and takes up less room in your luggage. The *Telegraph* journalist **Rosemary Behan**, who reported back to the paper throughout her gap travels, allowed herself the luxury of taking a silk sleeping bag liner which she used in dodgy hotels throughout Asia. Other handy equipment includes a travel towel, which can be used to dry or wash yourself. Unlike a conventional towel, which occupies space and turns smelly in the heat and damp of the tropics, this one will dry very quickly after it has been wrung out.

In the heat of the tropics you should carry at least two litres of water in order to prevent dehydration. The best water bottles are soft-sided bladder-style ones (look for the Platypus brand); some also have small separate compartments for a purifying agent like chlorine or iodine (mentioned below).

Belts with a zipped compartment worn under a shirt are very handy for carrying money unobtrusively. A bandana is also advisable in the tropics to keep the sun off your head, to mop up sweat, or to put round your face in windy desert conditions. Some even have backgammon and chess sets printed on them to provide portable entertainment.

When packing it's best to roll rather than fold clothes to save space, and put the heaviest objects at the bottom of the pack. Always carry liquids (like shampoo or water) inside a plastic bag in case they leak.

Do not panic that you will be cut off from the products you love. Prior to leaving for her voluntary placement in a law office in Belize, **Sara Ellis-Owen** emptied the shelves of Boots and also stocked up on favourite foodstuffs like Marmite and Earl Grey tea. She later realised that Belize City already had everything that she needed – the local supermarket even stocked Waitrose supplies – so try to do some research about the shopping facilities at your destination before weighing down your luggage.

Other specialist travel merchandisers include the award-winning Itchy Feet in Bath (01225 442618; www.itchyfeet.com), and the mail-order companies Catch 22 in Lancashire (01942 511820; www.catch22products.co.uk) or Travel with Care in Wiltshire (www.travelwithcare. com). For more specific information on what to stuff your backpack with if you plan to camp consult the *Camping Pocket Bible* by Caroline Mills (Crimson Publishing, 2011).

HANDY TRAVEL TIPS FOR BACKPACKERS

■ *Keep a record of vital travel documents like passport number, driving licence, travellers' cheques serial numbers, insurance policy, tickets, emergency number for cancelling credit cards, etc. Make two copies: stow one away in your luggage and give the other to a friend or relation at home. An even shrewder method is to take a scan of your passport and store it digitally in your email account so that you can access it instantly in an emergency.*

PRACTICAL ADVICE FOR TRAVELLERS

WHAT TO TAKE

- *Make sure your passport will remain valid for at least three months beyond the expected duration of your trip; some countries require six months' worth of validity.*
- *Carry valuable items (like passport, essential medicines, digital cameras, and of course money) on your person rather than relegating them to a piece of luggage which might be lost or stolen.*
- *Only take items you are prepared to lose.*
- *When deciding on clothes to take, start at your feet and work your way up the body; then try to shed up to half. If you find that you really need some missing item of clothing, you can always buy it en route.*
- *Take waterproof and dustproof luggage.*
- *If going to a developing country where it is a constant struggle to keep clean, take a bar of Vanish laundry soap as well as some nice-smelling moisturiser or soap for your skin.*
- *Remember to ask permission before taking photographs of individuals or groups. In some cultures it can be insulting.*
- *Take advantage of the toilets in expensive hotels and fast food chains.*
- *Take a list of consular addresses in the countries you intend to visit, in case of emergency.*

MAPS AND GUIDES

Good maps and guides always enhance one's enjoyment of a trip. If you are going to be based in a major city, buy a map ahead of time. If you are in London or Bristol, visit the famous map shop Edward Stanford Ltd (020 7836 1321), whose catalogue can be searched online at www.stanfords.co.uk; or try Daunt Books for Travellers (020 7224 2295; www.dauntbooks.co.uk). The Map Shop in Worcestershire (0800 085 4080/01684 593146; www.themapshop.co.uk) and Maps Worldwide in Wiltshire (0845 122 0559; www.mapsworldwide.co.uk) both do an extensive mail order business in specialised maps and guidebooks. In the US an excellent source is www.omnimap.com.

Phrase books, dictionaries and teach-yourself language courses can be more useful once you arrive in a country than at home.

ELECTRONIC ITEMS

Few serious travellers will want to leave home without a decent digital camera and the wherewithal to upload photos on to a blog or otherwise for the folks back home. Flickr.com and Picasaweb are just two of the many free image hosting sites where travellers share personal photos.

Try to minimise the gadgets you are carrying. If you can't live without your hair dryer or travel iron, find out what the voltage and frequency are in the countries you intend to visit and invest in an earthed adaptor. Plug adaptors suitable for North American, British, and European plugs can be bought from major electrical stores. For converting voltage (eg, between European and North American equipment) you need a transformer.

The miniaturisation of gadgetry these days means that travellers can travel light after loading up their iPod or MP3 player with music. Some consider this essential equipment in order to pass the time on long bus journeys and to block out the sound of dorm-snorers. Along with a pair of sunglasses, something plugged into your ears can also prove useful in protecting you from unwanted attention. You may want to consider travelling with a laptop or palmtop computer; a surprising number of places now provide WiFi access to the internet. If you are going to be based in one place, you might investigate plumbing your computer in, eg by taking apart a wall socket or telephone. Once you're connected, you simply sign up with a local or international Internet Service Provider (ISP).

MEDICATIONS

Prescribed drugs (except contraceptives) that you take with you should be accompanied by a doctor's letter explaining why you need them. Do not carry non-prescribed drugs stronger than aspirin or anti-malarials, and then only in the original packs. Customs officers are highly sensitive about drugs of all kinds, and can be suspicious of some available over-the-counter in Britain but that are available only on prescription in other countries.

If you are planning a long trip, take a prescription from your doctor. It can be endorsed by a doctor abroad and used to obtain drugs.

GIFTS

When you encounter the kindness of strangers it is sometimes appropriate to bestow a small gift to acknowledge your appreciation. In developing countries, a supply of postcards, photos of your hometown, or stamps to give to children as a memento of your visit are often appreciated. Symbols of Western, particularly American, culture like T-shirts and baseball caps are also highly prized by many.

After spending some months working as a volunteer in Cambodia, **Polly Botsford** knew what she would do differently another time:

> *When I go back I will take a lot more presents from England. Ask your host country contacts if there is anything which is particularly expensive/unobtainable where you are going and bring bucket-loads of whatever it is.*

Choosing what to take for friends or relations, or to ingratiate yourself with friends-of-friends on whom you wish to impose, is an art. If your beneficiaries are British expats, then virtually anything British might be appreciated: from a copy of *Private Eye* to Marmite or Scotch whisky.

Scott Burke, founder of a volunteer placement company in the USA called Cosmic Volunteers, has a good suggestion – especially for anyone who is going to be working with children in a school or orphanage. When suffering acute culture shock in Nepal and in danger of abandoning his plan to become a volunteer English teacher, he found the solution:

> *What ended up saving me was...Mr Bubbles. That's right: a four-ounce bottle of bubbles I had brought with me to Nepal on the advice of a friend. 'A great icebreaker with kids,' she had said. I took the bottle, walked outside and started blowing bubbles alone in my front yard.*

Sure enough, in a few minutes several children appeared, seemingly from nowhere. Without exchanging even one word for the next two hours, the children and I blew bubbles and laughed and ran around. Back in my room, I sat back down on that bed, took a deep breath and thought to myself: Maybe I can do this.

If you are going to be working with children, donations that are highly prized include wax crayons (preferable to coloured pencils since they don't need sharpening), colouring books, balloons, tennis balls, and trainers. StuffYourRucksack.com is a charity set up by the TV broadcaster Kate Humble for conscientious travellers wishing to make a practical difference when they travel. Small charities use the website to post wish lists of things they need, so that travellers can pack and then deliver some useful items.

STAYING IN TOUCH

The revolution in communication technology means that you are never far from home. Internet cafés can be found in almost every corner of the world where, for a greater or lesser fee, you can access your email, keep in touch with friends via Facebook, check relevant information on the web, or upload and distribute digital photos. However, with WiFi becoming more available in accommodation and cafés worldwide, some travellers now consider a laptop or smartphone an essential piece of equipment. **Barry Irvine** is lucky enough to have a lightweight MacBook Air that he takes with him everywhere (except the time he accidentally left it on a rock during a hike in Bolivia and spent a frantic hour searching a hillside for the right rock):

> My advice is to take pretty much anything with WiFi. In Africa it doesn't make much difference – the internet there is appalling except for South Africa – but I found my MacBook Air invaluable for keeping my blog up-to-date whilst I was travelling throughout Latin America. Nearly every hostel had free WiFi and practically everyone travels with at least a netbook these days. Not everybody will be able to afford a MacBook Air, but for me it was the perfect travel companion – lightweight and yet a full-sized computer. It's just rather unfortunate that my first one got stolen in Ecuador! So anything from a mobile phone with WiFi (eg, iPhone) to an iPad, or netbook or lightweight laptop are invaluable. You save money by not going to internet cafés all the time and save time by not having to wait for computers to become free at hostels. Also, with an iPhone you can make Skype calls for free using the WiFi.
>
> Facebook was an essential tool, not just for keeping in touch with the people back home, but also with other travellers that you meet along the way. It's amazing how often you see a recent acquaintance saying, 'I'm in such-and-such' and you say, 'I'm there too in Hostel X. Wanna meet up?' A mobile phone is only really useful as an alarm clock – too expensive to actually use. Much better to use Skype credit if you want to call home – most internet cafés have headphones/speakers too. Again, if you're carrying a computer that doesn't have a built-in mic then a headset is a useful item.

You can get the weight down even more with a WiFi-enabled smartphone, which was **Mark Perriton's** solution on his round-the-world cycle trip:

> I have taken a Nokia E71 smartphone with me, which does all that I need. It has a 5-megapixel camera, a music player, and email and web browsing functions. I spent time looking into the cost of roaming in my phone and found that it was very expensive, so I always get a local sim card if I am staying in a country for any time. The key things to me are weight and keeping the number of bits of technology to a minimum. The risk if you take lots of kit is that it gets stolen or breaks.

Kath McGuire's pre-gap year budget did not quite stretch to a smartphone, plus she did not want to draw attention to herself as she backpacked through Asia. She had also been worried about how easy it would be to charge it along the way, which proved to be unfounded: 'I am carrying a Palm III, which has been useful as a calculator, alarm clock, and most importantly a means of reading books and writing memos – which I can later upload to a computer as text files.'

Sending photos home electronically has become a piece of cake, as is setting up your own website, blog (ie web log), or even vlog (video log) to share travel tales with family, friends, and interested strangers. Lots of companies will help you create your own blog free of charge: for example, Wordpress (www.wordpress.com) is free and easy to use. The other main contender for free blog hosting is blogspot.com (go to www.blogger.com/start). If you do decide to keep a blog, remember that less is more: the folks back home probably don't have the time to read all the ins and outs of your long bus journeys and negotiations with hoteliers. Try to record the most interesting highlights for public consumption.

To avoid floating off into a news vacuum, some people subscribe to the BBC daily email service, which sends out a selection of news stories according to the interests you register (newsvote.bbc.co.uk/email). Others relish the prospect of no longer having a clue who is who in the Cabinet or what scandal has befallen footballers and their wives.

Fixing yourself up with web-based email and Skype accounts before leaving home is now virtually compulsory. Not only does it allow you to keep in touch with home and with friends met on the road, it is also very handy for managing your finances and staying in touch with professional resources. The most heavily-subscribed service for travellers is still Hotmail (www.hotmail.com or www.hotmail.co.uk), which has made many improvements over the past couple of years to stay ahead of Google's Gmail.

The danger for people who rely too heavily on technology is that they spend so much time on Facebook in cybercafés that they end up not having the encounters and adventures they might have otherwise. Just as the texting generation is finding it harder to cut ties with home knowing that a parent or a school friend is only a few digits away wherever they are, so too travellers who spend an inordinate amount of time online risk failing to look round the destination country in depth and missing out on meeting locals in the old-fashioned, strike-up-a-conversation, getting-in-and-out-of-scrapes way. They will also be deprived of another old-fashioned treat: arriving at a poste restante address and experiencing the pleasure (sweeter because deferred) of reading their mail.

MOBILE PHONES

Roaming charges for mobiles can cost an arm and a leg. Contact your mobile phone company to check on coverage; if not, you may need to take it into a shop to have the phone 'unlocked'. Also check what deals your provider offers, which can be spectacularly complex. Vodafone's 'Passport' is a free tariff option available with any handset, which allows you to make calls at your home tariff after paying a 75p connection fee, and texts for 11p. It is available in most of Europe, Australia, New Zealand, and Japan, but not North America (www.abroad.vodafone.co.uk).

If you are going to be on the move a lot, you might want to investigate a gadget that can charge your mobile and iPod using solar power: the Solio charger (www.solio.com) retails from about £50.

A plethora of companies in the UK and USA sell pre-paid calling cards intended to simplify international phoning. You credit your card account with an amount of your choice (normally starting at £10 or £20), or buy a card for $10 or $20. You are then given an access code which can be used from any phone. Lonely Planet, the travel publisher, has an easy-to-use communications card called eKit which offers low cost calls, voice mail, and email (lonelyplanet.ekit. com). A company called 0044 (0044.co.uk) sells foreign sim cards which allow you to take your mobile with you and call at local rates while you're away. Their global sim card costs £20, compared with £30 from GoSim (gosim.com).

Warn friends not to call your UK mobile while you are away; you will be paying for all incoming calls from abroad. If you are staying in one country for more than a few weeks and use your phone a lot, consider getting either a cheap local mobile phone or a local sim card for your UK mobile. Even better, ensure your UK contacts have the special access codes available for low-cost dialling from landlines to your destination. One of the most often-recommended discount companies (for people phoning abroad from the UK) is www.telediscount.co.uk, which offers unbeatable prices: in many cases you can make international calls at local rates.

Gaptrac (www.gaptrac.co.uk) provides a range of state-of-the-art functions, and uses GPS to record your route for friends and family to follow in real time. After joining for £10 plus VAT per month, you are assigned a user name and password to pass on to followers who can then access your blog, photos, and even audio files.

TRAVEL ARRANGEMENTS

Those who are joining an organised voluntary or expeditionary scheme will no doubt receive plenty of advice on how to book flights and onward travel. Independent travellers should be looking at discounted tickets, last minute bargains, and no-frills airlines (see Part 7: Travel and Adventure, for detailed advice).

ACCOMMODATION

Places where travellers tend to congregate always have a good selection of reasonably-priced accommodation. In many parts of the world the status of backpacking is rising, and the growing range of facilities pitched at this important sector of the more mature backpacking market is impressive.

Those who haven't stayed at a hostel since their student days will be surprised at the revolution that has taken place. Hostels generally offer higher standards of comfort than a generation ago and have become far more attractive to older travellers (not least because they have abolished the dreaded compulsory chore). Nowadays many hostels offer single, double, and family rooms in addition to the standard dormitories. In major cities youth hostels often represent the cheapest accommodation, and in remote areas they often represent the most beautiful. Many are located in prime sites and some are in beautifully-restored old buildings.

Hostels offer the cheapest beds in Europe, ranging from about €10 to €25+ per night, depending on location. Hostels are a good way to meet people and find out about the area, but you will not have much privacy. Hostels fall into two categories: 'official' and independent. The original Youth Hostels Federation is now called Hostelling International (www.hihostels.com) and consists of 4,000 hostels in 60 countries. Annual membership costs £15.95 for those over 26 (01629 592700 in the UK; www.yha.org.uk). Rules and guidelines apply, often including curfews (good if you don't want to be woken up in the early hours by drunk party animals) and dorms are usually single-sex. You can stay at youth hostels without being a member, but will pay a supplement. Private hostels are unpredictable, but often have fewer rules and more colour. Good hostel websites include www.hostelbookers.com, www.hostelworld.com, and www.hostels.com – all of which allow online bookings.

The cheapest accommodation of all is a tent: an attractive option if you're travelling into remote areas like national parks where accommodation is in short supply, or if you are ever caught at dark without a roof over your head. The drawback of course is the extra weight of a tent and sleeping bag, and discretion is always recommended when camping by the side of the road. If you are camping on private land, always seek permission from the local farmer or enquire locally. Finding a supply of water may present problems; never be tempted to camp in a dried-up river bed, since a flash flood can wash you away.

These are the steps Stephanie Fuccio followed, in vaguely chronological order, in preparation for a trip to Guatemala:

- Followed gut feeling and decided it was time to head down to Guatemala.
- Researched volunteer opportunities and Spanish schools.
- Bought plane ticket.
- Sub-let her rented San Francisco apartment through Craigslist.com and created a three-page sublet agreement that would have made her lawyer boss from a decade ago proud: 'I will be a long way away, and don't want to think about my SF life when I am down there.'
- Looked for travel partners for parts of the trip via Lonely Planet Thorn Tree, Bootsnall, and an ad on Craigslist's SF community page.
- Started to contact locals and expats who live in Guatemala.
- Gave notice at present job.
- Spent time going over her budget with a fine-tooth comb: 'My usual method of travel is to save money then travel, or, if planning a long period of travel, work along the way to finance, come home, and work more. This time I am not travelling on savings so much as travelling on rent money.'
- For peace of mind she paid some bills before she left, since she was not likely to be working right away when she returned.
- Set up an online blog.
- Researched necessary immunisations and travel advisory warnings.
- Downloaded all music into iTunes, in case she decided to take an iPod: 'I prefer to listen to local music/radio when I am in a place, but I have also noticed that familiar sounds are settling during times of strong culture shock or stress'.
- Sorted through tons of papers lying around her apartment: sorting out what projects she could realistically complete before leaving in a few weeks, and what needed to be postponed until her return. Breaking down projects no matter how big or small and assigning a day to work on them helped a lot: 'I also noticed that if there were a project that I kept putting off, then it tended to go into the "Better off as an idea than reality" pile.'
- Made a packing checklist that included travel towel, earplugs (essential), sunblock, and other things that might have been forgotten.
- Researched travel insurance. She used Google and followed links from respectable travel websites like Lonely Planet, Rough Guides, Bootsnall, and Budget Travel Magazine, and rejected any she couldn't extend once she was on the trip. Her main concerns were health (since she was doing some hiking) and theft protection (since she was taking her digital camera and iPod).

TRAVEL INSURANCE

European nationals are eligible for reciprocal emergency health care within Europe. However, outside Europe, a good insurance policy is absolutely essential. Increased competition among travel insurers has brought costs down over the past few years, though it will still be necessary to set aside a chunk of your travel fund. Travel policies do not automatically cover certain activities deemed to be dangerous, such as winter sports and manual work (eg on a volunteer project). Anyone wanting to engage in adventure or extreme sports like bungee jumping, scuba diving, or sky diving, should do some comparison shopping – since by studying the fine print, you may find a company that will cover your preferred activity without the need of investing in special cover. You are expected to inform your insurer ahead of time if you plan to indulge in any potentially risky activities.

The UK has reciprocal health agreements with more than 40 countries worldwide that entitle you to emergency care, though it is still recommended to have your own comprehensive private coverage to cover extras, like loss of baggage and, more importantly, emergency repatriation. Many countries in Africa, Asia, Latin America, and the USA do not provide any reciprocal cover and travelling without travel insurance can literally break the bank. Medical care in an emergency might cost an individual tens of thousands of pounds.

All travellers must face the possibility of an accident befalling them abroad. In countries like India, Turkey, and Venezuela, the rate of road traffic accidents can be as much as 20 times greater than in the UK. Certain activities obviously entail more risk. For example, broken bones are common on ski treks and evacuation can be difficult in mountainous areas where trekking is popular. If you are thinking of travelling with a tour group, ask the company how they deal with medical emergencies and whether repatriation is included in their group policy.

If you're travelling independently, you will find that almost every enterprise in the travel business will be delighted to sell you insurance because of the commission earned. Ring several insurance companies with your specifications and compare prices. Europ-Assistance Ltd (0844 338 5533; www.europ-assistance.co.uk) is the world's largest assistance organisation, with a network of doctors, air ambulances, agents, and vehicle rescue services managed by more than 200 offices worldwide – all offering (at a price) emergency assistance abroad 24 hours a day. Many companies charge lower premiums, though you will have to decide whether you are satisfied with their level of cover. Most offer a no-frills rate which covers medical emergencies, and a premium rate which covers extras that might be considered non-essential – like loss of personal baggage. If you are not planning to visit North America, the premiums will be much less expensive. Note that if the Foreign & Commonwealth Office advises against travelling to a certain country, your travel insurance will be invalidated if you ignore this advice.

Some companies to consider are listed here with a rough idea of their premiums for 12 months of worldwide cover (including the USA). Expect to pay in the region of £25 per month for basic cover and £35 for more extensive cover.

USEFUL CONTACTS

PRACTICAL ADVICE FOR TRAVELLERS

- **Age UK** – formerly **Age Concern**, (0845 600 3348; www.ageuk.org.uk). Specialises in travel insurance for over 60s and over 70s (no upper age limit), with policies provided by Fortis Insurance Ltd. Pre-existing medical conditions can be covered. Sample price of £97 covers one month of volunteering in Tanzania.

- **Austravel**, (0870 166 2020; www.austravel.com/travel-info/insurance). Specialist in travel to Australia and New Zealand, and sells a range of competitively-priced insurance policies for budget travellers and families, eg £130 for three months' cover per adult. Cover for adventure sports is available too.

- **Automobile Association**, (www.aatravelinsurance.com). Their policies cover pensioners, but are pricy.

- **Club Direct**, (0800 083 2466; www.clubdirect.com). Basic backpacker cover.

- **Columbus Direct**, (0870 033 9988; www.columbusdirect.com). One of the giants in the field of travel insurance. From £220 for 12 months' worldwide cover.

- **Direct Travel Insurance**, (0845 605 2700; www.direct-travel.co.uk). Consistently among the cheapest. Maximum stay away is 31 days for over-65s.

- **Europ-Assistance Ltd**, (0844 338 5533/5555; www.europ-assistance.co.uk). Maximum duration of 91 days costs £284 for worldwide cover.

- **gosure.com**, (0845 222 0020; www.gosure.com). Among the cheapest for travellers under 65.

- **Lockton International**, (020 7933 0000; www.lockton.com). Providers of International Loss/Damage Vehicle Insurance for people of any nationality living or working outside their country of origin, including travellers on expedition, diplomats, expatriates, teachers, aid workers, and journalists: in their key markets of Africa, South America, Asia, the Middle East and Eastern Europe.

- **MRL Insurance**, (0845 676 0691; www.mrlinsurance.co.uk). £121 for four months' economy cover. Also offer policies to travellers up to age 89.

Emergency medical claims are normally processed efficiently, but if you have to make a claim for lost or stolen baggage you may be unpleasantly surprised by the amount of the settlement eventually paid, especially if you have opted for a discount insurer. Loss adjusters have ways of making calculations that prove that you are entitled to less than you think. The golden rule is to amass as much documentation as possible to support your application: most importantly medical receipts and a police report in the case of an accident or theft.

TRAVEL INSURANCE

HEALTH AND SAFETY

Travel inevitably involves balancing risks and navigating through hazards real or imagined. With common sense and advice from experts, you can minimise potential problems. If you are planning to travel outside the developed world, you will have to research what health precautions are essential, possible, or recommended. You will also have to consider how to minimise loss or theft of money and belongings – something to be considered when you are deciding what to pack.

The Foreign & Commonwealth Office of the UK government runs a regular and updated service; you can ring the Travel Advice Unit on 0845 850 2829 (£0.04 per minute) or check their website at www.fco.gov.uk/travel. This site gives frequently updated and detailed risk assessments of any trouble spots, including civil unrest, terrorism, and crime. Some believe that the FCO travel warnings err on the side of caution to the detriment of NGOs struggling to attract volunteers, so try to balance the official warnings with a first-hand account from someone who lives in the place you are considering. The director of the charity Sudan Volunteer Programme describes what he sees as the FCO bias:

> *We continue to be dogged by the negative and, I believe, misleadingly indiscriminate travel advice issued by the FCO, which puts off potential volunteers, or more particularly, their families. It stems it seems to me from the alarming experiences of embassy staff, which induces them to put up ever higher fences to guard their premises, and of course, this siege mentality brings about an ever-greater ignorance of the actual conditions. There was one threat to embassy security about two years ago and one murder of an American official in Khartoum in January 2008. There were otherwise no attacks in the recent years on foreigners in Khartoum or smaller northern towns. I do not belittle these outrages but they cannot be described as 'indiscriminate', as used in the FCO warning.*

Several years ago the FCO launched a 'Know Before You Go' campaign, to raise awareness among backpackers and independent travellers of potential risks and dangers and how to guard against them, principally by taking out a water-tight insurance policy. The same emphasis can be detected on the FCO site www.gogapyear.co.uk. The 50-page leaflet *World Wise*, prepared by Lonely Planet for the FCO and available to read online at www.fco.gov.uk/resources/en/pdf/2855621/world-wise, might raise some travel issues you hadn't thought of. Arguably much health and safety advice is over-cautious: advising travellers never to ride a motorbike or accept an invitation to a private house. Adult travellers will have to decide for themselves when to ignore advice and trust their instincts.

A couple of specialist organisations in the UK put on short courses to prepare clients for potential dangers and problems on a gap year or expedition. Needless to say, these are normally aimed at naïve 18-year-olds whose parents are paying for the course. Managing director John Cummings of provider Safetrek in Devon (01884 839704; www.safetrek.co.uk) notes that more grown-ups have been requesting their personal safety and awareness training. The over-40s are interested not just in what to do when abroad, but how to leave their homes secure. He acknowledges that a lot of it is common sense but not necessarily common practice. People in the older age group are undoubtedly more confident than their gap year counterparts straight out of school, but more worried about things going wrong at home in their absence. John Cummings also suspects that older men are more inclined to react too quickly to an incident, thereby making matters worse, so thinks that they could benefit from training which urges them to remain calm and walk away. The one-day courses costing £140 are offered in Exeter or Bristol, and still mainly attract young gappers. Another training provider in this area is Objective Travel Safety (01788 899029; www.objectivegapyear.com).

News of tragedies affecting travellers crop up in the news from time to time: for example, the case of 50-year-old nurse Jennifer Pope from Greater Manchester, who stopped making contact with her family after four happy months of working and travelling in South America. Nine months later a man was arrested for her abduction and murder in Ecuador. All that can be said by way of reassurance is that these events are exceedingly rare.

The preparatory courses mentioned above cover general safety issues like how to prevent pickpockets. Prometheus Medical Ltd (01568 613942; www.prometheusmedical.co.uk/prometheus/courses/Surviving-Adventure/home) offers scenario-based training mainly out of doors, and is designed for career breakers, expeditioners, and individuals taking part in overseas projects, to help participants feel that they could manage an emergency. Courses are led by a medic, mountaineer, or former Special Forces member.

Similarly, Wilderness Medical Training in Cumbria (01539 823183; www.wilderness medicaltraining.co.uk) puts on courses in expedition medicine for lay people as well as doctors. Their foundation course is called 'Far From Help', which teaches the use of prescription medicines. Courses last from two days (from £265) to seven days for their annual Expedition Skills course (£720).

TRAVELLERS' HEALTH

No matter what country you are heading for, you should obtain the Department of Health leaflet T7.1 *Health Advice for Travellers* (updated May 2006). This leaflet should be available from any post office or doctor's surgery. Alternatively you can request a free copy on the Health Literature Line (0300 123 1002) or read it online at www.dh.gov.uk, which also has country-by-country details.

Increasingly, people are carrying out their own health research on the internet; check sites such as the NHS's www.fitfortravel.scot.nhs.uk and www.travelhealth.co.uk. The website of the World Health Organization (www.who.int/ith) has valuable country-by-country information and a listing of the countries in which a yellow fever certificate is a requirement of entry. The BBC's Health Travel Site (www.bbc.co.uk/health/travel) is a solid source of information about travel health, ranging from tummy trouble to water quality and snake bites.

The free European Health Insurance Card (EHIC) entitles EU nationals to emergency health care in any member state. However, it does not cover repatriation, so many travellers choose to obtain private travel insurance as well. You can pick up an EHIC application form from main post offices or apply for one online (www.ehic.org.uk). If you have a pre-existing medical condition it's important to anticipate what you might require in a crisis. Ask your GP or specialist support group for advice before you leave. If you're travelling with a tour operator, let the company know about your condition in advance. Even if you suffer from seasickness or vertigo, it might be worth mentioning on a form if these situations might arise. Under extreme climatic conditions, chronic or pre-existing conditions can be aggravated. Try to ascertain how easy it will be to access medicines on your trip, whether you'll be able to carry emergency supplies with you, and how far you will be from specialist help. Always carry medications in their original containers and as a precaution you might carry a note from your doctor with an explanation of the drugs you're carrying and the relevant facts of your medical history. This could also include details of any allergies: for example, an intolerance of antibiotics. This might be of use if you are involved in an accident or medical emergency.

In an age of mass communication it is usually possible to manage a medical condition while travelling. If you plan to travel to an area with poor medical standards and unreliable blood screening, you might want to consider equipping yourself with sterile syringes and needles. The Department of Travel Medicine at the Hospital for Tropical Diseases recommends that you should carry a specially-prepared sterile needle kit in case local emergency treatment requires injections; Travelpharm (see below) sells various ones starting at £10.

Any visits beyond the developed world, particularly to tropical climates, require careful preparation as you will face the risk of contracting malaria or water-borne diseases like typhoid and hepatitis A. You will need to provide your medical practitioner with precise details about where you intend to travel. Visit a medical centre at least a month before departure because some immunisations like those for yellow fever must be given well in advance.

Some of the advice given below may seem intimidating, especially while preparing for travelling in the developing world; you might begin to feel as if you're joining an SAS induction course. Expert medical advice is widely available on how to avoid tropical illness, so you should take advantage of modern medicine to protect yourself. And be prepared to pay for the necessary inoculations that are not covered by the NHS (apart from typhus and anything you can get in the UK). It is always worth asking at your surgery since if they are able to give good advice (and the internet has made that possible for any doctor or practice nurse worth their salt), the injections may be considerably cheaper than at a private specialist clinic. To give an example of how high the costs can be, check the price list on the MASTA website (see next section) where immunisations against hepatitis A with typhoid cost £84, Japanese Encephalitis £52, cholera £60, and so on.

INOCULATIONS AND PROPHYLAXIS

Depending on where you live, it is entirely possible that your GP will not be keeping abreast with all the complexities of tropical medicine – particularly malaria prevention – for different areas of the world, etc. Some are downright ignorant. The only disease for which a vaccination certificate may be legally required is yellow fever. Many countries insist on seeing one if you are arriving from an infected country, though it is a good idea to get protection if you are planning to travel to a yellow fever zone (much of Africa and almost all of Latin America).

A company that has become one of the most authoritative sources of travellers' health information in Britain is MASTA (enquiries@masta.com; www.masta.com). It maintains a database of the latest information on the disease situation for all countries, and the latest recommendations on the prevention of tropical and other diseases. This advice is provided via a personalised Health Brief based on your destinations and the nature of your trip, which is emailed to you from their website for a charge of £3.99. Along with vaccination recommendations it also provides practical advice such as protection against malaria, information on disease outbreaks, and other non-vaccine preventable health risks for travellers. MASTA's network of travel clinics administers inoculations and sells medical kits and other specialist equipment like water purifiers, mosquito nets, and repellents. Note that arguably the advice errs on the side of caution (which means they also make more profit).

Private specialist clinics abound in London but are thin on the ground elsewhere. A worldwide searchable listing of specialist travel clinics is maintained by the International Society of Travel Medicine (www.istm.org), though many countries are not included.

USEFUL CONTACTS

- **The Hospital for Tropical Diseases**, (Mortimer Market Building, Capper Street, Tottenham Court Road, WC1E 6AU; www.thehtd.org). Offers appointments at its Travel Clinic (020 7388 9600) and operates an automated Travellers Healthline Advisory Service (020 7950 7799), which charges 50p a minute (average phone call lasts about seven minutes).
- **Nomad Travel Clinics**, (020 7823 5823; www.nomadtravel.co.uk). Several London locations including Victoria; also in Bristol, Manchester and Southampton. They offer walk-in appointments though you may have to wait at busy times.
- **The Royal Free Travel Health Centre**, (At the Royal Free Hospital on Pond St in London; 020 7830 2885; www.travelclinicroyalfree.com). A well-regarded private clinic.
- **Trailfinders Travel Clinic**, (194 Kensington High St; 020 7983 3999; www.trailfinders.com). Long-established clinic.
- **Travelpharm**, (0115 951 2092; www.travelpharm.com). Online shop which carries an extensive range of mosquito nets, anti-malaria drugs, water purification equipment, and travel accessories. The website also carries lots of health information. Note that if you want to buy medications online you will have to send a prescription with your order; GPs normally make a charge for this service, eg £15.
- Americans seeking general travel health advice should ring the **Center for Disease Control & Prevention Hotline** (+1 877 394 8747; www.cdc.gov). CDC issues travel announcements for international travellers rated from mild to extreme, ie minimal risk to a recommendation that non-essential travel not take place.

For routine travellers' complaints, it is worth looking at a general guide to travel medicine such as *The Essential Guide to Travel Health: Don't Let Bugs, Bites and Bowels Spoil Your Trip* by Dr Jane Wilson-Howarth (Cadogan, 2009).

MALARIA

Malaria is undoubtedly the greatest danger posed by visits to many tropical areas and should be taken very seriously. If you don't take precautions in malarial zones, you are virtually bound to get the parasite. Because of increasing resistance, it is important to consult a specialist service as those listed above. You can also become better informed by looking at specialist websites such as www.hpa.org.uk/infections/topics_az/malaria. You need to obtain the best information available to help you devise the most appropriate strategy for protection in the areas you intend to visit. Research indicates for example that the statistical chance of being bitten by a malarial mosquito in Thailand is once a year, but in Sierra Leone it rises to once a night. Start your research early since some courses of malaria prophylaxis need to be started up to three weeks before departure. It is always a good idea to find out in advance if you are going to suffer any side effects as well.

Falciparum malaria is potentially fatal. Last year there were 1,378 recorded cases of malaria in the UK (the number has been declining in recent years), six of which were fatal. The two main prophylactic drugs are Doxycycline and Malarone (atovaquone), though Larium is also in use. Doxycycline is a cheap antibiotic and anti-malarial, but some people suffer from the side effects of nausea on an empty stomach and increased skin-sensitivity to sunlight. One tablet must be taken daily from a week before entering a malarial zone until four weeks after leaving; tablets purchased online cost about 14p each. Malarone by contrast costs £2.25 per tablet, so some people buy only a week's supply before arriving in their destination and then buy the drug at a local pharmacy where it will be much cheaper than in the UK. **Lisa Bass** spent a complete gap year in Madagascar and shared her thinking about how to protect yourself when malaria is so prevalent. She recommends Coartem (trade name for artemether lumefantrine):

People do get malaria down in Fort Dauphin, but it is very effectively treated using Coartem – a drug that can be bought without a prescription in the towns. Apparently there is another variant of this drug now which is also very good. The type of malaria you tend to get down here isn't too bad – although obviously you want to avoid it if you can. However, once diagnosed, the people reported starting to feel much better after just six hours after taking the drug. Then it is just a matter of lots of rest and building yourself back up over about the next few days. I took Larium when I was here last time, which made me very disorientated on waking up in the morning and sent me a bit weird when I drank coffee (so I didn't). I'm out here for a year now and was going to take Doxy for the first couple of months but this really didn't suit me at all. So I'm currently on nothing at all. I use lots of DEET and cover up at night. Although I still get bitten a bit I would rather take my chances than feel permanently ill.

Unfortunately these prophylactic medications are not foolproof, and even those who have scrupulously swallowed their pills before and after their trip as well as during it have been known to contract the disease. **Gosbert Chagula**, who spent his gap year working in the field of human rights legislation in Ghana, was unlucky with the mosquitoes that bit him:

The low point was catching acute malaria. That was probably the worst illness I've ever experienced; it wasn't just the fact I had malaria, it was the fact it kept on returning. I estimate I went to the hospital in Kumasi on at least eight separate occasions and at some points it seemed that the doctors didn't know what was wrong with me. They knew it was malaria, yet they had no answers as to why it kept returning with a vengeance. With hindsight, I would not have compromised on malaria tablets. I chose to take the cheaper doxycycline, instead of the far more expensive (and effective) Larium.

It is essential to take mechanical precautions against mosquitoes. If possible, screen the windows and sleep under a permethrin- or DEET-impregnated mosquito net since the offending mosquitoes feed between dusk and dawn. (Practise putting your mosquito net up before leaving home since some are tricky to assemble.) Some travellers have improvised with netting intended for prams, which takes up virtually no luggage space. If you don't have a net, cover your limbs at nightfall with light-coloured garments, apply insect repellent with the active ingredient DEET, and sleep with a fan on to keep the air moving. Try to keep your room free of the insects too by using mosquito coils, vaporisers, etc. DEET is strong enough to last many hours. Wrist and ankle bands impregnated with the chemical are available and easy to use.

Prevention is vastly preferable to cure. It is a difficult disease to treat, particularly in its advanced stages. If you suffer a fever up to twelve months after returning home from a malarial zone, visit your doctor and mention your travels, even if you suspect it might just be flu.

Paula Donahue is a doctor in Canada as well as an inveterate traveller, with a cautionary tale. She and her 13-year-old son decided to take an extended trip to Madagascar, partly because Gabriel was attracted to the exotic name and partly because they had met some charming Madagascan musicians at the annual jazz festival in New Orleans earlier that year. Naturally she was more familiar with the health risks than most and researched them thoroughly. Given the worrying side-effects of anti-malarials, especially in children, and the care with which she intended to prevent mosquito bites, she decided not to take antimalarial drugs. They came back from a wonderful month in Madagascar unscathed. Gabriel felt a bit feverish a couple of days after returning to Ontario but it was assumed that he had caught the same flu that his stay-at-home sister and her friends all had. Four days later he was hooked up to every high tech machine in the hospital and was fighting for his life. Six months later he had regained the 25lb he lost and returned to full strength and vigour but it was a horrible experience and, as his mother admits, forced her to give back the Mother-of-the-Year award she had received for organising their Madagascar trip. Paula now thinks she knows the occasion on which their defences were penetrated: on a day when they went for a walk to spot lemurs in the bush, Gabriel had forgotten his long trousers, refused to borrow a pair because of the heat, and as a consequence got bitten. Paula says that the next time she takes her children to a malarial zone she will steel herself to the possible side effects and prescribe the recommended anti-malarials.

FOOD AND WATER

Tap water throughout the developing world is unsafe for travellers to drink because there is always a chance that it contains disease organisms to which the westerner has had no chance to develop immunities. Do not assume that you can get by with substitute beverages such as tea or beer or even bottled soda water. In hot climates, it is imperative to drink large quantities of water to avoid dehydration, possibly as much as six pints a day. The most effective method of water purification is boiling for at least five minutes. However, this is seldom convenient and in hot weather the water never gets cooler than lukewarm.

A more manageable method of water sterilisation is to use chemical purifiers. Simply pick up the appropriate tablets of chlorine dioxide or tincture of iodine from a chemist before departure, checking how long they take to become effective (ten minutes is preferable to 30 in a hot climate when you're gasping for a cold drink). You can also buy a product that neutralises the unpleasant taste of iodine. Remember that ice cubes, however tempting, should be avoided. Drinking water can also be purified by filtering. MASTA and Nomad market various water purifiers; among the best are the Aquapure Traveller (from £35) and the MSR Sweetwater Microfilter for £70.

Deciding what food is safe to eat is not always easy. You should aim to eat only freshly cooked food and avoid raw vegetables unless they have been peeled or washed thoroughly in purified water. Many people are nervous to eat street food in developing countries. In fact, food served in such places is usually safe provided it has been thoroughly cooked and does not look as though it has been hanging around in a fly-invested environment. A vegetarian diet is less likely to give trouble than meat or fish, and you should try to eat lots of yoghurt since the bacteria help to combat any bugs in the stomach.

Up to 50% of travellers will suffer the trots, or 'Delhi belly', and a mild case of diarrhoea is virtually inevitable for travellers outside the developed world. Doctors warn that however many precautions with food and water you take, it is simply impossible to guard against it completely. If left to its own devices, most bouts clear up within two or three days, although in an extreme case the fluid loss may leave you weak and tired. You should keep drinking to avoid dehydration. This is particularly important for the young or the elderly. Rehydration tablets, which replace lost salt and sugar in the right proportions, are a possible item for your first-aid kit.

Diarrhoea will clear up more quickly if you can get a lot of rest and stop eating altogether. When you begin eating again, stick to as simple a diet as possible, eg boiled rice and tea (without milk). If the problem persists, try a recommended medication such as kaolin and morphine, or codeine phosphate. The antibiotic Ciprofloxacin can speed up recovery, but you'll need to obtain a prescription from a doctor before you leave.

CULTURE SHOCK

Not all travellers' ailments are as straightforward to treat as mild diarrhoea. Enjoying yourself won't be easy if you are suffering the adverse psychological effects of culture shock. Adult gappers who elect to spend time in a developing country are invariably shocked to some degree by the levels of poverty and deprivation. Shock implies something which happens suddenly, but cultural disorientation more often creeps up on you. Adrenaline usually sees you through the first few weeks as you find the novelty exhilarating and challenging, and you will be amazed and charmed by the odd gestures the people use or the antiquated way that things work. As time goes on, practical irritations intrude and the constant misunderstanding caused by those charming gestures – such as a nod in Greece meaning 'no', or in Japan meaning 'yes, I understand, but don't agree' – and the discomfort of those impossibly crowded buses may begin to get on your nerves.

However, most mature gappers who have researched their destination or volunteer situation beforehand learn to cope with the cultural differences even if they sometimes find them exasperating. While teaching and living in Vietnam, **Beth Buffam** felt that her life had been taken over by her minder:

> *My main problem during the six months I was in Hanoi with the Ministry of Trade was communication, as very few people spoke any English. I had a delightful liaison person, Hue, who unfortunately didn't speak much English. Since I knew quite a bit of Vietnamese and wanted to*

learn more, at first this was a plus – but eventually it became a huge problem. Most requests I made to Hue were answered with a smile and a sigh. Although Hue couldn't or didn't solve my problems, she loved to spend time with me, hand in hand, arm tightly in arm, walking around. It felt controlling and uncomfortable, and unpleasant given the fact that eventually I didn't feel very close to her.

People were VERY respectful, but almost too much so. For meals, it was extremely difficult for me ever to pay for my own or everyone's food. I really wanted to be 'one of the guys', but it was always: 'It's our custom, we pay for our guests'. Even after six months? And I got tired of the fact that although I'm strong and carried a lot of heavy books most of the time, when Hue and I had some work to do (like moving tables), she rushed to make sure I didn't lift a finger.

I also felt like a puppet, pushed and pulled. People were always telling me what to do, never asking, and inviting me to their homes on minimal notice ('But my wife is cooking right now...'). So many invitations which all assumed a Yes answer. Finally, after four months there, I realised the existence and value of the word 'No'. Another irritant was invariably being introduced as: 'This is Beth. She is 59 years old. She has one son but no husband. Her son is 36 years old.' So much for keeping personal matters personal!

When **Nikki D'Arcy** from Watford volunteered in a home for the elderly in Peru with Cross-Cultural Solutions, she only gradually overcame her fears that she would be able to cope. Like so many other westerners who have immersed themselves in a developing community, she was left full of admiration:

Despite considering myself an independent, confident person, the thought of completely immersing myself in another culture was still slightly daunting. I won't lie. During my time there, I saw some things that saddened and shocked me; I didn't realise that people could live in such poverty. But I also got to know those people and saw such amazing strength in them. They were so happy to invite me into their lives, to share their stories, and were so full of life it put me to shame for moaning about the tiny problems we have. Even after a few days, I felt my attitudes and perceptions changing. I began to really understand what is important in life. Not the material things that so many of us seem to become obsessed with, but family and friends and enjoying life. Don't get me wrong, I already knew that, but I don't think you can fully understand it until you see people who have nothing, and I mean literally nothing – sometimes not even a roof – but yet they meet up with their friends and dance and sing and laugh like they don't have a care in the world. They are truly inspirational.

THEFT

From London to La Paz crooks lurk, ready to pounce upon the unsuspecting traveller. Theft takes many forms, from the highly trained gangs of children who artfully pick pockets in European railway stations, to violent attacks on the streets of American cities. It is also not unknown to be robbed by fellow-travellers from hostels, beaches, etc, or by corrupt airport officials in cahoots with baggage handlers.

How to carry your money and valuables should be given careful consideration. The first rule is not to keep all your wealth in one place. A money belt worn inside your clothing is good for the peace of mind it bestows; when choosing one, avoid anything too bulky and therefore indiscreet.

In fact, a simple money belt can easily be manufactured at home by any handy seamstress from a left-over length of cotton or silk (preferable to man-made fibres). Just cut a strip of cloth several inches longer than your waist with a six-inch bulge in the middle large enough to accommodate bank notes and travellers' cheques folded lengthwise. If heavy rain is a possibility, put the money in a plastic bag first. Use Velcro to close the flap over your money and also to fasten the belt around your waist under your clothes. It is a good idea to wear your belt for a few days before departure to make sure that it is comfortable and to prove to yourself that it won't fall off. Keep large denomination travellers' cheques and any hard currency cash there, plus a large note of the local currency. Then if your wallet or purse is stolen, you will not be stranded.

To reduce the possibility of theft, steer clear of seedy or crowded areas and moderate your intake of alcohol. If you are mugged, and have an insurance policy which covers cash, you must obtain a police report (sometimes for a fee) to stand any chance of recouping part of your loss. Be particularly careful on long distance bus or train journeys when you are likely to fall asleep. Career breaker **Barry Irvine** tells the sad story of what happened to him on a bus to Quito in May 2010:

> One of the guys (whom I thought was from the bus company) was trying to be 'helpful' and offered to put our bags in the overhead bins. There was no way I was letting my bag out of my sight so I put it under the seat in front of me and then under my feet. I kept dozing in and out of sleep and at various points thought I felt my bag moving but I assumed it was the movement of the bus. Just before we arrived at Quito I moved my bag back in front of me and suddenly noticed that it didn't seem as full as normal. That's when I discovered that my beloved MacBook Air, the charger, and my sunglasses were missing. After looking under my seat (obviously a futile effort) and searching around the bus for the man and his potential accomplice, I sat back down again feeling stupid and upset. The situation could have been a lot worse. In the same compartment of my bag, my money belt (usefully not around my waist: I think I've learned another lesson here!) with hundreds of dollars and all my bank cards in it, still remained. And my passport in the front compartment was still there too. I told some Americans my story and they said that just before we got on the bus the driver had mentioned that there were thieves operating on this bus route and to keep your bags in your lap and not put them in the overhead lockers. It's a shame we missed that message!
>
> Whatever happens don't let your daypack out of your sight. Despite what anyone who appears to work for the bus company says, always keep it in front of you with your feet through the straps. If you do fall asleep in the bus, then you're less likely to have someone riffle through it.

If you end up in dire financial straits without a cash or credit card, you will have to contact someone at home to send you money urgently. You can contact your bank at home (usually online) and ask them to wire money to you. This will be easier if you have set up an internet bank account before leaving home, since they will then have the correct security checks in place to authorise a transfer without having to receive something from you in writing with your signature. You can request that the necessary sum be transferred from your bank to a named bank in the town you are in – something you have to arrange with your own bank – so you know where to pick the money up.

If a private individual has kindly agreed to bale you out, they can transfer money in several ways. Western Union offers an international money transfer service whereby cash deposited at one branch by your benefactor can be withdrawn by you from any other branch or agency, which the sender need not specify. Western Union agents – there are 90,000 of them in 200 countries – come in all shapes and sizes (eg travel agencies, stationers, chemists), but unfortunately it is not well represented outside the developed world. The person sending money to you simply turns up at a Western Union counter, pays in the desired sum plus the fee – which is £14 for up to £100 transferred, £21 for £100–£200, £37 for £500 and so on. For an extra £7 your benefactor can do this over the phone with a credit card. In the UK, ring 0800 833833 for further details, a list of outlets, and a complete rate schedule. The website www.westernunion.com allows you to search for the nearest outlet.

Thomas Cook and the UK Post Office offer a similar service called MoneyGram (www.moneygram.com). Cash deposited at one of their foreign exchange counters is available within ten minutes at the named destination, or can be collected up to 45 days later at one of 176,000 co-operating agents in 190 countries. The fees are very slightly less than Western Union's and the Post Office website (www.postoffice.co.uk) explains how it works. In an emergency your consulate can help you get in touch with friends and relations, normally by arranging a reverse charge call. British Consulates have the authority to cash a personal cheque to the value of £100, supported by a valid banker's card.

CONSULAR HELP IN EMERGENCIES

Widespread confusion persists concerning the help available from the UK government to its citizens in a crisis. In the first place it is the Consulate or Consular Services department which is responsible for looking after UK nationals, whereas the Embassy does business with the host country.

A British Consul can:
- Issue an emergency passport
- Contact relatives and friends to ask them to help you with money or tickets
- Tell you how to transfer money
- Cash a sterling cheque worth up to £100 if supported by a valid banker's card
- As a last resort give you a loan to return to the UK
- Put you in touch with local lawyers or doctors
- Arrange for next of kin to be told of an accident or death
- Visit you in case of arrest or imprisonment and arrange for a message to be sent to relatives or friends
- Give guidance on organisations who can help trace missing persons

But a British Consul cannot:
- Intervene in court cases
- Get you out of prison
- Give legal advice or start court proceedings for you
- Obtain better treatment in hospital or prison than is given to local nationals
- Investigate a crime
- Pay your hotel, legal, medical, or any other bills
- Pay your travel costs, except in rare circumstances
- Perform work normally done by travel agents, airlines, banks, or motoring organisations
- Find you somewhere to live or a job or work permit
- Formally help you if you are a dual national in the country of your second nationality

MY GROWN-UP GAP YEAR:
MARGARET HOLLAMBY

Margaret Hollamby from Sussex spent one autumn volunteering in Ecuador. Despite some mild disappointments with her placement and accommodation, she made the most of her opportunities and overall had a great experience. Because she is diabetic she did not want to be in a remote non-English speaking placement, so chose to work in the nursery of a women's prison in Quito.

After having thought about quitting my job as a learning support maths teacher for the previous two years, I finally decided to do it. My husband had died four years earlier and for the first couple of years after this it was good to stay in the job - 'Don't make life changes too quickly', people had advised me, and I feel they were right. I have always been an adventurous type of person but having an ill husband and bringing up children puts all this somewhat on hold. However, with both my children at university there was an opportunity to have a bit of an adventure myself. After a bit of web searching I found a website about Gap and Career breaks for adults.

I didn't find Quito a particularly attractive place to be. It is noisy and very smelly with pollution, partly due to the low grade fuel used and partly to its altitude of 2,800m. Street crime is common and there are constant reminders of this with armed guards outside big shops and banks. My voluntary work in the prison was enlightening, but if I'm honest also a little disappointing. I was only expected to work for three hours, five days a week, which was much less than I had anticipated. With some of my spare time, I booked one-to-one lessons in the Academia Latinoamericana de Espanol. The voluntary work wasn't giving me much opportunity for conversation, so at least this way I could keep my Spanish improving. In addition I organised some more voluntary work teaching English at the Jovenes Contra Cancer Fundacion for young cancer patients.

Living with the family also wasn't quite what I expected, but it was OK. The family consisted of an elderly woman (also diabetic) and her daughter. The only conversation I had was at breakfast and dinner. It made me appreciate my home so much. My host 'Mum' certainly found it difficult to comprehend my lifestyle of regular runs in the park, in all weathers. Things

I liked in Quito were the interesting museums, the botanical gardens, the park (for running and Sunday morning aerobics), and most surprising of all, free entry on Sunday to a performance of Taming of the Shrew by the Ecuadorian Ballet.

I'd dreamed of visiting the Galapagos ever since I learned about them as a teenager, but didn't think I would really ever get there. A week's trip to the Galapagos Islands rounded off my adventure and it goes without saying that this was a big highlight. Overall my Ecuador experience was something I shall never forget and I hope to do something similar again in the future.

PART 4

DOING SOMETHING WORTHWHILE

BECOMING A
VOLUNTEER

The impulse to 'give something back' or 'do something worthwhile' can ring in the ears as empty clichés. But in the aftermath of recent devastating natural disasters like the Haiti earthquake, Pakistan floods, and before that the Tsunami – and increasing global awareness of the discrepancy between rich and poor created by the Make Poverty History campaign – there has been a noticeable shift among travellers with a social conscience. Many prefer to combine travel with trying to make a contribution to people less fortunate than themselves, rather than pursuing hedonism and relaxation. They are signing on with companies that offer a chance to participate in some worthwhile way (if only briefly), rather than just gawp and lounge.

In an age when the old jobs-for-life contract between employer and employee is breaking down, individuals are increasingly looking for rewarding experiences outside of work that will add value to their lives. They want to find activities that can bestow pride and a sense of achievement. Work may provide an outlet for some of these yearnings, but many individuals prefer to search elsewhere and the voluntary sector at home and abroad is a major beneficiary.

The first tentative step that working people might take in this direction is to volunteer locally. In the UK, many companies like Marks & Spencer and HSBC have long run programmes to encourage their employees to take an active part in their communities. Major companies promoting social responsibility in this way such as Barclays, PwC, and Nike encourage staff to become involved: for example, in literacy and numeracy projects in schools. The leading UK volunteering charity CSV works hard to encourage employee volunteering (www.csv.org.uk/services/employee+volunteering).

The British government strongly supports corporate initiatives to promote volunteering. Hardly anyone can be unmoved by news reports of disasters or by appeals from local and international charities on behalf of the struggling and the suffering – abandoned children, needlessly blinded farmers, performing bears, and so on. Usually a feeling of responsibility flickers past our consciences and is quickly suppressed, but a career break allows you to believe that you can get usefully involved. However, stepping in to right such wrongs is never straightforward and potential volunteers soon learn that a willingness to help is not sufficient. Aid work is a difficult field to break into, and agencies are increasingly cautious in the selection process for candidates to go overseas. You might think that being able-bodied and financially privileged might be sufficient, but relevant experience and professional qualifications are almost always required.

The Tsunami disaster on December 26th, 2004, focused minds on helping in an emergency in an unprecedented way. The outpourings of financial help from around the world were reinforced by an upsurge in the number of people wanting to donate their time to help. As with all emergency relief work, skilled and experienced professionals were in demand while well-meaning amateurs potentially just got in the way. In the immediate aftermath, the United Nations Volunteers (www.unv.org) drew up an emergency roster of potential volunteers keen to help in the relief effort and reconstruction in Southeast Asia. To be included on that, you had to have had experience in disaster response, be available at short notice, have worked in South Asia, be at least 25 years of age with a completed technical/university degree, and fluent in English with some knowledge of local languages. Quite a tall order.

If all of this sounds discouraging, ordinary mortals should be aware that many organisations offer fee-paying volunteers the chance to experience life in the developing world by working alongside local people or on wildlife projects for a short period. The next chapter has details of programmes of dozens of charities and companies that can make it easy for the man or woman who is tired of the commute on the Northern Line or the M42 to go abroad as a volunteer, provided that the ex-commuter is willing to pay – normally in the range of £100–£400 a week. It is also possible to bypass the middleman – ie the agency or charity in your country – and go direct to small grass-roots projects, some of which are experienced at incorporating paying volunteers from the developed world. It is for each individual to weigh up the pros and cons of paying a fee to a mediating agency, which is what **Polly Botsford**, a lawyer from London, did when arranging a project in Cambodia through Outreach International as part of her six-month gap year:

> *I went to a couple of extraordinarily off-putting open days full of anxious sixth formers and their less anxious parents. It may be that you do not need to go through an organisation. Many people I met had just turned up in a country and got a feel for what was going on. Organisations can be expensive and could be spoon-feeding. I do feel quite sorry for students who really do want to go and discover the world for themselves, because sometimes it can be over-packaged, particularly perhaps for the more 'mature' traveller. On the other hand, the agency did provide useful contacts and structure and was particularly good in finding friendly language tutors, which was invaluable. There was no way I would have picked up Khmer as much as I did without that tuition.*

If you decide that you do not need the safety net of a sending organisation in your own country, the internet makes it possible to connect with local charities directly. **Geoffroy Groleau** is an economist and consultant from Montréal who decided to spend some months in India, and wanted to dedicate part of his time to volunteering in the development field. He stumbled across the website of an Indian NGO and arranged to work for a month with Dakshinayan, which works with tribal peoples in the hills of Rajamhal and nearby plains. Although Geoffroy ended up thinking that his enjoyment took precedence over his usefulness, he still enjoyed his 'gap' from professional life enormously:

> *The application process is simple and can be conducted fully over the internet. The registration fee, which must be provided before setting out for the project, is the primary source of revenue for Dakshinayan. So there I was, stepping onto a train from New Delhi, heading to Jharkhand.*
>
> *The project provides an opportunity to acquire a better understanding of the myths and realities surrounding poverty in the developing world, and specifically about the realities of rural India. The tribal people of these villages do not need or want fancy houses or televisions, but simply an education for their children and basic healthcare in order to improve the life they have been leading in relative isolation for centuries. It was interesting for me to see that they lead a quiet and simple life based on the rhythm of harvests and seasons, in marked contrast to most westerners. The primary role for volunteers is to teach English for a few hours every day to the*

kids attending the three Dakshinayan-run schools. I should also mention the numerous unforgettable football games with enthusiastic kids at the end of sunny afternoons. One should be aware that Dakshinayan is an Indian NGO fully run by local people, which in my view is another positive aspect. But it also means that volunteers will have to adapt to Indian ways.

Volunteers should expect to learn more from the people there than they will ever be able to teach. Remember that the villagers know much more about their needs than we do, and they have learned long ago to use effectively the resources around them. On the other hand, the contacts with the outside world that the volunteers provide is a valuable way for the villagers to begin to understand the world that surrounds them. In my experience, the hardest things were adapting to the rather slow rhythm of life, and to the fact that as a volunteer you will not manage to change significantly the life of the villagers – other than by putting your brick in a collective work that has been going on for many years.

The contact for Dakshinayan is Mr Siddharth Sanyal (Midadali Chadderjee, 2/1A, Mahenbra Road, Kolkata 700025; +91 99345 72399; www.dakshinayan.org). Volunteers join grass-roots development projects every month and contribute $300 for a month.

Some have found useful an ebook called *The Underground Guide to International Volunteering* by Kirsty Henderson (www.nerdynomad.com/volunteering), which is based on her own experiences of setting up worthwhile volunteer placements on her own.

VOLUNTOURISM

Committing to three, six, or 12 months might be more than some people can manage in the first instance. If you want to test the waters, one solution is to book a holiday that incorporates an element of volunteering. The coinage 'voluntourism' has been used slightly sneeringly by some commentators; however, these trips provide a snapshot of the needs of a specific locality and serve to introduce the paying visitor to the potential rewards of a more serious commitment of time and energy. The US site www.voluntourism.org advocates the benefits of this kind of trip for both parties, while the book *Hands-on Holidays* by Guy Hobbs (Crimson Publishing, 2007) describes hundreds of short volunteer travel opportunities.

Not all providers of voluntourism trips are equal. The rest of this chapter gives you tips on how to choose the good ones, especially page 147: Choosing an Agency. Some are marketed through www.responsibletravel.com, which has links to a number of volunteering holiday providers. The following companies organise what might be called mini-gaps:

- **Camps International**, Ringwood, Hampshire (0844 800 1127; www.campsinternational. com). Volunteer and adventure trips to Kenya and Borneo lasting up to two weeks, marketed as 'Career Break' trips.
- **Different Travel**, Southampton (07881 698623; www.different-travel.com). Participants on charity treks and expeditions spend up to a few days assisting volunteer projects: for example, in Ethiopia, Tanzania, Morocco, Zambia, Vietnam, Nepal, India, China, Borneo, and Peru.
- **Go Differently**, (01799 521950; www.godifferently.com). Voluntourism trips and ethical holidays to Thailand, Vietnam, Laos, Cambodia, and India.

- **Great Projects**, (www.thegreatprojects.com). See entry in the Directory of Programmes (page 171).
- **Impact Travel**, see entry in the Directory of Programmes (page 174)
- **Hands Up Holidays**, (020 7193 1062 in the UK; 201 984 5372 in North America; www.handsupholidays.com). Ethical tour operator working with local NGOs around the world to arrange trips lasting four to 23 days worldwide.
- **Vivisto**, Winchester (0845 603 5719; www.vivisto.co.uk). Conservation and Community experiences lasting two to 12 weeks in a range of countries.

The MondoChallenge Foundation (www.mondochallengefoundation.org) has come up with a way of giving travellers a brief taste of volunteering while benefitting the charity. Their 'ambassadors' are invited to spend a little of their time while on holiday visiting Mondo projects in Nepal, India, Tanzania, and the Gambia: for example, visiting the schools or encouraging HIV-affected women in their business activities. Whilst in-country these so-called ambassadors might like to get involved in some ecotourism, teacher training, business development, or wherever their interests lead them.

REWARDS OF VOLUNTEERING OVERSEAS

By volunteering somewhere in the world on a humanitarian or environmental project, you can give your career break a structure and a goal, and integrate into a foreign society rather than just pass through on a holiday. Importantly, you will also acquire skills that are not available during the course of your normal professional life. A career break offers the chance to test and stretch yourself and make an enduring contribution, if not to the world then at least to your own development. If you want to use a career break to discover a country or culture, then volunteering is an attractive option. One (legitimate) reason for choosing a volunteering experience might be straightforwardly selfish, as in the case of 30-something IT professional **Barry Irvine**: 'I decided I wanted to travel but was a bit afraid of travelling on my own, which wasn't something I'd ever really done before. I therefore decided to do some volunteer work, since I'd then be working with people every day and it would be easy to meet others.' And so it proved.

Volunteers who return from stints abroad frequently rhapsodise about their experience and regard their time as a volunteer as an extraordinary episode in their lives. During a holiday in Southeast Asia, **Dale Hurd** was enormously impressed by the friendliness and dignity of the people and the beauty of a culturally fascinating country, but at the same time appalled by the poverty and deprivation. Having long before decided to do some voluntary work overseas as soon as she retired from teaching, Dale knew immediately that she had no alternative but to return to Cambodia to do something more constructive than sightseeing. Through Outreach International, she devoted six months to a project training Khmer teachers and working with children who work on a rubbish dump in Phnom Penh, which in normal circumstances you would not expect to prompt someone to write about their experiences under the title 'The Time of my Life':

Sitting here, back in the freezing English spring, I look at my hundreds of photographs and dream I'm back in Cambodia in Phnom Penh, dripping in sweat, dodging motodops, blinded by the radiant smiles of the enchanting Khmer people. I had elected to train teachers at a French school called Pour un Sourire d'Enfant, which rescues children living near a vast rubbish dump – spending their days and most of their nights scavenging what bits of junk they can sell to finance their survival. They were in considerable danger from hypodermics, from pressurised tins that can blow up in their faces, and from the huge machines that sometimes carelessly run them down. I visited the dump early one morning when the stench was suffocating: the sight of small filthy children dragging round the mounds of squalor was unforgettable. I was warned to be careful when I filmed as the adults felt insulted and degraded; theirs was not a life they had made through choice but through desperation. Despite this situation, where humanity seemed to have hit rock bottom, the children smiled and laughed: eager to communicate and make friends.

The vocational school, where I spent most of my time, comprised seven sectors: mechanics, gardening, secretarial, hairdressing and spa, maternity nursing, hotel work/housekeeping, and restaurant. The beauty of this was that not only did they get a general education but students were also able to graduate fully trained to go straight into a job. I'll never forget the graduation ceremony when I not only got a huge lump in my throat, but thought: one less prostitute, one less drug pusher – as I watched each immaculate, smiling student receive a certificate.

I could go on indefinitely about the experiences I had. I learnt an enormous amount about Cambodia and about myself. I found depths of tolerance within me that I never knew I had: when in England would I ever happily sit and wait for a bus for three hours, munching bananas and watching the world go by as I did at Snoul? When before had I got as much job satisfaction, or feel daily like a princess when the students said 'Oh, Dul, you are so beautiful today,' when all I'd done was put on a clean shirt? I miss – terribly – the camaraderie and laughter of the teachers. I miss the heady fragrance of the Jacaranda and the tantalising smells of cooking food in the streets; I miss Raidth running up from downstairs calling, 'Mummee,' with something delicious to eat; I miss Naieng the landlady playing badminton every night in the yard and nursing me so kindly when I was ill; I miss my students who greeted me so joyfully every day; I miss the landscape, slowly turning from blinding greens to dull golds and browns. Above all I miss the Cambodian smile. I miss everything. I had the time of my life and I can't wait to go back.

In addition to the energising break in routine, you may be able to improve or acquire a language skill, and of course will learn something of the customs of the society in which you are volunteering. Not only will you gain practical experience in the fields of construction, conservation, archaeology, or social welfare, you will acquire a more nuanced understanding of the complexities of delivering aid. But best of all, you will probably experience some wonderful hospitality and friendship.

A number of organisations offer integrated programmes that might combine work, adventure, and language learning. For example, Trekforce (now part of Gapforce – see Directory entry) has a five-month programme in Belize for candidates of all ages, consisting of a jungle survival expedition, English teaching, and Spanish course. Meanwhile, Frontier (www.frontier.ac.uk) actively assists volunteers to pursue a career in conservation by offering a BTEC qualification in Tropical Habitat Conservation or Expedition Management. Although these and similar organisations are popular among young people taking a gap year between school and university, they encourage older volunteers to participate as well.

INSPIRE VOLUNTEERING
Music teacher Lucy Fisher used her summer holiday to volunteer in India.

Inspire Volunteering offers sustainable programmes overseas where volunteers can make a real difference to the lives of underprivileged communities.

Lucy Fisher volunteered to teach in India during her school summer break.

'I spent six weeks in New Delhi teaching music and other subjects in a school and vocational centre for children and adults. I had never really considered travelling before, but after graduating from university and working as a music teacher for two years, I was beginning to feel that it was becoming a bit mundane and I needed to develop my skills.

'I wanted to experience something completely different, broaden my horizons and, most of all, set myself a new personal challenge. I have a mild form of cerebral palsy which limits my mobility, so for me this trip was more than simply an opportunity to travel and teach, it was a risk and a chance to push the boundaries. I can assure you from personal experience that it was the most crucial and productive decision I've ever made!

'My time in India exceeded all my expectations. I had seen pictures of India so I had some idea of what to expect, but seeing it for yourself is something quite different! At first it was chaotic and quite unnerving, but it's amazing how quickly you adapt.'

During her volunteer teaching placement, Lucy found that 'the children were very keen to learn and the amount of faith the staff had in my ability to teach was very reassuring. Every day I would walk into classes of children stood to attention, with bright eyes and smiling faces.'

While slightly unnerved by the prospect of teaching her first solo lesson, it 'exceeded all my expectations and it was all completely adlib. No special resources or teachers, just me, the kids, a bit of creative thinking and positivity – teaching Indian style!

'My adrenaline was pumping because something I had done seemed to make a small but significant difference to these children. It was a joy to see and it was wonderful being given the opportunity to try out my own ideas in this way. I soon forgot all my inhibitions and found myself well and truly in the Indian spirit!'

Inspire Volunteering offers a range of volunteer teaching programmes across the world, where travellers like Lucy have the opportunity to do something meaningful during their holidays or while on a career break. Inspire programme durations range from two weeks to six months and cater for people with a wide variety of skills.

CAREER BREAK OR CAREER DEVELOPMENT?

Does the term 'career break' do justice to the range of experiences obtained and new skills acquired by those who venture forth on a volunteering sabbatical? 'Almost certainly not,' says Anthony Lunch, founder of MondoChallenge – 65% of whose volunteers fit this category. The need to get away is frequently a desire to challenge oneself in new directions, to move outside one's comfort zone, to experience different ways of life, and to work in a new geographical location. There is usually also an element of wanting to put something back; of doing something useful for people less fortunate.

Undertaking a challenge of this kind often turns out to be more of a career *development* experience than just a break in one's normal routine. New skills are learned very quickly. Teaching in a small school in India, for example, when one has never taught before, provides daily practice in planning and rapidly hones communication skills. For women, the ability to work effectively in what is often a male-orientated society, provides a sharp focus on negotiating skills and on the art of diplomacy.

Volunteers taking part in a small business programme face other challenges. 'They can forget the Excel spreadsheets and three-year plans', say Anthony Lunch. 'It is today's actions and tomorrow's plan that really matter when trying to create livelihoods.' A Proctor & Gamble marketing manager once likened his experience on an HIV business project in Tanzania to a 'six-week MBA programme,' which illustrates how a career break can be qualitatively different from a long holiday.

AGENCY FEES

As soon as you start to search for volunteering opportunities in books (like this) or on the internet, you will quickly discover that volunteering can be expensive. Mediating agencies charge fees that are sometimes very high: typically £2,500–£3,500 excluding airfares. Participants must either pay the fees themselves or fund-raise. Most organisations provide very detailed advice on how to obtain sponsorship and raise money.

Like many before her, **Rosie Prebble** was taken aback at first when she saw the price of volunteering at an orphanage in Romania through Projects Abroad, but concluded it was money well spent:

> It appeared quite expensive, especially as I had never done anything like this before. I paid about £2,500 (I can't quite remember) plus my airfare, but when I realised what it covered it did not seem so expensive after all. Projects Abroad paid for transport to and from the airport, full board accommodation with a host family, laundry, full insurance including medical care, and a phone or sim card that works in the country. They support you at your placement, organise social events with all the other volunteers and, if you find yourself alone at a weekend, invite you into their homes and show you the special places to go.

Internet search engines are dominated by the high profile international volunteer operations offering a packaged volunteer experience, which may not suit everyone. Paying to volunteer is an issue with which adult gappers have to grapple. Attitudes to the fees charged by sending agencies (a typical monthly cost exceeds £1,000) differ enormously from a feeling that they are good value, to a conviction that they are a complete rip-off. For example, it does not seem entirely reasonable for a company (as Sunrise International UK does) to market volunteering career breaks in China, which cost the hapless participant £749 plus flights to spend just two weeks in Beijing teaching English.

Essentially, some sending agencies are tantamount to specialist tour operators and charge accordingly for the infrastructure they provide. Occasionally suspicions are aired in the media and elsewhere that the service offered by the big agencies does not justify the fee. For example, advertising executive William Eccleshare (whom the *Independent* described as 'The brainiest man in adland') took advantage of a gap between high level appointments to contribute his time to a worthwhile cause, and later wrote about his experiences in the *Financial Times*:

> *Faced with a few months enforced garden leave earlier this year, I decided to use some of my sabbatical for a worthwhile cause. Volunteering for a tsunami relief project in Sri Lanka seemed ideal. Certainly my friends appeared to think so. It's interesting how keen others are to see a life-long slave to capitalism do something with a vaguely altruistic air to it ...We donned our pristine Homebase gardening gloves (the company had advised us to bring two pairs each) and started shifting rubble – whole bricks, clay, mortar – away from the wrecked houses and into a pile nearby. On the second day we were told to stop doing that and just separate the whole bricks for re-use into one pile; leave the rest of the rubble where it was, and put the clay into the foundations of what would become a new house. The next day the plan changed again: we were told the bricks we had spent the last two days saving were waterlogged and useless, and we should just put loose clay or cement in the foundations. It rapidly became apparent that what we were doing was pretty futile. By the end of the week, one of the group sighed and said that she wouldn't be surprised if we were simply moving back the same rubble that had been shifted by a previous team... I thought we could have achieved much more if the trip had been better planned. And I kept wondering about the money I'd spent (about £1,400 when you added airfares and other travel costs to the £800 fee).*

In concluding, he accepts a charge of naïveté but feels that the marketing makes it difficult to see a commercial company for what it is, when all the rhetoric is about helping others. It should be the company's responsibility to provide as clear and honest a briefing as possible about what the volunteer can expect to achieve.

The sending agencies differ enormously in how serious they are about the sustainability and usefulness of the projects to which they send volunteers, and it is not always easy to distinguish among them. A source of guidelines on what to investigate when trying to choose among providers is the website www.ethicalvolunteering.org. The site's creator, Kate Simpson, did a PhD in gap year provision.

Many of the companies in the Directory following this chapter are committed to supporting community development. Some sources of volunteer projects have a much lower profile on the internet than others, but may suit your purposes better:

■ **Globalteer**, (www.globalteer.org). Registered UK charity with HQ in Cambodia, which promotes sustainable volunteering and recruits for development projects in many countries.

- **Ecoteer**, (www.ecoteer.com). Based in Plymouth. Collection of 150 projects worldwide that need volunteers, and are willing to provide food and accommodation at no, or at little, cost. Ecoteer provides contact information to members (joining fee is £15) so they can organise their placement directly with the projects. Teaching English projects are among the most common. Membership is open to people of all ages.
- **The 7 Interchange/Se7en**, (www.the7interchange.com). 'Seven' stands for Social & Environmental Volunteer Exchange Network. Maintains list of free and low-cost volunteering opportunities worldwide and maintains a register of prospective volunteers. Volunteers are put in direct contact with host projects that need help.

Most volunteers who have gone abroad through one of the sending agencies agree that they could (or would) not have had the same experience without the backing of an organisation. Some of the most satisfying volunteer experiences have been with small specialised charities, which may have a couple of committed representatives in the UK who know the project well. Madagascar seems to be a country where these are easy to find (see Blue Ventures, Azafady, and the Dodwell Trust in the Directory). To take just a couple of examples: Volunthai is active in northern Thailand, and Ecologia in a community for orphans in western Russia (see Directory entries).

With the benefit of hindsight, volunteers conclude that they did not need all the expensive services provided by a mainstream sending agency. You can simply Google 'Volunteer Ecuador' or 'Volunteer Zambia', and find local projects which can be joined for next to nothing. Again, patient searching of the web will unearth opportunities for volunteering, perhaps through one of the mainstream databases like www.idealist.org, www.traveltree.co.uk, or www.wwv.org.uk. One specialist website is www.volunteersouthamerica.net, founded in 2005 by Steve McElhinney after he had been looking himself for 'grass-roots, zero-cost volunteer work' in Argentina. Finding volunteering opportunities that did not involve paying a large amount of cash to a middle-man or third party was more difficult than he anticipated and he has spent hundreds of hours trying to track them down. He now posts his findings on the site and keeps it updated. Another Latin American specialist website with a similar ambition is www.volunteerlatinamerica.com, which will prepare a customised volunteer guide to suitable grass-roots organisations for a fee of £25. A website that is international in scope is www.independentvolunteer.org.

Older travellers with experience of the developing world may conclude that they do not need the safety net of a sending agency. **Till Bruckner** is a veteran world traveller who has developed a strong preference for fixing up teaching and voluntary placements independently after arrival, rather than with the help of an agency. In fact, he did go to Africa initially through a London-based organisation and later regretted that he hadn't put the £500 fee he had paid the agency into a donation box, since he feels that the money would have been much better spent by an international charity than on his placement as a teacher in a relatively privileged setting:

If you sign up as a volunteer with an organisation in your home country, it's hard to tell if you're needed at all. It might be run by a local businessman who wants to polish his ego and reputation by seeming charitable, or it might simply fail to address local needs. Some companies are offering nothing more than cultural adventure holidays with a politically correct twist and CV value. Nothing wrong with that, as long as people don't delude themselves that they're contributing to a better world by flying halfway around the planet (spraying the ozone layer with kerosene as they go).

My advice to anyone who wants to volunteer in Africa (or anywhere else) is to go first and volunteer second. That way you can travel until you've found a place you genuinely like and where you think you might be able to make a difference. You can also check out the work and accommodation for yourself before you settle down. If you're willing to work for free, you don't need a nanny to tell you where to go. Just go.

However, for those who find this prospect daunting (and unless you are a mature and seasoned traveller you probably will), you will want to pre-arrange a more structured placement.

It is not surprising that indigenous volunteer coordinators gravitate to model projects and well-organised charities, which may not actually be the ones that are the most needy. **Madeleine Wheare** noticed this conflict for herself. At the beginning of 2010 she left her comfortable home in the Cotswolds to spend a couple of months working with a charity in Kerala that endeavours to assist in creating sustainable livelihoods for local communities. The local rep, a legendary figure known as Babu, was lining up potential new volunteer placements at another secondary school which they visited together:

It looks good – well organised and disciplined, with hard working students and lots of parental support. Maybe too good! We volunteers discussed whether we think we should be working with more down and out people (disorganised and low-standard) or up and coming people who have had some advantages in life. Fascinating topic!

CAUTION

Potential volunteers should not get carried away imagining that they will be able to change the world. It is undoubtedly the case that some of the promotional literature, distributed by profit-making companies out to enlist paying volunteers, shamelessly tries to exploit people's altruistic urges. The reality is that the experience of volunteering overseas is invariably of more benefit to the volunteer than to the community being helped. Some people argue that volunteer-tourism is the new colonialism: that poor suffering communities are being exploited as do-gooders' playgrounds. This negative interpretation should be resisted because all it does is quash the impulse to help others. It may be true that some volunteer schemes have been set up with the needs of the foreign volunteers taking priority over those of the local community. The local people may well enjoy the presence of the foreigners but in terms of contributing to ongoing change or building infrastructure, many of the programmes have little lasting impact. Older volunteers tend to have more awareness of the limitations of their contribution: for example, retired teacher **Barbara Plane** from Newcastle looked back on her volunteer teaching with mixed feelings:

Despite all my travels, I was so naïve at the beginning. I will come away having learnt a lot from what I've seen and from the people I've met, and if I ever come again I would do it so differently. I wonder if westerners, full of good intentions, are really helping? Just because they speak English (and for some I would even question that!) doesn't mean they can teach it!

All the same, this is not colonial exploitation as some have argued. Nothing is removed from the foreign village except the experience for the western participant, which can be transforming.

The insights gained by volunteers are often the most important long-term effect, resonating long after a gap year is over. Even those who have given the matter little thought when they are signing up for a £3,000 volunteering adventure in Africa or Southeast Asia, often end up with their eyes being opened to the difficulties of delivering aid across cultural divides. Typical gap year volunteers might find themselves working in a school in Ghana or Nepal or Costa Rica. Every day for three months they will stand in front of a class of 60 or 80 children, trying to help them improve their spoken English by devising games for them to rearrange sentences in order, teaching them Beatles songs or nursery rhymes, and having them compose haikus or put on a play. You could take a jaundiced view and say that in the scheme of things this contribution is negligible and mainly provides a chance for the local classroom teachers to put their feet up in the staff room. But our volunteer is sure to go home with a heightened sensitivity to cultural differences. Even if the development outcomes that follow on from a typical short volunteer placement are limited, foreign participants usually bring variety and laughter to the lives of children and adults they meet, forming bonds along the way. These issues are worth thinking through before committing yourself, so that you are more likely to choose with care your sending agency. A good agency will promote worthwhile programmes which grow out of local input, while avoiding local rascals and rip-off merchants.

But however good the agency, cultural differences cannot be overcome. While appreciating the wonderful people and the warm welcome she received from the charity to which she was attached in Trivandrum, India, **Madeleine Wheare** could not help feeling frustrated at the complete lack of progress and the sense of overwhelming frustration with the business end of things during her months there in 2010:

> *I tried not to have too many expectations before I left. I wanted to be totally open to the experience but I did want to feel useful, and I did often wonder whether my own need to feel useful made me feel more frustrated. My expectations of what I could achieve were a great deal higher than the people I worked with. They were delighted with very small improvements. The cultural work ethic was extremely counter-productive to work being completed accurately and on time. The lack of follow-through sowed the seeds of future problems, and good workmanship was hard to find. One could never really build on anything.*
>
> *In India, I have found it is very difficult to get closure on anything. One thing usually leads to three consequences and a seemingly straightforward action takes one or two weeks to complete – and that is if you don't get bogged down in the details. The need to keep focussed is never greater than when you are here. In a way, I find it makes it harder to relax when I know there are always a multitude of things I should be doing to advance such and such an idea or initiative. Not very restful!*

Some of the glossy marketing material distributed by the most commercial specialist operators shows only pristine beaches, glamorous bikini-clad volunteers, jolly campfires, and smiling babies, with an upbeat text to match. It might be instructive to quote a more realistic version, taken from the literature of an Icelandic exchange organisation:

> *As much as we would like Peru to live up to European standards, we have to warn you that institutions do not prepare for your arrival by organising a weekly work schedule or other special instructions. It's a big challenge to live and work in a poor Latin American country. It demands courage, some experience, and the ability to adapt. It can be overwhelming, especially at first, to*

have to adjust to completely new conditions, communicate in a foreign language, etc. Things are not as you are used to: the climate, the food, the atmosphere – everything is different. During your work you will be faced, daily, with a harsh social reality and experience things very differently from the way a tourist would.

Voluntary projects abroad often demand a large measure of flexibility. More mature volunteers with experience of the working world are often better placed than young students to cope in situations where the tasks are not pre-determined, and where you may be left not knowing what you are supposed to do or be asked to carry out tasks for which you are ill-prepared. And they may also have more practical ideas for improving the experience of the next batch of volunteers, as **Barbara Plane** noted after her stint in Nepal:

We gave Bindu a list of small things we think would be beneficial upstairs in the lounge/ eating area – eg, plates, knives and forks, a washing up bowl – and they arrived the same day! I also suggested a Visitors' Book that people could sign and make comments (not about the hotel – more about the sending agency, PoD), about places to eat, places to visit, tips, and what to do and not to do – that sort of thing. I for one would have found that most helpful. We've also started a 'Resource Pack' for future PoD volunteers.

Privately-run projects are particularly susceptible to causing disappointment if the individuals in charge fail to maintain high standards and continuity. For example, volunteers have travelled to remote corners of the world to work on eco-projects only to find that the managers run them for profit. One eager volunteer turned up for an eight-week music project in Rio de Janeiro, only to find that it was the summer holidays and then Carnaval, and the college was deserted most of the time. Another was promised a garden design placement in Sri Lanka, where the only task was weeding the headmistress's private garden because local males were not permitted to do this chore.

People who work in the developing world often experience just as much culture shock on their return home as they did when they first had to adapt to difficult conditions abroad (see Part 11: Back to Normal or a Change for Life?). Anyone who has spent time living amongst people for whom every day is a struggle to survive, may find it very difficult to return to their privileged and comfortable life in the west. Many returned volunteers claim to feel sickened by the excesses of consumer culture and misplaced value systems. After returning from an HIV education programme in Zambia, **Caroline Kippen** commented, 'I really value what is important in life now, although that makes things difficult managing my expectations now I am back home – people just don't see things the same way I do!'

Volunteering is nothing like a conventional holiday and even volunteers for organisations with glossy seductive brochures often find the tasks they are assigned to be more physically and emotionally demanding than they anticipated. Teaching English to a group of smiling 8-year-olds in a West African village sounds fun and exotic when contemplated at home, but can actually land you in a very testing situation, which might involve few creature comforts and demand a measure of stoicism. During a longer-term placement some volunteers are bound to face homesickness, loneliness, or illness.

Raleigh stresses that for its volunteer expedition leaders, attitude of mind, not age, is the crucial factor in coping with the tough conditions of the Borneo jungle or Indian tribal village.

If you have any concerns about physical endurance, it's best to consult your GP for a full medical first. Explain the conditions you are likely to face and ask for advice. Fitness is always an asset.

Regional crises can flare up, making volunteering potentially risky: for example, most volunteer agencies have withdrawn from troubled Zimbabwe. To avoid nasty surprises you should do some research beforehand of political issues relating to democratic and religious freedoms, human rights, and so on. Two starting points might be the Freedom House website at www.freedomhouse.org (despite the American bias), and the Paris-based Reporters Sans Frontières (Reporters Without Borders) at www.rsf.org.

MY GROWN-UP GAP YEAR: JENNY HICKMAN

A mini-gap in Uganda wove such a powerful spell over Australian Jenny Hickman that she contrived to go back for a longer period the following year.

Several people conspired to make 2008 the year marked for me to have the experience of a lifetime. And I thank those co-conspirators immensely: my ex-employer in the finance industry for making my stressful job of ten years redundant; my nephew for rekindling my love of travel; two of my friends for sparking the idea of working as a volunteer in Africa; the charity Soft Power Education for enabling me to follow the dream; my partner for his wholehearted support; and last but not least, the people of the beautiful country of Uganda.

I had found out about the non-religious British charity, Soft Power Education, from a friend who had recently travelled through Africa. After I received my redundancy pay-out and despite the doubts of family and friends whose only knowledge of Uganda was Idi Amin and the movie 'The Last King of Scotland', I travelled to Uganda together with my 17-year-old nephew. We spent four weeks with Soft Power, doing volunteer work painting at a pre-school. When we arrived back home we both realised that Uganda had woven a spell around us and the amazing time we had experienced had made us both determined to do something different in our lives. My nephew decided to go back to school to finish his studies. I decided to do a course to teach English as a second language. If only I hadn't waited until my 50s to discover the joys of teaching conversational English!

Listening to my heart and inspired by words I'd read on a greeting card - 'the best discoveries are made outside your comfort zone' - the spell drew me back to Uganda to work with Soft Power Education once again. I was very much out of my comfort zone, travelling alone and taking on the task of implementing English lessons for women in the rural villages of Kyabirwa and Bujagali, near Jinja, Uganda. The villagers welcomed me into their homes and hearts, and for four and a half months I shared in their lives. These people have so little but willingly shared everything with me, giving me items of food by way of thanks for my teaching, and, most wonderfully of all, giving me their friendship and love. I really felt at home, and the lack of life's little luxuries seemed very unimportant compared with the genuine feeling of happiness I enjoyed during my time in Uganda. I could also afford the relative luxury of living in a campsite next to the River Nile with electricity (except during frequent blackouts), a shower, and a flushing toilet.

The women have the daily household chores of working in their gardens where they grow most of their food; fetching water in jerry cans from the river or the pump in the village; washing the family's clothes at the river; collecting firewood for cooking; and, if the family is fortunate, tending their goat, pig, or cow. And we think the male/female imbalance exists in our households!

Every day something would happen to touch my heart: a child waiting for a cuddle on my way to lessons, a young boy calling me his dahdah (grandmother), or walking with a young girl carrying a load of firewood on her head through the rain and mud. The success of the English classes was both rewarding and humbling. I felt proud of myself for achieving something so meaningful to the wonderful women I taught, but I felt prouder of these women as I watched them not just learn English, but blossom and grow in self-confidence. I gained so much more from them than I could ever have given them; it surely was the experience of a lifetime!

Now, just a few months later, I find it hard to believe I am that woman who rode into town on the back of a boda boda (motor bike), who was covered in red dust or mud every day but kept smiling, who formed amazing friendships with women half a world away, and who was overwhelmed by the gifts, letters of thanks, and heartfelt farewells.

VOLUNTEERING ABROAD THROUGH A UK AGENCY

A growing number of British companies and organisations make it possible for people of all backgrounds to take a career break of three, six, or 12 months volunteering abroad. While some specialise in fixing up placements for gap year students between school and university, others cater to an older age group, and many accept volunteers on a year out whatever their age.

Because the student gap year market has almost reached saturation, many mediating agencies for 18-year-olds have broadened the scope of their programmes to appeal more specifically to an older clientele. A number of the leading companies report that the real growth market has been among the over-30s, with the over-50s close behind. Any upper age limits may be flexible and should be challenged by a keen and energetic candidate.

MondoChallenge has always encouraged older volunteers to join its range of community-based projects on three continents. Its volunteer profile indicates that as many as 65% of volunteers are on a career break, 21% are post-university, and 3% are retired, while the rest are students. Each agency has its own application procedure and it is best to telephone or look on their websites for detailed instructions. Many of these volunteer recruitment companies hold open days when you can meet the permanent staff and hear from former volunteers. If you have anxieties, try to establish precisely what safety net is in place in case of difficulties or emergencies.

OPPORTUNITIES FOR PROFESSIONALS

Mainstream voluntary bodies like VSO (Voluntary Service Overseas), International Service, Skillshare Africa, and many others, act as matching agencies for overseas partners looking for specialist skills and expertise from the developed world.

VOLUNTARY SERVICE OVERSEAS (VSO)

VSO is an international development charity that works on long-term partnerships with overseas organisations, and which is perhaps the most famous and longest established of volunteer-sending agencies in the UK. Doing a stint as a volunteer with VSO (www.vso.org.uk) is a classic career break which thousands of Britons apply to do every year. Every year VSO recruits many people from around the world, with a steadily rising average age (now 42) and a maximum of about 75. Volunteers are recruited via its offices in the VSO Federation (UK, Netherlands, Canada, etc). In addition to its standard one- to two-year placements, short-term specialist assignments are available for highly experienced professionals who can work at senior levels, as are business partnership placements for volunteers from the corporate world who can be seconded for periods of six to 12 months. VSO has an international website (www.vsointernational.org), which gives an overview of the whole of VSO and a number of case studies. VSO recruits volunteers in the fields of education, tourism advising, health, natural resources, technical trades and engineering, business and social work, and many others. About half of all VSO projects worldwide are related to education, and there is a growing need for expertise in small business advisers.

During the 53 years since its creation in 1958, VSO has earned a reputation for the success of its programmes and its professional approach to recruiting volunteers. Recruitment is rigorous and intended to make sure that volunteer skills are matched most effectively with projects in the developing world. The advantage of volunteering with VSO is that its track record means that it is relatively well funded. Volunteers have their expenses covered and are also given a salary in line with local salaries, plus various grants such as an equipment grant, national insurance, extensive training, reasonable accommodation with a private room, and return travel. Most reassuringly, the health insurance package is described as the 'Rolls–Royce' of policies, providing comprehensive coverage. Additionally, a payment is made on the return home to act as a cushion.

This level of support requires a corresponding level of commitment and responsibility, because most applicants will be asked to dedicate one or two years of their lives to their projects. VSO's Business Partnership Scheme also encourages company bosses to allow volunteers to work overseas for shorter periods of between three and 12 months, partly to demonstrate their commitment to corporate responsibility. Companies like Accenture, PwC, AstraZeneca, and Shell have participated. The selection procedure takes place in several stages. Applications are assessed initially on paper to match volunteer skills to the requests made to VSO by its partners. If a certain skill does not meet a requirement then an application might be put on hold until opportunities arise. Then each applicant's personal situation is assessed to see whether it affects their suitability. For example, does the applicant have children, a partner, financial stability, emotional stability? Often a couple will apply and only one member of the couple will be able to find a suitable placement. References from current employers are checked at this stage and also a routine check takes place with the police to ensure that the applicant doesn't have a criminal record. Successful applicants then undergo intensive training in the UK and after arrival to prepare them for their assignments, including workshops on health and language immersion. An IT trainer in her late 40s, Jan Lee decided that before she turned 50 she was finally going to follow through on her New Year's resolution to do something different:

> *After spending some time searching the internet, I discovered that VSO seemed to offer me all that I wanted – the opportunity to travel; the chance to live in and experience at first hand another culture; an appropriate job where I could fully utilise my skills and share my knowledge with local people in a developing country; and, perhaps most importantly for a 50-year-old single female embarking on her first real adventure, the protection and support of a large and well-respected organisation.*
>
> *I soon began the process: filling in application forms; attending the selection day which weeds out those who are not fully committed, those with marked prejudices, those who are burning with a desire to change the world, and other inappropriate candidates; and attending the various training offered by VSO to prepare you as much as possible for what you might meet overseas. My medical showed up a previously unknown condition which involved an operation and a six-month delay to my departure, but by November of that year I was ready to depart for Laos (which I learned is in Southeast Asia and not Africa) as an IT adviser to a government department dealing with Agriculture and Fisheries.*

Any potential volunteer needs to know that the relationship with the host group will be delicate. Cross-cultural differences will be a challenge to accommodate and it is the volunteer who will have to do more adapting than the host project. Sometimes the advertised role will be different from the one expected and inevitably some local attitudes to volunteers are ambivalent. On the one hand a placement from a charity like VSO is prestigious and lends credibility to the indigenous programmes, but on the other you might be perceived as something of a nuisance – a disruptive challenge to the established hierarchy. The trick is to earn the trust of your co-workers and to act as a catalyst for change, rather than simply imagine you can act in an executive fashion. One past volunteer recommends not to sit around feeling frustrated and unhappy if the placement is not working out, but try to negotiate improvements. If that doesn't work, consider asking VSO if it is possible to change jobs in-country.

OTHER AGENCIES RECRUITING PROFESSIONALS

A range of charitable organisations support 'operational' agencies such as Oxfam, UNICEF, UNHCR, etc, by recruiting for certain positions within their programmes. The types of assignment for which the client agencies need personnel almost always require previous field experience: typically at least six months with a known non-governmental organisation (NGO) in a developing country. The mediating agencies find people for specific jobs; not jobs for specific people. They receive many requests from those without previous field experience who wish to do short-term assignments, but it is increasingly rare for such people to be placed – especially if they are first-timers who cost the agencies a lot of money in training and travel expenses. Competition for such placements is high, and international development work has become a competitive profession. Agencies are increasingly cautious in the selection process for candidates to go overseas, because they have to ensure that the donors' money is being spent in the best possible way. Even with a relevant degree and further specialist qualifications, it can still be difficult to secure a position in the aid field.

Within most professions, an organisation refers specialists to appropriate volunteer vacancies overseas, including vets, dentists, pharmacists, pilots, even accountants. **Debbie Risborough** got her job with Concern in Sudan through MANGO: Management Accountants for NGOs – not to be confused with the fashion label (see www.mango.org.uk). A current list of humanitarian vacancies for professionals is carried on www.reliefweb.int, while another useful resource in the USA is NGOabroad (www.ngoabroad.com): a service that helps people enter international humanitarian work, in addition to providing frugal, customised international volunteer options.

Skillshare International (www.skillshare.org) sends more than 100 qualified and skilled staff to work professionally in partnership with local people on development work throughout southern and east Africa, and India. Positions are varied and have included teachers for agricultural studies, business advisers, curators, fund-raisers, catering tutors, ceramics/3D design lecturers, physiotherapists, engineers, bricklaying instructors, and so on. Placements are for two years, and flights, national insurance payments, a modest living allowance/salary, rent-free accommodation, health insurance, small home savings allowance, and equipment grants are provided. Applicants should be between the ages of roughly 25 and 65, and should have relevant qualifications and at least two years' post-qualification work experience. In 2011 Skillshare was looking to develop some shorter term opportunities lasting three to 12 months for suitable volunteers over 18.

If you are spending time in one place in the developing world you are bound to make the acquaintance of the aid community, who will be plugged into the needs of local NGOs and international agencies. While **Till Bruckner** was staying in the Sudan he noticed that overseas branches of Oxfam, Save the Children, etc, had huge volumes of reports to write, something that the local staff sometimes struggled to do in polished English. He discovered that his assistance was welcomed by some and so advises others to do likewise (see Part 11: Back to Normal or a Change for Life?, for further ideas on how to break into the world of professional development).

The first voluntary agency to spring to an American's mind is the Peace Corps (+1 800 424 8580; www.peacecorps.gov) which sends volunteers, normally with appropriate skills and experience, on two-year assignments to 77 countries. The average age of volunteers is 28, so considerably younger than with VSO. The Peace Corps has undoubtedly done good work over the years though some volunteers come away with reservations about its focus. **Kristie McComb** was a Peace Corps volunteer in Burkina Faso, and gradually concluded that the programme places less emphasis on development than on cultural exchange, ie sharing American culture with the host country nationals and then sharing the culture of your host country with Americans on your return:

The cool thing for Americans is that you don't have to be qualified in anything to be accepted by the Peace Corps. There are many generalised programmes where you can learn what you need to know once you get there, through the three-month pre-service training. I would encourage interested parties to be honest about what they can and cannot tolerate since not all volunteers are sent to live in mud huts. In a world changed by terrorism it is comforting to know how much of an active interest the US government takes in the safety and well-being of its citizens abroad. However, some people might find this stifling and not adventurous enough. How well PC keeps tabs on volunteers in any given country depends on the local PC leadership but, regardless, you are still in a high profile group of well locatable people. Risk reduction is the buzz word in Washington these days.

Overall I am happy with my experience though I am often frustrated by the inertia, the corruption, and the bureaucracy that makes me question whether anything will ever change. But you do gain a lot by (if nothing else) witnessing poverty on a regular basis. You quickly learn to recognise the difference between a problem and an inconvenience, and to see how lucky we are as Americans to have some of the 'problems' we have.

LISTING OF INTERNATIONAL VOLUNTARY ORGANISATIONS

- **British Red Cross**, London (0844 871 1111; www.redcross.org.uk). Their policy is not to send volunteers overseas. With branches in countries worldwide, only local volunteers are deployed.
- **Concern Worldwide**, Dublin, Ireland (+353 1 417 7700; www.concern.net). See website for UK offices. Concern believes in working directly with local people, so recruits few volunteers in the British Isles.
- **International Service**, York (01904 647799; www.internationalservice.org.uk). Founded as the United Nations Association, IS recruits professionals for two-year placements in Brazil, Bolivia, Burkina Faso, Mali, and Palestine.
- **Doctors of the World UK**, London (020 7515 7534; www.doctorsoftheworld.org.uk). Must have a minimum of two years' healthcare experience post-qualification. Minimum placements are two to three months in emergency programmes; maximum one year. Around 90 projects in 50 countries throughout Africa, the Americas, Asia, and Europe.
- **Médecins Sans Frontières UK**, London (020 7404 6600; www.msf.org.uk). MSF sends 2,000 medical volunteers to 60 countries, providing medical support to victims of war and disaster, and normally for nine to 12 months. Most opportunities are for qualified medical professionals, though there are also places for administrators and accountants. A knowledge of French is an asset.
- **Merlin**, London (020 7014 1600; www.merlin.org.uk). Deploys medical volunteers at short notice to work in emergencies worldwide.
- **Oxfam**, Volunteering Team, Oxfam House, John Smith Drive, Cowley, Oxford OX4 2JY (0300 200 1300; www.oxfam.org.uk/what_you_can_do/volunteer/internship). Oxfam recruits only full-time development professionals for overseas, but relies on volunteers in the UK. Internships are available in several divisions and are mostly based in Oxford.

- **Progressio**, London (020 7354 0883; www.progressio.org.uk). Formerly the Catholic agency CIIR. Recruits development workers for one or two years.
- **RedR/IHE**, London (020 7840 6000; www.redr.org.uk). Disaster relief agency that trains and mobilises relief personnel for deployment to afflicted regions.
- **Skillshare International**, Leicester (0116 254 1862; www.skillshare.org). Activities described above.
- **United Nations Volunteers**, Bonn, Germany (+49 228 815 2000; www.unvolunteers. org). Keeps a resource bank of skilled professionals, and also sends volunteers who have several years' professional experience to development projects for at least one year, though six-month assignments are available.
- **VSO**, Carlton House, 27A Carlton Drive, Putney, London SW15 2BS (020 8780 7500; enquiry@vso.org.uk; www.vso.org.uk). Offices in Canada, Netherlands, and other countries.

MY GROWN-UP GAP YEAR: DEBBIE RISBOROUGH

Although Debbie Risborough was, at age 38, enjoying her job as an accountant for a small friendly company, she was bored and decided she wanted to travel and try something completely different. Like everyone in this position, the idea of abandoning everything to get on a plane left her nerves in tatters, especially with her mother treating her as though she had gone mad and would never return. The year out was to be funded initially by savings, though she knew eventually she would have to make use of the £4,000 credit limit on each of her four credit cards and her overdraft facility of £1,400.

In total I was away about 14 months. I decided to do voluntary work as I am not a very good tourist, and I also needed things to be planned upfront so that I would not worry about what would happen next. I made a list of all the countries that I wanted to visit and looked for voluntary work in them. Three months was a good length of time in most countries as tourist visas last that long. My trip included India for six weeks (three weeks with Indian Volunteers for Community Service, and three weeks travelling); South Africa for three months with Sneewitje Creche; Australia for one month of holiday (since I had nothing planned, a month was enough for me); Fiji (nine weeks with Greenforce on a marine expedition and about ten days travelling); Argentina for three months teaching English with Travellers Worldwide while taking a Spanish course at the University of Buenos Aires; and finally two months of holiday in Canada where I liked it so much I stayed on until my ticket was due to expire.

The India stay was quite a short time as I wasn't sure how I would cope with the change in culture. I chose the Greenforce expedition because I had always wanted to learn to dive and that was an opportunity to do that. The Travellers programme in Argentina seemed good value for money. In fact, Argentina turned out to be the high point as everything just worked and I loved it all. The low point was the last few weeks of the Greenforce placement: the weather was not good, I was stuck on an island with 15 18-year-olds for company (it really didn't matter how nice they all were), and I knew I had another three weeks to go!

In general, the reality far exceeded my expectations as I didn't really know what to expect so was really nervous. The only part of the trip I had built up in advance was the Fiji expedition, so it was not surprising that reality kicked in here. I am still amazed that I managed to effectively travel around the world on my own and nothing bad happened. I didn't lose anything, get anything stolen, or have any nasty stories to tell. I am truly thankful for that.

When I returned I was totally amazed at how life continued. When I got back I was on a mission to work in the NGO field, and temp in the meantime. I managed to get a temporary job after ten days back in the UK and obtained a year's contract with an NGO in Sudan within four months by consulting the website of MANGO, which matches accountants with overseas aid agencies. The job was as finance officer for Concern Worldwide in Darfur, which progressed to country accountant due to a vacancy - so I am still using my accountancy qualification, but in a field that I am really interested in. During that year in Sudan, I managed to get married to a Sudanese national and am now pregnant and back in the UK to have the baby.

When I came back from my travels I needed to take out a loan for £10,000 to pay everything off. All in all I think I probably spent about £16,000, which was quite expensive but worth every penny. The biggest expenses were the plane ticket (£1,772), the Greenforce expedition (£2,750) and the Travellers Worldwide fee (£1,710).

My future plans are to start a business buying handicrafts from third world projects and selling to the UK market, and to sail around the world.

Luckily my husband is supportive of all this and I just have to work out how it can be done with no money and family responsibilities!

In general my gap year was a mental breakthrough for me. I managed to get out of the need for working for money, the necessity of earning a living, and craving for stability with partner, house, etc. I actually went out and did something that I really wanted to do. That gave me the inspiration to do other things that I really wanted to do. I may not now have a house or the latest car, but I have managed to find a life partner and I have not regretted the trip one bit. On the contrary, I feel that I did the right thing at the right time and learnt a lot of useful skills, which I am putting into use all the time.

TRAVELLERS WORLDWIDE
Deanne Michelle Peterson recalls her experience volunteering in South Africa.

I embarked on this journey in revolt to my recently turning 40. As a business owner, wife and mother, a month-long journey to Africa seemed like something far reaching and beyond my reality.

I wanted to see and do as much as I could but with family and work obligations, time was an issue. My journey with Travellers Worldwide gave me the opportunity to see all of the things a holidaying tourist would do, while the volunteering gave me the chance to meet many local people, and get to know more about the culture and the people of SA. I was able to see and do more than I ever imagined possible in one month.

Before this journey, I was stuck in my everyday routine. But after a month of diving with great white sharks, working with orphans and street kids, animal safaris, zip-lining through jungles, and sky-diving(!!), I have returned invigorated and with a new lease of life! I also made friends from all over the world. Travellers is an amazing organisation that offers life-changing experiences to people of all ages, I will highly recommend it to everyone. Thank you for the experience of a lifetime!

SHORT-TERM VOLUNTEERING

WORKCAMPS

Voluntary work in developed countries often takes the form of workcamps, which accept un-skilled people of all ages for short periods. The term 'workcamp' is falling out of favour and is often replaced by 'international project'. As well as providing volunteers with the means to live cheaply for two to four weeks in a foreign country, workcamps enable volunteers to become involved in what is usually useful work for the community; to meet people from many different backgrounds (many of whom will be young); and to increase their awareness of other lifestyles, social problems, and their responsibility to society.

Within Europe, and to a lesser extent further afield, there is a massive effort to coordi-nate workcamp programmes by the umbrella body Service Civil International (www.sciint.org). Prospective volunteers should apply in the first instance to an organisation in his or her own country, all linked from the SCI website. The vast majority of camps take place in the sum-mer months, and camp details are normally available online from March/April – with most placements being made between April and June. The joining fee for an overseas workcamp is usually around £150 within Europe, and £200 outside Europe, which includes board and lodging but not travel.

Many projects are environmental and involve the conversion/reconstruction of historic buildings and building community facilities. Interesting projects have included building ad-venture playgrounds for children, renovating an open-air museum, forest fire spotting in Italy, conservation work, plus a whole range of schemes with the disabled and elderly, and the study of social and political issues. Specialised workcamps may appeal to mature volunteers with special interests and/or skills. **Jeffrey Lawson** from Florida ended up spending part of the autumn in Sweden, having traced a 'mixed age' workcamp that suited him through the work-camps organisation Volunteers for Peace (www.vfp.org). In contrast to many voluntary projects he checked, he found this one to be 'amazingly inexpensive' at $280 (and with no sleeping bag required):

With mixed feelings of satisfaction and self-doubt, I decided to volunteer for a three-week con-struction project in October in a small town in Sweden. As a premature retiree on the north side of 50, I was looking for an opportunity that combined moderate adventure (new places, faces, and functions) with moderate self-sacrifice (without breaking my back or bank account) in ap-pealing surroundings that would challenge my skills in a hands-on contribution to a local cause. I found all of that and enjoyably more in the town of Gamleby, a water-front settlement of about 4,000 souls situated 250km south of Stockholm. As indicated in the brief online description, the workcamp was held at a small varv (boatyard) that had been established specifically to restore and preserve historic Swedish wooden sailing vessels and traditional shipbuilding techniques.

Gamleby was my first overseas volunteer experience, and what attracted me was its con-nection to my Scandinavian heritage and my interest in wooden boats. What nearly deterred me was the scant information about the nature of the work (the advertised primary objective of the project was to complete a blacksmith shop), the nature of the participants, and particu-larly my concern as how a 'senior citizen' would fit in among the multi-national 20-somethings I anticipated as workmates. I shared a room with Fabio (30), an affable, self-employed carpen-ter from the Italian part of Switzerland. Two other males, aged 30 and 42, hailed from Holland and Germany and our only female volunteer, just 22, was from Moscow.

I found the physical labor tiring, but the work did not trouble me. Apart from one or two days, the weather was beautiful: a late autumn for Sweden, with golden maple leaves fluttering to carpet the ground.

Our hosts were very pleased with our work. In fact, in the Friday edition of the regional newspaper of our second week, we were the featured front page story. The locals we met smil-ingly shook our hands and expressed appreciation for our efforts. Would I go back? Yes, indeed, and I hope one day to accept my hosts' open invitation to return and sail aboard the three-masted schooner VEGA.

SCI's UK branch is International Voluntary Service (IVS-GB) in Edinburgh (0131 243 2745; info@ivsgb.org). The cost of registration on IVS workcamps outside the UK is £190, which in-cludes £35 membership in IVS. IVS has linked up with the four other main agencies listed below to form VINE-UK (www.vineuk.co.uk), all of which organise International Volunteer Exchange programmes. The other organisations in the network are Concordia International Volunteers (www.concordiavolunteers.org.uk); UNA Exchange, Cardiff (www.unaexchange.org); Volunteer Action for Peace/VAP (www.vap.org.uk); and Xchange Scotland (www.xchangescotland.org).

ARCHAEOLOGY

Taking part in archaeological excavations is another popular form of voluntary work, but vol-unteers are usually expected to make a contribution towards their board and lodging. Also, you may be asked to bring your own trowel, work clothes, tent, etc. Archaeology Abroad (020 8537 0849; www.britarch.ac.uk/archabroad) is an excellent source of information, as they annually publish on a CD details of excavations needing volunteers; in the past year between 700 and 1,000 definite places on sites were offered to subscribers. They do stress, however, that applications from people with a definite interest in the subject are preferred. An annual subscription costs £23.

For those who have no experience of archaeology, the chances of finding a place on an over-seas dig will be greatly enhanced by having some digging experience nearer to home. Anyone who wants to participate on an archaeological dig in the UK should consult information from the Council for British Archaeology in York; some of its fieldwork listings are freely available on their site (www.britarch.ac.uk/briefing/field.asp).

A great many archaeological digs and building restoration projects are carried out each year in France. Every May, the Ministry of Culture (Direction de l'Architecture et du Patrimoine, Sous-Direction de l'Archéologie) publishes a national list of summer excavations throughout France requiring up to 5,000 volunteers, which can be consulted on its website (www.culture.

gouv.fr/fouilles). Without relevant experience you will probably be given only menial jobs, but many like to share in the satisfaction of seeing progress made.

Israel is another country particularly rich in archaeological opportunities. Information on volunteering is available on the website of the Israeli Ministry of Foreign Affairs (www.mfa. gov.il; search for 'Archaeological Excavations 2011'). After choosing an excavation of interest, you make contact directly with the person in charge of the research, some of them in the Department of Classical Studies at Tel Aviv University and others at universities elsewhere in Israel or abroad. Fees charged can be steep, eg $400 per week. Most camps take place during university holidays between May and September, when temperatures soar. Volunteers must be in good physical condition and able to work long hours in hot weather. Valid health insurance is required.

MY GROWN-UP GAP YEAR:
ANNALISA WINGE BICKNELL

By her early 40s, Annalisa had climbed high in the finance industry to be International Head of Business Development in a London bank. She was delighted when her bosses agreed to allow her to take a six-month sabbatical and was in the comfortable position to be able to fund the period of leave herself. By the end of the series of environmental projects she joined around the world through Earthwatch, she had spent £15,000 but she had fed her soul, and had experienced the world in a way that is not open to many people in the West.

After having worked for 18 years and enjoyed a successful international career, I decided I needed a break and to do something for a worthwhile cause. I wanted to commit myself to it over a long enough period that it was noticeable and really worthwhile. I think for me a sabbatical meant stepping out from the middle of the road onto a completely unknown road – the road of exploration – and opening myself up to new experiences. I received a lot of encouragement, good wishes, and some envy of my courage to take this leap from fellow employees, friends, and family - although a few worried that I was leaving a good job with no contractual return ticket.

I asked around and searched the internet for a charitable organisation that needed a pair of hands and offered the opportunity to explore a side to life which hitherto had been unknown to me. When a friend mentioned Earthwatch I checked them out online. As I read the various projects they were committed to and about the opportunities they offered to volunteers, a huge grin appeared on my face. That is how I knew that I had found the right organisation with which to spend my sabbatical. The good thing about Earthwatch's projects is that they don't have many requirements, apart from needing a helping hand and enthusiasm. A certain level of fitness was required for certain projects, and of course, a financial contribution.

So I planned to spend my six-month break volunteering on five Earthwatch projects back-to-back. I deliberately chose projects that did not offer comfort which I could get at home, and thereby would open my eyes to what a lot of people endure in life. One of the projects I opted to join for a month was the Chinese Village Traditions in Jia Xian County in Shaanxi Province, which aims to document a lifestyle that has changed little in the past few generations. It was out of this world. I slept on a concrete bed with four others, with a pillow full of beans, a cow next door, and a pit toilet. I lived the simplest of lives with people who know the values of food and family. They were living off the earth and using the earth; they were so much in tune with their environment. I grew as a person and got to really understand that so many of us confuse 'want' with 'need'.

Mongolia is one of those remote places you hear of, but you don't know about. This country fascinated me, as did the project run by a team of scientists collecting data on the threatened Mongolian argali sheep. The expedition to this region of semi-arid grasslands and rocky outcrops was pure camping - the research camp consisted of five gers [huts] with no electricity and no running water. You slept on the ground and it was freezing. I was thrilled when the scientists named a sheep after me, and there is now an argali sheep with a satellite collar on it wandering about the Mongolian steppe called Annalisa.

The sabbatical opened my eyes, giving me experiences I never would have gotten as a tourist or on a business trip. I got to live amongst the natives as they do themselves, which was extraordinary. There are still so many people in the world who do not understand one another. In our global community, we do sometimes need to step outside our comfort zones and let others in.

The only disappointment I had was with my employer, who didn't keep their promise to keep my job open. I was just unlucky because my return from the sabbatical was at the start of a scary recession. However, I have no regrets for taking a sabbatical, not even for a second, because the reward I got far outweighed not having taken it at all and keeping my job. Due to finding no job upon my return, I continued to volunteer for Earthwatch at their head office in Boston for three months where I helped them review their sales strategy in view of the downturn in the market. I decided to do things that I wouldn't have had the opportunity to do whilst working, ie pursuing interests and hobbies I had been wanting to do for years. So, although I hadn't planned or desired the aftermath of my sabbatical, it has turned out to be very productive and satisfying.

CONSERVATION

Saving the planet is an issue that is quickly climbing up the international agenda, as climate science proves how urgent the situation is. Scaling down one's consumption is often part of a gap year spent travelling or learning, but to make a more lasting contribution, it is worth slotting into a conservation project at home or abroad. Most gappers fix up a placement in advance, though this is not essential.

Animal lovers will find a wealth of opportunities. To take just one of the main conservation organisations, Global Vision International (www.gvi.co.uk) can arrange for people to work with vervet monkeys in South Africa, langur monkeys on Java, lemurs in Madagascar, turtles in Panama or the Greek Peloponnese, orangutans in Sumatra, various species in the Galapagos Islands, and many others. Elsewhere, the six-week expeditions in Borneo with the Orangutan Foundation or The Great Projects are popular with career breakers, as are wildlife assignments in Africa with the main agencies listed in the Directory of Specialist Programmes in the chapter that follows. **Phil Bond's** lack of fitness in hot humid Borneo was instantly forgotten when an orangutan came over to him, put her hand in his lap, and her baby played with the zip on his pocket.

Neil Munro was in his 60s when he joined a lion-breeding project at a game park in Zimbabwe called Antelope Park (www.antelopepark.co.zw). He gravitated to two cubs who had had a traumatic start in life, perhaps because he had just emerged from a four-year family trauma in his own life. Neil knew nothing about lions before he went and had had limited contact with animals, but discovered to his pleasure that he was a natural. He was not overly frightened of the lions. Even on the occasion when two cubs did jump on him he didn't lose his nerve, and only biffed them on the side of the face as the guides had instructed, to show them who was in command. He was good at 'thinking like a lion' and worked patiently and devotedly to win the trust and affection of the two damaged cubs in his care. He has been back since his original stay to visit 'his' cubs, who clearly remembered him. He is now looking into the possibility of selling some land to fund further long-term stays in this beautiful corner of Africa.

Short-term conservation holidays are available through the BTCV (British Trust for Conservation Volunteers), which runs a programme of mainly two-week International Conservation Holidays in a dozen countries including Iceland, France, Bulgaria, USA, Cameroon, and Japan. Further details are available from the BTCV Conservation Centre in Doncaster (01302 388888; shop.btcv.org.uk). Accommodation, meals, and insurance are provided; sample prices are £460 for a week of nest-building on the Black Sea, to £510 for two weeks planting trees in a Cameroonian village, excluding flights.

The Involvement Volunteers Association Inc. based in Australia (www.volunteering.org.au) arranges short-term individual, group, and team voluntary placements in many countries, including Australia, New Zealand, Hawaii, Fiji, Thailand, India, Lebanon, and Finland. Many projects lasting from two to six weeks are concerned with conservation, while others assist disadvantaged people. The One-Placement Package cost is AUS$1,200, while for two placements the fee is AUS$2,070.

Well-known organisations like Raleigh and Coral Cay recruit expeditionary groups, which operate as a project team for a period of two to three months. These agencies provide fee-paying volunteers to help staff scientific expeditions. These are in effect specialist tour operators, and it seems that there is a booming market for this sort of working holiday among the affluent, who are looking for a holiday with a difference or a platform from which to launch a career break. The Directory in Part 5 includes many entries from scientific expedition organisations and wildlife programmes that use self-financing volunteers, such as African Conservation Experience, Biosphere Expeditions, Blue Ventures, Earthwatch Institute, Operation Wallacea, and Personal Overseas Development.

Ann Knight is a 63-year-old married grandmother and horsewoman from Worcester, who works as a teaching assistant at a special school:

Every year I go on a riding holiday in different countries, but in the summer of 2010 I wanted a change – opting to work as a volunteer at Naan ku se, a wildlife sanctuary near Windhoek in Namibia. I booked through Amanzi, who were fantastic, giving me all the information I needed and booking my flights. I was nervous before I left, and my family were very anxious, but once there everything fell into place, making me feel that I'd achieved something special when I returned.

The experience was amazing, being so close and hands-on with a variety of animals. The coordinators and fellow volunteers, most of whom were independent travellers, were very friendly – with the camaraderie adding to the enjoyment, and allowing us to share the ups and sometimes downs of working a six-day week. In groups of five or six, we did a variety of tasks: some easy like food prep, big cat feeding (cheetahs, leopards, lions), walking the young leopard or caracel, fence patrol (looking for and repairing any damage), and enclosure patrol. Other tasks were not so easy, such as clearing a large perimeter of blackthorn trees/bushes in preparation for the installation of electrical enclosure fencing: a job that was extremely hard and painful. But every one of us did their share in rotation.

I was fortunate in being given permission to take charge of two horses, to organise riding for those interested and to ride out myself, which was a bonus I hadn't expected. If I could have done it differently it would be to go for longer and to travel overland to Cape Town, seeing and visiting more of Namibia en route, then spending time at a sanctuary in South Africa. To anyone considering this type of break I would say: don't hesitate. Just get the information, costs, etc, and book it.

ORGANIC FARMS

With an upsurge of interest in organic and local sourcing of foods, the organic farming movement is attracting a rapidly-increasing following around the world, from Tunbridge Wells to Turkey, with an ever-rising number of farms converting, at least partially, to organic methods of production. The international system of working-for-keep on organic farms is another good way of visiting unexplored corners of the world cheaply through WWOOF (World Wide Opportunities on Organic Farms). The International WWOOF Association (IWA) has a global website (wwoofinternational.org) with links to both the national organisations in the countries that have a WWOOF coordinator, and to those which do not: known as WWOOF

Independents. National WWOOF coordinators compile a list of member farmers willing to provide bed and board in a non-monetary exchange with volunteers who help out, and who are genuinely interested in furthering the aims of the organic movement. Guest-workers are expected to work around six hours per day in return for free accommodation and food. Most WWOOF organisations offer an online application process, but the cost of joining each WWOOF branch varies. WWOOF UK membership costs £20. Countries that have national WWOOF organisations have to be joined separately: for example, Denmark, Sweden, Germany, Switzerland, Austria, Italy, Australia, New Zealand, Canada, Ghana, Japan, Korea, and many more.

Before arranging an extended stay on an organic farm, consider whether you will find such an environment congenial. Many organic farmers are non-smoking vegetarians and living conditions may be primitive by some people's standards, so if you are used to slipping out from work for a cappuccino or a burger for lunch, you might want to think carefully before organising a career break on an organic farm.

A free internet-based exchange of work-for-keep volunteers can be found at www.helpx.net, where the majority of farms are located in Australia and New Zealand.

VOLUNTEERING
WITHOUT MALARIA PILLS

Going abroad is not essential to becoming a volunteer. Thousands of opportunities within the UK do not require volunteers to pack a rucksack or learn survival skills. If the thought of leaving home for an extended period and living in some wild and woolly place is unappealing, daunting, or just plain unmanageable, volunteering closer to home may easily be incorporated into a gap year.

Some of the people most desperately in need of a career break (and uniquely placed to arrange one) are those people who work from home: freelance cartoonists, web designers, translators, crafts people, childminders, copyeditors, and so on. For many, feelings of isolation can be overwhelming, and they think back with fondness on the busy camaraderie of the office life left behind. Many feel that their social (not to say love) lives have gone into hibernation, and they long for some new social outlets. One way of achieving this end is to join a congenial local project as a volunteer.

You might want to use a career break to find out about a different profession through volunteering. For anyone considering a career in youth and community work, counselling or social services, conservation or outdoor education, and many others, it is standard practice to spend time initially as a volunteer. Anyone contemplating taking time out of the workplace this way can start gradually by volunteering locally while working full-time. This is becoming easier with the creation of schemes like Business in the Community (www.bitc.org.uk), which has persuaded hundreds of companies to donate some of their employees' time to a local charity or community group.

The best place to start familiarising yourself with volunteering opportunities at home is to consult your local Volunteer Centre, which forms part of Volunteering England (www.volunteering. org.uk) and links volunteer centres all over the country. For example, each London borough has its own. Each office is staffed by professional advisers who will develop a profile of your abilities and interests and then match you with a local organisation. They act as a high street recruitment agency for local charities, non-profit bodies, and community groups, and on average have databases containing between one and three thousand opportunities. A national survey in 2009 revealed that numbers of volunteers are climbing as unemployment rises, as a result of the recession and government cuts. Scotland's equivalent is called Volunteer Development Scotland (www.vds.org.uk).

Other sources of possible vacancies include public noticeboards in libraries, and the local hospital, etc. Local councils also work with volunteers and it's worth approaching the department that interests you, eg social services.

Volunteering England, which advises voluntary bodies, suggests you consider these issues first:

■ *Before making contact with an organisation, think about what you want to know from them, and what they are likely to ask you.*

■ *How much time can you give? At what time of day?*

■ *What do you want to get from volunteering, eg meeting people, or gaining new skills?*

■ *What skills or experience can you offer?*

■ *Will out-of-pocket expenses be paid? Does the organisation insure its volunteers?*

■ *Will you need to obtain a police check from the Criminal Records Bureau?*

Volunteering in the UK can be a stepping stone to opportunities abroad, or provide a taster of work in the field of development as it did for **Jen Dyer**. Although Jen had been enjoying her work in the office of a conservation expedition company, she decided to take a break to find out more about careers in the humanitarian and development sector. After much research she discovered that an internship was the best option, since proper jobs required previous experience and qualifications she didn't have. She applied for all of the different internships Oxfam was advertising at the time and was interviewed by two departments, the Programme Resource Centre and the Media unit:

My internship was for over three months for three days a week. I lived with a friend who was located conveniently close to Oxford, which meant that I had lower rent and could finance my internship by continuing to work part-time in my paying job. Oxfam paid my expenses, which meant my living costs were very low and I just had to resist unnecessary items.

I have gained many contacts through Oxfam and am hoping that when I travel to Honduras with Operation Wallacea this summer, I will be able to visit Oxfam's agricultural scale-up programme and see development work firsthand. Here in the office I have been pestering other staff members to have coffee and chats with me to hear their experiences and how their career in this sector came about...I have enjoyed my internship entirely, and it has been a wonderful experience where I have learnt an inordinate amount, not just about Oxfam's work but about working in a large NGO, and in fact in a large company, as well as making some great friends.

PRACTICALITIES

The choices for volunteering in the UK are infinite and include both residential and non-residential work. Residential posts range from a week (say, helping at a holiday centre for disabled children or rebuilding a dry stone wall) to a year (for instance, at an outdoor centre for disadvantaged youths or at the Centre for Alternative Technology in Wales). By piecing together short stints as a volunteer in different places, it is possible to experience a range of activities and settings on a gap year within the UK.

Volunteer organisations that take on people to work with children or vulnerable adults have a statutory obligation to run a police check on new volunteers. It is the responsibility of the organisation rather than the individual to apply to the Criminal Records Bureau or CRB (0870 90 90 811; www.crb.homeoffice.gov.uk), although you may be asked to pay the fee.

Many organisations arrange accommodation: sometimes free, as in the residential social care placements made by CSV (www.csv.org.uk); sometimes at a modest cost, as in the week-long conservation projects organised by the BTCV (British Trust for Conservation Volunteers). Most BTCV conservation holidays for paying volunteers are for short periods of a weekend or a week, but it is also possible to become a volunteer field officer for up to a year at one of BTCV's centres. Long-term volunteers are not restricted by age or qualification, and are eligible for income support for the duration of their placement. CSV places volunteers away from home around the UK for four- to 12-month placements, in a large variety of projects in the social care field. This includes working with the homeless, schools, and hospitals, and mentoring young offenders and teenagers in care. Volunteers are given free board and accommodation and paid pocket money of £34 per week. CSV aims to recruit individuals up to the age of 35, though they also run a Retired & Senior Volunteers Programme for volunteers over 50. The CSV Employee Volunteering programme encourages companies to release employees on a part-time basis to volunteer locally in schools, etc.

Peter Luckham was at the upper end of the age range when he decided to give his managerial job in IT a rest and become a CSV volunteer, a scheme he remembered hearing about at university. For the first part of his six-month sabbatical he supported 63-year-old Eddy, who is partially blind and has learning difficulties. His next project was to work as a learning mentor at a special school in Hackney, for boys with emotional and behavioural difficulties. It was while working there that he decided to resign from his job in London with a big investment bank and now works on a self-employed basis for a small IT consultancy, which serves local small businesses in and around Bournemouth:

> *Originally I felt as though I was living in an isolated world, worrying about mortgages and pensions, but disconnected from the world around me. Now I'm in a continuous process of discovery. Volunteering has helped me have a wider experience of dealing with different people. It has helped me prove that I can do other things outside the IT world and that I don't need to be as dependent on the perceived security that a very commercially-focussed career provides. The experience of being a volunteer provided the space and a new structure to find out a little more about me, and what I really want. I wanted to give something back – maybe I have a little middle class guilt complex.*

VOLUNTEERING RESOURCES

The *World Service Enquiry* of the respected charity Christians Abroad (www.wse.org.uk) provides information and advice to people of any faith or none who are thinking of working overseas, whether short or long term, voluntary or paid. They offer a one-to-one consultancy service ranging in price from £80 to £240. Other useful consultative services include:

- **2Way Development**, Fitzroy House, 18 Ashwin Street, London E8 3DL (020 7193 6167; www.2waydevelopment.com). Offers a different kind of service to people looking for international voluntary experiences. They provide independent, professional support to volunteers in the organisation of placements overseas, in all sectors of work. The one-off fee of £750 includes personal consultation, referral to ethical volunteering opportunities with NGOs, assistance with preparation, and ongoing support.
- **Working Abroad**, The Coombe, Spring Barn Farm, Kingston Road, Lewes BN7 3ND, UK (01273 479047; www.workingabroad.com). As well as being a web-based resource of voluntary opportunities worldwide, Workingabroad.com will prepare a personalised report after you complete a detailed request form; the fee is £29 by email, £36 by post. Also places volunteers on various conservation and social projects worldwide: working with sea turtles in Grenada and Kenya, cheetahs in Botswana, national parks in Iceland, teaching Tibetan refugees in Dharamsala, teaching kids in Brazil, etc.
- **Christian Vocations**, (01926 487755; www.christianvocations.org). Publishes a searchable online directory of short-term opportunities with Christian agencies.
- **REACH**, (www.reach-online.org.uk). Brings together voluntary organisations in the UK and volunteers with career skills; mainly mature professionals and executives who are not in full-time work. Registration necessary to view vacancies.

The revolution in information technology has made it easier for the individual to become acquainted with an amazing range of possibilities. One worthwhile website directory is www.traveltree.co.uk. It covers gap year ideas and volunteering opportunities worldwide, as well as internships and educational travel. Transitions Abroad maintains great online resources for volunteering (www.transitionsabroad.com), though they aren't dated so it is not easy to know how current they are. The best of the websites have a multitude of links to organisations big and small that can make use of volunteers. For example, www.idealist.org (from Action Without Borders) is a US-based easily-searchable site that will take you to the great monolithic charities like the Peace Corps, as well as to small grassroots organisations. At the time of writing it offered nearly 18,000 listings of opportunities with non-profit and community organisations in 150 countries.

WorldWide Volunteering (WWV) is a non-profit making organisation designed to help people of all ages get involved with volunteering and find a placement which suits them. WWV's online database of 1,700 organisations, offering a potential total of 1.5 million placements, is free for all to use from the website www.wwv.org.uk. The site also carries volunteers' stories.

If you are interested in short- or long-term voluntary projects in Britain, you might start by browsing do-it.org.uk and timebank.org.uk, both with databases of volunteering opportunities in the UK.

MY GROWN-UP GAP YEAR: TINA FREEMAN

In response to the grief of losing one of her two sons, Tina searched the net for a volunteer teaching programme that would suit her. She liked the personal approach of POD and also the fact that TEFL training was provided on-site in Tanzania. She never dreamed that she would also spearhead a 'knitting revolution' as described in an article for safaritalk.net (which she has given this book permission to quote).

Before I left home I was given a knitting bag with about 14 pairs of knitting needles and a few odd balls of wool. As I was reading up about Yamba, the project and environment, I was shocked to learn how cold it gets in the mountains. I heard how children with only the holey clothes on their backs would jump up and down to try and get warm before trying to go to sleep. So I thought with the wool and needles maybe I could show a few of the ladies in Yamba how to knit little squares and to sew them together to make blankets. I thought even though I hadn't knitted anything since I was very young (except a failed attempt to knit my son a scarf), I could manage to teach them how to knit a simple square: knit, knit, knit, and maybe even purl. They very soon learnt knit and purl, and it was at this time I realised I had forgotten how to cast off. As the squares took size and shape I had to remember - fast! (I later realised that it wasn't the best way - but it worked).

The lessons were given weekly after school and I was only going to be in the village for seven weeks. They seemed to think that I was going to show them how to make a hat ... a hat!! OK - I like a challenge. I thought - rib to start should be OK to teach, but a hat! I had a few attempts and finally success (of sorts - it was sort of pixie styled - all pointy). I wrote a very simple pattern out 14 times (translated into Swahili) and by the next lesson I was presented with a sea of multi-coloured hats - not just completed, but stripy as well. By this time we were buying wool for them from Tanga (five hours away) to keep up!

And what did I hear they wanted to make next? - A sweater! I thought I could send them a pattern from the UK, maybe simplified, even translated, but it seemed that they really wanted to be shown. I made no promises, but studied the jumpers I had brought with me and attempted to make a sweater myself, before attempting to teach them. All I managed to show them before I had to leave was the V-neck shape and roughly how to achieve it. I heard, via email, long after my departure from Yamba that the ladies were still knitting. On a rather quiet Christmas Eve I received another email - this time with attached photos - of Yamba ladies and their children and their multi-coloured stripy V-neck raglan sweaters. Tears came to my eyes.

PART 5

DIRECTORY OF SPECIALIST PROGRAMMES

CHOOSING AN AGENCY
DIRECTORY
KEY US ORGANISATIONS

GENERAL ADVICE

Specialist agencies and organisations can arrange the logistics and save you a great deal of time and anxiety. They make placements, provide orientation and sometimes group travel and, crucially, provide back-up – usually in the form of an in-country representative who can sort out problems. Mediating agencies come in all shapes and sizes. Some are ethical non-profit charities that have links with local grassroots projects; some are bastions of the business establishment with long-standing programmes in a range of countries. Still others are profit-making companies and are always seeking new projects in developing countries to which they can send paying volunteers. It is not always easy telling the difference between the various types of sending agency.

A plethora of organisations, both charitable and commercial, offer a wide range of packaged possibilities: from teaching in Himalayan schools to work experience as a journalist in Bolivia. Many of these organisations focus on the gap year market, targeting school leavers taking a year off before university. The boom in year-out travel for 18-year-olds heading abroad after doing A-Levels has resulted in an explosion of specialist companies. An increasing number of programmes from Siberia to Sulawesi is available to almost anyone able to pay.

Competition among the companies that once targeted school leavers has become so acute that many of the agencies have been trying to broaden the appeal of their programmes to an older clientele. The directory that follows gives brief details of the programmes offered by companies, agencies, and charities that place mature candidates in voluntary positions worldwide, sometimes integrated with language courses, expeditions, diving courses, etc.

With the marked growth in the number of adults undertaking such projects, the mediating agencies are beginning to design programmes for the older age range. There has been a recent tendency for projects of shorter duration – eg two to four weeks – to be introduced, to cater for the well-heeled older person who does not want to take off more than a few weeks at once. Organisations that started out offering experiences to young folk have realised that without changing anything except how they package and market their experiences, they can attract another population. It is possible that the majority of participants on a given scheme will still be school leavers though, which might potentially limit the social pleasures in store for a career-breaker. Anyone who is concerned about this possibility should simply enquire of the sending agency what the average age and full age range will be on the project that interests him or her. On her otherwise fantastic 14-month gap year, 38-year-old **Debbie Risborough** did not experience the buzz she expected to from a diving expedition she had booked in Fiji:

> *All the other people on the trip were in their gap year prior to uni so I was the odd one out, which I found very difficult. I would have preferred a wider age range in the group. One of the low points was knowing that I was stuck on an island with 15 x 18-year-olds for company for weeks and weeks and it really didn't matter how nice they all were.*

While 18 is usually quoted as the minimum age, an upper age limit is seldom specified. Even if an agency specifies 30 or 40, these upper limits tend to be flexible and an energetic candidate may have little trouble in being accepted. Most of these programmes are open to anyone with an adventurous spirit, good health, reasonable fitness, a willingness to rough it, and enough money to pay for it. Many mature volunteers end up not minding working alongside

18-year-olds as much as they thought they would. **Nigel Hollington** knew that he wouldn't mind since he had always enjoyed the company of young people during his long teaching career. Over the ten weeks of his wildlife project in Zambia, differences of age and background seemed to melt away and he enjoyed the company of his 18-year-old roommate Mark. Stereotypes of carefree youth versus cautious middle age were overturned when they set off together to do a bungee jump. Nigel knew that Mark was absolutely terrified but felt that he could help him by remaining calm, so they achieved it together.

Another grown-up gapper, 43-year-old **Paul Edmunds**, worked on the outskirts of Accra in Ghana with mainly gap year students. He feels that the 18-year-olds who choose to do something worthwhile like this are a self-selecting group, and tend to be more sensible and plucky than typical 18-year-olds. However, because of his age, he did sometimes feel impatient with the emphasis placed by his agency (Travellers Worldwide) on safety and security. Occasionally he found living in a family, who assumed it was their role to act *in loco parentis*, rather claustrophobic, and he sometimes regretted that he wasn't able to live independently – kind and welcoming as his host family was. For example, he struggled with the Ghanaian diet and sometimes found the meals served by his host inedible, yet it was awkward going out to find a more palatable alternative.

CHOOSING AN AGENCY

Unless you have a reasonably specific plan for your gap year, you can become overwhelmed by the number of possibilities out there. Career gapper **Polly Botsford** has come to distrust the current mantra of extending choice and feels that there are too many destinations and options: 'You have this sense that you want to be original. My approach was to let the plans evolve. I let ideas sit awhile and talked to lots of people over the course of about a year.' Of course, there is no better starting point than this book for providing a survey of the options. Specialist websites www.thecareerbreaksite.com and www.acareerbreak.co.uk also carry lots of useful information, links, and first-hand accounts. In the USA, Briefcase to Backpack (http://b2b.meetplango.com) exists to offer travel advice for career breaks and sabbaticals. All of these have been started by entrepreneurs, who have come back from their own gap years with a mission to spread the word.

The word 'voluntourism' is sometimes used in the context of the more superficial kind of volunteer experiences, as offered by the profit-driven companies that commercialise and com-modify the experience of helping in developing countries. Not long ago the director of VSO expressed her concern at the rise of this phenomenon, and that many year-out programmes represented a new form of colonialism. This in turn prompted some of the gap year companies committed to their development work to respond in the editorial pages of newspapers with the following:

> *Your prominent coverage of the views of Judith Brodie, director of VSO UK, puts into relief a criti-cal need for greater transparency and accountability amongst organisations operating within the UK's largely unregulated gap year and volunteer travel industry. The proliferation of poorly-planned, spurious, and increasingly profit-oriented gap-year schemes poses a growing threat to the legitimacy of reputable UK-based volunteer organisations, large and small, working throughout the sustainable development sector.*

The question remains of how to separate the wheat from the chaff. The non-profit trade asso-ciation, the Year Out Group, aims to promote and advise on structured years out. Their website (www.yearoutgroup.org) has links to its 37 member organisations and contains guidelines and questions to ask when comparing year out providers, most of which are common sense, eg find out whether it is a charity or a profit-making company, look at safety procedures and in-placement support, ask for a breakdown of costs, and so on. However, the Year Out Group is primarily a trade association and Tourism Concern has expressed concern that it is not as selective in its membership as it might be, since it has no external auditing procedure and no funds to investigate claims made by members. Note that the Year Out Group cannot intervene in any dispute between member companies and disgruntled clients.

A good organisation should be able to tell an applicant exactly what work they will be doing and precise contact details for the overseas project. Ask the company what financial contribution they make to the development project and about their ethical tourism policy. Some gap year companies wait until a paying customer has signed up before finding a placement abroad and these are often less satisfactory. Sustainable development means: 'Development which meets the needs of the present without compromising the ability of future generations to meet their own needs'.

Matching your preferred dates is a basic requirement. Organisations whose literature contains dire warnings of the consequences of procrastination often have last-minute vacancies, so it is worth ringing around whenever you decide you want to go for it.

Another consideration is the financial soundness of the company. Not all gap year companies have financial protection for the consumer in the form of an ATOL license and personalised insurance certificates. The 1992 Package Travel Act states that any company that arranges a package (and this is simply two or more elements of travel such as flights, accommodation and transport) should have coverage in place: whether it be a bond, ATOL licence, or insurance policy.

Comparing the style and literature of competing companies can be instructive. You might be suspicious of companies that use terms like 'brand' and 'product' for their volunteer schemes. Open days, when you can meet the permanent staff and hear from former volunteers, are a better way of getting an insight into the ethos of a company. **Kath McGuire** knew exactly what she wanted when she started her search online:

I found the website of VESL when I was looking online for volunteer projects. I chose them because they were doing the sort of project I wanted (teaching, three months), because they were affordable, and they impressed me with the fact that they run selection days that involve an interview – they don't just take your money and send you to a project regardless of your appropriateness for it.

Check feedback sites online for candid reviews – as on the site www.abroadreviews.com, which offers 'unbiased reviews of international programmes'. The site www.go-volunteerabroad.com gives each of its listed programmes a star rating based on users' feedback. Gapadvice.org provides independent and unbiased information, research, and advice on gap years for people of all ages, and devotes a section of its site to career breaks. It is also worth paying attention to the companies that win acclaim in the Volunteering category of the annual Virgin Responsible Tourism Awards announced each November at the World Travel Market. For example, the winner in 2010 was Blue Ventures (see Directory entry), while honourable mention went to Biosphere Expeditions, BTCV, and The Great Projects: all mentioned elsewhere in this book.

People with a church affiliation and Christian faith have a broader choice of opportunities, since a number of mission societies and charities are looking for Christians. Whereas some religious organisations focus on practical work – such as working with street children, orphans, in schools, building libraries, etc – others are predominantly proselytising, which will only appeal to the very committed. Potential volunteers should be wary of joining a group that advocates a cultural or religious superiority or acts insensitively to local customs.

When trying to differentiate among gap year providers, the guidelines provided on www.ethicalvolunteering.org might prove helpful. The academic Kate Simpson has compiled a searching list of questions under the heading 'How to be an ethical volunteer: Picking the worthwhile from the worthless'. An agency that cares deeply about these issues and which accepts only grown-up volunteers is people & places (see Directory entry).

MY GROWN-UP GAP YEAR: LISA BASS

In her mid 30s Lisa Bass had just finished doing up her house, and had a secure job she loved managing emergency responses for the British Red Cross in Yorkshire. She had gone straight from school to uni to a job, and then had commitments that kept her from realising her ambition to work abroad. But when she found herself with no ties and her employers said they were willing to grant her a three-month career break, she knew she wanted to seize the opportunity 'before life got in the way again', ignoring her friends and family who thought that this wasn't quite career-minded enough. But then she was faced with the daunting task of choosing what to do.

In terms of choosing where to go and with which organisation - it was harrowing. Going through all the different websites and seeing all the need that there was in the world for volunteers to go and do, at times, life-saving work - you did at times feel guilty at just picking one project above the others. The choice was overwhelming and you had to stay focussed on what you wanted out of the three months, as well as what you had to give, so that you made a choice with both your heart and your head. Just because a project working with orphans in rural India touched your heart didn't mean that you were necessarily the right person to go and work there for three months.

I realised that there were just too many variables, and had to start to narrow the choice down a bit. I did this by thinking that taking my three months off was a once-in-a-lifetime opportunity, so, if I could go anywhere in the world, where would it be? Immediately I knew that it would be Madagascar, so then all I needed to pick one that was most suited to my needs and skills. One of the things that really came over from the Azafady web site was the straight talking, no nonsense, honest approach to what the scheme was about - warts and all! It was a welcome change from some of the others and I chose it.

There were so many high points. The chief of the village we were first working in met us and told us how he had been praying for our safe arrival so that we could help them build the well. He explained that since the first well had been built in another hamlet, no children under five had died. In a country that has an infant mortality rate of up to one in ten, that really struck us about the difference a couple of weeks of our time actually meant. I don't think any of us doubted from that moment on why we were here. One of my most emotional moments was when we all went down to the well we had just built with the villagers and pumped water for the first time. It was nothing short of a miracle that in that barren, parched landscape, clear drinking water was suddenly appearing and this would enable lives to be saved every day from here on in.

Another highlight was from my time later on in the local Azafady office, doing policy work. Gradually I realised how much I was learning and changing, as the Malagasy staff worked with me on developing policies that had to marry up international law and Malagasy culture. I felt that I was stretched in a way that I had never been before and I gained an appreciation and deep understanding of a culture and belief system that was so different to what I had grown up with, and really changed for the better my outlook on how I approach work.

I had wanted something that was hard but rewarding, and totally different from sitting at a desk job with the pace of life that has become the norm in Britain. And I found it - getting up at 5.30am each day to a fantastic sunrise, working in a brilliant and motivated group of volunteers, living with local guides and villagers who taught you everything about the local culture and history, and knowing that every single placement that you worked on made a real difference to the lives of the villagers that you had come to know.

Returning back home was a nightmare! I gave myself a month to make sure that this wasn't just a bad case of holiday blues, then gave in my notice at work, and started fundraising to go back to Madagascar for a year to work for Azafady. My time away was a completely life-changing experience. It allowed me the time and freedom to really look at what I wanted from life and showed me a way, with a little determination, that I could have it. I've given up a good job, great social scene, and comfortable house back in the UK to live in a place where the electricity and water are sporadic, food is basic to say the least, and there is no salary at the end of the month. And yet, I know that I have got the best of the deal! It just goes to show, you should never underestimate the difference to your life ten weeks can make.

DIRECTORY

The Directory sets out the programmes of charities and companies that are equipped to arrange all or part of a gap year. Organisations that specialise in placing North American volunteers are listed at the end of this chapter, though some US organisations welcome all nationalities onto their programmes.

2WAY DEVELOPMENT
Fitzroy House, 18 Ashwin St, London E8 3DL
(0)20 7193 6167
volunteer@2waydevelopment.com
www.2waydevelopment.com

PROGRAMME DESCRIPTION: 2Way Development arranges skilled, long-term volunteer placements within local not-for-profit organisations in the developing world, that work in pursuit of sustainable development and social justice. Skills of volunteers are matched with areas of need within local development-related charities. Volunteers are looking to gain experience in international development, or expanding their skills by taking a career break.

DESTINATIONS: Africa, Asia, Latin America, Middle East

NUMBER OF PLACEMENTS PER YEAR: 150

PREREQUISITES: Nationalities include British, American, Canadian, Australian, and New Zealand. Average age 28. Educational and/or professional background in a skill (not specified) is needed.

DURATION AND TIME OF PLACEMENTS: Three to 24 months (six months average)

SELECTION PROCEDURES AND ORIENTATION: Careers interview offered initially free of charge to establish volunteer's motivations. Full application online. Event days are held every month in central London, where volunteers can meet staff to evaluate their decision. All volunteers receive a personal adviser, three placement options, and an individual role description for their placement.

OTHER SERVICES: Pre-departure training course, help with visas and accommodation, preparatory handbooks and country guides, fundraising pack and online account, in-country airport collection, monthly placement reviews and remote mentoring, CV re-write, contact with volunteer alumni, networking and careers events.

COST: £750

CONTACT: Katherine Tubb, Director

ADVENTURE ALTERNATIVE
PO Box 14, Portstewart, Northern Ireland BT55 7WS
(0)2870 831258
office@adventurealternative.com
www.adventurealternative.com

PROGRAMME DESCRIPTION: Programmes primarily for gap year students, career breakers, medical students or medical professionals, in Kenya, Nepal, and Borneo. Combine two to 12 weeks of teaching/community/charity/ medical or environmental work, group activities (eg, climbing, trekking, rafting, safaris) and independent travel. In Kenya, participants teach and work in clinics and primary education in rural and slum schools, or in an orphanage or rescue centre for street children. In Nepal, participants help to build a village school or work in a Kathmandu primary school. In Borneo, community and tree planting projects take place deep in the Sarawak jungle.

DESTINATIONS: Rural and inner city slums in Kenya, Himalayan Nepal, and Sarawak (Malaysia)

NUMBER OF PLACEMENTS A YEAR: 50 for Kenya, 30 for Nepal, 20 for Borneo

PREREQUISITES: Hard-working, committed enthusiastic volunteers who are not fazed by the hardships of living in a developing country. All nationalities and ages welcome.

DURATION AND TIME OF PLACEMENTS: Two to 12 weeks, but can be flexible

COST: From £650 for short expeditions; sample price is £1,250 for two months in Kenya; £1,850 for three months (includes food and accommodation), plus estimated £800 for flights, inoculations, insurance and other necessities.

CONTACT: Gavin Bate, Director; Chris Little or Andy MacDonald, Expedition Coordinators

AFRICAN CONSERVATION EXPERIENCE
Unit 1, Manor Farm, Churchend Lane, Charfield, Wotton-Under-Edge, Gloucestershire GL12 8LJ
(0)1454 269182
info@ConservationAfrica.net
www.ConservationAfrica.net

PROGRAMME DESCRIPTION: Conservation placements on game reserves in southern Africa. Tasks may include tracking elephants, hand-rearing a rhino, studying dolphin behaviour, and restoring and maintaining the bushveld habitat.

DESTINATIONS: Southern Africa including South Africa and Botswana, plus Mauritius

PREREQUISITES: Open to people of all ages who have reasonable physical fitness and ability to cope mentally. Enthusiasm for conservation is essential. Specific projects are recommended for 'grown-ups' which allow for better social interaction within the group.

DURATION AND TIME OF PLACEMENTS: Two to 12 weeks throughout the year

SELECTION PROCEDURES AND ORIENTATION: Candidates are matched to a suitable project on the information provided on their application form, but do have final say on their choice of project. Prospective participants can meet company representatives at various talks and events in the UK and elsewhere.

COST: Students can expect an average total cost of about £2,200 for two weeks, up to £5,200 for 12 weeks, which includes international flights (from London), transfers, accommodation, and all meals. Support and advice given on fundraising.

CONTACT: Alexia Massey and Katrina Steele

AFRICAN IMPACT
6 Carlton Close, Noordhoek 7985, Cape Town, South Africa
+27 (0)21 785 4319; USA: +1 800 606 7185; UK: (0)800 098 8440
kylie@africanimpact.com
www.africanimpact.com

PROGRAMME DESCRIPTION: Short-term voluntourism opportunities on community projects (teaching, medical, and sports) and on lion conservation projects. Internships and professional courses also available.

DESTINATIONS: Zambia, Zimbabwe, South Africa, Zanzibar, Mozambique, Kenya, etc

NUMBER OF PLACEMENTS PER YEAR: 1,200

DURATION AND TIME OF PLACEMENTS: Two to eight weeks on community projects; two to four weeks on lion projects, preferably starting on the first or third Monday of every month

COST: Sample prices are £1,045 for a fortnight volunteering with lions in Livingstone; £1,725 (in 2011) for six-weeks teaching in Kenya

CONTACT: Kylie Taute, Destination Manager

AIDCAMPS INTERNATIONAL
483 Green Lanes, London N13 4BS
(0)845 652 5412
info@aidcamps.org
www.aidcamps.org

PROGRAMME DESCRIPTION: Teams of volunteers of all ages work with partner NGOs on a range of projects, such as building rural primary schools, resource centres, etc. Independent AidCamps placements are also available in conservation work, orphanage care, teaching, medical placements, etc.

DESTINATIONS: India, Nepal, Sri Lanka, and Cameroon

PREREQUISITES: Average age of volunteers is 40. If someone has particular skills/interests to offer, AidCamps will liaise with partner NGOs to try to arrange an appropriate independent placement.

DURATION AND TIME OF PLACEMENTS: Mainly short-term projects lasting three weeks. Longer-term scheme called 'Independent AidCamps' suitable for gappers of all ages and 'Family AidCamps' for those with children under 18. Average duration is five weeks, but can be between two weeks and several months.

COST: Group participants pay up to £1,000 for three weeks, nearly three-quarters of which goes directly to the aid project and on volunteer costs. Homestay accommodation for Independent and Family AidCamps costs roughly £50 per week.

CONTACT: Stephen Youd-Thomas, Office Manager

ALL AFRICA VENTURES

Box 2031, Jeffreys Bay, 6331, South Africa
+27 836 615 393
allafricavolunteers@gmail.com
www.allafricavolunteers.com

PROGRAMME DESCRIPTION: Run their own community surf volunteer and wildlife volunteer projects in Jeffreys Bay, and cooperate with partner organisations elsewhere in South Africa to offer other volunteer opportunities.

DESTINATIONS: South Africa

NUMBER OF PLACEMENTS PER YEAR: 50–100

PREREQUISITES: Average age 16–45. All nationalities accepted. No specific qualifications needed, only life skills.

DURATION AND TIME OF PLACEMENTS: One to three months

SELECTION PROCEDURES AND ORIENTATION: Applications due at least four weeks in advance of arrival

COST: Varies with programme. Volunteer fee covers meals and lodging, and programme sponsorship. Accommodation is in volunteer lodge (for community project), or log cabins in game area (for wildlife project).

CONTACT: Tyron van Tonder, Company Owner

ALL OUT AFRICA

PO Box 153 Lobamba, Swaziland
+268 416 2260
info@alloutafrica.com
www.alloutafrica.com

PROGRAMME DESCRIPTION: Travel organisation that offers packages combining volunteering and tourism. Projects are aimed at engaging people from around the world in research and action for a sustainable Africa. Social projects include orphan care, teaching, sports development, and building in Swaziland; teaching, childcare and medical/social work project in Cape Town; and childcare or teaching in Botswana and Mozambique. Conservation projects focus on research and monitoring of marine and terrestrial wildlife, with some hands-on conservation action. Volunteers help to collect and analyse field data on whale sharks, humpback whales, turtles, coral fish, Marabou storks, tortoises, rodents, bats, and vultures in Mozambique and Swaziland.

DESTINATIONS: Swaziland, South Africa, Botswana, and Mozambique

NUMBER OF PLACEMENTS PER YEAR: 250

PREREQUISITES: Ages 18–65. No special skills needed except for medical project in Cape Town. Attempts are made to match a volunteer's skills to a particular project.

DURATION AND TIME OF PLACEMENTS: Standard length of stay is four weeks, though two-, six-, eight-, or 12-week stays (or longer) are also possible. Arrival day is the first Monday of each month.

SELECTION PROCEDURES AND ORIENTATION: Applications should be submitted at least a month before start date. Volunteers receive project briefs and a travel pack in advance and an orientation tour on arrival. The whale shark marine project incorporates a scuba dive course.

COST: From £993 upwards. In Swaziland and Cape Town volunteers stay in backpacker lodges; in Mozambique in a beach volunteer house; and in Botswana with host families, all onsite. Private accommodation can be organised subject to availability.

CONTACT: Gabby Lee, Bookings Officer

PROGRAMME DESCRIPTION: Volunteer opportunities throughout Africa, helping with wildlife conservation, medical, teaching, orphan care, and sustainable community programmes. Volunteers can work with big cats and orphaned wildlife at the Namibia Wildlife Sanctuary or at the Lion Rehabilitation Project at Victoria Falls; assist medical staff at the remote Bushman Medical Clinic or look after AIDS orphans in Cape Town and St Lucia; teach disadvantaged children in schools in Zambia or in a coastal village on Zanzibar Island; or coach sports in primary and secondary schools.

DESTINATIONS: Botswana, Kenya, Mozambique, Namibia, South Africa, Tanzania, Uganda, Zambia, and Zimbabwe

NUMBER OF PLACEMENTS PER YEAR: 300–400

PREREQUISITES: All ages, including people taking a career break, mature volunteers and gap year students

DURATION AND TIME OF PLACEMENTS: Three days to 12 weeks, with flexible start dates

SELECTION PROCEDURES AND ORIENTATION: Comprehensive pre-departure pack and full orientation on arrival

OTHER SERVICES: Amanzi Travel also offers courses where you can learn to be a Game Ranger or Field Guide, as well as a range of adventure overland trips

COST: From £185 for short stays to £3,365–£5,295 for three months

CONTACT: Gemma Whitehouse, Managing Director

PROGRAMME DESCRIPTION: Assistance given to committed volunteers who want to work in rural Kenya. Summer placements are community-based, eg living with Maasai, helping set up a football academy, and coordinating a nature conservancy. New creative/musical placements in Amazonian rainforest community.

DESTINATIONS: Kenya, Brazilian Amazon (Combu: reachable only by boat, not far from city of Belém)

PREREQUISITES: Enthusiasm, tolerance, and dedication. Background in education would be helpful, but desire to help is often enough

DURATION AND TIME OF PLACEMENTS: Four-week placement in July/August; otherwise any time of year with orientation

SELECTION PROCEDURES AND ORIENTATION: Online interviews via email and Skype

OTHER SERVICES: At the end of each programme, AVIF can offer recommended providers for safari, or a climb of Kilimanjaro or Mount Kenya with an experienced guide, or diving and relaxing at Diani Beach on the Indian Ocean

COST: AVIF does not charge fees. Volunteers cover their costs, ie international airfares plus subsistence (eg $30 a week).

CONTACT: Ms Alison Lowndes, Founder Trustee. Further information about AVIF can be found on Facebook, Flickr and on the websites of associated hosts in Kenya.

PROGRAMME DESCRIPTION: Azafady is a UK-registered charity and Malagasy NGO, providing opportunities to work with a grassroots organisation tackling conservation issues and extreme poverty in Madagascar. Working closely with local communities, volunteers can choose to join the award-winning 10-week Pioneer Programme, and work on projects as diverse as well construction, school-building, tree planting, environmental or health education, help on the Lemur Research and Conservation Programme; or to join the Short-term Programmes for two or three weeks to assist with school-building or English teaching. Programmes are particularly suited to those interested in development and ecology (who may be looking for experience as an entry point into an ethical career), or who simply want to make a difference and have a meaningful career break experience.

DESTINATIONS: Southeast Madagascar

NUMBER OF PLACEMENTS PER YEAR: Approx. 100

PREREQUISITES: Enthusiasm and cultural sensitivity. All ages welcome; past age range is 18–70. Training given. Volunteers learn basic Malagasy so that they may work together with members of rural communities and gain a unique insight into the culture.

DURATION AND TIME OF PLACEMENTS: Two to 10 weeks, with main start dates in January, April, July and October

COST: Successful applicants pay personal pre-project costs such as flight, vaccinations, and visa, and are required to raise a minimum charitable donation of between £595 and £2,650 – depending on project and duration. Volunteers are provided with extensive fundraising resources and advice.

CONTACT: Sarah Lamb, Volunteer Coordinator

BASE BACKPACKER HOSTELS
PO Box 5188, Wellesley St, Auckland 1141, New Zealand
☏ +64 9 358 4877
✉ info@stayatbase.com
🖥 www.stayatbase.com

PROGRAMME DESCRIPTION: Network of superior centrally-located backpacker hostels in New Zealand, offering good value and quality local experiences. Beds are available for every budget and one-stop-shop services for travellers of all ages, which include expert travel centres, New Zealand Job Search services, high speed wireless internet cafés, and bars. New Zealand Job Search is located in Base Auckland, Level 3, 229 Queen

St (+64 9 357 3996; info@nzjs.co.nz; www.nzjs.co.nz) and operates as a job agency for those on working holiday visas.

DESTINATIONS: Throughout New Zealand; hostels in Auckland, Bay of Islands, Rotorua, Taupo, Wellington, Christchurch, Queenstown, and Wanaka

NUMBER OF PLACEMENTS PER YEAR: Unlimited number of visas valid for up to 23 months, available to UK nationals aged 18–30

PREREQUISITES: Working holiday visa necessary to use NZ Job Search

COST: Starter pack includes 12 months registration with Job Search, airport pick-up, two nights accommodation on arrival, etc, for NZ$345

CONTACT: Email info@nzjs.co.nz for full price list and more info

---

BASE CAMP GROUP
30 Baseline Business Studios, Whitchurch Road, London W11 4AT
☏ (0)20 7243 6222
✉ contact@basecampgroup.com
🖥 www.basecampgroup.com

PROGRAMME DESCRIPTION: Instructor Courses and Performance Camps in snow, water and adrenaline sports – including skiing, snowboarding, kitesurfing, surfing, and mountain biking – all suited to gap years, career breaks, and holidays

DESTINATIONS: Diverse range of locations in France, Canada, Argentina, Morocco, South Africa, and Egypt. For snow sports: Meribel and Val d'Isère (France); Whistler, Kicking Horse and Banff (Canada); and Bariloche (Argentina). For water sports: Dahab (Egypt); Taghazout (Morocco); and the South African coast. For adrenaline sports: Whistler (Canada).

NUMBER OF PLACEMENTS PER YEAR: 300

DURATION AND TIME OF PLACEMENTS: Two to 11 weeks

PREREQUISITES: Course specific (see website)

OTHER SERVICES: Qualifications are also offered. For snow sports: BASI in Europe, and CSIA/CASI in North

America. For water sports: BSA and IKO. For adrenaline sports: PMBI.

COST: £300–£800 per week depending on length of programme and nature of sport. Usually includes all local requirements such as accommodation, food, coaching, exams, etc, but not flights.

CONTACT: Helen Nicholls and Fergie Miller, Course Advisers

BIOSEARCH EXPEDITIONS
Wayfarer Lodge, Welbourn, Lincs LN5 0QH
(0)1400 273323
expeditions@biosearch.org.uk
www.biosearch.org.uk

PROGRAMME DESCRIPTION: Expeditions to track and record game in the Nyika National Park of Malawi, to build up a biodiversity index for the park in co-operation with Malawi Department of National Parks & Wildlife and other institutions.

DESTINATIONS: Malawi. Preparatory weekend courses held at Hilltop Farm, Lincolnshire.

NUMBER OF PLACEMENTS PER YEAR: Over 25 attend weekend training camps in the UK

PREREQUISITES: All nationalities and range of ages accepted, from university students up to 70. Biosearch are actively encouraging more mature team members with established amateur and professional skills. Training weekends require no qualifications, just the desire to learn about adventure travel and bush living. Candidates for expeditions should have an inclination to natural history and conservation.

DURATION AND TIME OF PLACEMENTS: Standard one-month expeditions in December and July/August. Two-day training weekends in UK are open to all (whether or not they join a team in Malawi).

SELECTION PROCEDURES AND ORIENTATION: 48-hour training weekends held before expedition departures (see website for details)

OTHER SERVICES: Training continues on arrival in the bush. Accommodation is in small tents on expedition; otherwise in comfortable accommodation.

COST: £1,900–£2,500 for African expedition, depending on season

CONTACT: Peter Overton, Project Director

BIOSPHERE EXPEDITIONS
The Henderson Centre, Ivy Lane, Norwich
NR5 8BF
(0)870 446 0801
uk@biosphere-expeditions.org
www.biosphere-expeditions.org

PROGRAMME DESCRIPTION: Biosphere Expeditions is an international non-profit-making organisation, offering hands-on wildlife conservation holidays to all who seek adventure with a purpose. Volunteers with no research experience assist scientific experts. Projects include studying snow leopards in the Altai Republic of Central Asia, surveying leopards and cheetahs in Namibia, monitoring marine mammals in the Azores, protecting coral reefs in Honduras, studying Arabian leopards in Oman, and pumas and jaguars in Brazil.

DESTINATIONS: Worldwide

NUMBER OF PLACEMENTS PER YEAR: 300

PREREQUISITES: No special skills or fitness required to join, and no age limits whatsoever

DURATION AND TIME OF PLACEMENTS: Six days to two months, starting year round

COST: £900–£1,930 (excluding flights) for one or two-week expeditions. At least two-thirds of contributions benefit local project directly.

BLUE VENTURES
309 a/b Aberdeen Centre, 22–24 Highbury Grove, London N5 2EA
enquiries@blueventures.org
www.blueventures.org

PROGRAMME DESCRIPTION: Volunteers needed for award-winning marine conservation project. Blue Ventures conducts marine research, and works with local communities to sustainably manage marine resources in South West Madagascar, northern Belize, and eastern

Malaysia. Volunteers participate in all research programmes, community projects, and alternative livelihood schemes. Non-diving conservation work might involve cetacean surveys, accompanying local fishermen, or beach clean-up operations.

DESTINATIONS: The village of Andavadoaka in south-west Madagascar has been the Blue Ventures expedition site since 2003. Blue Ventures is now repeating this success in the fishing community of Sarteneja in northern Belize, and on the beautiful island of Tioman in the Malaysian South China Sea.

PREREQUISITES: No diving or scientific background required as all necessary training is provided on site. The Blue Ventures international team of volunteers comprises all ages and walks of life.

DURATION AND TIME OF PLACEMENTS: Typical stay of six weeks, although shorter and longer stays are available

OTHER SERVICES: The Blue Ventures volunteer programme has been awarded a number of international responsible tourism awards and has pioneered successful conservation efforts

COST: £2,200 for six weeks, for volunteers requiring dive training; £2,000 for PADI Advanced divers or equivalent. Short stays of a fortnight are available from £900 at Tioman project. Volunteers will be expected to provide personal diving kit (ie, mask, snorkel, wetsuit, fins), torch, sleeping bag, malaria prophylactics, inoculations, and flights.

CONTACT: Kathleen Edie, Expedition & Volunteer Coordinator

THE BRITISH INSTITUTE OF FLORENCE
Piazza Strozzi 2, 50123 Florence, Italy
(C) +39 055 26 77 81
info@britishinstitute.it
www.britishinstitute.it

PROGRAMME DESCRIPTION: Housed in two magnificent buildings on either side of the River Arno in the heart of the historic centre of Florence and minutes from all the city's museums, galleries, and churches, the British Institute of Florence has a long tradition of excellence in its teaching, and is recognised as a centre for learning by

the Tuscan Region. The Institute offers students the opportunity of experiencing the life and culture of Florence within the framework of a structured programme of study. Courses are offered in Italian language, history of art, and life drawing. A regular programme of events including lectures, concerts, and films, is held in the Institute's Harold Acton Library overlooking the River Arno.

DESTINATIONS: Florence, Italy

DURATION AND TIME OF PLACEMENTS: One to 12 weeks throughout the year

OTHER SERVICES: Accommodation can be arranged in local homes, pensione, and hotels. Price for homestay accommodation starts at approximately €30 per night. There is a fee of €25 for arranging accommodation.

COST: Fees vary according to the course chosen – eg a four-week Italian language course is €630, and a four-week History of Art course is €615. Four-week combined Italian and History of Art course is €1,150.

BUNAC
16 Bowling Green Lane, London EC1R 0QH
(C) (0)20 7251 3472
enquiries@bunac.org.uk
www.bunac.org

PROGRAMME DESCRIPTION: Founding member of the Year Out Group. Primarily a non-profit national student club offering work and volunteer programmes worldwide to young people, BUNAC accepts candidates up to the maximum visa age for some work abroad programmes and imposes no maximum age for volunteering. Work New Zealand and Work Australia are open to non-students 18–30 or 35-years-old for one of the New Zealand visas. Volunteer placements of varying lengths are offered in a range of countries, plus a Teach-in-China programme. BUNAC acts as an aide before and after arrival in the country of travel, and a 'security blanket' if anything goes wrong.

DESTINATIONS: Australia and New Zealand for Work Abroad programmes. Volunteering for two to eight months in Cambodia, Costa Rica, Ghana, India, Peru, South Africa, and USA. (BUNAC's main destination is the USA, but its paid work and camp counselling programmes are primarily for full-time students.)

PREREQUISITES: Ages 18–30/35 depending on visa

DURATION AND TIME OF PLACEMENTS: Two to eight months depending on destination, with departures throughout the year

OTHER SERVICES: BUNAC has an in-house travel agency, GS World Travel (020 7250 0222; www. gsworld-travel.co.uk), which arranges flights. BUNAC also offers an online TEFL training course (partnered with i-to-i).

COST: £5 BUNAC membership fee; plus programme fees from £295 for up to 12 weeks of conservation volunteering in the USA, to £2,095 for five months of paid teaching in China

---

CACTUS LANGUAGE TRAINING
4 Clarence House, 30–31 North St, Brighton BN1 1EB
✆ (0)845 130 4775
✉ info@cactuslanguagetraining.com
🖥 www.cactuslanguage.com and
www.cactustefl.com

PROGRAMME DESCRIPTION: Cactus helps over 15,000 people learn a language every year via language holidays abroad, and evening courses in 41 locations and 24 languages across the UK. In Latin America, language courses can be combined with volunteering placements. Cactus also acts as a business language and TEFL training consultancy. Cactus TEFL delivers up-to-date information on hundreds of TEFL courses throughout the world, which can be used to compare prices.

DESTINATIONS: Language courses in Germany, France, Spain, Italy, Greece, Russia, China, and 30+ other countries

PREREQUISITES: All ages and nationalities welcome

OTHER SERVICES: Cactus offers an advice service for anyone new to TEFL

COST: From £359 for two-week course in Tenerife with option of learning to surf (additional cost)

CALEDONIA – LANGUAGES, CULTURE, ADVENTURE
33 Sandport Street, Leith, Edinburgh EH6 6AP
✆ (0)131 621 7721/2
✉ info@caledonialanguages.co.uk
🖥 www.caledonialanguages.com

PROGRAMME DESCRIPTION: Established in 1994, Caledonia's main focus is arranging language, culture, and adventure travel abroad. They offer short- and long-term language courses with accommodation (usually homestay, but other options are available) throughout Europe and Latin America. They also arrange volunteer work placements in Latin America, work experience programmes, language + activity courses (eg Spanish + dance in Spain, Cuba, Argentina and the Dominican Republic; Spanish + trekking in Cuba; Portuguese + trekking in Brazil; French + sailing in Nice), and language + learning courses (eg, Italian + History of Art in San Giovanni; Spanish + cooking in Malaga, or French + cooking in Aix-en-Provence). Volunteer community projects in Latin America for language clients include working with children in Lencois, Brazil; conservation in the cloud forests of Costa Rica; kindergarten in Peru; or teaching English in Ecuador. Work experience programmes are sometimes available working with partner language schools, companies, and organisations, according to the client's skills and experience.

DESTINATIONS: Caledonia's partner language schools are in France, Spain, Portugal, Italy, Germany, Austria, Russia, Argentina, Peru, Chile, Bolivia, Ecuador, Costa Rica, Brazil, Mexico, Dominican Republic, and Cuba. Cuba is one of Caledonia's main destinations; tailormade programmes can be made year round to include dance, percussion, music, touring, and trekking, with or without language course.

PREREQUISITES: All levels are offered, from complete beginner to advanced. A higher level of Spanish or Portuguese is needed to work on volunteer and work experience programmes.

DURATION AND TIME OF PLACEMENTS: Minimum one week (or three to four weeks if combined with volunteer placement), and up to 12 months. Classes start all year round.

SELECTION PROCEDURES AND ORIENTATION: For volunteer and work experience programmes, a short language course is taken in the country for cultural and linguistic familiarisation before work can begin. Briefing meetings on the proposed work and occasional pre-placement site visits are arranged. Full back-up support is given by the language school in-country.

COST: Volunteers and work experience applicants must pay an arrangement fee of £250 plus VAT, and fees for the pre-placement language course in the overseas country (eg, £1,355 for four weeks in Brazil, encompassing 20 lessons per week with half-board single room accommodation). Accommodation is with local families.

CONTACT: Kath Bateman, Director

CAMP AMERICA

37a Queen's Gate, London SW7 5HR

✆ (0)20 7581 7373

✉ enquiries@campamerica.co.uk

🖥 www.campamerica.co.uk

PROGRAMME DESCRIPTION: Camp America has been placing people from Europe, Asia, Africa, Australia, and New Zealand on American summer camps since 1969. Camp counsellors look after the children and/or teach sports activities, music, arts, drama and dance, etc.

DESTINATIONS: Throughout the USA

NUMBER OF PLACEMENTS PER YEAR: 7,000+ (from around the world) for 900 camps

PREREQUISITES: No upper age limit, though the vast majority are under 23. Camp America is looking to recruit skilled adults for a variety of job choices. Experience in sport coaching, religious counselling, teaching, childcare, health care, and lifeguarding is preferable.

DURATION AND TIME OF PLACEMENTS: Must be willing to depart between 1 May and 27 June for a minimum of nine weeks. Up to 10 weeks of travel time available between camp and visa expiry at the end of October.

SELECTION PROCEDURES AND ORIENTATION: Face-to-face interview with locally appointed Camp America interviewer. Also, Camp America hosts recruitment fairs in the winter to allow participants to meet and interview with Camp Directors from a variety of summer camps in London, Manchester, Edinburgh, and Belfast. Selectors aim to evaluate applicants' background, training, and main skill areas to make suitable placements. Personal interview at US Embassy is also required for a J-1 visa. Early application is advised.

COST: Medical insurance and application fees apply. All programmes offer free return flights from London and other selected international airports to New York, along with transfer to the camp, free accommodation and meals, up to 10 weeks of travel time after camp duties, Cultural Exchange USA visa sponsorship, 24-hour support, medical insurance, and pocket money – which ranges from $600 to $1,650 (depending on age, experience and role).

CESA LANGUAGES ABROAD

CESA House, Pennance Road, Lanner, Cornwall TR16 5TQ

✆ (0)1209 211800

✉ info@cesalanguages.com

🖥 www.cesalanguages.com

Founder member of the Year Out Group.

PROGRAMME DESCRIPTION: Beginner, intermediate, and advanced courses in French (Cannes, Nice, Montpellier, Rouen, Tours, Antibes, Bordeaux, Paris, or, for a more exotic option, Guadeloupe); Spanish (Seville, Nerja, Salamanca, Malaga, or Madrid in Spain, plus Argentina, Peru, Chile, Mexico, Costa Rica, or Ecuador); German (Berlin, Heidelberg, Lindau, Munich, Cologne, or Vienna and Kitzbuhel in Austria); Italian (Florence, Rome, Sorrento, Siena, and Viareggio); Portuguese; Chinese; Russian; Dutch; Greek; and Arabic (in Morocco). Courses for mature students (50+) in Spain, Italy and France; Italian/Spanish/French + Cookery; German or Spanish + Skiing; Spanish + Diving/Surfing; French + Surfing/Sailing

DESTINATIONS: As above

NUMBER OF PLACEMENTS PER YEAR: 500+

PREREQUISITES: None

DURATION AND TIME OF PLACEMENTS: One to 48 weeks, with possibility of studying in more than one location during a year-out programme. At least one start

date per month year round. Set dates apply to Language + Activities or Mature Student programmes.

SELECTION PROCEDURES AND ORIENTATION: Certain courses will require a specific language level, however, most are open to all abilities. Advice and support are provided prior to and throughout the course by CESA staff, and in-country support is available from the language school.

OTHER SERVICES: DELE preparation offered in Spain; DELF, Alliance Francaise, and CCIP exams in France; TRKI exams in Russia. Full range of CEFR (European) exams offered in Germany and Austria. Accommodation options include student apartments or residences, on-campus accommodation, host families, sole-occupancy apartments and hotels.

COST: Languages for Life eight-week course in Seville or Madrid costs from £1,856, including shared apartment accommodation and 20 hours' tuition per week. A four-week course with college residence accommodation and 20 lessons a week in Heidelburg costs from £724.

CONTACT: Katherine Hughes

CHALLENGES WORLDWIDE
54 Manor Place, Edinburgh EH3 7EH
(0)845 200 0342
info@challengesworldwide.org
www.challengesworldwide.org

PROGRAMME DESCRIPTION: Challenges Worldwide is a leading international development charity that recruits, trains, and manages expert volunteers to carry out short assignments for social enterprise in developing countries. Volunteer assignments aim to make a sustainable contribution to partner organisations, whilst building new skills and experiences of our expert volunteers in an international context. Expert volunteers share their professional skills and experiences with local partner organisations. Volunteers with professional experience are needed in: Strategic Planning, Business Development, Project Management, Finance, Human Resources, IT, Marketing and Communications, Fundraising, Research, and Law.

DESTINATIONS: Belize, India, Sri Lanka, Kenya, Tanzania, and Cambodia

NUMBER OF PLACEMENTS PER YEAR: 120

PREREQUISITES: Average age is mid 30s, although volunteers can be aged 23–65. Volunteer assignments fall into three categories, based on the level of experience required by the volunteer.

DURATION AND TIME OF PLACEMENTS: Three to six months with possibility of shorter assignments. Recruitment takes place all year round.

SELECTION PROCEDURES AND ORIENTATION: Volunteers are provided with end-to-end support, including pre-departure training, weekly reports and appraisals

COST: The fee for a self-funded assignment is £1,800. Volunteer covers cost of flights, insurance, accommodation, and living expenses, though in some cases partner organisation will contribute to these.

CHANGING WORLDS
11 Doctors Lane, Chaldon, Surrey CR3 5AE
(0)1883 340960
ask@changingworlds.co.uk
www.changingworlds.co.uk

PROGRAMME DESCRIPTION: Member of the Year Out Group. Small, family-run company that aims to provide individual attention and full cultural immersion through challenging and worthwhile work placements, with a safety net if required. ATOL Licence number 6885. Voluntary work placements in schools, journalism, hospitals, legal firms, orphanages, outdoor education, zoos, etc, and paid work placements in hotels and hospitality.

DESTINATIONS: Argentina, Australia, Brazil, China, Dubai, Germany, Ghana, Honduras, India, Kenya, Latvia, Madagascar, New Zealand, Romania, Serbia, South Africa, and Thailand

NUMBER OF PLACEMENTS PER YEAR: 120

PREREQUISITES: Must have initiative, determination, adaptability, and social skills, plus skills relevant to the job if possible. Open to all ages, apart from paid work placements in New Zealand – which are open to candidates under 30. Volunteers to Argentina and Honduras are expected to know or learn Spanish, and volunteers to Brazil are expected to learn Portuguese.

DURATION AND TIME OF PLACEMENTS: One, three, six, or nine months. Placements start throughout the year.

SELECTION PROCEDURES AND ORIENTATION: Interview days held in Surrey every six to eight weeks. All participants attend a pre-departure briefing; for those going to a developing country, this is a two-day residential course. Participants are met on arrival in-country and attend orientation with the local representative before proceeding to placement. Local representatives act as support during placement.

OTHER SERVICES: Changing Worlds is a member of Interhealth, which can provide health screening to all participants and act as travel health advisers.

COST: From £1,595 for six months in Germany, to £3,725 for six months in Argentina. Prices include return flights, but exclude insurance (approximately £260 for six months) and visas.

CONTACT: David Gill, Director (david@changingworlds.co.uk)

CORAL CAY CONSERVATION
Elizabeth House, 39 York Road, London SE1 7NQ
(0)20 7620 1411
info@coralcay.org
www.coralcay.org

PROGRAMME DESCRIPTION: Hundreds of volunteers participate in Coral Cay expeditions every year, to assist in conserving fragile tropical marine and terrestrial environments, building local capacity to protect these ecosystems long-term. The overall aim of CCC is to use good science to support the preservation of coral reefs, and to support the dependent communities. Volunteers undertake dives to understand biodiversity and to gather scientific data, which is used to compile reports for journals to establish new marine protected areas (MPAs).

DESTINATIONS: Currently three expedition sites: Southern Leyte in the Philippines, Tobago, and Cambodia. Possibility of setting up new terrestrial project in Kenya (see website for updates)

NUMBER OF PLACEMENTS PER YEAR: 200–500

PREREQUISITES: No previous experience is required. Volunteers come from a diverse range of backgrounds, ages, and cultures.

DURATION AND TIME OF PLACEMENTS: Expeditions depart monthly throughout the year. Volunteers stay for two to 30 weeks or longer.

OTHER SERVICES: Scuba dive training is available up to PADI Dive Master level

COST: Sample prices are £1,550 for four weeks as a dive trainee, and £2,750 for 12 weeks if a qualified diver. Prices vary according to length of stay, type of project, and level of training required. Prices exclude flights and insurance; fundraising advice is given. Occasional special offers such as free PADI rescue diver, Reef Check International Ecodiver, and PADI Emergency First Response.

COSMIC VOLUNTEERS
PO Box 11895, Philadelphia, Pennsylvania 19128, USA
(C) +1 215 609 4196
(email) info@cosmicvolunteers.org
(web) www.cosmicvolunteers.org

PROGRAMME DESCRIPTION: Tax-exempt charity (33-0998120), which has been sending volunteers abroad since 2001. Volunteering, internships, and specialist travel programmes in developing countries. Volunteer programme includes teaching, medicine, orphanages, journalism, social work, HIV/AIDS, Buddhist monks, environment, sports, organic farming, and turtle conservation.

DESTINATIONS: Bolivia, Cambodia, China, Ecuador, Ghana, Guatemala, India, Kenya, Nepal, Peru, Philippines, South Africa, Thailand, Uganda, and Vietnam

NUMBER OF PLACEMENTS PER YEAR: 250+

PREREQUISITES: For all ages (16–70+) with average at about 23. Must have open mind and be fluent in English. Most medical placements available only to health professionals and trainees.

DURATION AND TIME OF PLACEMENTS: One week to 12 months

SELECTION PROCEDURES AND ORIENTATION: Applicants accepted year round. Must sign up at least 30 days before programme start date.

OTHER SERVICES: Spanish language classes are available in Bolivia, Ecuador, Guatemala, and Peru

COST: Varies with programme: from $795 one-time fee for Vietnam, to $1,995 for 12 weeks in Ghana

CONTACT: Scott Burke, Founder and Director

CROSS-CULTURAL SOLUTIONS
Tower Point 44, North Road, Brighton BN1 1YR (UK); 2 Clinton Place, New Rochelle, NY 10801 (USA)
(C) (0)845 458 2781/2782 (UK); +1 800 380 4777 (USA)
(email) infouk@crossculturalsolutions.org
(web) www.crossculturalsolutions.org

PROGRAMME DESCRIPTION: A not-for-profit international volunteer organisation founded in 1995, and registered charity in the UK (Number 1106741). Opportunity for participants to work side-by-side with local people, on community-led initiatives. Volunteer programmes are designed to combine hands-on service and cultural exchange with the aim of fostering cultural understanding.

DESTINATIONS: Brazil, China, Costa Rica, Ghana, Guatemala, India, Morocco, Peru, Russia, South Africa, Tanzania, and Thailand

NUMBER OF PLACEMENTS PER YEAR: Approx. 3,000

PREREQUISITES: No upper age limit. No language or specialist skills are necessary. All nationalities welcome, provided they speak English.

DURATION AND TIME OF PLACEMENTS: One to 12 weeks. Start dates are offered all year round.

COST: Programme fee starts at £1,949 for two weeks, to £4,449 for 12 weeks. Covers the cost of lodging, meals, bottled water, and ground transport; plus individual attention and guidance from an experienced Programme Manager, co-ordination of the placement, cultural and learning activities, a 24-hour emergency hotline, and travel and medical insurance. Airfares not included.

CSV (COMMUNITY SERVICE VOLUNTEERS)

5th Floor, Scala House, 36 Holloway Circus,
Queensway, Birmingham B1 1EQ

(0)800 374991 or (0)121 643 7690

volunteer@csv.org.uk

www.csv.org.uk

PROGRAMME DESCRIPTION: CSV is the largest voluntary placement organisation in the UK. It provides a voluntary placement to those aged 16–35 who commit to moving away from home for four to 12 months. CSV volunteers help people throughout the UK in a huge range of social care projects, eg working with the homeless, mentoring young offenders, supporting children in special schools, or helping the disabled to live independently in their homes – and at the same time learn new skills.

DESTINATIONS: CSV volunteers are full-time and live away from home anywhere within the UK

NUMBER OF PLACEMENTS PER YEAR: 1,000

PREREQUISITES: Full-time programme is for volunteers under 35. No specific qualifications or experience is needed. Volunteers must have commitment and be flexible, as volunteers are placed where their help and skills are needed most. A full UK driving licence is useful but not required. Open to UK or EEA citizens who are residents in the UK. Other international volunteers from specific countries can apply through one of CSV's international partnerships (www.csv.org.uk/international-volunteers-fact-sheet). Retired & Senior Volunteers Programme is for people over 50 to volunteer in their local community.

DURATION AND TIME OF PLACEMENTS: Four to 12 months, beginning at any time of the year

SELECTION PROCEDURES AND ORIENTATION: Interview days are held across the UK and start dates are available throughout the year. Volunteers receive regular supervision and back-up support from their local CSV office.

COST: No joining fee. CSV volunteers receive free accommodation and subsistence (which includes food and money to live on), and also travel expenses and relevant training. The current weekly allowance (for 2010) is £34 plus £40 food allowance if meals are not provided on the placement.

DEVELOPMENT IN ACTION

78 York St, London W1H 1DP

(0)7813 395957

info@developmentinaction.org

www.developmentinaction.org

PROGRAMME DESCRIPTION: Non-profit-making development education organisation (formerly Student Action India). Voluntary internship type placements to partner Indian non-governmental organisations. Grassroots development projects range from teaching children in urban slums, administration, and fundraising, to fieldwork and research. Volunteers are also required to produce a development education project to be used as a resource in the UK.

DESTINATIONS: India; with projects in Pune, Udaipur, Indore, Bhopal, Pondicherry, and Mumbai surrounding areas

PREREQUISITES: Motivation, an interest in global issues, and commitment to the aims of DiA. No upper age limit or nationality restrictions

DURATION AND TIME OF PLACEMENTS: Two-month summer placements or gap year five-month placements beginning in September

SELECTION PROCEDURES AND ORIENTATION: University recruitment talks/careers fairs take place between January and March (see website for details). Application deadlines around the end of January and March; interviews held in February and April/May. Pre-departure training over one weekend plus one week training on arrival.

COST: £800 for summer; £1,600 for five months (covers placement, training support and accommodation). Flights, insurance, visa, and subsistence costs are extra.

CONTACT: Michelle Leeder, UK Coordinator

THE DODWELL TRUST

16 Lanark Mansions, Pennard Road, London
W12 8DT

(0)20 8740 6302

dodwell@madagascar.freeserve.co.uk

www.dodwell-trust.org

PROGRAMME DESCRIPTION: Hands-on experience in English teaching, working with children, French-language conversation tuition, conservation, research, or zoology (depending on time of year).

DESTINATIONS: Madagascar

NUMBER OF PLACEMENTS PER YEAR: 60–70

PREREQUISITES: No skills required. All nationalities welcome, provided English is spoken. Age range normally 20–55. Older volunteers welcome and families with children. Placements matched with volunteers' skills and interests where possible: for example, local radio, French practice, tennis, song groups, conservation, and animal studies at zoo.

DURATION AND TIME OF PLACEMENTS: Three weeks to eight months. Flexible timing.

SELECTION PROCEDURES AND ORIENTATION: Interviews not essential, though frequent optional meetings and briefings are held in London. Two-day training and orientation course on arrival in Madagascar at placement. Volunteers normally placed in pairs.

COST: In-country placement costs from £670 for three weeks; £1,340 for 12 weeks. Self-contained accommodation with cooking facilities provided, in quaint small towns in highlands, rainforest, or seaside. Volunteers are responsible for obtaining their own visas and health insurance.

CONTACT: Christina Dodwell, Head of Projects

DRAGONFLY COMMUNITY FOUNDATION
1719 Mookamontri Soi 13, A. Meuang Nakhon Ratchasima, 30000 Thailand
 +66 4428 1073
 dan@thai-dragonfly.com
 www.thai-dragonfly.com

PROGRAMME DESCRIPTION: Charitable foundation in Thailand working on building, orphanage, and education projects. Volunteers are recruited to help with English teaching in schools and orphanages, and to build mud brick buildings as an affordable and environmentally friendly alternative to standard concrete buildings.

DESTINATIONS: Thailand

NUMBER OF PLACEMENTS PER YEAR: 50

PREREQUISITES: Good working knowledge of English (or Thai!), flexibility, and an open mind

DURATION AND TIME OF PLACEMENTS: Teaching project requires a minimum two-month commitment, up to four months. Building projects are more flexible, and any help that can be given is accepted if possible.

SELECTION PROCEDURES AND ORIENTATION: Preliminary contacts online; application forms processed by email followed by Skype interview

OTHER SERVICES: TEFL courses through local providers for teaching volunteers; choice of online option or courses based in beach towns in Thailand

COST: Teaching project training fee 3,000 Thai baht (£65); lunches and accommodation normally provided by schools. For building projects volunteers must cover their own costs. Donations to various projects gratefully accepted.

CONTACT: Dan Lockwood, Volunteer Projects Coordinator

EARTHWATCH INSTITUTE
Mayfield House, 256 Banbury Road, Oxford OX2 7DE
 (0)1865 318838
 info@earthwatch.org.uk
 www.earthwatch.org/europe

PROGRAMME DESCRIPTION: Founded in 1971, Earthwatch is an international environmental charity which offers conservation volunteering opportunities on scientific research expeditions worldwide: not eco-tourist trips. Earthwatch currently supports hundreds of expeditions on 61 projects in 29 countries. To ensure research addresses pressing global environmental issues, Earthwatch preferentially funds projects that fit the focus of one or more of the following priority research areas: climate change, oceans, ecosystem services, and cultural heritage. As an environmental charity it uses volunteers to help gather data. Expeditions are designed at the request of scientists who are trying to find solutions to pressing environmental problems.

DESTINATIONS: Volunteer field assistants needed throughout Europe and worldwide. European projects include monitoring whales and dolphins in Scotland, and contributing to climate change research in Oxford's Wytham Woods. International projects range from turtle conservation and coral reef research, to protecting wildlife in Kenya or the Peruvian Amazon.

NUMBER OF PLACEMENTS PER YEAR: Approximately 4,000

PREREQUISITES: Normal age limit is 18+ with no maximum, though there are some family teams (minimum age 10) and teen teams (for ages 16–18). All nationalities accepted.

DURATION AND TIME OF PLACEMENTS: Projects last one to 22 days throughout the year (see www.earthwatch.org/europe for expedition dates)

SELECTION PROCEDURES AND ORIENTATION: No previous experience or special skills necessary. Volunteers fill out a questionnaire and health form before participating on the project; no interview is required.

OTHER SERVICES: All volunteers receive a briefing pack prior to joining an expedition giving detailed information about the project, logistics, and general information about the area. All volunteers receive training at the expedition site before they start assisting the scientists. Accommodation provided, from study centres at the Arctic's edge to tents in the rainforest, or wildlife lodges in Kenya.

COST: From £195 to £2,195, given as a charitable donation to support the research. Cost covers training in the field, food, accommodation, medical emergency evacuation, and the offsetting of greenhouse gases. It does not include travel to the rendezvous site.

ECOLOGIA YOUTH TRUST
The Park, Forres, Moray IV36 3TD
(0)1309 690995
volunteer@ecologia.org.uk
www.ecologia.org.uk and www.kitezh.org

PROGRAMME DESCRIPTION: The Trust promotes creative change in Russia through youth, ecology, and education, working closely with the Kitezh Community of foster families. Volunteers, including gap year students and two or three adults, are placed at the Kitezh Children's Community for orphans in Kaluga region, western Russia, where they live with families, interact

with children, and take part in community life. Russian language is not essential, although students of Russian will quickly become fluent. Intensive Russian language courses are offered in spring and summer.

DESTINATIONS: Kaluga, Russia

PREREQUISITES: Reasonable knowledge of Russian language or experience teaching English as a foreign language, experience working with children (sports, arts and crafts, music, drama), building, cooking, and gardening. An interest in children and a willingness to participate fully in the life of the community are essential.

DURATION AND TIME OF PLACEMENTS: One to three months; additional months are at the discretion of the Kitezh Council

SELECTION PROCEDURES AND ORIENTATION: Introductory questionnaire followed by telephone interview required. Police check in country of residence required. Extensive preparatory materials are sent, including feedback from previous volunteers. Informal orientation given on arrival; weekly meeting with volunteer supervisor; and ongoing support from Ecologia Youth Trust via email.

COST: One month costs £1,105; two months £1,320. Costs include visa support, visa registration, transfer from Moscow to Kitezh return, and accommodation and food in Kitezh. Insurance, consular fee, and airfare are not included; flight costs from £220 from London. Cost of extended stay £130 per month.

CONTACT: Liza Hollingshead, Director

ECOTEER
23 Bearsdown Close, Plymouth PL6 5TX
(0)1752 426285
contact@ecoteer.com
www.ecoteer.com

PROGRAMME DESCRIPTION: Ecoteer is a non-profit organisation, with a collection of around 150 projects worldwide that need volunteers and are willing to provide food and accommodation at no, or at little, cost. Ecoteer projects prefer older volunteers because they have more experience and skills than younger volunteers. Volunteer openings are at eco lodges, conservation projects, farms, teaching, and humanitarian projects. Ecoteer provides contact information to members so they can organise their placement directly with the projects.

DESTINATIONS: Worldwide

NUMBER OF PLACEMENTS PER YEAR: 180

PREREQUISITES: Varies among projects. Most of the projects are remote, so require volunteers to be tolerant with a willingness to participate.

DURATION AND TIME OF PLACEMENTS: Minimum one month; no maximum

COST: Membership is £15 per year; £25 for a lifetime membership. Membership gives access to contact details for NGOs, etc, registered with Ecoteer, access to Ecoteer forums, and the chance to advertise yourself as a volunteer.

CONTACT: Daniel Quilter, Owner

EDUCATORS ABROAD LTD

5 Talfourd Way, Royal Earlswood Park, Redhill, Surrey RH1 6GD

(0)1737 785468/768254

craig@educatorsabroad.org

www.educatorsabroad.org

PROGRAMME DESCRIPTION: Company that manages and operates the English as a Foreign Language Teaching Assistant Program, for students and adults from the UK and other countries. Volunteer/college-sponsored programme open to adults as a non-credit certificate option, as well as to students. Participants assist teachers and students in ESL and EFL classes by bringing their native fluency in English to schools around the world.

DESTINATIONS: Over 25 countries on all continents

DURATION AND TIME OF PLACEMENTS: Four or 10 weeks throughout the year

COST: $500 placement fee plus $2,300–$4,200 depending on programme option; plus travel, and in some cases room and board. Host schools assist with arrangements for accommodation and board.

CONTACT: Dr Craig Kissock, Director

EXPERIENCE MEXECO LTD

38 Award Road, Fleet, Hampshire GU52 6HG (UK); #59 Valentín Gómez Farías, San Patricio Melaque, Jalisco (Mexico)

(0)1252 629411 (UK); +52 1 315 355 7027 (Mexico)

info@experiencemexeco.com

www.experiencemexeco.com or www.mex-ecotours.com

PROGRAMME DESCRIPTION: Sea turtle conservation, English teaching projects, community fundraising for special needs schools, physiotherapy placements, and other community-based projects.

DESTINATIONS: Pacific coast of Mexico

NUMBER OF PLACEMENTS PER YEAR: 30–35

PREREQUISITES: All nationalities and ages (average 19–26). All backgrounds welcomed as any necessary training is provided. Spanish is not a necessity as local staff speak English and Spanish.

DURATION AND TIME OF PLACEMENTS: One to three months

SELECTION PROCEDURES AND ORIENTATION: Applications should be in no less than one month before desired start date, though earlier preferred. Interview not required.

COST: £799–£899 for one month; £1,899–£1,999 for three months. Covers accommodation (homestay, private, or small tents on turtle project) and food throughout placement, plus insurance and 24-hour in-country support, but excludes flights.

CONTACT: Daniel Patman, Director

EXPERIENCE QUEST

15a Cambridge Grove, Hove, East Sussex BN3 3ED

(0)1273 777206

info@experiencequest.com

www.experiencequest.com or www.questoverseas.com

PROGRAMME DESCRIPTION: Sister organisation of Quest Overseas, a founding member of the Year Out Group. In addition to programmes of short two or three-week holidays, Experience Quest also offers tailor-made group expeditions in Africa and South America, combining worthwhile volunteer projects and challenging adventure travel: for example, trekking, safaris, scuba diving, and white water rafting. Expeditions combine work on well-supported volunteer projects, such as working with children or animals, undertaking scientific research, or constructing a school classroom.

DESTINATIONS: Africa and South America

NUMBER OF PLACEMENTS PER YEAR: 200+

PREREQUISITES: No qualifications needed, just enthusiasm

DURATION AND TIME OF PLACEMENTS: Tailor-made group expeditions from two weeks to three months

SELECTION PROCEDURES AND ORIENTATION: Application deadline is two weeks before departure

OTHER SERVICES: All participants receive a joining pack and access to help and advice. Tailor-made groups will be invited to a UK-based training event, which covers all topics in preparation for overseas travel and project work.

FLYING FISH

25 Union Road, Cowes, Isle of Wight PO31 7TW

✆ (0)1983 280641

✍ mail@flyingfishonline.com

💻 www.flyingfishonline.com

PROGRAMME DESCRIPTION: Member of the Year Out Group. Flying Fish trains water- and snow-sports staff, and arranges employment for sailors, divers, surfers, windsurfers, skiers, and snowboarders. Founded in 1993, Flying Fish provides travel, training, adventure, and professional qualifications for those looking to enjoy some time out, take a gap year, or start a career in water or snow sports. A year out with Flying Fish starts with a course leading to a qualification as a surf or windsurf instructor, a yacht skipper, or sailing instructor, divemaster and dive instructor, or a ski or snowboard instructor. For those not looking to work in the sports industry, training at professional level makes a challenging recreational course – offering personal adventure and the ability to perform at a high level.

DESTINATIONS: Training courses are run at Cowes in the UK, at Sydney and the Whitsunday Islands in Australia, Vassiliki in Greece, and Whistler in Canada. Jobs are worldwide, with main employers located in Australia, the South Pacific, the Caribbean, and the Mediterranean.

NUMBER OF PLACEMENTS PER YEAR: 900; almost equal numbers of men and women

PREREQUISITES: Ages 18–60+, from all around the world

DURATION AND TIME OF PLACEMENTS: Two to 19 weeks, with start dates year round

SELECTION PROCEDURES AND ORIENTATION: Applicants submit an application and, if looking for a career in the industry, may be asked to attend job interviews.

COST: Fees range from £1,100 to £11,000. Accommodation and airfares are provided, with normal wages during employment.

FRONTIER

50–52 Rivington St, London EC2A 3QP

✆ (0)20 7613 2422

✍ info@frontier.ac.uk

💻 www.frontier.ac.uk

PROGRAMME DESCRIPTION: Frontier offers a range of volunteering opportunities in conservation and community work, and also internships such as journalism and medicine.

DESTINATIONS: Nearly 50 countries worldwide

NUMBER OF PLACEMENTS PER YEAR: 500+

PREREQUISITES: No specific qualifications required as training is provided. Marine expeditions include free scuba diving training. Possibility of studying in the field for a BTEC Advanced Diploma in Tropical Habitat Conservation, or a BTEC Advanced Certificate in Expedition Management.

DURATION AND TIME OF PLACEMENTS: Four, eight, 10, or 20 weeks

SELECTION PROCEDURES AND ORIENTATION: Open days are held twice monthly (Saturday mornings and Wednesday evenings, as listed on website). After an application has been submitted and a telephone briefing taken place, applicants will hear within a week whether they have been accepted. Prior to the expedition, a briefing weekend is held in the UK.

COST: Depending on location and duration, international volunteers raise from £1,200 for four weeks, £1,700 for eight weeks, £2,000 for ten weeks and £3,000 for 20 weeks – which covers all individual costs, including a UK weekend briefing, scientific and dive training, travel, visas, insurance, food, and accommodation, but excludes flights.

GAPFORCE
21 Heathmans Road, London SW6 4TJ
(0)20 7384 3028
info@gapforce.org
www.gapforce.org

PROGRAMME DESCRIPTION: Member of the Year Out Group; merger of brands Trekforce and Greenforce. Participants work as Fieldwork Assistants on various marine and terrestrial projects, carrying out tasks such as tracking animal movements and studying coral reef species. Training is provided, including diver training for the marine expeditions and language training for the terrestrial expeditions. Internships, sport volunteering, teaching, community work, and many other projects also arranged worldwide. Participants on Trekforce expeditions to Belize, Borneo, and Amazon live with remote tribes, learn about their culture and customs, explore jungles, deserts and mountains, help build sustainable communities, and assist with rainforest conservation and scientific projects. Programmes can incorporate a combination of expedition jungle training, project work, a Spanish language course, teaching in rural communities, trekking, adventure, and dive phases. A 16-week expedition leader course also available.

DESTINATIONS: Fiji, the Bahamas, Tanzania, India, Nepal, China, South Africa, Ecuador, and Australia (for working holiday makers, visit www.ozforce.org)

NUMBER OF PLACEMENTS PER YEAR: 1,000

PREREQUISITES: No previous experience is necessary and no qualifications are required, as training will be provided in the field

DURATION AND TIME OF PLACEMENTS: Six, eight, or ten weeks in Fiji (conserving coral reef); up to 12 months in China, Ecuador, Australia, and Africa.

SELECTION PROCEDURES AND ORIENTATION: Applicants may attend one of the regular informal open days in central London. A briefing pack is provided on application, giving information about fundraising and relevant medical advice, etc, and participants can attend a training day prior to joining the project (cost included in contribution). The first week of the expedition is spent undertaking further training and familiarisation with the project and host country.

COST: Sample prices are £2,300 for six weeks, and £2,600 for ten weeks dive training and project in Fiji; £4,200 for a five-month Belize expedition. Fees cover training and instruction, food, accommodation, and in-country transport, but not insurance and international flights. Fundraising advice is given to all participants.

GAP YEAR FOR GROWN UPS
1st Floor, 1 Meadow Road, Tunbridge Wells
TN1 2YG
(0)1892 701881
info@gapyearforgrownups.co.uk
www.gapyearforgrownups.co.uk or www.
realgap.co.uk

PROGRAMME DESCRIPTION: Part of the Real Travel Group, including Real Gap Experience for the 18–30 market. Choice of volunteer and travel options around the world, including a bespoke 'Design-your-own-gap-year' service. Range of travel and volunteer programmes includes working with children and adults in deprived communities, conservation volunteering, working with wildlife, paid work, learning a new skill (such as a language), PADI dive course, or farm skills on an outback property.

DESTINATIONS: Australasia, Africa, Asia, Eastern Europe, Latin America, North America, and Round-the-World.

PREREQUISITES: Programmes vary, but most are open to all ages and backgrounds

DURATION AND TIME OF PLACEMENTS: Two weeks to six months, with four weeks being typical. Departures year round

COST: Varies with programme. Sample fees are £1,049 for teaching project on the Galapagos Islands, and £1,399 for four weeks of volunteering at an orphanage in India (exclusive to grown-ups).

GAP YEAR IN ASIA
See WLS International Ltd

GAP YEAR THAILAND
1 Vernon Avenue, Rugby CV22 5HL
(0)1788 552617 or (0)7899 887276
david@gapyearthailand.org.uk
www.gapyearthailand.org.uk

PROGRAMME DESCRIPTION: Professional education organisation, whose key team members have a background in teacher education in universities in the UK, or in the Rajabhat Universities (teacher training universities) in Thailand. The programme is approved and endorsed by the South East Asian Ministers of Education Organisation. Gap Year Thailand specialises only in Thailand, providing placements for volunteers as assistant teachers, teaching English (particularly conversational English) in schools or universities.

DESTINATIONS: Thailand

NUMBER OF PLACEMENTS PER YEAR: 20+

PREREQUISITES: Minimum age 18, but more mature volunteers are preferred by the schools and universities. Must speak English as a first language. Teaching qualification not needed.

DURATION AND TIME OF PLACEMENTS: Minimum two months, up to six months or more

SELECTION PROCEDURES AND ORIENTATION: Applications accepted throughout the year, followed by telephone interviews. Pre-departure briefing weekend

with some TEFL training, and further training in the orientation programme on arrival.

COST: £980, including accommodation – which can be homestay with family or in a teacher's house

CONTACT: Dr David Lancaster, Chief Executive

GLOBALTEER
Globalteer House, TheaChamrat Road, Wat Bo Village, Salakamroeuk Commune, Siem Reap, Cambodia
+855 (0) 63761802
info@globalteer.org
www.globalteer.org

PROGRAMME DESCRIPTION: Globalteer provides financial support and volunteers to teach and assist in the daily running of their partner in-country projects in five countries. In Cambodia, they work with four projects in Siem Reap to assist over 800 underprivileged Khmer children, and build water filters for rural communities. In Mondulkiri, Cambodia, the projects assist the indigenous Bunong hill tribe people, the elephants, and conserve the forest. There are also projects to help orphaned and street children in Peru and Colombia, and projects working with wildlife in Thailand and Indonesia.

DESTINATIONS: Cambodia, Thailand, Indonesia, Peru, and Colombia

PREREQUISITES: No maximum age as long as volunteers are fit and healthy, and can tolerate some climatic extremes. Knowledge of English preferred.

DURATION AND TIME OF PLACEMENTS: One week to three months

SELECTION PROCEDURES AND ORIENTATION: Applications should be sent at least two months in advance. Late applications accepted where there is availability. Each project has a volunteer coordinator to liaise with local staff.

COST: Each project asks for a donation for the volunteer placement depending on duration, which helps to fund the project. Donations (as listed on website) cover accommodation, airport pick up, in-country support, administration costs, and a direct donation to the project.

CONTACT: Each of the nine projects across five countries has a separate email contact, available from info@globalteer.org

---

GLOBAL VISION INTERNATIONAL (GVI)
3rd Floor, The Senate, Exeter EX1 1UG
(0)1727 250250
info@gvi.co.uk
www.gvi.co.uk

PROGRAMME DESCRIPTION: GVI offers 150+ projects in over 40 countries worldwide, on conservation and community expeditions, volunteer projects, and internships throughout Africa, Latin America, Europe, and Asia. Internships for prospective volunteers include training to become a safari field guide in South Africa, marine biology and conservation in Mexico and the Seychelles, and childcare in indigenous communities throughout Latin America. Training options and support for career prospects available on selected projects. Some projects are also available to families.

DESTINATIONS: Mexico, Costa Rica, Guatemala, Honduras, Nicaragua, Panama, Belize, Ecuador, Brazil, Peru, Nepal, India, Sri Lanka, Thailand, South Africa, Kenya, Namibia, Ghana, Uganda, Seychelles, Tanzania, Madagascar, Indonesia, Borneo, and Vanuatu

DURATION AND TIME OF PLACEMENTS: One week to two years

SELECTION PROCEDURES AND ORIENTATION: Online application, plus application assessment

COST: From £475 for some short-term projects in Latin America, to £3,995 for a year-long internship in South Africa. Price for marine conservation expedition in the Seychelles starts at £1,745 for five weeks, including scuba diving equipment, training and accommodation.

GLOBAL VOLUNTEER NETWORK
PO Box 30-968, Lower Hutt, New Zealand
+64 4 569 9080
info@volunteer.org.nz
www.globalvolunteernetwork.org

PROGRAMME DESCRIPTION: Volunteers recruited for a variety of educational, community aid, health/medical, environmental/conservation, construction, and wildlife programmes, and cultural homestays in 22 countries.

DESTINATIONS: Cambodia, China, Costa Rica, Ecuador, Ethiopia, Ghana, Guatemala, Honduras, India, Kenya, Nepal, New Zealand, Peru, Philippines, South Africa, Thailand, Uganda, Vietnam, and South Dakota (USA)

NUMBER OF PLACEMENTS PER YEAR: Approx 2,000

PREREQUISITES: No special skills or qualifications needed in most programmes. All ages and nationalities placed, although projects in China and Romania accept only Australian, Canadian, European, Irish, British, American and New Zealand nationals.

DURATION AND TIME OF PLACEMENTS: Two weeks to 12 months, depending on the placement. Applications accepted year round

OTHER SERVICES: Fundraising treks are also offered to Everest Base Camp, Mount Kilimanjaro, and Machu Picchu.

COST: US$350 application fee to GVN covers personal staff support, programme guide, fundraising guide and software, access to your online journal, and online video 'Preparing for your trip'. Programme fees start at US$597 per month in China. Fees cover training, accommodation and meals during training and placement, supervision, and project transport (but not international airfares).

CONTACT: Colin Salisbury, Founder and President

GLOBAL VOLUNTEER PROJECTS
7–15 Pink Lane, Newcastle upon Tyne NE1 5DW
(0)191 222 0404
info@globalvolunteerprojects.org
www.globalvolunteerprojects.org

PROGRAMME DESCRIPTION: Range of volunteer and work experience projects, especially for people hoping to go/change into medicine or the subjects allied to medicine – such as physiotherapy, dentistry, and nursing – and people looking for work experience in journalism. Opportunities also available to help with teaching, conservation, and orphanage work in local communities. Most programmes include basic language courses as well as 'culture' courses, such as drumming in Ghana, yoga in India, or learning Swahili in Tanzania. Orphanages and panda project are the most popular with career breakers.

DESTINATIONS: Ghana, Tanzania, China, India, Cambodia, Mexico, and Romania

NUMBER OF PLACEMENTS PER YEAR: 100–200

PREREQUISITES: All ages

DURATION AND TIME OF PLACEMENTS: Two weeks to one year. Most join for one month (summer) or three months. Projects available throughout the year.

SELECTION PROCEDURES AND ORIENTATION: Applications must be submitted at least four weeks prior to departure. References must be provided and CRB checks are compulsory for projects involving work with children. Journalism projects include time on a media course (unless you have a background in media or a media related degree), and some of the medical projects include time in lectures at a medical college. Participants require visas for nearly all programmes; visa support given.

COST: Ranges from £995 to £1,795 for one-month projects

CONTACT: Kevin Dynan, Founder and Director

THE GREAT PROJECTS

Studio Six, 8 High St, Harpenden, Herts AL5 2TB

(0)845 3713070 or (0)1582 469950

volunteer@w-o-x.com

www.thegreatprojects.com

PROGRAMME DESCRIPTION: Trading name of Way Out Experiences Ltd. Formerly the Great Orangutan Project but now expanded to other species. Highly commended in 2010 in the Virgin Responsible Tourism Awards, in Best Volunteer Organisations category. Company aims to provide privileged access to wildlife (orangutans, baboons, dolphins, etc) on hand-picked conservation projects in selected countries.

DESTINATIONS: Borneo, Uganda, Peru, and India

PREREQUISITES: All welcome. 85% are more mature volunteers, eg on career breaks.

DURATION AND TIME OF PLACEMENTS: Two or four weeks

SELECTION PROCEDURES AND ORIENTATION: Trips are escorted by at least one tour leader or facilitator, so orientation and training on handling and rehabilitating the species takes place on-site.

COST: £995–£1,250 for two weeks; £1,850–£2,000 for four weeks, including everything except flights. 25%–40% of this fee goes as a contribution to the project.

CONTACT: Afzaal Mauthoor, Managing Director

HANDS AROUND THE WORLD

PO Box 117, Monmouth, South Wales NP25 9AR

(0)1600 740317

info@hatw.org.uk

www.hatw.org.uk

PROGRAMME DESCRIPTION: HATW seeks to help vulnerable children around the world by sending volunteers on short-term placements. Volunteers work alongside local people as encouragers and skill-sharers. Building projects sometimes available, for which participants do not need building skills.

DESTINATIONS: Africa, India, and Brazil

NUMBER OF PLACEMENTS PER YEAR: 40

PREREQUISITES: Ages 21–75; average age 45. All nationalities accepted, though must be available in the UK before placement. HATW particularly encourages people with childcare-related skills to apply – such as primary school teachers, foster carers, teaching assistants, physiotherapists, and occupational therapists – though all are welcome. Must be prepared for simple living conditions as provided free by host: often a mattress on the floor, a 'hole-in-the-ground' toilet, and no electricity.

DURATION AND TIME OF PLACEMENTS: Three weeks to six months, though minimum preferred stay is two months

SELECTION PROCEDURES AND ORIENTATION: Applications must be submitted at least 12 weeks prior to departure. All prospective volunteers must meet for an informal chat normally at HATW office in South Wales, or if necessary, on Skype. All accepted volunteers are sent a handbook of tips for preparing for their project, health and safety advice, packing list, emergency plan, country profile, insurance details, child protection statement of commitment, and information on debriefing policy. In addition, all volunteers attend a three-hour orientation session that covers cultural sensitivities, health and safety, local language, and ways to get the most out of the project. Volunteers are put in touch with their host and with past volunteers. They are also sent a fundraising handbook containing tips, ideas and templates.

COST: £2,000 contribution (no matter the length of the placement), which includes flight costs, visa and insurance, and a donation to HATW. Volunteers pay for their own immunisations, anti-malarials, food, internal transport, and any holiday breaks.

CONTACT: Joanna Touray, Education & Development Manager

HELP (HIMALAYAN EDUCATION LIFELINE PROGRAMME)

30 Kingsdown Park, Whitstable, Kent CT5 2DF

✆ (0)1227 263055

✉ help@help-education.org

💻 www.help-education.org

PROGRAMME DESCRIPTION: HELP enables young people from poor communities in the Himalayas (Nepal and India) to improve their employment opportunities through education, by providing financial and volunteer resources to their schools. Volunteer teachers and nurses work in needy schools targeted by HELP.

DESTINATIONS: Needy schools in the Kathmandu Valley, Pokhara, and western region of Nepal, as well as in Sikkim, Ladakh, and Uttarakhand in India.

PREREQUISITES: Ages 19/20–60+. Teaching experience and/or TEFL qualifications are essential. Those without are expected to take a short intensive TEFL course before their assignment. Volunteers should be mature and resourceful people who can hit the ground

running. Qualities needed include resilience and adaptability, an open mind, and an interest in other cultures, good mental and physical health, plus tact and diplomacy. A love of, and experience with, children is vital.

DURATION AND TIME OF PLACEMENTS: Two months normally (one month is acceptable for practising teachers fitting their volunteering into their school holidays). Volunteers can stay for a maximum of six months (for visa reasons).

SELECTION PROCEDURES AND ORIENTATION: Applications accepted year round. Telephone interview is conducted after receipt of the online application form. Volunteers receive a briefing pack, and advice is given by email and/or over the phone.

COST: From £390, depending on volunteer's status and length of stay, including accommodation with host families or in school hostel.

CONTACT: Jim Coleman, Executive Director

HOPE AND HOME

Travel & Volunteer Program, Lazimpat, Kathmandu, (PO Box 119, Kathmandu) Nepal

✆ +977 1 4439097

✉ info@hopenhome.org or hopeandhome@gmail.com

💻 www.hopenhome.org

PROGRAMME DESCRIPTION: Community-oriented volunteer and adventure opportunities for international volunteers, in a quest to find sustainable solutions for education, health, conservation, and development issues through volunteering. Volunteer opportunities are in the fields of teaching English, ecotourism, orphanages, community health, nature conservation, school and community maintenance, and homestay/cultural exchange.

DESTINATIONS: Nepal (Kathmandu Valley, Kavre, Pokhara, Chitwan and Nawalparasi)

NUMBER OF PLACEMENTS PER YEAR: 55–60

PREREQUISITES: Ages 18–35. All that is needed is a genuine desire to help people.

DURATION AND TIME OF PLACEMENTS: Two weeks to three months

SELECTION PROCEDURES AND ORIENTATION: Online applications accepted year round

OTHER SERVICES: Language class, heritage sightseeing, cultural information, and project information provided.

COST: Volunteer fees entirely fund programme, and include homestay accommodation and food. From $350 for two weeks, $700 for six weeks, to $1,000 for three months.

CONTACT: Rabyn Aryal, Director

IALC (INTERNATIONAL ASSOCIATION OF LANGUAGE CENTRES)
Lombard House, 12/17 Upper Bridge St,
Canterbury, Kent CT1 2NF
℡ (0)1227 769007
🖳 info@ialc.org
🖥 www.ialc.org

PROGRAMME DESCRIPTION: Language school association that accredits private language schools, with 100 members in 24 countries. Diverse range of language programmes in French, German, Italian, Japanese, Chinese, Portuguese, Russian, and Spanish, ranging from short-term general courses to specialised courses combining language with culture, cookery, dance, art, sport, etc. Some IALC schools offer work experience or volunteering.

SELECTION PROCEDURES AND ORIENTATION:
Canterbury office is not a booking office. Contact details for member schools appear on the IALC website.

OTHER SERVICES: Accommodation is normally a choice of family stay, hall of residence, guesthouse, or flat-share

CONTACT: Jan Capper

ICYE UK (INTER-CULTURAL YOUTH EXCHANGE)
Latin American House, Kingsgate Place, London
NW6 4TA
℡ (0)20 7681 0983
🖳 info@icye.org.uk
🖥 www.icye.org.uk

PROGRAMME DESCRIPTION: ICYE is a registered charity (charity No. 1081907), and a unique user-led organisation facilitating cultural exchanges throughout the world. ICYE-UK is a member of the international ICYE

Federation, with over 60 years of volunteering experience. ICYE's core programme is a reciprocal six to 12 month exchange programme. Recently it has introduced a short-term programme (STePs) to give applicants the flexibility to volunteer as a break from employment, studies, or as part of a longer trip. All ICYE programmes place an emphasis on inter-cultural understanding and integration into local communities, and the vast majority of ICYE volunteers live with host families. Many ICYE projects are social and community-based, such as working with street children, HIV/AIDS education, working in disability support, or volunteering as a teaching assistant. Eco-projects such as conservation work and caring for animals are also available in some partner countries.

DESTINATIONS: Throughout Africa, Asia, Latin America and Eastern Europe (see website)

NUMBER OF PLACEMENTS PER YEAR: ICYE sends around 80 volunteers overseas every year, as well as hosting around 45 international volunteers at worthwhile projects throughout the UK.

PREREQUISITES: No formal qualification or previous experience is necessary, but applicants must be open-minded and committed to intercultural learning and volunteering. ICYE's Long Term Programme is open to 18–30 year olds, although older applicants can be considered on a case-by-case basis. The Short Term Programme is open to volunteers of any age over 18 years old.

DURATION AND TIME OF PLACEMENTS: The Long Term programme begins in August and January, and lasts six or 12 months. The Short Term programme offers year-round departures (starting the first Monday of every month), and placements last three to 16 weeks.

COST: ICYE's programme fee includes return flights, insurance, visa support, accommodation, daily meals, pocket money (long term only), pre-departure and on-arrival training, language course (long-term only), full international administration, and on-going support. The 12-month programme fee is £4,495 and six months is £3,795. The short-term programme starts from £1,600 for four weeks, and varies according to country and length of stay. ICYE offers full fundraising support. Volunteers also have the opportunity to apply for bursaries of £750–£1,500.

173

CONTACT: Jenny Williams (Long-term Coordinator); Sarahgwen Sheldon (Short-term Coordinator for Latin America, Asia and Europe); Charlotte Dando (Short-term Coordinator for Africa)

IKO PORAN ASSOCIATION

Rua do Oriente 280/201, Santa Teresa, Rio de Janeiro (RJ), CEP: 20.240-130, Brazil

☏ +55 21 3852 2917

✉ rj@ikoporan.org

🖥 www.ikoporan.org

PROGRAMME DESCRIPTION: Volunteers are assigned to various autonomous development projects. Iko Poran is always forging new links with Brazilian NGOs, who can use the services of volunteers.

DESTINATIONS: Brazil (Rio de Janeiro only)

NUMBER OF PLACEMENTS PER YEAR: 300–400

PREREQUISITES: Average age range 20–30, but accept volunteers up to 70. All nationalities welcome.

DURATION AND TIME OF PLACEMENTS: Three to 24 weeks, according to volunteer's availability. Maximum of 24 weeks is for visa reasons.

SELECTION PROCEDURES AND ORIENTATION: Applications accepted up to one week before arrival. Volunteers fill out an extensive application form detailing their interests, abilities, and reasons for joining an international volunteer programme. Police certificate needed by volunteers who want to work with children.

OTHER SERVICES: Upon arrival, volunteers are picked up from airport and given an orientation that includes a welcome pack, info on neighbourhood facilities and public transport, maps and guides, safety tips, and so on. A 20-hour Portuguese language course is included in the programme fee.

COST: Programme fee is R$2,100 (US$1,235/£750) with the Portuguese course or US$941/£572 without the language lessons. Fee covers lodging in one of Iko Poran's comfortable volunteer houses for the first four weeks and a donation of R$400 to the project. Additional weeks cost R$180, including accommodation.

CONTACT: Luis Felipe Murray, General Coordinator

IMPACT TRAVEL

The Beeches, Grammar School Lane, Kirkham, Preston PR4 2DJ

☏ (0)1772 672098

✉ info@impacttravel.co.uk

🖥 www.impacttravel.co.uk

PROGRAMME DESCRIPTION: Impact Travel believes in socially-responsible travel and that communities where a meaningful relationship has been developed with local schools should be given ongoing support. Selected few gap year-style volunteer projects in India and Nepal, such as working in needy schools and orphanages. Also offers short escorted trips, including participation for a week in a community volunteer project.

DESTINATIONS: India and Nepal

NUMBER OF PLACEMENTS PER YEAR: 30

PREREQUISITES: No age or nationality restrictions

DURATION AND TIME OF PLACEMENTS: One week to one year for volunteering, but most are no longer than one month

SELECTION PROCEDURES AND ORIENTATION: Discussions arranged to suit the volunteers. Cultural awareness training and specific advice on teaching preparation is available so that volunteer teachers are ready to face their classrooms.

COST: From £200 for one week (project only), to £800 for one-month placements with accommodation. Escorted flagship tours costing £2,000 include extensive travel itinerary, quality accommodation (with homestay options), transport, and an insight into the communities visited.

CONTACT: Jeremy Mannino, Company Partner

INSPIRE VOLUNTEERING

Town Hall, Market Place, Newbury RG14 5AA

☏ (0)1635 45556

✉ info@inspirevolunteer.co.uk

🖥 www.inspirevolunteer.co.uk

PROGRAMME DESCRIPTION: Inspire provides ethical and sustainable volunteer opportunities in underprivileged communities overseas. Each volunteer's skills and aspirations are matched to projects in genuine need, ensuring that volunteers maximise their impact and experience. Volunteers work closely with local communities, NGOs, and charities to support teaching, childcare, healthcare, livelihood support community and conservation programmes, helping to achieve the long-term development goals of the FutureSense Foundation, a UK registered charity.

DESTINATIONS: India, Tanzania, Nepal, Sri Lanka, Romania, South Africa, Ecuador, Chile, The Gambia

NUMBER OF PLACEMENTS PER YEAR: Approximately 200

PREREQUISITES: Volunteers must be aged 18 or over. All nationalities accepted. Business experience necessary for business development programmes. Relevant experience useful for other programmes, but not essential. Volunteers must have enthusiasm, flexibility, and good communication skills.

DURATION AND TIME OF PLACEMENTS: Programmes last from two weeks to six months, with flexible start dates all year round

SELECTION PROCEDURES AND ORIENTATION: Application can be made online or by phone, with acceptance subject to an informal interview and receipt of references. Volunteers are provided with pre-departure briefing, and given local orientation by in-country teams on arrival.

OTHER SERVICES: Inspire offers specialised travel programmes in India, Nepal, and Tanzania. Trips include treks, safaris, and cultural tours, and are fully guided.

COST: Costs vary depending on location and project type, but start from £545 for a two-week placement. All accommodation and some meals are included.

CONTACT: Prakriti Malhotra

INTERNATIONAL ACADEMY
Sophia House, 28 Cathedral Road, Cardiff
CF11 9LJ
(0)29 2066 0200
info@international-academy.com
www.international-academy.com

PROGRAMME DESCRIPTION: Ski and snowboard instructor training courses, run in partnership with the resident ski and snowboard schools in various resorts worldwide. Courses lead to recognised CSIA, CASI, BASI, NZSIA, or SBINZ qualifications. Professional programmes aimed at personal development and the improvement of technical/teaching skills.

DESTINATIONS: Courses are run in Whistler Blackcomb, Banff/Lake Louise, and Castle Mountain in Canada; Val d'Isere/Tignes and Chatel in France; Verbier in Switzerland; and Cardrona Alpine Resort in New Zealand

DURATION AND TIME OF PLACEMENTS: Five to 12 weeks

COST: £3,950–£8,450, depending on course duration and resort

CONTACT: Alan Bates, General Manager

IST PLUS LTD
Rosedale House, Rosedale Road, Richmond, Surrey TW9 2SZ
(0)20 8939 9057
info@istplus.com
www.istplus.com

PROGRAMME DESCRIPTION: Work, teaching, and study abroad programmes for UK students, graduates, and professionals. Programmes that are open to grown-up gappers include Professional Career Training (PCT) in the USA (for ages 20–40), Work & Travel Australia (maximum age 30), Work & Travel New Zealand (maximum age 30), Teach in China (maximum age 65), and Teach in Thailand (maximum age 65). IST Plus also offers a Volunteer Programme, helping disadvantaged children in Thailand (recommended maximum age 30).

DESTINATIONS: China, Thailand, USA, Australia, and New Zealand

NUMBER OF PLACEMENTS PER YEAR: Unlimited

COST: Australia £320; New Zealand £195; Asian teaching programmes £995–£1,095; PCT in the USA starts at £740, excluding travel; Volunteer Thailand programme from £325

Volunteering abroad with Inspire opens up a world of new opportunities and experiences, and provides an ideal way to use your skills to make a difference.

Tony Arthur volunteered at care homes in Romania, where he found great reward in sharing the skills he had gained from years of teaching and travel. Having come to the end of a teaching career that had taken him as far as Russia and Uganda, Tony was keen to make use of his retirement and found himself drawn to the challenge of volunteering in Romania. During his placement Tony worked in care homes and schools in Miercurea Ciuc, where he taught English and cared for children from difficult backgrounds.

For Tony, 'volunteering was a very positive experience and one that was richly rewarding. Children in Miercurea Ciuc are starved of the individual attention and luxuries that we take for granted, so to be able to teach and share new experiences with them was incredibly fulfilling'.

Tony's background in teaching meant that as well as helping the children to improve their English, he was able to spend time coaching local teachers in lesson planning techniques and improving their conversational English.

Tony's advice for other travellers is to 'be flexible and patient. Don't travel with any preconceptions and be prepared to adapt and go with the flow!' Volunteers who are prepared to immerse themselves in their project work can gain a real insight into the culture of their host community.

Having enjoyed his time in Romania in 2010, Tony is set to return to the same volunteer project this year. He is also keen to explore options for teaching in India and Tanzania, as well as getting involved with the work of the FutureSense Foundation, a UK-registered charity that volunteers work to support on the Inspire programme.

Tony's experiences highlight the positive impact volunteering can have on both volunteers and host communities. Inspire Volunteering offers a range of programmes that give volunteers like Tony the chance to make the most of their time off and share their skills with those in greatest need.

Volunteers often get involved with extra-curricular activities at schools

IT training in a Tanzanian village

Dini Peterson at Street Kids Project in Knysna, South Africa. Photo kindly supplied by Dini Peterson.

Volunteers supervise small grant schemes in Tanzania, enabling families affected by HIV/AIDS to sustain livelihoods

Volunteer vs. Monks' XI

Ann Knight volunteering at the Naan ku se wildlife sanctuary in Namibia. Photo kindly supplied by Ann Knight.

A rural agricultural project in Darjeeling, India

Assisting at a Maasai women's market

clic

... just clic!

Spanish Courses

in Seville and Cadiz

*amar, vivir
y sentir
en español*

Teacher Training Institute

English Teacher Training

CELTA and DELTA

Seville **T** 954 502 131
Cadiz **T** 956 255 455

www.clic.es   clic@clic.es   www.tefl.es

International House Sevilla y Cádiz
A MEMBER OF THE INTERNATIONAL HOUSE WORLD ORGANISATION

Volunteers run arts and crafts activities in Ecuador

i-to-i TEFL

Woodside House, 261 Low Lane, Leeds LS18 5NY

☎ (0)113 205 4610

🖥 www.i-to-i.com or www.onlinetefl.com

PROGRAMME DESCRIPTION: i-to-i TEFL specialises in online and short TEFL courses, including a 20 hour weekend course of hands-on, face-to-face training. Free TEFL Jobs Placement Service is offered to participants to put them in touch with possible employers in South Korea, Japan, Ecuador, etc. i-to-i also offers fee-paying candidates teaching internships in China, Poland and Thailand.

DESTINATIONS: Online TEFL course can be taken anywhere, as long as there is internet access. Classroom courses are in various locations in the UK, Europe, Asia, and the US.

PREREQUISITES: No previous experience needed – only have to be fluent English speaker

DURATION AND TIME OF PLACEMENTS: Courses are flexible and course extensions can be arranged

SELECTION PROCEDURES AND ORIENTATION: No pre-course test. TEFL Job Placement Service or paid internships are available to candidates who meet application criteria (see website). Once accepted, i-to-i's partners provide full information, visa assistance, and in-country orientation.

COST: Online TEFL training from £129

i-to-i VOLUNTEER & ADVENTURE TRAVEL

Woodside House, 261 Low Lane, Horsforth, Leeds LS18 5NY

☎ (0)113 205 0076

✉ info@i-to-i.com

🖥 www.i-to-i.com

PROGRAMME DESCRIPTION: A founding member of the Year Out Group, i-to-i is a commercial company now owned by giant tour operator TUI Travel PLC. i-to-i is partnered with more than 500 projects in 23 countries, involving teaching, conservation, community work, building, sports, and humanitarian tours.

DESTINATIONS: Argentina, Brazil, Cambodia, China, Costa Rica, Ecuador, Honduras, India, Indonesia, Kenya, Malaysia, Nepal, Peru, Philippines, South Africa, Sri Lanka, Tanzania, Thailand, Uganda, Vietnam, and Zambia. Community teaching and conservation projects take place in most countries, whilst more career-focussed programmes – including marketing, media, and tourism – are available in selected countries.

NUMBER OF PLACEMENTS PER YEAR: Approximately 5,000

PREREQUISITES: Most projects require no experience or qualifications, although some skills-development placements (eg, media) require a CV. Teaching programmes include an i-to-i TEFL training course prior to arrival in country (see entry above).

DURATION AND TIME OF PLACEMENTS: From one week to a full year out, starting year round

SELECTION PROCEDURES AND ORIENTATION: Volunteer placements include full pre-departure support, but there is no formal selection process. i-to-i provide full project information packs and in-country orientation, plus accommodation and meals. All teaching placements include a free i-to-i online TEFL course.

COST: Sample costs are £799 for four weeks working with underprivileged families in Goa, India; and £1,799 for 12 weeks working with disadvantaged children in South Africa (excluding airfares)

JAPAN EXCHANGE & TEACHING (JET) PROGRAMME UK

JET Desk, Embassy of Japan, 101–104 Piccadilly, London W1J 7JT

☎ (0)20 7465 6668

✉ info@jet-uk.org

🖥 www.jet-uk.org

PROGRAMME DESCRIPTION: The JET Programme is a well-established initiative in the field of cultural exchange, and provides opportunities for those contemplating a career break or change of career. The Japan Exchange & Teaching (JET) Programme is a Japanese government-run scheme to promote international understanding and improve foreign language tuition. UK graduates have the opportunity of working in educational institutions throughout Japan for a minimum of one year.

DESTINATIONS: Throughout Japan

NUMBER OF PLACEMENTS PER YEAR: Approximately 200 places are offered to UK candidates, however the number varies each year

PREREQUISITES: Must have a Bachelor's degree in any subject and be under 39 years of age by the time of departure. Neither teaching qualifications nor Japanese language ability is needed for the Assistant Language Teacher (ALT) positions; however the Coordinator for International Relations (CIR) role does require Japanese language ability sufficient for everyday working situations.

DURATION AND TIME OF PLACEMENTS: 12-month renewable contracts starting in late July. Normal working hours are 35 per week, although teaching hours are between 15 and 20.

SELECTION PROCEDURES AND ORIENTATION: The application deadline is usually the last Friday in November. Interviews take place in London and Edinburgh in January and February, with decisions given in April. JET finds placement, organises visa and insurance, hosts two-day pre-departure orientation in London or Edinburgh in July, beginners' TEFL training and basic Japanese language course, two-day orientation in Tokyo upon arrival, language books, and return flights provided.

COST: None. There is no application fee and return airfares are provided to those who complete their contract. Salary of 3,600,000 yen paid (currently worth over £27,000).

KAYA RESPONSIBLE TRAVEL
Technology House, Lissadel Street, Salford, Manchester M6 6AP
✆ (0)161 870 6212
✉ info@kayavolunteer.com
🖥 www.kayavolunteer.com

PROGRAMME DESCRIPTION: Responsible travel organisation supporting grassroots voluntary projects worldwide, and giving volunteers an opportunity to contribute to positive action and enjoy travelling the world more responsibly. Volunteers are placed in local projects in the fields of environmental conservation and community development, in Asia, Africa, and Latin America. Work experience can be combined with travel, and a chance to live and work alongside the community.

DESTINATIONS: Belize, Bolivia, Costa Rica, Brazil, Ecuador, Peru, Mexico; Ghana, Tanzania, Zambia, Kenya, Zimbabwe, S Africa, Mozambique, Botswana; India, Nepal, Thailand, Vietnam, Philippines

NUMBER OF PLACEMENTS PER YEAR: 250+ in 2010; up to 500 in 2011

PREREQUISITES: Volunteers are aged 18–80; average age around 33. All level of skills accepted. Anyone with enthusiasm, passion, openness, and a willing attitude to hard work can contribute to some of the world's neediest communities. Volunteers with specific skills such as medical, teaching, business, and construction are matched with appropriate placements.

DURATION AND TIME OF PLACEMENTS: Two weeks to six or 12 months

SELECTION PROCEDURES AND ORIENTATION: Rolling applications throughout the year. Bookings preferred three months in advance, though last-minute placements are also possible. Business visas needed for some projects, for which Kaya assists. CRB check is required in some cases. Pre-departure training packs are given and all volunteers are picked up at the destination airport and taken to their homestay or volunteer accommodation.

COST: Project fees vary from project to project and country to country, but start from £625 for two weeks, with an additional fee of £175 per week after that. Discounts can be negotiated for stays of longer than 13 weeks, and for multiple projects and/or locations.

CONTACT: Nicci Hawkins, Placement Adviser

LANGUAGE COURSES ABROAD LTD
67-71 Ashby Road, Loughborough, Leicestershire LE11 3AA
✆ (0)1509 211612
✉ info@languagesabroad.co.uk
🖥 www.languagesabroad.co.uk

Language Courses Abroad Ltd. is a UK-based language travel agency, offering in-country full immersion language courses at more than 100 schools. Trading name is Apple Languages (www.applelanguages.com).

PROGRAMME DESCRIPTION: Standard or intensive language courses offered as combination of group course and private lessons, or as specialist language course with activity programme. Language courses are offered in Spanish, French, German, Italian, Portuguese, Russian, Chinese, Japanese, Greek and others.

PREREQUISITES: All ages, including clients in their 30s, 40s and older. Club 50+ language courses are offered in a number of destinations for people in their 50s and older (details on www.languagesabroad.co.uk/third_age).

DURATION AND TIME OF PLACEMENTS: One to 36 weeks

OTHER SERVICES: Accommodation can be shared self-catering student apartments, private studio apartments, host families, student residences, or hotels

CONTACT: Scott Cather (Language Travel Adviser)

THE LEAP OVERSEAS LTD
121 High Street, Marlborough, Wiltshire
SN8 1LZ
(0)870 240 4187 or (0)1672 519922
info@theleap.co.uk
www.theleap.co.uk

PROGRAMME DESCRIPTION: Voluntary placements in Africa, South America, Asia, and Australia, that incorporate a variety of experiences and locations. Projects are involved with eco-tourism, conservation, and community projects. For example, in Kenya volunteers can escort guests on safari, track elephant in the bush, and teach football or English to local kids.

DESTINATIONS: Placements are based in game parks, jungle, and coastal locations in Africa (Kenya, South Africa, Mozambique, Tanzania, and Zambia), South America (Guyana, Costa Rica, Argentina, and Ecuador), Asia (Cambodia and India), and Australia

NUMBER OF PLACEMENTS PER YEAR: Approx 300. The majority of participants are school-leavers aged 18–20, though career breakers are specially catered for and sent together with others of a similar age.

PREREQUISITES: Ages 18 and up. Must be committed, enthusiastic, and motivated, able to work well in a team, and prepared to get stuck in.

DURATION AND TIME OF PLACEMENTS: Departures in January, April, July, and September for six or 10 weeks

COST: From £1,700 for six weeks; solo placements lasting up to three months cost £2,400 – including accommodation, food, transport, and back-up; and excluding travel, visas, and insurance

CONTACT: Guy Whitehead, Director

MADVENTURER
The Old Smithy, Corbridge, Northumberland
NE45 5QD
(0)845 121 1996
team@madventurer.com
www.madventurer.com

PROGRAMME DESCRIPTION: Madventurer combines development projects and adventurous overland travel for all ages. Expeditions that give career breakers, gap year individuals, and students the opportunity to undertake a range of voluntary work for a grassroots community or environmental project (building, teaching, sports instruction, healthcare, and orphanage) with the option then to travel on an overland adventure (trekking, rafting, touring). Placements can sometimes be arranged to complement area of academic study. The specially-designed career break projects are for individuals aged 24 or over who are looking for a unique experience during their time out from work.

DESTINATIONS: Peru, Ghana, Tanzania, Kenya, Fiji, India, Thailand, Vietnam, Uganda, and South Africa

PREREQUISITES: Career break, as well as gap year projects for all ages (17–70)

DURATION AND TIME OF PLACEMENTS: Two, four, six, eight, ten, 12, or 14 weeks or longer

SELECTION PROCEDURES AND ORIENTATION: Full-time crew support venturers, both before departure and overseas on project sites. Thorough pre-departure information, advice, support, and fundraising pack provided.

COST: Sample prices for six-week trips: £1,245 in Asia; £1,345 in Africa and Peru; £1,445 for Fiji (not including flights)

CONTACT: Elaine Lawler, Office Manager (elainel@madventurer.com) or John Lawler, Chief of Operations (chief@madventurer.com)

MONDOCHALLENGE

Town Hall, Market Place, Newbury, Berkshire RG14 5AA

✆ (0)1635 45556

✉ info@mondochallenges.co.uk

🖳 www.mondochallenge.co.uk

PROGRAMME DESCRIPTION: MondoChallenge works closely with overseas NGOs and charities to provide career break volunteer opportunities in some of the poorest regions of the world. Volunteer programmes are community-based and include teaching, livelihood support, childcare, healthcare, and development work. Volunteers live and work within local communities, giving them the chance to immerse themselves in a new culture while using their skills to help others.

DESTINATIONS: India, Tanzania, Nepal, Sri Lanka, Romania, South Africa, Ecuador, Chile, The Gambia

NUMBER OF PLACEMENTS PER YEAR: Approximately 200

PREREQUISITES: Volunteers must be aged 18 or over. All nationalities accepted. Business experience is required for business development projects. Other experience useful but optional. Volunteers must have enthusiasm, flexibility, and good communication skills.

DURATION AND TIME OF PLACEMENTS: Programmes last from two weeks to six months, with flexible start dates all year round

SELECTION PROCEDURES AND ORIENTATION: Application can be made online or by phone, with acceptance subject to an informal interview and receipt of references. Volunteers are provided with pre-departure briefing and given local orientation by in-country teams on arrival.

OTHER SERVICES: MondoChallenge offers specialised travel programmes in India, Nepal, and Tanzania. Trips include treks, safaris, and cultural tours, and are fully guided.

COST: Costs vary depending on location and project type, but start from £545 for a two-week placement. All accommodation and some meals are included.

CONTACT: Prakriti Malhotra

NONSTOP ADVENTURE/NONSTOP SKI & SNOWBOARD

Unit 3B, The Plough Brewery, 516 Wandsworth Road, London SW8 3JX

✆ (0)845 365 1525

✉ info@nonstopadventure.com

🖳 www.nonstopadventure.com (www.nonstopski.com and www.nonstopsnowboard.com)

PROGRAMME DESCRIPTION: Ski & Snowboard instructor, and improvement courses. Qualifications offered: Internationally-recognised CSIA (Canadian Ski Instructor Alliance), CASI (Canadian Association of Snowboard Instructors), NZSIA (New Zealand Snowsports Instructor Alliance), and the French 'Test Technique' and 'Préformacion'. Also CAA (Canadian Avalanche Association) Recreational Avalanche 1 certificate, and St John's Ambulance Basic First Aid certificate. Freestyle and race coach qualifications can also be obtained.

DESTINATIONS: Canada (Fernie, Whistler, Banff, and Red Mountain); New Zealand (Porters and Club Fields); France (Serre Chevalier)

NUMBER OF PLACEMENTS PER YEAR: 500 (30% are aged 30+)

PREREQUISITES: Participants should have at least 1 week's previous snow experience. Couples welcome.

DURATION AND TIME OF PLACEMENTS: Ski & Snowboard courses are between two and 18 weeks

OTHER SERVICES: Work experience may be arranged with local ski school, and contacts with other ski schools for instructing jobs can be provided. Ski accommodation in twin rooms (some quad, triple, and single rooms available) in houses/lodges equipped with kitchens and living rooms, with stereo and cable TV.

COST: £2,300–£7,150 which includes flights, transfers, accommodation, weekday meals, lift pass, resort transport, professional coaching, weekend trips, and (depending on course booked) CSIA/CASI examination, first aid course and avalanche course.

CONTACT: Adam Hillier, Course Adviser

OPERATION WALLACEA
Wallace House, Old Bolingbroke, Nr Spilsby,
Lincolnshire PE23 4EX
📞 (0)1790 763194
📧 info@opwall.com
💻 www.opwall.com

PROGRAMME DESCRIPTION: Marine and rainforest scientific research projects in Indonesia (SE Sulawesi), Honduras, Guyana, Mexico, and Madagascar; desert and marine projects in Egypt; conservation in Peruvian Amazon; bush and marine projects in South Africa and Mozambique; turtle and manatee monitoring and marine projects in Cuba. Projects aim to carry out large-scale biodiversity monitoring programmes in all areas to build a picture of threats, both human and environmental, and to then create a management plan for area protection. Operation Wallacea projects lead to sustainable conservation, to enable local people to protect their own environment from destructive practices.

DESTINATIONS: Indonesia, Honduras, Egypt, South Africa, Mozambique, Madagascar, Cuba, Mexico, Guyana, and Peru

PREREQUISITES: Minimum age 18. Enthusiasm needed. Volunteers from all walks of life and ages assist with surveys of marine, desert, bush, and rainforest habitats.

DURATION AND TIME OF PLACEMENTS: Two, four, six or eight weeks between June and September

SELECTION PROCEDURES AND ORIENTATION: No deadlines. Dive training to PADI and OW training given onsite (reef ecology, jungle training, bushcraft, etc) are included in the cost of the expedition.

COST: £975 for two weeks, £1,850 for four weeks, £2,500 for six weeks, and £2,950 for eight weeks; all excluding flights.

CONTACT: Pippa Disney

ORANGUTAN FOUNDATION
7 Kent Terrace, London NW1 4RP
📞 (0)20 7724 2912
📧 info@orangutan.org.uk
💻 www.orangutan.org.uk

PROGRAMME DESCRIPTION: Volunteers are based in Central or West Kalimantan, Indonesian Borneo: the Foundation's current release site for ex-captive and rehabilitated orangutans. Volunteers will get to spend time at Camp Leakey, the historical research site of Dr Biruté Galdikas, and may also work in other areas of the National Park. Previous projects have included: general infrastructure repairs, trail cutting, constructing guardposts, and orangutan release sites. Volunteers should note that there is no direct work or contact with orangutans.

DESTINATIONS: Central or West Kalimantan, Indonesian Borneo

NUMBER OF PLACEMENTS PER YEAR: 36

PREREQUISITES: Participants must become members of the Orangutan Foundation (£20 per year). They must work well in a team, be fit and healthy, and adaptable to difficult and demanding conditions. There is no upper age limit.

DURATION AND TIME OF PLACEMENTS: Six weeks: three teams of no more than 12, departing April, June, and September.

SELECTION PROCEDURES AND ORIENTATION:
All potential UK volunteers are expected to attend an interview at the Foundation office in London, or phone interviews can be conducted.

COST: Approx £775: includes all accommodation, food, equipment, materials, and transport for the duration of the programme, but does not include international and internal travel to the project site. Prices are confirmed before places are offered, and will depend on inflation and exchange rates.

CONTACT: Cat Gibbons, Development & Volunteer Coordinator (cat@orangutan.org.uk)

PROGRAMME DESCRIPTION: Social care and conservation placements throughout the world

DESTINATIONS: Mexico, Guatemala, Costa Rica, Honduras, Ecuador, Peru, Argentina, Brazil, Paraguay, Ghana, Kenya, South Africa, Tanzania, India, Nepal, Thailand

NUMBER OF PLACEMENTS PER YEAR: 3000

PREREQUISITES: All ages and backgrounds accepted

DURATION AND TIME OF PLACEMENTS: One to four weeks, with possibility of combining two or more placements.

SELECTION PROCEDURES AND ORIENTATION: Informal training given on arrival by local staff or long-stay volunteers.

COST: One-off registration fee of £125, plus £20–£60 per week to cover room and board on-site. Accommodation is usually self-catering in shared houses or apartments with other volunteers: two or three volunteers to a room. Sample prices are from £47 for four weeks in Latin America to £100 one-off payment in Thailand, and free accommodation provided in Paraguay.

PROGRAMME DESCRIPTION: Member of the Year Out Group. Outreach International is a specialist career break organisation that places committed volunteers in carefully selected, meaningful projects. One of the few genuinely carbon-neutral companies. All projects conform to BS 8848: the kitemark granted to companies and organisations that maintain high standards of safety and

procedures. Individuals are assigned a clear role and a position that cannot be filled by local people. Managerial roles include administering a project in Cambodia for victims of human trafficking, teaching in schools on the Pacific coast of Mexico, creating an educational programme for street children in Ecuador, working at a physiotherapist clinic on Galapagos, and teaching art and crafts to disabled women in Nepal. There are also more general roles that include helping vulnerable children in orphanages, supporting doctors in medical clinics, and carrying out marine or rainforest conservation. Volunteers are normally placed in pairs and never in a large group. Placements provide a good opportunity for individuals wishing to pursue a career in international development.

DESTINATIONS: Ecuador and the Galapagos Islands, Mexico, Costa Rica, Kenya, Sri Lanka, Peru, Nepal and Cambodia

NUMBER OF PLACEMENTS PER YEAR: Up to 100 individual volunteers

PREREQUISITES: Ideal for confident people with a desire to travel, learn a language, and offer their help to a humble community. Some of the projects need volunteers with skills or qualifications in physiotherapy, law, report writing, accountancy, IT, and in management. The majority, however, do not need specific skills. Energy, enthusiasm, and commitment are more important than official qualifications.

DURATION AND TIME OF PLACEMENTS: Short and long-term placements lasting a month or more. Flexible departure dates, though the most popular departure times are January, April, June, and September.

SELECTION PROCEDURES AND ORIENTATION: Projects are visited regularly by the Outreach International director. He aims to meet all applicants within three weeks of applying and to let them know what the chosen placement will involve. Each placement has its own project manager, and volunteers have 24-hour in-country support from a full-time coordinator.

COST: £2,950 for three months – includes full insurance (public liability, health and baggage), comprehensive language course, in-country support, food, accommodation (in private rooms with en suite facilities), local travel, all project costs, fundraising, teacher training, and pre-departure briefing days in the UK. Extended stays cost approximately £500 per month.

CONTACT: James Chapman, UK Director

PEAK LEADERS
Mansfield, Strathmiglo, Fife KY14 7QE
(0)1337 860779
info@peakleaders.com
www.peakleaders.com

PROGRAMME DESCRIPTION: Ski, snowboard, surf, and mountain bike instructor courses and performance camps, with possible job offers on completion of some of the courses. Range of sports instructor courses lasting four to 12 weeks in some resorts worldwide; suitable for career breaks, as well as holidays with a difference and career changers. Snow sport courses involve coaching in powder, moguls, free skiing, free riding, park and pipe, and ski tuning. Avalanche awareness, mountain first aid, team leading, back country, freestyle, ski school shadowing, and off-piste skiing also available. Courses can be tailored to individual requirements.

DESTINATIONS: Courses are in Switzerland (Saas Fee, Verbier); Canada (Whistler and Banff); Argentina (Bariloche in Patagonia); New Zealand (Queenstown). Mountain Bike Rider camps in Whistler, and Surf Camps in Southwest France.

DURATION AND TIME OF PLACEMENTS: Four to 12 weeks. Instructor training in Argentina and New Zealand finishes in September/October, the Saas Fee course finishes in November, and high-quality, well-organised candidates may be able to get jobs in Europe or Canada by Christmas.

OTHER SERVICES: Optional extras are offered, such as skidoo driving, backcountry training, Spanish and French language, and stopover in Buenos Aires. Job advice available.

COST: From £3,250 for short courses to £7,250, inclusive of instruction, flights (in some cases), hotel with half board, lift tickets and certification.

PROGRAMME DESCRIPTION: Volunteer recruitment organisation, which won the coveted Virgin Responsible Tourism Award in 2009 for best volunteering organisation. Places volunteers of all ages with skills and experience to share, mainly aged 25+. Also works in partnership with Explore on their volunteer programme. Various volunteer placements, as requested by local communities liaising with host country partners' project management teams. Examples include: community development work in the Gambia and Cambodia; education development in South Africa, India, and Peru; and marine research and healthcare support in Morocco.

DESTINATIONS: South Africa, Gambia, Mozambique, Swaziland, Madagascar, Nepal, India, Peru, Morocco, and Cambodia

NUMBER OF PLACEMENTS PER YEAR: 200–300

PREREQUISITES: Most volunteers are aged 30–65, with a maximum of about 75 – though there is no maximum age if volunteers are healthy and can do the work. All nationalities accepted. Volunteers' skills and abilities are more important than age and are matched with needs of individual projects, eg early childhood development, education, or health care training or experience, IT skills, practical and trade skills.

DURATION AND TIME OF PLACEMENTS: Most are four to eight weeks, though some are shorter and others last up to 12 weeks

SELECTION PROCEDURES AND ORIENTATION: Flexible start dates; normally two months are needed for screening and placement preparation. Telephone or face-to-face interview required, plus Criminal Records screening or equivalent.

OTHER SERVICES: Each volunteer receives comprehensive pre-departure information, including a briefing on responsible volunteering and the communities in which they will be working.

COST: £1,030 for four weeks – including orientation, half-board accommodation (normally homestay or locally owned guesthouse), airport transfers, and support throughout. All volunteer fees are paid direct to the host country, and at least 80% of it stays there. Each project description includes details of how and where the volunteer's money will be spent. Volunteers are clearly told in advance how the donation element will be spent for the specific project on which they are working.

CONTACT: Kate Stefanko, Placement Director, or Sallie Grayson, Programme Director

PROGRAMME DESCRIPTION: POD is a non-profit organisation arranging ethical and supported volunteering opportunities around the world. POD works with long term projects that they know personally and where there is genuine benefit to local communities. Volunteers are needed to help work with disadvantaged children, communities, animals, and conservation projects including: caring for elephants and wild animals; joining an Amazon jungle conservation project; marine conservation; community building projects; volunteering at orphanages and care homes; teaching English and running summer English camps.

DESTINATIONS: Belize, Cambodia, Nepal, Peru, South Africa, Tanzania, Thailand and Vietnam

PREREQUISITES: No specific requirements for most placements, just a positive attitude

DURATION AND TIME OF PLACEMENTS: From one week to six months, with flexible start dates throughout the year

SELECTION PROCEDURES AND ORIENTATION: All applicants submit an online application and, depending on the project, receive a telephone interview and references are taken. A Criminal Records Bureau Check may also be conducted. A detailed information pack is sent to volunteers. Pre-departure and local training and introductions are undertaken on arrival in-country.

OTHER SERVICES: These working holidays can be incorporated into existing travel plans

COST: Volunteer fees start at £375. Sample fees: two weeks at an orphanage in Cambodia or elephant care in South Africa for £449–£499. Placements include training, support, and accommodation. Sample price for longer placements: one-off fee of £375 for dog and cat care in Thailand, plus from £50 per week living costs; 12 weeks village teaching in Tanzania for £1,595.

CONTACT: The POD Team, headed by Mike Beecham and Alex Tarrant

---

PROJECTS ABROAD

Aldsworth Parade, Goring, Sussex BN12 4TX

(0)1903 708300

info@projects-abroad.co.uk

www.projects-abroad.co.uk

PROGRAMME DESCRIPTION: Founding member of the Year Out Group. Company arranges voluntary teaching posts, as well as placements in care, conservation, animal care, medicine, journalism, and other fields around the world.

DESTINATIONS: Argentina, Bolivia, Brazil, Cambodia, China, Costa Rica, Ethiopia, Fiji, Ghana, India, Jamaica, Mexico, Moldova, Mongolia, Morocco, Mozambique, Nepal, Peru, Romania, Senegal, South Africa, Sri Lanka, Tanzania, Thailand, Togo, and Vietnam. Destinations and placements can be combined.

NUMBER OF PLACEMENTS PER YEAR: 6,000–8,000

PREREQUISITES: Volunteers range from 16 to 70

DURATION AND TIME OF PLACEMENTS: Very flexible, with departures year round. Placements last from two weeks to 12 months.

SELECTION PROCEDURES AND ORIENTATION: Paid staff (350 in total) in all destinations who arrange and vet placements, accommodation, and work supervisors. They meet volunteers on arrival and provide a final briefing before the placements.

COST: Placements are self-funded and the fee charged includes insurance, food, accommodation, airport pick-up and drop-off, and overseas support. Three-month placements cost between £1,695 and £3,000+, depending on placement and destination, and exclude travel costs.

PROJECTS ABROAD PRO

Aldsworth Parade, Goring, Sussex BN12 4TX

(0)1903 708300

info@projects-abroad-pro.org

www.projects-abroad-pro.org

ORGANISATION DESCRIPTION: Projects Abroad PRO is the skilled and qualified arm of volunteer organisation Projects Abroad. They are looking for people with a skill or qualification who want to make a difference, using their knowledge to help some of the poorest communities in the world. Projects for professionals are available in Business Development, Culture & Media, Education, Engineering, Environment, Human Rights, Medical and Social Work.

DESTINATIONS: Argentina, Bolivia, Cambodia, China, Costa Rica, Ethiopia, Ghana, India, Jamaica, Mexico, Moldova, Mongolia, Morocco, Nepal, Peru, Romania, Senegal, South Africa, Sri Lanka and Thailand

NUMBER OF PLACEMENTS PER YEAR: 100+

PREREQUISITES: Each project has specific requirements regarding qualifications, but generally speaking, Projects Abroad PRO is looking for the following individuals:

■ professionals with a diploma in the relevant area

■ retired seniors

■ university graduates

■ individuals with at least two years' experience in the relevant area but who hold no degree or diploma.

■ individuals who hold non-professional qualifications in the relevant area.

DURATION AND TIME OF PLACEMENTS: Two weeks upward – projects run throughout the year and volunteers are able to select their own start date

SELECTION PROCEDURES AND ORIENTATION: Application required with professional reference (two references for qualified medical volunteers). Projects Abroad in-country staff arrange and vet placements, accommodation and work supervisors. In-country training and operations include airport pickups, Projects Abroad office induction, orientation of surroundings and environment, volunteer handbook training and project supervisor introductions.

COST: Project fees range from £995–£2,000. Placements are self-funded by volunteers. The fee includes accommodation, food, medical and travel insurance, airport transfers and overseas support. The project fee depends on the placement duration and destination.

CONTACT: Ian Birbeck, Recruitment Director

RALEIGH
Third Floor, 207 Waterloo Road, London SE1 8XD
(0)20 7183 1270
info@raleigh.org.uk
www.raleighinternational.org

PROGRAMME DESCRIPTION: Raleigh is a leading youth and education charity established in 1984, which runs adventure and challenge expeditions for volunteers from a wide range of backgrounds, nationalities, and life stages, with the aim of increasing the leadership skills of individuals and their awareness of their role as active global citizens. Altogether, more than 30,000 people have taken part in Raleigh's expeditions. Volunteer managers (aged 25–75) use their professional and personal skills to support young people in undertaking sustainable community, environmental, and adventure projects overseas. These projects are designed in partnership with government ministries, local communities, and NGOs, to ensure that they are worthwhile and sustainable. Volunteer managers will either be based at Raleigh fieldbase in the expedition country, or on project sites. The experience is well suited to anyone interested in education development, looking for a constructive and challenging way to spend a career break, or as a motivational tool for a possible change of career.

DESTINATIONS: Borneo (Malaysia), Costa Rica combined with Nicaragua, and India

NUMBER OF PLACEMENTS PER YEAR: More than 300 Volunteer Managers, distributed over 12 expeditions per year

PREREQUISITES: Applicants must be aged between 25 and 75. Some roles require volunteers to have relevant skills and experience; however, volunteer managers come from a wide range of backgrounds. The most important prerequisite is that volunteers have a 'can-do' attitude, and the energy and desire to benefit communities and young people from around the world. Roles available include: Project Manager, Trek Leaders Administrator, Finance Manager, Logistics Coordinator and Manager, Driver, Communications Officer, Photographer, Videographer, Medics (doctors, nurses, and paramedics), and Spanish Interpreter.

DURATION AND TIME OF PLACEMENTS: Volunteers can choose between eight and 13 weeks (which includes two weeks thorough in-country training before the expedition begins, and a week after the expedition ends).

SELECTION PROCEDURES AND ORIENTATION: Volunteer Managers can apply online. Successful applicants will be invited to attend an assessment weekend in the UK, which is an intensive two-day course designed to recreate expedition life and give a taste of what each role entails. Once accepted onto the programme volunteer managers will need to attend a compulsory Development Weekend, where they will meet other volunteer managers on their expedition and the country director, learn more about planned projects, medical and kit advice, receive training for group work and facilitation with young people in challenging environments, and practical cross-cultural management techniques.

COST: Depending on the length of expedition, volunteer managers are asked to contribute between £1,350 and £1,950 to cover their training costs, living expenses, and medical insurance. Bursaries are available for some roles (eg medics and qualified outdoor professionals). As a registered charity, Raleigh encourages its volunteers to fundraise towards the cost of their expedition. Full fundraising support is provided.

PROGRAMME DESCRIPTION: Restless Development, formerly SPW (Students Partnership Worldwide), is a youth-led development agency and non-profit making charity, currently working in Africa and South Asia. Its development model has been cited as a model of best practice by UNICEF, the World Bank, and others. Range of tiered International Placements, which means assignments are appropriate to the volunteer's level of experience and skills, and the placements provide structured and professional experience in the field of international development. European, American, and Australian volunteers aged 18–28 are recruited to work in partnership with counterpart volunteers from Africa and Asia. In pairs or groups they live and work in rural communities for five to nine months. Their input builds awareness and begins to change attitudes and behaviour to important health, social, and environmental issues amongst young people and communities. All volunteers take part in training, which covers health, hygiene, sanitation, nutrition, and the environment – with a particular emphasis on HIV/AIDS prevention and care. Technical Assistant placements are for skilled and high capacity young professionals, to fulfil specific placement objectives in specific areas such as strategy, programme quality, research, fundraising, finance, marketing, and others, in one of the charity's offices in Africa and Asia.

DESTINATIONS: Long-term community development placements: Uganda and Nepal; Technical Assistant placements: India, Nepal, Sierra Leone, South Africa, Tanzania, Uganda, Zambia, and Zimbabwe

NUMBER OF PLACEMENTS PER YEAR: Long-term community development placements: 28 places for European, American, and Australian volunteers; Technical Assistant placements: up to 20 placements open to applicants from around the world

PREREQUISITES: Volunteers need to be physically and emotionally healthy, hard working, open-minded, enthusiastic, and have good communication skills. Some technical placements require specific backgrounds.

DURATION AND TIME OF PLACEMENTS: Long-term community development placements: five to nine months; Technical Assistant placements: two weeks to six months, with starting dates throughout the year

SELECTION PROCEDURES AND ORIENTATION: For long-term community development placements, every applicant is required to attend an Information and Selection day in London, where they can meet staff and returned volunteers. Applicants are then required to complete an application form and participate in a selection interview. All selected applicants will attend a three-day training session prior to departure, with a one-month, in-country training at the beginning of their placement. For Technical Assistant placements, applicants complete an application form and participate in a selection interview. These placements are advertised in four batches throughout the year. All selected applicants will receive training prior to departure and an in-country induction at the start of their placement.

COST: Long-term community development placements: minimum donation of £3,600 to the charity. All costs are then covered by Restless Development, including open return flight, accommodation, basic living allowance, insurance, in-country work permit, UK briefings and general administrative support, and extensive overseas training and support. Technical Assistant placements: costs vary depending on the placement.

PROGRAMME DESCRIPTION: The TOTEM programme enables people to work in one of 200 villages for spells of three weeks (or longer) as volunteers in India. Volunteers can choose between Environmental Management Programme, Social Development Programme, and Health and Sanitation Development Programme.

DESTINATIONS: Himachal Pradesh, India

NUMBER OF PLACEMENTS PER YEAR: 150

PREREQUISITES: For ages 20–60. All candidates are welcome to apply. The key acceptance criterion is whether the candidate has enough international travel experience to handle the basic conditions in a grass-roots organisation.

DURATION AND TIME OF PLACEMENTS: Three-week placements for working professionals, starting on the fifth day of every month (though start dates are flexible). Extensions can be negotiated for up to six months. Short duration (two weeks) workcamps are also conducted by RUCHI, where volunteers are involved with light physical work on a small-scale project.

COST: $1,000 for three weeks; cost for longer placements negotiable. Fee includes transport from Kalka or Chandigarh railway station, use of private car with driver when at RUCHI, accommodation, and all vegetarian meals. The participation fee for the two-week workcamp is 14,000 rupees (less than £200), which does not include transport, and the living conditions are very basic.

CONTACT: Dharamvir Singh

SAGA VOLUNTEER TRAVEL
The Saga Building, Enbrook Park, Folkestone, Kent CT20 3SE
volunteer@saga.co.uk
www.saga.co.uk/volunteer

PROGRAMME DESCRIPTION: Saga Volunteer Travel operates as a non-profit part of the Saga Group. Any profit is donated to the Saga Charitable Trust on an annual basis to help support projects worldwide. Range of volunteer placements.

DESTINATIONS: South Africa, Nepal, Sri Lanka and St Lucia

COST: From £1,999 for four weeks (including flights and hotels as part of a complete package)

SCHOOLHOUSE VOLUNTEERING
Schoolhouse, Anderson Road, Ballater, Aberdeenshire AB35 5QW
(0)1339 756333
info@school-english.com
www.schoolhousevolunteering.com

PROGRAMME DESCRIPTION: Well-researched and supported volunteer English teaching placements in government schools, through the Ministry of Education in Colombo and other organisations in Sri Lanka and Tamil Nadu, India.

DESTINATIONS: Sri Lanka and India

PREREQUISITES: Must be native or fluent English speaker. Teaching qualifications are not essential as there is a range of placements to match a range of skills and experience. However, newly-qualified teachers seeking experience, those wishing to explore teaching with a view to training in the future, teachers seeking a refreshing sabbatical or holiday, and retired teachers may be particularly interested. Volunteers must be good communicators, be enthusiastic and open to contributing to and learning from new and challenging experiences. Ideally candidates can attend pre-placement training in Scotland.

DURATION AND TIME OF PLACEMENTS: One month to one year

SELECTION PROCEDURES AND ORIENTATION: A free (optional) two- to three-day residential pre-departure training course is given at Schoolhouse premises in Scotland. The course aims to prepare volunteers and enable them to get the most out of their volunteer teaching experience, both in terms of contribution and self-development. Volunteers stay in campus accommodation, with selected host families or in a shared house or flat with other volunteers. Applications welcomed year round. After submitting the online application form (on the Schoolhouse site), Schoolhouse will develop a rapport with applicants to ensure an effective matching and good preparation.

COST: £595 for one month (covers placement admin, training, airport pick-up, accommodation, most meals, and ongoing support during placement)

CONTACT: Alan and Cathy Low, Schoolhouse Volunteering

PROGRAMME DESCRIPTION: Non-profit organisation providing holistic support to economically-disadvantaged children in the district of El Porvenir, located on the north coast of Peru. SKIP works to strengthen and empower families so they can enable children to realise their right to an education. Projects include teaching in both English and Spanish, youth work, social work, and psychology – including group and individual work with children, young people, and parents. Opportunities also in an economic development team, providing microfinance loans and business training and advice to parents.

DESTINATIONS: El Porvenir, Trujillo, Peru

PREREQUISITES: All ages. SKIP can provide training suitable for volunteers who want to learn about working in an NGO. Volunteers must be comfortable working with and around children.

DURATION AND TIME OF PLACEMENTS: Minimum of one month

SELECTION PROCEDURES AND ORIENTATION: Rolling applications accepted year round. Specific vacancies are advertised on www.idealist.org. Telephone interviews held in some cases.

COST: $350 per month for the first two months, then $250 for three to five months, $180 for six to eight months and $125 for nine to 12 months. Accommodation in the volunteer house (for up to 22 volunteers) or with a local host family is included, but not food and travel.

CONTACT: Liz Wilson, Director

PROGRAMME DESCRIPTION: British registered non-religious charity, working to enhance the education facilities for hundreds of Ugandan children. Volunteers needed for a range of projects in the Jinja area: two pre-schools for orphans and vulnerable children, a school refurbishment programme, to assist with hands-on learning experiences at the Amagezi Education Centre used by upper primary pupils from 26 partner schools, a special needs project, and the Murchison Project – which brings conservation education to the communities surrounding the National Park. Particular areas of interest for 'grown-ups' are TEFL teachers and those with experience in working with SEN children.

DESTINATIONS: Uganda

NUMBER OF PLACEMENTS PER YEAR: About 100 independent volunteers and 150+ in student groups

PREREQUISITES: Long-term volunteers range from 18 to 70 years old. Summer groups are mainly university students. No qualifications needed. All nationalities accepted. Soft Power is looking for highly independent and motivated individuals, who are looking for a grass roots volunteering experience where they can be involved in a wide range of activities.

DURATION AND TIME OF PLACEMENTS: One day to 12 months. Volunteers accepted year round.

SELECTION PROCEDURES AND ORIENTATION: Arrival should be arranged at least a month in advance. Airport collection and accommodation are arranged, but volunteer covers those costs. Volunteer coordinator meets volunteers soon after arrival and gives orientation on all the projects.

COST: Volunteers must cover their own living and travel expenses, as well as a donation to the charity (minimum £75 a week). Accommodation can be everything from camping to living with local community family to staying in a five star lodge.

CONTACT: Sharon Webb, General Manager

PROGRAMME DESCRIPTION: SVP works with undergraduates and graduates who are native English speakers and who wish to teach English in Sudan. Teaching tends to be informal in style, with four to five hours of contact a day. Volunteers can plan their own discussions and teaching schemes – such as arranging games, dramas, competitions, and tests for assessing skills learned by the students. Accommodation is in flats shared with other volunteers.

DESTINATIONS: Sudan: mostly in and around Khartoum area, and especially Omdurman

PREREQUISITES: TEFL certificate, experience of travelling in developing countries, and some knowledge of Arabic are helpful but not obligatory. Volunteers must be in good health and be native English speakers, and have experience of living away from home. Older candidates with teaching experience are welcome to participate.

DURATION AND TIME OF PLACEMENTS: Preferred minimum of eight months. Shorter summer placements are possible.

SELECTION PROCEDURES AND ORIENTATION: Applications accepted year round. Two referees are required. Prior to departure, medical check-up required plus selection interviews, orientation, and briefings take place. Volunteers are required to write a report of their experiences and to advise new volunteers.

COST: Volunteers must raise the cost of the airfare to Sudan (currently £485) plus £65 (cost of the first three months insurance). Volunteers must be able to support themselves for the first three to four weeks in Khartoum while their permits are obtained prior to travelling, and the first month in their placement town as most universities pay the allowance in arrears. Accommodation is provided.

CONTACT: David Wolton (at email above)

SUNRISE VOLUNTEER PROGRAMMES
71A Church Road, Hove BN3 2BB
📞 (0)1273 738205
✉ info@sunrint.com
💻 http://en.sunrint.com

PROGRAMME DESCRIPTION: Paying volunteers are recruited for China: for example, to teach English in special needs schools and hospitals, or to volunteer at a Panda Base.

DESTINATIONS: Beijing (mostly); Panda Base is near Chengdu

NUMBER OF PLACEMENTS PER YEAR: 80

PREREQUISITES: Ages 17–55 and all nationalities. Must be native speaker of English and have a college degree.

DURATION AND TIME OF PLACEMENTS: Two weeks to three months

SELECTION PROCEDURES AND ORIENTATION: Sunrise sends applicant's CV and supporting documents to Chinese organisation, which then endeavours to find a placement.

COST: Sample project package fee is £749–£899 for a fortnight, excluding visas and airfares. Accommodation included in Central Beijing hostel or other accommodation (occasionally homestay) near projects.

CONTACT: Gavin Tan, Programme Founder

TRAVELLERS WORLDWIDE
2A Caravelle House, 17/19 Goring Road, Worthing, West Sussex BN12 4AP
📞 (0)1903 502595
✉ info@travellersworldwide.com
💻 www.travellersworldwide.com

PROGRAMME DESCRIPTION: Founder member of the Year Out Group. Volunteer programme for people taking a career break, gap year, or wanting to do something constructive in retirement. Voluntary work overseas on different types of project; open to all individuals and groups. Projects include teaching conversational English (and other subjects like sports, music, drama, art, maths, geography, IT); care and orphanage placements; conservation programmes, including rehabilitation of endangered species, marine projects, and African wildlife courses; structured work experience in sectors such as law, journalism, media, and medicine; language courses (eg, Spanish, Mandarin, Brazilian Portuguese, Swahili, Tamil); and cultural courses (meditation, photography, tango, music, martial arts).

DESTINATIONS: Argentina, Australia, Bolivia, Brazil, Brunei, China, Ghana, Guatemala, India, Kenya, Malawi, Malaysia, New Zealand, Peru, South Africa, Sri Lanka, Tanzania, Thailand, Zambia, and Zimbabwe

NUMBER OF PLACEMENTS PER YEAR: 1,000+

PREREQUISITES: Open to all ages 17–90. Approximately 30%–40% of Travellers volunteers are aged between late 20s and retirees. No formal qualifications required. Travellers runs a weekend TEFL course in the UK (check details at www.tefltime.com).

DURATION AND TIME OF PLACEMENTS: Two weeks to one year, with flexible start dates all year round

COST: Sample charges: from £675 for two weeks to £1,425 for 12 weeks, with additional weeks at £80 each. Prices include food and accommodation plus transport, airport pick-up, local support, and back-up by Travellers staff overseas; but do not include international travel, visas, or insurance. (Travellers can arrange the latter but many volunteers prefer the flexibility of organising their own.)

TRAVELWORKS

Muensterstr. 111, 48155 Muenster, Germany

℘ (0)844 576 5411 (UK); +49 2506 830 3299 (from outside UK)

⌂ info@travelworks.co.uk

▣ www.travelworks.co.uk

PROGRAMME DESCRIPTION: TravelWorks is a tour operator, offering gap year volunteering projects and paid work programmes in over 30 countries around the world. Well-established in Germany, they began offering their programmes to the English-speaking market in 2008. In addition to a large range of programmes for young gappers, TravelWorks has two career break programmes in India. The 30+ programmes offer volunteers a better opportunity to use any skills, experience, or education.

DESTINATIONS: Rajasthan and Himachal Pradesh

PREREQUISITES: For ages 30–65. (No upper age limit on most of TravelWorks' other non-specialist gap year programmes.)

DURATION AND TIME OF PLACEMENTS: Four, eight, or 12 weeks

SELECTION PROCEDURES AND ORIENTATION: Comprehensive travel support offered

COST: £1,220 for four weeks, £1,790 for eight, £2,335 for 12; excluding airfares. Accommodation on

career-break programme offers slightly more comfort and privacy than for younger volunteers.

CONTACT: Laura Hoesman, Content Manager (lhoesman@travelworks.co.uk)

VENTURECO WORLDWIDE

The Ironyard, 64-66 The Market Place, Warwick CV34 4SD

℘ (0)1926 411122

⌂ mail@ventureco-worldwide.com

▣ www.ventureco-worldwide.com

PROGRAMME DESCRIPTION: Specialists in Adventure Volunteering. Career experiences in Latin America consisting of three phases: learning a language, volunteering, and exploring. Development projects are funded by the VentureCo Trust, a UK registered charity. ATOL license 5306. Member of the Year Out Group. Combination of language courses, community development projects, and expeditions allows career gap travellers to explore off the beaten track, learn about the host country, and give something back to the communities where they stay.

DESTINATIONS: Several itineraries operating across Latin America

NUMBER OF PLACEMENTS PER YEAR: 175

PREREQUISITES: Career Gap Ventures for those 21 and over. No upper age limit. Must have enthusiasm and an open mind.

DURATION AND TIME OF PLACEMENTS: Ventures range from two to 15 weeks. Departures year round.

SELECTION PROCEDURES AND ORIENTATION: Attendance at an Open Evening, held in London on the first Tuesday of every month, can be booked by phone or online. Pre-departure travel course held in the UK, lasting one or three days depending on Venture. Planning, leading, and organisation roles throughout the Venture are shared amongst the team.

COST: Venture costs range: £635 for a two-week volunteer project, £1,895 for a six-week Summer Venture, and £4,700 for a full 15-week Career Gap Venture. Cost includes a three-day Travel Safety Course, all food, accommodation, in-country transport, language tuition, project funding, and all expedition activities. Flights, airport taxes, insurance, and visas are not included.

CONTACT: Seth Harris (Venture Coordinator) and Mark Davison (Director)

VERBIER-SUMMITS PARAGLIDING

Chalet Anguillita, Chemin de la cote 15, 1934 Verbier, Switzerland

☎ +41 (0)79 313 5677

🖱 stu@verbier-summits.com

💻 www.verbier-summits.com

PROGRAMME DESCRIPTION: Paragliding holidays in the Alps, specially suited to people taking career breaks

DESTINATIONS: Switzerland

NUMBER OF PLACEMENTS PER YEAR: 200

PREREQUISITES: All nationalities. Average age 30–45. Participants receive a thorough training, both theory and practical. Participants with no flying experience can leave with a pilot's licence.

DURATION AND TIME OF PLACEMENTS: One-week beginner's course, to eight-week instructor's course

COST: From £1,000 for one week, to £5,000 for eight weeks. Includes luxury accommodation and five star cuisine.

CONTACT: Stuart Belbas, Director

VESL (VOLUNTEERS FOR EDUCATIONAL SUPPORT & LEARNING)

17 Silk Hill, Buxworth, High Peak, Derbyshire SK23 7TA

☎ 0845 094 3727

🖱 info@vesl.org or enquiries@vesl.org

💻 www.vesl.org

PROGRAMME DESCRIPTION: VESL is a charity registered in the UK (no. 1117908) and as an NGO in Sri Lanka and Thailand, and sends volunteers to work on projects in Asia. Volunteers and qualified teachers are sent to run English language summer schools in remote communities.

DESTINATIONS: India, Thailand, and Sri Lanka

NUMBER OF PLACEMENTS PER YEAR: Up to 60

PREREQUISITES: Minimum age 18, though most volunteers are older. Volunteers should be enthusiastic, motivated, and up for a challenge. TEFL experience and some experience overseas are helpful, but not a requirement.

DURATION AND TIME OF PLACEMENTS: Four to six week summer programmes in July and August, and three to six month projects throughout the year. Some volunteers are also required to help run teacher workshop programmes in August each year.

SELECTION PROCEDURES AND ORIENTATION: Applications accepted throughout the year. All candidates must be able to attend a selection day and training weekend (dates and places in the UK to be notified).

COST: Programme fee ranges from £900 for summer placement to £1,350 for three months, which covers cost of setting up the projects, training, orientation, insurance, accommodation, food, in-country travel, and comprehensive back up and support. VESL is run mainly by volunteers, so costs are kept to a minimum.

CONTACT: Tom Harrison, Programme Director

VOLUNTEER AFRICA

PO Box 24, Bakewell, Derbyshire DE45 1YP

🖱 support@volunteerafrica.org

💻 www.volunteerafrica.org

PROGRAMME DESCRIPTION: UK charity recruits volunteers to work on community projects in Tanzania, eg in rural development or working with children.

DESTINATIONS: Singida region of Tanzania

PREREQUISITES: All ages above 18

DURATION AND TIME OF PLACEMENTS: Two, four, seven, ten, 11 or 12 weeks

OTHER SERVICES: Other vacancies in Africa with various charities and aid agencies are posted on the same website

COST: Fees are £600 (two weeks), £1,050 (four weeks), £1,380 (seven weeks), £1,710 (10 weeks), £1,950 (11–12 weeks): a proportion of which is a donation to the host programme

CONTACT: Moya Cutts, Volunteer Coordinator

VOLUNTEER PETEN

Parque Ecologico Nueva Juventud, San Andres, Peten, Guatemala

📞 (502) 5711 0040

✉ volunteerpeten@hotmail.com

💻 www.volunteerpeten.com

PROGRAMME DESCRIPTION: Not-for-profit organisation, which recruits volunteers to help protect and manage a 150-acre reserve in San Andres; to provide environmental education to all the schools in the area; to aid and assist small community organisations, schools, and families; and to provide quality volunteer opportunities for travellers and students. Volunteer projects are concerned with Ecological Management or Education. Ecological Management includes maintaining a 150-acre reserve, trail management, gardening, tree nursery management, medicinal plants, reforestation projects, and ecological restoration projects. Education includes environmental education, general education in local schools, library management and activities, extracurricular activities, and adult education. Volunteers also work on various construction projects throughout the year.

DESTINATIONS: San Andres, Peten, Northern Guatemala

NUMBER OF PLACEMENTS PER YEAR: 180

PREREQUISITES: Average age 25. Volunteers should be open-minded and hard working.

DURATION AND TIME OF PLACEMENTS: Four to 12 weeks

SELECTION PROCEDURES AND ORIENTATION: Rolling acceptance of volunteers. Orientation, tour of facilities and projects, use of equipment and tools, and daily supervision by staff.

COST: $450 for four weeks, $800 for eight weeks, and $1,150 for 12 weeks – which includes room and board with local family, training, all activities, and use of resources on a project.

CONTACT: Matthew R. Peters, Director

VOLUNTHAI (VOLUNTEERS FOR THAILAND)

86/24 Soi Kanprapa, Prachacheun Rd, Bahng Sue, Bangkok 10800, Thailand

📞 +66 1202 403 1540

✉ info@volunthai.com

💻 www.volunthai.com

PROGRAMME DESCRIPTION: Volunteer teaching in 20 target schools with homestay. Volunteers teach conversational English in the classroom for three to four hours a day.

DESTINATIONS: Rural areas in remote provinces of Thailand

NUMBER OF PLACEMENTS PER YEAR: 100

PREREQUISITES: Ages 21–70. College degree required. Must be speaker of English (native or non-native). Must be willing to live with and learn from the locals.

DURATION AND TIME OF PLACEMENTS: Two to four weeks minimum

SELECTION PROCEDURES AND ORIENTATION: Rolling admissions. Online interviews. Volunteers are met in Bangkok for an introduction, and then go to the headquarters in rural Chaiyaphum for a brief training in Thai culture and language. A Thai teacher is available at the homestay to help with questions.

COST: Modest monthly fee ($325 for first month; $150 for subsequent months) to cover comfortable homestay and meals. Volunteers pay for their own travel costs.

CONTACT: Michael Anderson, Founder

VSO (VOLUNTARY SERVICE OVERSEAS)

Carlton House, 27A Carlton Drive Putney, London SW15 2BS

📞 (0)20 8780 7500

✉ enquiry@vso.org.uk

💻 www.vso.org.uk (UK) and www.vsointernational.org (international)

PROGRAMME DESCRIPTION: International development charity, which works on long-term partnerships with overseas organisations worldwide. Offices also in Dublin, Ottawa, Nairobi, New Delhi, Quezon City, and Utrecht. (More detailed information about VSO may be found in Part 4: Doing Something Worthwhile.) Volunteers are assigned to suitable projects abroad, primarily in the fields of education, health, natural resources, technical trades and engineering, IT, business, management, and social work.

DESTINATIONS: Worldwide

PREREQUISITES: Must have professional skills or experience that can be matched with an overseas need. Average age of volunteers is 42; maximum age about 75. High level of commitment required.

DURATION AND TIME OF PLACEMENTS: One to two years. Short-term specialist assignments now available for highly experienced professionals who can work at senior levels. Business partnership placements for volunteers from the corporate world who can be seconded for periods of six to 12 months.

SELECTION PROCEDURES AND ORIENTATION: Rigorous selection procedures and extensive training provided

COST: None. Volunteer receives living expenses and wages in line with local workers, plus accommodation, flights, insurance and training.

WARREN SMITH SKI ACADEMY
Chemin d'Amon 22, 1936 Verbier, Switzerland
(0)1525 374757 (UK); +41 79 359 6566
(Switzerland)
theteam@warrensmith-skiacademy.com
www.warrensmith-skiacademy.com

PROGRAMME DESCRIPTION: Gap year Ski Instructor courses and ski performance improvement courses

DESTINATIONS: Verbier, Switzerland

NUMBER OF PLACEMENTS PER YEAR: 40 BASI trainees per year

PREREQUISITES: Minimum age 16; average age 35

DURATION AND TIME OF PLACEMENTS: Nine weeks; 3 July to 5 September 2011 in Saas Fee

OTHER SERVICES: Qualifications offered: BASI Level 1 and Level 2 qualifications. Academy has been known to achieve 100% pass rate.

COST: £7,499 with accommodation (half board, excellent food, en suite, in centre of Verbier); £5,299 without accommodation

CONTACT: Warren Smith, Director of Coaching

WAVA
67-71 Lewisham High Street, London, SE13 5JX
(0)800 80 483 80
smordarski@workandvolunteer.com
www.workandvolunteer.com

PROGRAMME DESCRIPTION: 'WAVA' stands for 'Work and Volunteer Abroad': rebranded in 2010 (formerly Twin Work & Adventure Abroad). WAVA offers three types of travelling experience: (1) Volunteering on projects in developing countries; (2) Internships in professional environments around the world; and (3) Seasonal paid and unpaid working holidays in developed economies.

DESTINATIONS: All over the world: North and South America, Europe, Africa, Asia and Oceania

NUMBER OF PLACEMENTS PER YEAR: 500+

PREREQUISITES: All ages. All nationalities are accepted, subject to visa requirements. Specific skills may be required depending on the programme. Participants need to be enthusiastic, willing to get actively involved, have an open mind, and sometimes a sense of humour.

DURATION AND TIME OF PLACEMENTS: From two weeks to one year

SELECTION PROCEDURES AND ORIENTATION: As part of WAVA's Responsible Travel Policy, they focus heavily on responsibly matching participants to programmes. The company advises participants to apply at least 12 weeks before their intended start date (although in many cases WAVA can fast track applications). The programme fee often includes a pre-departure briefing in London.

OTHER SERVICES: Because WAVA's programmes differ so much, a 'Foot rating' system is in place to categorise programmes according to the level of comfort and accessibility.

COST: From £390. Fees include pre-departure and in-country induction/training, a donation to the project, in-country transport, accommodation (volunteer house or on-project residence or local hostel/lodge), and food.

CONTACT: Sally Mordarski, Travel Administrator (smordarski@workandvolunteer.com)

WLS INTERNATIONAL LTD
29 Harley Street, London W1G 9QR
(0)203 384 4058
info@GapYearInAsia.com
www.GapYearInAsia.com

PROGRAMME DESCRIPTION: Affordable volunteering programmes in Asia

DESTINATIONS: China, Cambodia, India, Nepal, The Philippines, Thailand, and Vietnam

NUMBER OF PLACEMENTS PER YEAR: 350

DURATION AND TIME OF PLACEMENTS: One to 12 weeks

PREREQUISITES: All nationalities welcome. Most participants are aged 20–35, but no limit. Volunteers must have enthusiasm, flexibility, and a willingness to help. Candidates should be willing to prepare ideas for English lessons in advance of their trip.

SELECTION PROCEDURES AND ORIENTATION: Most candidates book a month in advance, but last-minute placements are available

COST: Sample prices: £505 for four weeks in Nepal (plus £50 for each extra week), and £585 per four weeks in the Philippines (plus £55 for each extra week). Accommodation in guesthouse or as homestay.

CONTACT: Matt Jones, Programme Manager

WORLDWIDE EXPERIENCE
The Oak Suite, Guardian House, Borough Road, Godalming, Surrey GU7 2AE
(0)1483 860560
enquiries@WorldwideExperience.com
www.WorldwideExperience.com

PROGRAMME DESCRIPTION: Conservation placements in Southern Africa and Asia, which give participants the chance to get actively involved in conservation on various game reserves, animal rehabilitation centres, and ocean research projects. Other projects include community and sports coaching placements, game ranger courses, a wildlife film academy, and a sculpting course.

DESTINATIONS: South Africa, Kenya, Malawi, India, and Sri Lanka

NUMBER OF PLACEMENTS PER YEAR: 1000+

PREREQUISITES: No particular skills needed. All nationalities accepted.

DURATION AND TIME OF PLACEMENTS: Two to 12 weeks. Placements are available all year round (gap year, summer break, and sabbatical).

SELECTION PROCEDURES AND ORIENTATION: Applications accepted year round. Interviews are informal and can be done by telephone. Open days are arranged throughout the year when Worldwide Experience crew meet potential volunteers. Full medical and personal checklist is supplied during preparation.

COST: From £1,599 for two weeks – inclusive of return flights from the UK, all road transfers, meals, accommodation (furnished and comfortable, shared between two), and placement activities. The 12-week placements without flights vary, from £1,785 working with colobus monkeys in Kenya to £4,549 at a rehabilitation centre for animals in the Limpopo region.

YHA
Recruitment Department, Trevelyan House, Matlock, Derbyshire DE4 3YH
(0)1629 592656
jobs@yha.org.uk
www.yhacareers.co.uk

PROGRAMME DESCRIPTION: Seasonal Team Members are required to help run the YHA's youth hostels in England and Wales. Team members undertake various duties, including catering, cleaning, reception work, and assisting the manager with all aspects of the day-to-day running of a hostel.

DESTINATIONS: England and Wales

NUMBER OF PLACEMENTS PER YEAR: 300

PREREQUISITES: Experience in one or more of the relevant duties is desirable, but lots of enthusiasm and excellent customer service is essential

DURATION AND TIME OF PLACEMENTS: Between February and October

SELECTION PROCEDURES AND ORIENTATION: Competitive salary and benefits package. Employee accommodation available at most locations, for which there is a nominal charge. Recruitment events and selection mainly from December to February and around Easter.

YOMPS

10 Woodland Way, Brighton, East Sussex
BN1 8BA

(0)845 006 1435

info@yomps.co.uk

www.yomps.co.uk

PROGRAMME DESCRIPTION: Multi-country trips suitable for career breaks, combining adventure, training courses, exploration, volunteering, and cultural experiences.

DESTINATIONS: South Africa, Namibia, Malawi, Kenya, Botswana, Zambia, Zimbabwe, Mozambique, Mexico, Ecuador, Venezuela, Chile, Peru, Honduras, Thailand, Fiji, and Switzerland

NUMBER OF PLACEMENTS PER YEAR: 200+

PREREQUISITES: All ages and nationalities welcome. Sometimes specific skills are required.

DURATION AND TIME OF PLACEMENTS: Two weeks to two years; average adventure lasts eight to 12 weeks

SELECTION PROCEDURES AND ORIENTATION: Applications accepted year round. Interviews sometimes required (by telephone). Field Manual provided pre-departure, and project orientation on arrival.

COST: Prices from £990 for four weeks volunteering in South Africa, to £4,225 for six-month Venezuela explorer. Prices include accommodation, which varies according to trip: for example, a chalet (in Switzerland), a tented camp (in South Africa), a seafront volunteer base (in Mexico), a coastal volunteer base on the southern shores of Lake Malawi, a specifically-designed overlanding vehicle (in southern Africa), under the stars (in Namibia), a rural guest house (in a rural area of South Africa), an Amazonian rainforest research base (in Ecuador), and camping out in the Patagonian wilderness (in Chile).

CONTACT: Antony Wilson, Director

KEY US ORGANISATIONS

Of the thousands of organisations large and small offering programmes of possible interest primarily to North American grown-ups planning a gap year (but often to people of any nationality), here is a selection of important ones for prospective volunteers, travellers, or learners. Before choosing, it is always best to search for online feedback: for example, at www.abroadreviews. com.

- **Adelante**, Seal Beach, CA (+1 562 799 9133; www.adelanteabroad.com). Internships, volunteer placements, teaching abroad, language classes and semester placements from one to 12 months in Spain (Barcelona, Madrid, Seville, Marbella and Jerez), Costa Rica, Mexico, Uruguay, and Chile.
- **Agriventure**, International Agricultural Exchange Association, Chestermere, Alberta, Canada (+1 403 255 7799; www.agriventure.com). Details of the international farm exchange may be found in Part 6: Working and Living Abroad.
- **AIDE (Association of International Development and Exchange)**, Austin, TX (+1 512 904 1137 or +1 866 6 ABROAD; reinventyourself@aideabroad.org; www. aideabroad. org). Variety of overseas placements in volunteer, internship work, and teach abroad programmes, lasting two weeks to 12 months in Argentina, Australia, Chile, China, Costa Rica, Ecuador, England, Guatemala, India, Ireland, Peru, South Africa, Spain, and the USA. Participants pay a programme fee to cover placement, airport pick-up, accommodation, meals, local support, medical insurance, and optional language courses.
- **AmeriSpan**, Philadelphia (+1 800 879 6640; www.amerispan.com). Specialist Spanish-language travel organisation with expertise in arranging language courses, voluntary placements, and internships throughout South and Central America.
- **ArchaeoSpain**, Connecticut (+1 866 932 0003; www.archaeospain.com). Summer archaeological programmes for anyone over 18 in Spain and Italy. Sample cost: $2,450 for a month working on a Roman excavation in Spain.
- **BUNAC USA**, Southbury, CT (+1 203 264 0901; www.bunac.org). Administers a number of work exchange programmes (some open only to students).
- **CCUSA (Camp Counselors USA)**, Sausalito, CA (www.ccusa.com.) Work Experience programmes in Australia/New Zealand (18–30), and summer camp counsellors in Russia and Croatia (no upper age limit).
- **CDS International Inc**, New York (+1 212 497 3500; info@cdsintl.org). Executive-level internships for young American professionals aged 23–34 in Germany. Programmes also in Russia (ages 25–35), Argentina, and Switzerland (both up to age 30).
- **Cross-Cultural Solutions**, New Rochelle, NY (+1 800 380 4777; www.crosscultural solutions.org). See Directory entry above with UK address.
- **Earthwatch Institute**, Boston (+1 800 776 0188; www.earthwatch.org). International environmental charity, which engages people worldwide in scientific field research

and education to promote the understanding and action necessary for a sustainable environment. Prices range from $759 to $5,750, excluding travel to the location.

■ **Educators Abroad**, Duluth, MN (contact@educatorsabroad.org; www.educatorsabroad. org). English as a Foreign Language Teaching Assistant Programme. Participants can be students or adults seeking college credit, or on a non-credit certificate option. They bring their native fluency in English to schools in over 25 countries on all continents. Placements last four or ten weeks throughout the year. Programme fee of $2,300–$4,200 depending on programme option, plus travel and, in some cases, room and board. Total cost from $3,000 for four weeks. Host schools assist with arrangements for accommodation and board. $500 placement fee, plus course fee and travel (total usually $3,000–$4,000).

■ **EIL (Experiment in International Living)**, Vermont (+1 800 345 2929; www. experimentinternational.org). Programmes lasting three to five weeks, including some language training.

■ **Explorations in Travel Inc**, Guildford, VT (+1 802 257 0152; www.volunteertravel. com). International volunteers for rainforest conservation, wildlife, community, and many other projects worldwide.

■ **Foundation for Sustainable Development**, San Francisco, CA (+1 415 288 4873; www.fsdinternational.org). Short summer and longer-term internships for students, professionals, and retirees, in the field of development in Argentina, Bolivia, Nicaragua, Uganda, Kenya, and India. Normally volunteers in Latin America will be expected to converse in Spanish. Prices from $3,000 for nine weeks.

■ **GeoVisions**, Connecticut (+1 203 453 5838; +1 877 949 9998; toll-free from UK: 0800 043 4822; www.geovisions.org). Volunteer or teach abroad in range of countries from Russia to Jordan, for one to three months. Average age of volunteers is 27, and some retired people join.

■ **Global Citizens Network**, St. Paul, MN (+1 800 644 9292; www.globalcitizens.org). Volunteer vacations in Kenya, Nepal, Mexico, Guatemala, Peru, Tanzania, Arizona, and New Mexico.

■ **Global Crossroad**, Irving, TX (+1 866 387 7816; www.globalcrossroad.com). Volunteer teaching and internships in 23 countries. Paid teaching in China (one to 12 months). Placement fees from $799, but more typically $1,399 for Peru.

■ **Global Service Corps**, San Francisco (www.globalservicecorps.org). Co-operates with grass-roots organisations in Thailand, Cambodia, and Tanzania, and sends volunteers and interns for two to three weeks or longer.

■ **Global Vision International**, Boston (+l 888 653 6028, www.gviusa.com). US office of British company of same name (see entry above).

■ **Global Volunteers**, St Paul, MN (+1 800 487 1074; www.globalvolunteers.org). 'Granddaddy of the volunteer vacation movement'.

■ **Kibbutz Program Center**, New York (+1 212 462 2764; www.kibbutzprogramcenter. org). Volunteer placement service for people aged 20–35 for Israeli kibbutzim; $100 registration fee, $250 programme fee.

■ **Living Routes**, Amherst (+1 888 515 7333; www.livingroutes.org). Semester, summer, and year-abroad programmes based in eco-villages around the world, which help people of all ages gain the knowledge, skills, and inspiration to build a sustainable lifestyle. Current programmes in India, Scotland, Senegal, USA, Mexico, Brazil, and Peru.

- **Operation Crossroads Africa**, New York (+1 212 289 1949; www.operation crossroad.safrica.org). Volunteer leaders over 25 needed for seven-week summer projects in Africa.
- **Peace Corps**, 1111 20th St NW, Washington, DC 20526 (+1 800 424 8580; www.peacecorps.gov). Sends US citizens on two-year volunteer assignments to 70 countries; the average age of volunteers is 27, with no upper limit.
- **Projects Abroad**, New York (+1 888 839 3535; www.projects-abroad.org). US office of British company (see Directory entry above).
- **ProWorld Service Corps**, San Francisco (+1 877 429 6753; www.proworldvolunteers.org). Offers a range of internships in fields from business to journalism lasting two to 26 weeks, with aid agencies in Peru, Belize, Mexico, Brazil India, Thailand, and Ghana. Fees start at $1,895, which includes project work with local NGOs, language training, room and board, and cultural activities. ProWorld has a UK contact number: (0)1865 596289.
- **Radical Sabbatical**, Annapolis, MD (+1 410 227 4827; www.radicalsabbatical.net). Meditation, yoga, and group travel. Short exploratory journeys worldwide for small groups of like-minded people (aged 45–60) who are dedicated to withdrawing from routine.
- **Volunteer Abroad** (+1 888 649 3788; www.volunteerabroad.ca). Worldwide volunteer placements lasting eight to 24 weeks run by Travel Cuts, the national student travel agency of Canada, but which are open to professionals taking a career break and retirees as well. Destinations are Nepal, Ghana, Peru, Ecuador, Costa Rica, Nicaragua, and Tanzania.
- **Wildlands Studies**, Santa Cruz, CA (+1 831 477 9955; www.wildlandsstudies. com). Conservation projects lasting six weeks in the USA (including Alaska and Hawaii), Belize, Thailand, Nepal, etc.
- **World Endeavors**, Minneapolis, MN (+1 612 729 3400; www.worldendeavors.com). Volunteer, internship, and study programmes lasting two weeks to two months in many countries, from Jamaica to the Philippines.
- **WorldTeach Inc**, Cambridge, MA (+1 617 495 5527; www.worldteach.org). Non-profit organisation that provides college graduates with one-year contracts to American Samoa, Bangladesh, Costa Rica, Ecuador, Namibia, Kenya, the Marshall Islands, China, Venezuela, Chile, Pohnpei, Mongolia, Rwanda, South Africa, and Guyana. Eight-week summer programmes in Bulgaria, China, Costa Rica, Ecuador, Poland, Namibia, and South Africa. Participants pay a volunteer contribution ranging from $500 to $7,990, but several programmes are fully funded by the host country.
- **Your World to Discover**, Richmond Hill, Ontario (+1 866 646 4693; www.yourworldtodiscover.ca). Range of gap year and volunteering programmes.

The Volunteer

Name: *Chetna Patel*
Age: *50*
Experience: *28 years of experience working in computing and qualification in IT Studies*

Project Partner

Ms Kaushalya is a teacher who runs the Mawala IT Centre in Wadduwa, a small town in the Western Province of Sri Lanka. The IT Centre was established in 2003 as a means of teaching computer skills to underprivileged children. Originally situated in Avisawella (70km south-east of Colombo), the centre was relocated to Wadduwa in 2004 and now provides free classes for local children on topics such as Microsoft packages and computing theory.

Role of the Volunteer

Chetna's role at the IT Centre included the following:

- *Using her knowledge of computing to teach IT skills to children aged between 6 and 18 with class sizes of up to 130 pupils at peak times during the summer.*
- *Taking extra sessions with A-level students in order to share her experiences of working in IT and helping them in areas such as preparing CVs, career advice and interview techniques.*
- *Working with Ms Kaushalya to assess and improve current methods of teaching and the content of her classes, based on her experience of what a modern professional needs from an IT training course.*
- *Marking exam papers at the end of a three month teaching course.*

Benefits to the community

Chetna's work alongside Ms Kaushalya helped to provide the following benefits to the local community:

- *Children of all ages who live in poverty with little access to education are given the chance to gain IT skills that they can use in the future.*
- *The pupils are provided with plenty of social interaction to help them develop as people.*
- *The children are provided with life skills that can be used in the future outside the centre and in the community.*

PART 6

WORKING AND LIVING ABROAD

WORKING ABROAD
TEACHING ENGLISH
WORKING IN TOURISM
INTERNATIONAL JOB EXCHANGES
WORKING IN THE USA
WORKING IN AUSTRALIA AND NEW ZEALAND
LIVING ABROAD

GAP YEAR THAILAND
'I developed skills that I never knew I was capable of...
I went to Thailand seeking an experience that would
enrich my career. What I got was so much more than that.'

To get a broad experience I chose to be placed in two schools, helping teach English, particularly spoken English; that was perfect for my requirements and helped me get more out of the venture.

It was certainly the challenge that I had been hoping for! I always believe you learn the most when you're out of your comfort zone and getting your teeth into a challenge. Looking back, my time in Thailand made me realise that I developed skills I never knew I was capable of and this has aided my confidence and belief of what I can achieve at home.

In addition to the rewarding work-based programme, my time outside the classroom was equally compelling. The teachers in both the schools I taught at were wonderful to me. So kind and so friendly and really interested in what my life was like in the UK. In fact, during a national holiday the teachers took me to Koh Samet island. It was great to feel included as part of the team as ten of us stayed on the island to see the 'fire-dancers' on the beach at night and to take an early morning swim in the ocean. I'm no stranger to travelling, but however much I love the 'backpacker' lifestyle, my time spent teaching in Thailand was just so much more rewarding.

Now I'm back home, it's not the end of the experience. Not only do I have all the precious memories, gifts and photos but I've made friends on the other side of the world and I have those new-found skills that I can use every day. A big thank you to the Gap Year Thailand team for helping to make this trip a reality!

Kimberley White

WORKING ABROAD

Who has not dreamed of living in a place far from home: perhaps a favourite holiday destination or a place that lives in your imagination? Perhaps you want to try living elsewhere as an experiment, to gauge how you might cope with moving abroad indefinitely. But how can you translate this yearning into the reality of spending an extended period of time somewhere else, of transforming yourself from a tourist into a temporary resident? The choices at your disposal are simply to set up home and stay there, which is expensive without an income (unless you are living in a country with a very low cost of living), to find paid work, or to undertake some formal studies. (Volunteering is covered in Part 4: Doing Something Worthwhile.)

The reasons why people choose to settle temporarily in a foreign place are multitudinous, but climate is the reason most often cited. Often it's something as straightforward as wanting to be near a partner who comes from that place or who has been posted there. Living abroad is by far the best way to master a foreign language. Two-week holidays can be unsatisfactory from many points of view, and may have engendered a desire to experience a foreign culture from the inside – rather than as an onlooker or even as a holiday-home-owner.

Using a gap year to dip your toe into foreign societies and cultures needs to be distinguished from becoming an expatriate, which by definition means that you have taken up residence in another country. On a personal level, it all depends on what you classify as home and how you regard your time abroad. Calling your time abroad a sabbatical or career break implies that you are suspending your normal professional routine temporarily and intend to return to 'real life'. Inevitably these definitions can become blurred over time.

If seeing the world is your motivation for a career break, finding an opportunity to live and work in a foreign country might give you the most rewarding experience. Travelling on its own may not answer your need to get under the skin of a different culture. By setting up a temporary home abroad, however, you'll have the chance to make new friends, learn another language, and experience, not just observe, how people in different parts of the world actually live. It will be a challenging experience, as you'll need to learn fast and find ways of landing on your feet in a place where customs and laws will be different from those back home.

For those who aren't going to be able to save enough beforehand to fund a long holiday from work, or can't rely on an income by renting out their house, money will have to be earned. Taking up paid work on the road may postpone penury or provide a bit more spending money. This may involve menial jobs like farm labouring, or more skilled work such as translating technical and academic papers. The latter kind is not always preferable, as **Chris Miksovsky** concluded. He found well-paid computer work in both Sydney and Melbourne offices with ease. However, after a few months he realised that the reason he had left home was to get away from spending his days in an office, so he headed north to work on a sheep and cattle station and was thrilled with the contrast.

Another potential advantage of working abroad is that it could look good on a CV, which is important if you're concerned that a career break might be viewed as an indulgence or waste of time by future employers. Of course, the acquisition of a language will always be a plus. So too an intimate knowledge of another country can be used to your advantage in many areas of commerce and the media.

Paul Jones, now in his 30s, had already given up a full-time position in the IT industry in his native Australia in order to go freelance. So when he took the decision to go overseas for a while, he was lucky enough to have the freedom to choose when:

> Having been working for a number of years and having transferable skills in IT, it made sense to find work in Europe in my field to finance my trip. Prior to leaving, I found a job by using the internet and having interviews over the phone. I still like the fact that I got my first job by having an interview on my mobile phone, which was the clearest while standing on a city street that provided a nice drowning-out kind of noise. Not the best conditions for an interview, but it worked. The job happened to be in the Netherlands where I hadn't particularly wanted to go, but that was the job that I was accepted for first, so I took it as a stepping stone. After a number of months in a job I didn't like in a country that I never found an affinity for, I found a job in Bristol which has been my base since.

Working abroad is one of the means by which people can immerse themselves in a foreign culture, to meet foreign people on their own terms, and to gain a better perspective on their own culture and habits. The kind of job you find will determine the stratum of society in which you will mix, and therefore the content of the experience. The professional who is engaged in a job swap with someone in their profession, or who is attached to an overseas office of their old employer, will have a less radical break than the adult on a gap year who decides to do something entirely different – like teach English in the Far East or scuba dive in the Red Sea. Round-the-world traveller and blogger **Lisa Lubin** tried whenever she could to top up her travel budget (mostly savings from her ten years of working in television production in Chicago):

> I have done random jobs all around the world: I started getting travel articles and photographs published; I got a job in Australia at a café and basically broke even; did some English tutoring in Istanbul (I even cat sat, so I had a free apartment for a month); worked a few days as a research assistant at the University of Cologne; did some voice-over work for an English-learners textbook publisher in Berlin (somewhere I love and may live for awhile); and ended up doing some PR work for an English Immersion program in Spain for one year, which covered all my travel expenses. There was always a way. It is amazing how many things fall into place if you are open, willing, and friendly.

VISAS AND PERMISSION TO WORK

The great hurdle to overcome in gaining work abroad, particularly in popular destinations like the United States and Australia, is obtaining the legal right to work. The situation is much more favourable in the European Union – where citizens of any member country can work, live, and study in any of the other member states with a minimum of bureaucracy. This is perhaps one of the greatest benefits of the single market, making a working stint in Denmark, Greece, Hungary, Malta, etc, wholly feasible for British and Irish nationals.

The European Union consists of the original 15 member states (Austria, Belgium, Denmark, Finland, France, Germany, Greece, Ireland, Italy, Luxembourg, the Netherlands, Portugal, Spain, Sweden and the United Kingdom), plus the ten that joined in May 2004 (Cyprus, Czech Republic, Estonia, Hungary, Latvia, Lithuania, Malta, Poland, Slovakia, and Slovenia), and Romania and Bulgaria since 2007. The standard situation among all EU countries is that EU nationals have the right to look for work in any member state, for up to three months, but the original EU member states have pretty well abolished the necessity for EU nationals to acquire a residence permit after three months. Usually some sort of registration process is necessary but the paperwork in most countries has been simplified. However, work permits/work visas outside the EU are not readily available. It is easy to understand why most countries in the world have immigration policies that are principally job protection schemes for their own nationals. Nevertheless, it can be frustrating to encounter bureaucratic hassles if you are merely taking a break from your employment at home and want to earn a little money by picking up a job here and there on your travels.

The standard procedure for acquiring a work permit or work visa is to find an employer willing to apply to the immigration authorities on your behalf months in advance of the job's starting date, while you are in your home country. This is usually a next-to-impossible feat unless you are a high ranking nuclear physicist, a foreign correspondent, or are participating in an organised exchange programme where the red tape is taken care of by your sponsoring organisation. In some countries, an exception is made for special employment categories such as teachers of English and live-in child-carers. Official visa information should be requested from the Embassy or Consulate of the country you intend to visit; the *London Diplomatic List* contains up-to-date contact details for all diplomatic representations in London and is published online by the Foreign & Commonwealth Office (www.fco.gov.uk). Being caught working illegally in any country potentially jeopardises any chance to work there in the future or even to visit as a tourist, and may even result in the ignominy of deportation.

For specific information on the red tape governing work in the USA and Australia, see relevant sections below.

PLANNING IN ADVANCE

At the risk of oversimplifying the range of choices, anyone who aspires to work temporarily abroad must either fix up a definite job before leaving home, or take a gamble on finding something on-the-spot. (A third option of bringing your job with you is discussed below under the heading 'Remote Working'.) As in any job hunt, it is much easier to land a job if you can present yourself face-to-face to a prospective employer, which is worth more than any number of speculative applications from home. If nothing else, your presence in the flesh reassures the employer that you are serious about working and available to start as soon as a vacancy crops up.

'Easy' ways to fix up a job abroad do exist: for example, to teach English in Taiwan, work on an organic farm, or look after children for a European family. The price you pay for having this security is that you commit yourself to a new life, however temporary, sight unseen. Also, wages in some cases are negligible, and may be on a work-for-keep basis.

It is a truism to state that the more unusual and interesting the job, the more competition it will attract. For example, it is to be assumed that only a small percentage of applicants for advertised jobs actually get the chance to work as history coordinators for a European tour company, assistants at a museum bookshop in Paris, or underwater photographic models in the Caribbean. However, other less glamorous options can absorb an almost unlimited number of people: for example, working as a counsellor or sports instructor on an American children's summer camp.

Employment and temp agencies from Brussels to Brisbane can be useful to those with the right qualifications, although most of them have had to retract during the economic downturn. The major players are Manpower (www.manpower.co.uk or www.manpower.com), Drake (www.drakeintl.com), and Adecco (www.adecco.com), with about 5,500 branches in 60 countries. No matter how briefly you have worked for an agency, request a letter of reference or introduction, which may allow you to bypass some of the registration procedures if you work through the same agency elsewhere.

Reputable international recruitment agencies in Britain, the USA, and elsewhere may be looking for personnel qualified in your area of expertise for short-term contracts in fields like accountancy and IT. For example, Robert Walters plc, with 42 offices in 20 countries (www.robertwalters.com), specialises in recruiting contract staff for jobs worldwide in the fields of accountancy and finance, banking, legal, information technology, sales and marketing, human resources, support, and administration. Interviews can be pre-arranged for candidates at their city of arrival and in the case of high calibre candidates, tele-conference links are set up.

IMPROVING YOUR CHANCES

A number of steps will improve your chances of convincing an employer in person of your superiority to the competition. For example, before leaving home you might take a course in a foreign language, or acquire a portable skill like teaching English as a foreign language, catering, or scuba diving – all skills which have been put to good use by people on a gap year working abroad.

Web forums, online communities, and expatriate messageboards like www.expatsinitaly.com can be incredibly useful. Even if you are not lucky enough to have friends and family scattered strategically throughout the world, contacts can be cultivated through these channels. All the same, it is always worth broadcasting your intentions to third cousins, pen friends to whom you haven't written since you were 12, and visiting professors, in case they divulge the addresses of some useful contacts. The more widely publicised your work and travel plans are, the better your chance of being given a lead. Any locals or expatriates you meet after arrival are also a potential source of help. Any skill or hobby, from jazz to running (eg seek out the Hash House Harriers popular with expatriates worldwide), can become the basis for pursuing contacts.

JOB-HUNTING ON ARRIVAL

One of the most useful sites is the free community noticeboard Craigslist, which started in San Francisco in 1995 but has spread to hundreds of cities – from Auckland to Buenos Aires, and Moscow to Cairo. With notification of about two million new job ads a month, it is probably the biggest job board in the world – as well as carrying accommodation listings and everything else. It also lists many unpaid jobs and internships. Another excellent source of free classifieds, including job ads in many cities, is Gumtree or its affiliate Kijiji (both owned by eBay), which

ANYWORK ANYWHERE

Anywork Anywhere provides an online Job Search, Volunteer Guides and Resources for Work & Travel throughout Europe and Worldwide, via the website www.anyworkanywhere.com.

It is free to search and apply for jobs, as well as to access the resources sections, with no need to register first. Many jobs provide accommodation and sometimes meals as well. You may need to turn up for a face to face interview, but many employers are willing to interview over the phone, accompanied by a solid CV and checkable references.

Whilst the majority of positions are full-time temporary, with contracts running from a couple of weeks to 12 months, there are also a handful of advertised permanent positions, and it's not unlikely – where the employee/employer relationship has been good – for some 3/5 month summer/winter positions to turn into long term working relationships.

You could find work in Summer Resorts, Ski Resorts, Fruit Picking & Packing, Pubs & Bars, Catering, TEFL, Education, Hotels, Entertainment, Activity Centres, Voluntary & Conservation, Holiday & Theme Parks, Care Work, Childcare and other varied and exciting opportunities we come across which we feel are interesting and of value to the site…

If you fancy something with a little moral depth, there are an abundance of voluntary opportunities, with a wide range of fees to suit all budgets. Either going via a mainstream 'Western World'-based organisation, many of which you would have heard already, or for the more adventurous, going direct to a local NGO or even smaller project on the ground, we try to maintain a balance of the two, knowing that everyone has their own ideal environment for this kind of expeditionary experience.

The site is vast. As well as listing jobs or voluntary opportunities, our comprehensive Guides section has lots of helpful info on visas, working holiday visas and other varied work & travel resources. From our embassy directory, listed by host country, easy to navigate map links, country specific links sections, voluntary guides and training & courses from snowboarding to cookery – find all this and much, much more.

www.anyworkanywhere.com

are strong in the UK, Australia, New Zealand, Canada, and many others. One way of gaining a toehold is to offer your services free in the first instance. If (for example) you want a job polishing the English of documents in a company office or teaching English in a school, but there appear to be no openings, volunteer to do some unpaid translation or assist with a class one day a week for no pay, and if you prove yourself competent, you will have an excellent chance of filling a vacancy when one does crop up.

SEASONAL WORK

For a complete break from the stresses of a professional life, perhaps casual or seasonal work is the answer. Two categories of employment appeal most to seasonal workers because they appeal least to a stable working population: agriculture and tourism. Farmers from Norway to Tasmania (with the notable exception of developing countries) are not able to bring in their harvests without assistance from outside their local communities, though piece-work apple-picking in Tasmania or strawberry-picking in Denmark is unlikely to appeal to many career breakers. The tourist industry in many areas could also not survive without a short-term injection of seasonal labour. Big cities create a wealth of employment opportunities for people not driven to compete in a professional capacity.

While opening up an enormous range of possibilities, the internet can be a bewildering place to job-hunt. One of the best specialist recruitment websites is www.seasonworkers.com, a site that has been designed to help people conduct a tailored search for a summer job, outdoor sports job, ski resort job, gap year placement or course, quickly and easily. The Jobs Abroad Bulletin is a useful one-man and one-woman site (www.jobsabroadbulletin.co.uk), which dispenses with pretty graphics to deliver actual job vacancy details each month. Email subscriptions to what is billed as an 'online magazine for working abroad and taking a gap year' are free. Another recommended source of interesting paid and voluntary positions around the world, from volunteering in the Maldives to helping to restore an Italian vineyard, are listed at www.anyworkanywhere.com (see advertisement on previous page). Also look at www.overseasjobcentre.co.uk/gap, from the same people.

The site www.eurosummerjobs.com links to the EURES search engines. EURES, the government-run Europe-wide employment service, operates as a network of EuroAdvisers who have specialist expertise on living and working in other member states. The searchable database of general vacancies can be found at the EURES Job Mobility Portal www.ec.europa.eu/eures/home. Other commercial sites may also have something worth applying for, like www.kareve.com or www.britishexpats.com.

REMOTE WORKING

One notable work-abroad trend has been for more and more people to carry on an online business from anywhere in the world. Graphic designers, copyeditors, and short-traders have all succeeded in doing business through their computers. Websites with telling names like laptophobo.com, NuNomad.com, and locationindependent.com appeal to the market addressed by an article in *Business Week*:

Do you ever wish you could win the lottery, chuck the rat race, and take off to explore the world? Heck – who hasn't? These days, however, there's a group of independent-minded, techno-savvy entrepreneurs who are turning that dream into a reality. They call themselves New Nomads, and they've transformed work-at-home into work-anywhere-you-damn-well-please.

One such peripatetic businessman is **Charlie Wetherall**, originally from Montana, who runs the website runawaytrader.com:

I was reflecting today about how I got into this runaway mode in the first place and recalled that I can blame Susan Griffith for some of it. Her book Work Your Way Around the World *offered a glimmer of hope that – someday – I could scrape up enough courage to escape the drudgery of my own existence and see some of the world. I never gave up on the idea of flitting about the globe and inventing a way to pay for that extravagance as I travelled. Now we can do business – that is, make a living – from practically anywhere on the planet. Sure, you may choose an occupation like ditch-digger or a police officer that requires your local presence, but you can also pick an income-producing gig that can be performed from anywhere on the world. All you have to do is figure out what you're good at, and take it on the road – and get paid for it. Simple as that. Thanks to wireless and other advanced computer technologies, it's now possible to make money buying and selling stocks as I do from almost anywhere in America, and anywhere in the world. As for me, it's strictly pay as you go. If I make money day trading, I go, and keep going. If I don't, I'm marooned. It's as simple as that. I want to know if I can day trade at basecamp on Mount Everest (that's a trip I'm scheduling for spring); I know I can get to all these exotic places but can I whip out my laptop and make a trade from wherever 'there' is?*

Most people earning while travelling have built websites that produce a steady income stream. **Kirsty Henderson** itemises her earnings from various web ventures on her website www. nerdynomad.com. Link-building to get your websites to the top of Google seems to be the preferred way to flourish. Websites use Google's AdSense to 'monetise' their content, which is measured in clicks.

TEACHING ENGLISH

Although the English language is still the language that literally millions of people around the world want to learn, finding work as an English teacher has become more difficult in recent years, as an increasing number of people of all ages are acquiring specialised training. The number of public and private institutes turning out certified TEFL teachers in the UK, Ireland, North America, and the Antipodes has greatly increased, creating a glut of teachers chasing the good jobs – especially in the major cities of Europe like Paris and Prague.

Having sounded that warning note, there are still areas of the world where the boom in English language learning seems to know no bounds: from Ecuador to China, Slovakia to Cambodia. A university degree is sufficient to find a respectable job in Thailand, Japan, China, Korea, Taiwan, and others. In small private schools and back-street agencies, being a native speaker and dressing neatly are sometimes sufficient qualifications to get a job. But for more stable teaching jobs in recognised language schools, you will have to sign a contract (usually a year to qualify for a visa).

THE OLDER TEACHER

An increasing number of early-retired and other mature people are becoming interested in teaching English abroad for a year or two. Although it may be true that in certain contexts, language institutes are more inclined to employ a bright young graduate, if only for reasons of image and marketing, there are plenty of others who will value maturity – especially the growing number of establishments that specialise in teaching young children. Peter Beech, Director of Anglo-Hellenic in Corinth, Greece, which trains and places teachers in jobs, has noticed an increasing interest from people who have already had a career in the UK, in teaching or in any field, who want to move abroad. One of his cases is **Jerry Melinn**, who enjoyed teaching English at an institute in Athens so much that he has signed on for another year:

> I suppose you could say I don't fit the profile of a TEFL teacher. Usually they are unattached, young, and out to see the world after finishing their university studies. I worked in the telecommunications industry in Ireland for almost 40 years and took advantage of an early retirement scheme when I was 56 years old. I didn't want to stop working and, as my four children were grown up, I decided – with the agreement of my wife – to try my hand at teaching English in Greece. I was interested in Greece because we have friends here and had been coming to Greece on holidays for many years.
>
> I have read some horror stories on the internet about teaching in Greece, but my experience has been great. The TEFL training course in Corinth (www.teflcorinth.com) prepared me well for teaching here at the Katsianos School of Foreign Languages in Athens. I have learned so much,

TEFL EXPRESS
www.teflexpress.co.uk
A 100-hour TEFL course led to Ho Chi Minh City, the Gobi Desert and the Great Wall...
...and an enviable career along the way.

Enda Harty's modesty belies his success. He is talented, charming and unavoidably likeable. TEFL Express caught up with him as he launches the TEFL Express Online business.

Enda, tell me how your career started?
I'd finished college, done some travelling and knew I'd like to see more of the world. I did a TEFL course in 2000, though without any teaching experience or long term plan.

It seems to have led you down an interesting road.
Yea, first stop Vietnam. My first teaching job did take a few months; an internship would have made things easier. I taught both adults and children in various centres in Vietnam and China over the next six years. My experience in reputable schools was invaluable when I moved somewhere new. In 2003 I was offered Director of Studies at Language Link, Beijing and then moved on to overseeing the running of 12 schools in China. I also developed new courses for teens which were very popular.

You enjoyed life in Asia?
Absolutely loved it! Vietnam is amazing – a unique culture and fantastic people. I had loads of fun and made great friends. China was intriguing and where most of my professional development happened. While I was based there I saw Cambodia, Laos, Mongolia, Thailand, Japan, and North Korea – deeply enriching cultural experiences, especially Laos and the Gobi desert – what a place!

I believe you got an Award in China? Why did you leave?
The City of Beijing gave me a Great Wall of Friendship Award for my Contribution to Beijing's Society and Growth. They have a big emphasis on learning English. Hungry for teachers! I'd started developing more courses and was interested in broadening the availability through the web when a beautiful Spanish girl lured me to Majorca! Now I'm based between the UK, Ireland and Majorca and really excited about taking online teaching where it hasn't gone yet.

made many new friends, and grown very attached to the school and especially the students. I have nothing but admiration for them as they come to lessons twice a week after Greek school, and the vast majority are well-behaved and good-humoured. The pay and conditions are the same as most schools in Greece: beginning at €700 a month with accommodation provided and all bills paid, as well as IKA (health insurance), which I thought was very good.

Whereas few companies openly impose an upper age limit, some age discrimination does regrettably take place – more noticeably in some countries than others. For older job-seekers it will be a matter of spreading their net as widely as possible by contacting as many relevant organisations, including voluntary ones, as possible. Older applicants may have to work harder to demonstrate enthusiasm, energy, and adaptability to prospective employers, but this should be no bar to someone committed to creating adventures later in life.

Australian journalists **Alexandra Neuman** and **John Carey**, aged 49 and 50 respectively, decided that having worked for 30-odd years it was time to do something different. They didn't want to do the sensible thing and wait till retirement, so started saving and planning and after a couple of years had enough to fund a year in Italy. At first Alex didn't work, but when they decided to extend their stay Alex needed to find work, and really the only work available was teaching English – which is what she is doing right now in the lovely town of Bergamo:

Above all you must bring with you tolerance, flexibility, and an upbeat attitude. The rewards are well worth it. I love living here. The upside to teaching is that the Italians working in the schools are great on the whole: everyone knows that the system is bad and tries to help each other through it. I have never met such kindness. The students are also great and if you have a class you get to know, teaching can be really fun. It's a good way to get to know people and to gain a sense of belonging and really getting involved. I know the bureaucracy is terrible and I get paid badly, but as I sit looking out of my hilltop apartment to the snow capped Alps and the grapes ripening on the vine just below my bedroom window, I think life is pretty wonderful!

TEFL TRAINING

The only way to outrival the competition and make the job hunt (not to mention the job itself) easier, is to do a training course in Teaching English as a Foreign Language (known as TEFL; pronounced 'teffle'). Intensive Certificate courses are typically delivered over four weeks and cost between £850 and £1,100. The two standard recognised Certificate qualifications that will improve your range of job options are the Cambridge Certificate in English Language Teaching to Adults (CELTA), administered and awarded by the University of Cambridge Local ESOL Exam Unit (address in Resources listing below), and the Certificate in TESOL (Teaching English to Speakers of Other Languages), offered by Trinity College London. Both courses involve at least 100 hours of rigorous training with a practical emphasis (full-time for four weeks, or part-time over several months; the latter option might suit grown-ups who are not ready to give up their jobs but want to equip themselves for a future break). Although there are no fixed pre-requisites apart from a suitable level of language awareness, not everyone who applies is accepted.

CLIC
(CENTRO DE LENGUAS E INTERCAMBIO CULTURAL)
Teaching English and living in Andalucia, Spain

The first time I came to Andalucia I was a 14-year-old school girl, and I spent two weeks in Almeria over Easter. I couldn't get over the colours, sights and sounds of the Semana Santa processions, as well as the warm March sunshine, and I vowed to come back. It took me 12 years, but it's a decision I have never regretted. I did a CELTA teacher training course and packed my bags, coming to Spain after an enjoyable two-year period in Japan.

The first thing which struck me was how everybody seems to live life on the streets, chatting while enjoying tapas, beers and wine until the early hours. Initially in Cordoba, the mixture of Arabic, Roman and Catholic Kings' architecture made it such a magical place, and the month of May, with a different festival every week, kept me there for five years. I also met my partner Miguel, with my Spanish quickly improving!

I loved my job teaching English to students from 5–75 years of age, beginners level to advanced, so I then moved from Cordoba to Seville for further job opportunities where I became involved in teacher training. Seville may be bigger but it also draws you like a magnet, with its elegance and feeling of aquí estoy ('here I am!'). The April fair, flamenco, football, and the warm spring and autumn days are all here to be savoured. The coast is only an hour away which can be a welcome escape midsummer, and being here when Spain won the World Cup was an unforgettable experience.

I have met so many interesting people through my working and personal life over the years and have discovered so many hidden corners of Andalucia, I wouldn't swap living here and teaching English for anything.

Claire Potter

A listing of the 280+ centres offering the CELTA course is available from the University of Cambridge, and can be searched on their website www.cambridgesol.org/teaching. Here is a small selection:

- **Basil Paterson College**, Edinburgh (0131 225 3802; www.basilpaterson.co.uk). Nine courses per year: £1,150.
- **Ealing, Hammersmith & West London College**, London (0800 980 2185; www.wlc. ac.uk). Five times a year: £945.
- **Embassy CES**, Cambridge (01223 345650; www.embassyces.com). Full-time, roughly four per year: £1,250.
- **International House**, 16 Stukeley St, Covent Garden, London WC2B 5LQ (020 7611 2414; www.ihlondon.com). Certificate course runs at least monthly: £1,250 plus exam fee of £108. Also offers courses at IH Newcastle (www.ihnewcastle.com) for £995.
- **Language Link**, London (020 7370 4755; www.languagelink.co.uk). £960 full-time; £995 part-time over 12 weeks. Language Link has a network of affiliated schools in Russia, China, Vietnam, Kazakhstan, and Uzbekistan.
- **St Giles College Highgate**, 51 Shepherd's Hill, London N6 5QP (020 8340 0828; www. stgiles-international.com). Nine times a year: £995. Also offered monthly at St Giles in Brighton and eight times a year in San Francisco ($2,495).
- **Stanton Teacher Training**, Stanton House, 167 Queensway, London W2 4SB (020 7221 7259; www.stanton-school.co.uk). £920, including Cambridge registration fee.

Centres offering the Trinity College Certificate include:

- **Golders Green Teacher Training Centre**, London (020 8731 0963; www.english languagecollege.co.uk). Five week course, seven times a year: £879 plus exam fee.
- **Inlingua Teacher Training & Recruitment**, Cheltenham (01242 250493; www. inlingua-cheltenham.co.uk). £1,095 plus moderation fee. May be able to help successful candidates obtain posts in inlingua schools in Ecuador, Italy, Germany, Russia, etc.
- **International House Bristol**, Bristol (0117 909 0911; www.ihbristol.com). £1,360 including moderation fee.
- **Oxford TEFL London**, London (www.oxfordtefl.com). Offered monthly: £995.

Cambridge CELTA courses are offered at more than 280 overseas centres, from the Middle East to Queensland, including eight in the USA and six in Canada. From 2011 Cambridge is piloting a partially online CELTA, which will still require 60 hours of observed teaching practice in person. The course will have to be done over at least ten weeks, and they predict that it won't be any cheaper.

Independent TEFL training course providers may be tracked down around the world, with a growing number of distance learning options available. Some companies are delivering complete courses online, for example i-to-i TEFL (see Directory entry), and others offer an additional chance to do face-to-face teaching practice such as TEFL Express (0800 048 8861; www. teflexpress.co.uk), Global English (www.global-english.com) and INTESOL Worldwide (www.in-tesoltesoltraining.com). It is strongly recommended that you ensure that the certificate course for which you are applying is accredited by an independent body.

Other centres for American readers to consider are Transworld Schools in San Francisco (www.transworldschools.com), San Diego State University/American Language Institute (www.americanlanguage.com), and the Boston Language Institute (www.teflcertificate.com), which offer highly regarded *sui generis* certificates with extensive job placement assistance.

Many advantages can be gained by signing up for a TEFL course in the place where you want to work. Most TEFL training centres have excellent contacts with language schools and can assist with the job hunt. Scores of independent providers provide TEFL training courses of varying lengths, though note that qualifications may not be recognised outside their own organisations.

TEFL RESOURCES

- **Teaching English Abroad** by Susan Griffith (Vacation Work/Crimson). The 2010/11 edition is the definitive guide to short and long-term opportunities for trained and untrained teachers.
- **British Council**, Information Centre, Manchester (0161 957 7755; www.britishcouncil. org). Distributes information on getting started in TEFL.
- **University of Cambridge ESOL Examinations**, Cambridge (01223 553355; www. cambridgeesol.org/teaching). Administers the Cambridge Certificate in English Language Teaching to Adults (CELTA) and other specialised qualifications in English Language Teaching.
- **Trinity College London**, London (020 7820 6100; www.trinitycollege.co.uk). Administers the Certificate in TESOL (Teaching English to Speakers of Other Languages). Course locations provided on website.

WHAT ENGLISH TEACHING INVOLVES

It is difficult to generalise about what work you will actually be required to do once hired as a TEFL teacher. At one extreme you have the world traveller who is hired by a businessman to correct English pronunciation on a one-to-one basis, and at the other you get teachers contracted to teach a gruelling 30-hour week, split between early morning and evening classes requiring extensive preparation.

Native speaker teachers are nearly always employed to stimulate conversation, rather than to teach grammar. Yet a basic knowledge of English grammar is a great asset when pupils come to ask awkward questions. The book *English Grammar in Use* by Raymond Murphy (Cambridge University Press, 1994) is recommended for its clear explanations and accompanying student exercises. Other useful books for unsupported English teaching placements include *Five-Minute Activities: A Resource Book of Short Activities* by Penny Ur, and *Games for Language Learning* by Andrew Wright, David Betteridge, and Michael Buckby (both Cambridge Handbooks for Language Teachers, 1992 and 1984), and *Lessons from Nothing* by Bruce Marsland (Cambridge University Press, 1998).

Each level and age group brings its own rewards and difficulties. Beginners of all ages usually delight in their progress, which will be much more rapid than it is later on. Not everyone, however, enjoys teaching young children (a booming area of TEFL, from Portugal to Taiwan), which usually involves sing-songs, puzzles, and games. Intermediate learners (especially if they are adolescents) can be difficult, since they will have reached a plateau and may be discouraged.

Adults are usually well-motivated, though may be inhibited about speaking. Teaching professionals and business people is almost always well paid. Discipline is seldom a problem, at least outside Western Europe. In fact, you may find your pupils disconcertingly docile and possibly also overly exam-oriented.

Most schools practise the direct method (total immersion in English), so not knowing the language shouldn't prevent you from getting a job. Some employers may provide nothing more than a scratched blackboard and will expect you to dive in using the 'chalk and talk' method. Brochures picked up from tourist offices or airlines can be a useful peg on which to hang a lesson, as can photographs of your home town. If you're stranded without any ideas, write the lyrics of a pop song on the board and discuss.

The wages paid to English teachers are usually reasonable, and in developing countries are quite often well in excess of the average local wage. In return you will be asked to teach some fairly unsociable hours since most private English classes take place after working hours, and so schedules split between early morning and evening are not at all uncommon. It is also possible to arrange an informal exchange of English conversation for discounted accommodation or lessons in the destination language. At least two Spanish companies, Vaughan Town (www.vaughantown.com) and Pueblo Ingles (www.puebloingles.com), offer one-week programmes whereby holiday resorts in Spain are 'stocked' with native English speakers and Spanish clients who want to improve their English. English-speaking participants receive free room and board, and transport from Madrid.

Of course many people on an extended break teach English on a voluntary basis. Thailand is a popular destination for career breakers: **Ed Reinert** worked as a salesman for 25 years before becoming a teacher in Thailand, while **Carlos Vega** was a computer technician who says, 'There is nothing else you can do here but be a teacher, even if you are not a teacher.' **Barbara Darragh** sent this account of volunteering in Thailand in 2010:

> *My first volunteer trip to Thailand was with an organisation set up after the tsunami. I then went to Chiang Mai for six months, and, after completing a month's TEFL course with See TEFL in Chiang Mai (www.seetefl.com), I offered my services to a local school. I loved working there and made many Thai friends who are always emailing me and asking me when I plan to return, which I hope to do again in September. It is very easy to find good cheap accommodation and the Thai people are so friendly. The children are a delight to teach and are so excited when you go into the school. The poorer schools where I volunteer would never normally be able to afford an 'English' English teacher. There is also plenty of paid work and I did have a private student; if I had wanted I could have had a lot more. As soon as people realise that you are an English teacher they want you to teach them or their family. I have never felt so rewarded in a job before, and the fact that I want to go back and work for nothing must say something.*

Those who are worried about financing a period abroad as a volunteer teacher should find out if it might be possible to earn some pocket money doing private teaching. For example, in Thailand it is fairly easy to do some supplementary English teaching, as **Steph Morrison**, a participant in the Gap Year in Thailand programme, reported at the end of 2010:

> *After only three weeks in Thailand, I've got two university students who wanted some tutoring – totalling five hours a week which they are prepared to pay me for. And one of the teachers in the secondary school has asked if I would spend an hour a week with him and his friend, just learning conversational English.*

ENGLISH FOR SPECIFIC PURPOSES

English for Specific Purposes (ESP) refers to the practice of teaching groups of employees the specific vocabulary they will need in their jobs, preferably by a native speaker of English with experience of that job. This means that anyone with a professional background – such as business, banking, tourism, medicine, science and technology, secretaries, etc – can try to be matched to an appropriate group of language learners, from airline staff to exporters. They want lessons in which they can pretend to be telephoning a client or chasing a missing order. People on a gap year are often far more suited to this kind of teaching than a freshly-qualified TEFL teacher would be.

When applying to an organisation that serves this business market, try to demonstrate your commercial flair with a polished presentation – including a business-like CV. **Andrew Sykes** felt that he owed the success of his job-hunt in France to his experience of accountancy, rather than to his TEFL Certificate:

> *I wrote to lots of schools in France and elsewhere that didn't stipulate 'Experience required' and was fairly disheartened by the few, none-too-encouraging replies along the lines of: 'If you're in town, give us a call'. Sitting in a very cheap hotel bedroom halfway down Italy in early November feeling sorry for myself and knowing that I was getting closer and closer to my overdraft limit and an office job back in the UK, I rang the schools that had replied. 'Drop in,' the voice said, 'and we will give you an interview.' So I jumped on the next train to Bordeaux, met the director on Monday and was offered a job on the Tuesday morning – initially on an hour-by-hour basis and then in December on a contract of 15 hours, which was later increased to 20 hours a week.*
>
> *What got me the job was not my TEFL certificate nor my good French: it was the fact that I was an ex-accountant. I had been one of the thousands enticed by the financial benefits of joining an accountancy firm after graduation, but I hated the job and failed my first professional exams. Ironically the experience gained during those years of hell was invaluable because in France most employers are looking for business experience (whereas in Italy they want teaching experience).*

You will in the end be teaching people, not objects, and any experience you can bring to the job (and especially the job interview) will help. However ashamed you may be of telling everyone in the pub back home that you were once a rat catcher, it may be invaluable if the school's main client is Rentokil.

THE JOB HUNT

Here is a list of some of the key English Language Teaching recruitment sites:
- *www.eslcafe.com*
- *www.TEFL.com*
- *www.tesljobs.co.uk*
- *www.youcanteachenglish.com/jobs*
- *www.jobs.edufind.com*
- *www.tefl.net*
- *jobs.guardian.co.uk/jobs/education/tefl. Job vacancy listings on the Guardian Unlimited website; also check the Guardian's TEFL pages (www.guardian.co.uk/education/tefl).*

The best time of year is between Easter and July. Very occasionally a carefully-crafted CV and enthusiastic personality are as important as TEFL training and experience.

Other websites that are country specific – eg www.ohayosensei.com (jobs in Japan) and www.ajarn.com (teaching in Thailand) can be goldmines of local information and job vacancies. The major language school chains hire substantial numbers of teachers, many of whom will have graduated from in-house training courses. Among the major employers of TEFL teachers are Bénédict Schools (www.benedict-international.com), Berlitz (www.berlitz.com), EF English First Teacher Recruitment and Training, (based in Shanghai; www.teachenglishfirst.com; www. ef-teachers.com), International House (www.ihworld.com), Language Link in London (www. languagelink.co.uk), Linguarama (www.linguarama.com), Saxoncourt (www.saxoncourt.com), and Wall Street Institute International (www.wallstreetinstitute.com).

For schools, a web advert offers an easy and instantaneous means of publicising a vacancy to an international audience. CVs can be emailed quickly and cheaply to advertising schools, who can then use email themselves to chase up references. Arguably it has become a little too easy to advertise and answer job adverts online. At the press of a button, your CV can be clogging up hundreds of computers. After sweating his way through a CELTA course one summer, **Fergus Cooney** (an aspiring musician from Scotland) turned to the internet to find a job:

> *After installing myself in the cheapest net café in Edinburgh I began reading and posting emails here, there, and everywhere. I also posted a message on Dave's eslcafe.com: a message stating 'Qualified teacher seeking job'. Within two days I was inundated with many dozens of replies requesting my CV and, more surprising, with job offers everywhere from Andorra to Zonguldak, through Italy, Poland, Turkey, Russia, and too many to count from Korea, Taiwan, and China. Jackpot, I thought. (I have since realised that many schools/agents must have an automatic reply system that emails those who advertise in the way I did.) I quickly began sifting through the replies but not as quickly as they kept arriving in my inbox. Before a few days had passed, I had become utterly confused and had forgotten which school was which; which Mr Lee-Soo was which, etc. So I deleted them all, got a new email address and posted a second more specific message on Dave's: 'Teacher with degree + CELTA seeks job in Italy/Spain'. This had the desired effect. A couple of days later my inbox began to fill, though not overflow, with replies. I still had to delete many from China etc, but could work with the rest and chose a school in Calabria.*

A choice he later came to regret but that is another story.

Other career-breakers simply wait until they arrive at their destination to look around for money-making teaching opportunities. American **Bradwell Jackson's** holiday travels throughout his 20s and 30s persuaded him to re-invent himself as a long-term world traveller and as of 2011 he was funding his travels by teaching English in Guiyang, in southern China. After reading my book *Work Your Way Around the World*, he made the decision to quit his job as a drug abuse counsellor, give most of his belongings to charity, sell his car, and wander the earth freely. He wondered if it was really possible to get a job teaching English so easily, and in Mexico City proved that it was. Later he depended on luck again when he ended up teaching in a most unlikely corner of the world: Nouakchott in Mauritania, West Africa. His most recent trip has been to Taiwan to investigate the teaching scene:

I couldn't believe all the English schools in Taipei. I presumed that the market must be saturated by now and that it would be too difficult to find a job, but after talking to the scuttlebutt-mongers at the Taipei Hostel (www.taipeihostel.com/teach), I found out that this was not the case. The hostel is English teaching central for foreigners, and the common room is where all the newcomers meet to get the latest on the English teaching situation. Once you get the lowdown from the old hands there, just pick a direction and start walking. After passing about three corners, you'll definitely see an English school: probably two. Have your introduction ready, march on in there and sell.

FREELANCING

An alternative to working for a language school is to set yourself up as a freelance private tutor. While undercutting the fees charged by the big schools, you can still earn more than as a contract teacher. Normally you will have to be fairly well-established in a place before you can attempt to support yourself by private teaching, preferably with some decent premises in which to give lessons (either private or group) and with a telephone.

It is always difficult to start teaching without contacts and a good working knowledge of the language. When you do get started, it may be difficult to earn a stable income because of the frequency with which pupils cancel. It is unrealistic for a newly-arrived freelancer to count on earning enough to live on in the first six months or so.

Getting clients for private lessons is a marketing exercise, and all the avenues that seem appropriate to your circumstances have to be explored. Here are some ways you can market yourself:

- Advertise your tutoring skills on a free community noticeboard online like Gumtree, or set up a Facebook group.
- Find out if the city you are in has a meeting place for locals and native English speakers. For example, in Istanbul there is a flourishing English Spoken Café (the location is announced on the Facebook group) where Turkish language learners can meet up with native speakers informally, and which would be a good hunting ground for private pupils.
- Put a notice up in schools and universities, supermarkets, or corner shops, and run an advertisement in the local paper.
- Send neat notices to local public schools, announcing your willingness to ensure the children's linguistic future.
- Compile a list of addresses of professionals (lawyers, architects, etc) who may need English for their work and have the resources to pay for it. Then contact them.
- Call on export businesses, distribution companies, travel agencies, or any businesses you think might have staff who need English for their jobs.

These methods should put you in touch with a few hopeful language learners. If you are good at what you do, word will spread and more paying pupils will come your way, though the process can be slow.

If you are more interested in integrating with the local culture than making money, exchanging conversation for board and lodging may be an appealing possibility. This can be arranged by answering (or placing) small ads in appropriate places. The American Church in Paris notice board is famous for this.

WORKING IN TOURISM

The travel and tourism industry employs a staggering 19 million people across the European Union, which represents nearly 13% of the workforce. A season of working as a tour guide, holiday rep, or sports instructor might exactly suit someone taking a gap year, though, on the whole, the work is hard and the pay low.

Everywhere you look on the internet, potentially useful links can be found. A surprising number of tour operators and other travel company home pages feature a Recruitment or Human Resources icon, which you can click to find out about jobs. Dozens of sites may prove useful such as www.resortjobs.co.uk (part of natives.co.uk). Two US-based sites – www.cool-works.com and www.jobmonkey.com – are recommended for seasonal jobs in the tourist industry. Check out the glossy magazine *Wanderlust* for independent travellers. It carries ads which might be relevant in its Job column (www.wanderlust.co.uk/travel-jobs): for example, vacancies with adventure travel companies for 25–35-year-old Spanish-speaking tour leaders in the eastern Mediterranean or in Latin America. Opportunities for cycle holiday leaders or hill-walking guides are also notified in specialist outdoor magazines. Often a first aid certificate and driving licence are required, and in some cases a specialist certificate such as the MLTE (Mountain Leader Training).

Many tourist destinations are in remote places where there is no local pool of labour. Itinerant job-seekers have ended up working in hotels and lodges in some of the most beautiful corners of the world, from the South Island of New Zealand to the shores of Lake Malawi. People with some training in catering will probably find themselves in demand; in addition to hotel and restaurant kitchens, cooks and chefs can put their talents to good use in a range of venues from luxury yachts to holiday ranches, and safari camps to ski chalets.

RESORTS

It is not at all unusual for people who have been working in business or industry for a few years to want to work in the sun for a while. You are always hearing about somebody's sister who has just run away from their office job to work with Club Med or Mark Warner in some holiday hotspot. While Mediterranean resorts in places like the Canaries, Ibiza, and Corfu are staffed mostly by young party animals, other locations are more suitable for a grown-up gap year. More mature candidates may be appreciated by companies catering to that market: a hope expressed by a woman from Yorkshire who posted a request for relevant information on the 'Living and Working Abroad' branch of Lonely Planet's Thorn Tree website:

I've done the career thing: 17 years in banking, finishing up as a relatively senior manager. But I'm opting out of the rat race now with a handy redundancy payment in my pocket. I passionately want to live on an unspoilt Greek island. I don't mind being paid peanuts, a pit for accommodation is fine, and a bicycle is an improvement on the transport I'll have in the UK (my feet). I haven't applied to just an ordinary holiday company but rather to a specialist in unspoilt Greek islands. Their prices are a little higher and their clientele a little older. I should know, since I've holidayed with them four times. Each time the rep was over 30, and once he was over 50 so I don't worry about being too old.

HOSTELS

At the age of 29, it hadn't occurred to **Steph Fuccio** to strap on a backpack until she spent time working in a travellers' hostel in San Francisco and met a series of creative travellers. They inspired her to save like mad and make a trip to the part of Italy from which her family originates. By making use of the international hostel site www.hostels.com, Steph had little difficulty pre-arranging a hostel job:

> *I was working at a really cute, small hostel in Rome called Hostel Casanova, and was working seven days a week (I was a bit scared about running out of money since this was the first leg of the trip). As well as getting to stay there for free, they paid me €20 per day in cash which was really nice. Rome was so cheap (from a San Francisco point of view) and with great weather, it was easy to save. I came to Italy with $700 cash and a plane ticket; I left with about $600 and a plane ticket to England and Ireland.*

TOUR OPERATORS

A list of special interest and activity tour operators (to whom people with specialist skills can apply) is available from AITO, the Association of Independent Tour Operators (www.aito.co.uk). When Roger Turski came to a crisis in his career and wanted a gap year, he knew immediately that he wanted to go to Africa to work at a safari lodge. He was able to arrange this with the help of an agency that specialises in making placements in eco-tourism in Africa and Asia:

> *I decided I needed a career sabbatical and wanted to combine this with my passion for the African Bush. At 39 years of age my desire was to spend time through voluntary work at a Game Lodge in Southern Africa. Within a few clicks of the internet I came across The Leap, and after a call to the director, I knew I had found the kind of thing I was looking for. I was thrilled at the type of experiences on offer, which were much closer to the career sabbatical I was after than some normal gap year projects.*
>
> *My time in Botswana was nothing short of magical. The safari company has four lodges as part of their operation (three in Botswana and one in Zambia) and I spent time in all of them, learning and experiencing a life that few imagine possible. Realising that I was there to work, I was quite happy to be given tasks that utilised some of my city-born skills. Initially I helped the company resolve some logistical issues they were having with maintaining correct levels of food and general supplies within each lodge. In doing this I picked up some new skills along the way, and have come away with a rudimentary but solid knowledge of how to run a safari operation. Eventually I moved on to helping with relief management of the camps whilst the permanent*

managers were on leave. This was quite a responsibility as the guests pay a premium price for a luxury safari holiday and demand the service that goes with it. I did of course have many, many opportunities to see the wildlife. Some events will stay with me for the rest of my life. Coming across your first pride of lions, alone in a completely open vehicle, is quite an experience.

OVERLAND TOUR LEADERS

Leaders are needed to escort groups on tours within Europe by a range of companies. Drivers need to have a Passenger Carrying Vehicle (PCV) or a Large Goods Vehicle (LGV) licence, the training for which can cost between £1,500 and £3,000. Working in Africa, Asia, and Latin America as an adventure tour leader is usually only for people in their late 20s and 30s willing to train for one of the specialist licences, and with some knowledge of mechanics. Competent and well-travelled expedition staff over 25 are in demand by the many overland companies and youth travel specialists, which advertise their tours and occasionally their vacancies in magazines like the London giveaway *TNT* (www.tntmagazine.com) or *Wanderlust*. See page 259 for a section on Adventure Travel, including a list of the main overland operators.

Occasionally opportunities arise that are true 'working holidays', ie you exchange your input as a guide or a cook in exchange for the chance to join an adventure tour free of charge. For example, at the time of going to print, the safari company Africa Expedition Support (www. africaexpeditionsupport.com) was looking for 'tour group facilitators' to cook and lead groups in East Africa, in exchange for flights from the UK, living expenses, and a small wage.

The job of expedition tour leader may sound glamorous, but it can be daunting unless you know well the countries and places through which you will be expected to chaperone your group. The journalist **Rosemary Behan**, who took her own gap year, gave an account in the *Daily Telegraph* of a small group tour she joined in southwest China:

Our group numbered seven plus our Australian guide. We were concerned to learn that she had never been to China before, but we hoped for the best. It soon became clear that our guide was seriously out of her depth, barely managing to shepherd us on to local buses and trains, let alone give us the expert insight into the country we had all hoped for. On the other hand, simply having someone to take responsibility for our daily transport and accommodation needs did allow us more time for reflection.

SKI RESORTS

Ski resorts generate many vacancies in the tourist industry. Staff are needed to be in charge of chalets, to patrol the slopes, to dispense and maintain hired skis, and of course to instruct would-be skiers. Either you can try to fix up a job with a British-based ski tour company before you leave (which minimises red tape because your wages are paid into a UK bank and you have a secure contract, though with low wages) or you can look for work on the spot, where there will be a lot of competition from the young and footloose. Recruitment websites include www.natives.co.uk, www.skiconnection.co.uk, www.seasonworkers.com, and www. freeradicals.co.uk – all of which aim to be one-stop-shops for recruitment of winter staff for

Europe and worldwide. Also check out www.snowworkers.com, which carries ski resort jobs in Japan and elsewhere. For ski instructing courses, see the section on Snow Sport Courses in Part 9: New Skills and New Projects. Some chalet companies hire older applicants: for instance VIP Chalets (0844 557 3119; www.vip-chalets.com) says that the 150 people they hire for their chalets in Val d'Isère, Méribel, Alpe d'Huez, La Plagne, Les Gets, Morzine, and Zermatt tend to be 'more mature than most; the average age last year was 31'. Le Ski (www.leski.com/alpinejobs) is another company that will consider older applicants to manage chalets in France.

After nearly a decade of working in London, first as a restaurant manager and then in the head office of a top restaurant company, **Laura Clarke** was beginning to get a little bored and very fed up with London: the noise, pollution, traffic, nine-to-five stress, delays, bomb threats, etc. On a skiing holiday she met Mike, who was working a season after being made redundant from his job in London. It felt like the right time to take the plunge and work a ski season herself. When she told her friends they said, 'About time too'. Apparently it was all she'd talked about for years. Her employer kept her job open for her but she had fallen in love with the Alps (as well as with Mike), and now she and her husband run a catered chalet company in La Rosière called Snowcrazy. They have even created the 'Ultimate Chalet Host Cookery Course', to enable others to leave the rat race and move to the mountains to run a chalet during a career break. Laura describes the advantages of her new life, as of the beginning of the 2010/11 season:

No stress, skiing almost everyday, improving ski technique, meeting new friends, having a great social life. Downsides: it's hard work physically and long days. I wish I'd done this when I was 18! We live in a beautiful place, it's quiet in the summer and busy in the winter. We go hiking and skiing whenever we want. We are really living the dream!

INTERNATIONAL JOB EXCHANGES

Even though you will be performing the same job on a job swap as you do at home, it will involve a significant change in your life and therefore qualifies as a gap year for grown-ups. You'll have the chance to relocate abroad, meet new colleagues, and put yourself in a new, challenging environment. If you're keen to live abroad without giving up your job and its income, then this could be an ideal way of taking a break from the usual routines at home and work.

Employees of multinational companies are sometimes lucky enough to be offered a posting abroad so that their career break is laid on for them. A growing trend is for companies to send personnel abroad on temporary secondments, rather than as full blown expats. The term 'flexpats' has been coined for this.

TEACHER EXCHANGES

The UK government supports the idea of teacher sabbaticals and local authorities may even make funding available. Qualified teachers can join a post-to-post exchange through the League for the Exchange of Commonwealth Teachers (0118 902 1171; www.lect.org.uk), which assists British teachers with at least five years' experience to arrange one-year or one-term exchanges with colleagues in Australia and Canada. LECT also manages a number of other professional development programmes for teachers.

The British Council administers the Fulbright UK/US Teacher Exchange from its Belfast office (fulbright@britishcouncil.org), which funds British teachers at any level but with a minimum of three years' experience to spend a term or a year in the US. Other teacher exchange programmes in the US to investigate include VIF, based in North Carolina (+1 919 967 5144; www.vifprogram.com), and the Alliance Abroad Group (www.allianceabroad.com).

Teacher exchanges can also be arranged independently. **Anne Hogan** was teaching at a college of further education when it occurred to her that she would love to spend a term in the US. She wrote to about ten English departments which were strong in her field of interest (children's literature) and received several replies. The most promising was from a college in North Carolina. Further investigation revealed that it looked a good place to spend the winter months. She negotiated directly with her counterpart who was satisfied to exchange a big house for a small one, and wasn't unduly concerned that Anne didn't own a car.

Organisations involved in teacher recruitment, including the British Council and VSO, normally welcome applications only from trained and experienced teachers. Similarly, the long established CfBT (www.cfbt.com) recruits teachers on behalf of foreign Ministries of Education, mainly for Brunei, Malaysia, and Oman.

Minna Graber had had over a decade's experience teaching classroom music in primary schools in the East End of London, when she set her heart on teaching in Romania after celebrating the New Year there some years before in a Carpathian village at the top of a mountain, complete with gypsy fiddlers and not a single internal combustion engine for miles around. She made contact with the non-profit-making organisation Sharing One Language, or SOL (www.sol.org.uk), which places volunteer teachers in state schools for one academic year in Eastern and Central European countries, especially Hungary, Slovakia, and Romania. Candidates must be graduates, preferably with a recognised TEFL Certificate. All posts include a local salary and free housing.

Although I wanted to teach in the northeast of the country, in the end the job offer was with one of the best schools in Bucharest where the students all go on to university, and a significant minority are these days applying for British university places. The wages sound terrible: 1,100 Lei a month (£215) after deductions for tax and National Insurance. I am very good at living frugally but find that I still have to take on a couple of private students to make ends meet. My students are all completely delightful. I love teaching them. They are respectful and talented. Nobody knows anything about Romania, and the upside of this is that it is a very tourist-free area and you enjoy status as a visitor from the outside world. People are interested and welcoming, largely because there are so few visitors.

Certified American and international teachers seeking appointments abroad in international schools should contact International Schools Services (www.iss.edu), which offers a recruitment/placement service year round and sponsors three large international recruitment fairs each year. Similarly, Search Associates (www.search-associates.com) tries to match qualified teachers with vacancies in international schools worldwide via its website, and also teacher/recruiter job fairs held annually in Sydney, Dubai, London, San Francisco, and others between January and July.

If you are a qualified teacher and think you might want to look for a job after arriving in an English-speaking country, you should take along your diploma and any letters of reference you have. It is a good idea to correspond ahead of time with the education authority in the district which interests you, to find out what their policy is on hiring teachers with foreign qualifications. Some countries with teacher shortages (like New Zealand, Hong Kong, and Singapore) advertise their vacancies abroad and even sometimes offer incentives such as a NZ$4,000 re-location grant and automatic two-year visas (www.teachnz.govt.nz). Private recruitment agencies can also help teachers find temporary jobs in other English-speaking countries (though most of the traffic is from overseas to the UK, especially London).

INTERNATIONAL TRAINING

Some professional organisations for law, agriculture, business, social work, etc, sponsor work exchanges for career development around the world, but particularly in the USA, Canada, Australia, New Zealand, and South Africa.

Doctors have a well-established network of contacts for finding temporary secondments to hospitals abroad. In response to the many enquiries it receives from medics looking for a stint abroad, the British Medical Association (BMA; www.bma.org.uk) carries information on planning a temporary career abroad. The *British Medical Journal* carries classified adverts for long and short-term postings abroad (www.bmjcareers.com). Similarly, nurses and physiotherapists are a highly mobile population. The Royal College of Nursing (international.office@rcn.org.uk; www.rcn.org.uk) provides information for its members who want to work abroad. Note that the special visa category (H1-C) for registered nurses to work in the USA expired at the end of 2009 and has not been renewed by Congress. Of course many medical charities recruit volunteers for the developing world (see Part 4: Doing Something Worthwhile).

In some of the capitals of the world, specialist agencies and human resources companies can set up internships for ambitious young professionals in the field of their choice for a fee. The website www.linktodiversity.com has links to a number of relevant companies, such as www.getin2china.com for China and www.tlaloc.com.mx for Mexico.

INTERNATIONAL VOCATIONAL EXCHANGES

Agriventure is the name of the International Agricultural Exchange Association's exchange programme, which operates in Australia, New Zealand, Canada, the USA, and Japan. Agriventure (01945 450999; www.agriventure.net) has many years' experience arranging for young agriculturalists up to the age of 30 to live and work with approved host families. Many types of agricultural and horticultural placements are available for between four and twelve months. Participants pay between £2,030 and £4,500, which includes airline tickets, visas, insurance, orientation seminar, and board and lodging throughout with a host family or enterprise. Trainees are then paid a realistic wage.

IEPUK Ltd (www.iepuk.com), the rural employment specialist, places suitable applicants in all rural industries, including agriculture, horticulture, and winemaking. For people with relevant equine experience, live-in vacancies in dozens of countries in Europe and worldwide can be tracked down.

WORKING IN THE USA

Visas are a perennial bugbear for anyone who is interested in doing paid work in the United States. The exchange visitor visa (J-1) is available only through approved exchange organisations responsible for work and travel programmes, mostly for students, and only to candidates who pass an interview at the US Embassy. Joining a Summer Camp Counsellor programme like Camp America (www.campamerica.co.uk) or BUNAC (www.bunac.org.uk) is the most straightforward way to spend time working in the USA with a J-1.

Apart from the J-1 visa available to people on approved Exchange Visitor Programmes, the other possible visas must be applied for by the employer on the applicant's behalf, which will take at least three months. The H category covers non-immigrant work visas in special circumstances. The H-2B is for temporary or seasonal vacancies that employers have trouble filling with US citizens. For example, the chronic shortage of workers on the ski fields of Colorado means that a certain number of employers can obtain the necessary Labor Certification confirming that there are no qualified American workers available to do the jobs. A petition must be submitted by the employer to the US Citizenship & Immigration Services (USCIS) and there is a strict quota. The maximum duration of the H-2B visa is one year.

The H-1B 'Specialty Occupation' visa for professionals with a degree is available for 'pre-arranged professional or highly skilled jobs' (often IT specialists), for which there are no suitably qualified Americans. The strict quota of H-1B visas is usually filled within two months of the opening date of April 1st for the following year. A university degree is a pre-requisite and all the paperwork must be carried out by the American employer, who must pay a training fee.

INTERNSHIPS AND WORK EXPERIENCE

Internship is the American term for traineeship, providing a chance to get some experience in your career interest, often as part of your academic course. These are typically available to undergraduates, recent graduates, and young professionals.

Several organisations in the UK arrange for students and young professionals to undertake internships and work experience in the US. IST Plus (www.istplus.com/pctusa) runs Professional Career Training programmes for candidates aged 21+, as well as helping full-time students and graduates within 12 months of graduating to arrange placements in the USA lasting one to 18 months. IST Plus supplies practical advice on applying for work and a searchable database of internships/work placements. Those who qualify get a J-1 visa. The programme fees start at £700 for three months and rise for longer stays.

CDS International in New York (+1 212 497 3500; www.cdsintl.org) offers a USA Internship Program lasting six weeks to 18 months, in a variety of fields including business, engineering, and technology. The opportunities for internships are open to young professionals, aged less than 35, who are within a year of university graduation. The participation fee for stays of up to six months is $950; longer stays cost $1,250.

Internship programmes are also available through other companies such as InterExchange (www.interexchange.org), Alliance Abroad Group (www.allianceabroad.com), and the Association for International Practical Training in Maryland (www.aipt.org).

WORKING IN AUSTRALIA AND NEW ZEALAND

Australia has reciprocal working holiday arrangements with Britain, Ireland, Canada, Netherlands, and many other countries. Applicants must be between the ages of 18 and 30 and without children. The visa is for people intending to use any money they earn in Australia to supplement their holiday funds. Working full-time for more than six months for the same employer is not permitted, and full-time study or training can last up to four months only. Most people apply for a Working Holiday Maker (WHM) visa online, though you can also submit a paper application to any Australian representative outside Australia. When you apply online for an e-WHM visa there is no need to provide proof of funds, nor do you send in your passport. Applying online via the Australian Department of Immigration website (www.immi.gov.au) is normally straightforward and hassle-free, and should result in an emailed confirmation inside the promised 48 hours, which is sufficient to get you into the country. Your passport isn't physically inspected until you arrive in Australia, when you must take it along to an office of the Department of Immigration & Citizenship to obtain the visa label. In either case the fee for the WHM visa is AU$235 (currently £150).

A number of agencies such as BUNAC, CCUSA, and Real Gap offer working holiday packages for both Australia and New Zealand to anyone eligible for the working holiday visa (under 31), from basic DIY packages including the first couple of nights accommodation (from £200), to more deluxe versions that include visa, insurance, job offer guarantee, and other benefits.

The dense network of 'backpackers', ie private hostels, is a goldmine of information. Foreign job-seekers often find employment in the hostels themselves, or leads for jobs in the countryside. Many gap year dreams revolve around campfires by moonlight and close contact with wildlife and nature. One way of experiencing the authentic Aussie outdoors is to sign up for a one-week course as a station/farm assistant (jackaroo or jillaroo). Horsecraft, cattle mustering, ute driving, and trail biking are tasks that may occupy your days. The course organisers often provide a referral service to other stations in case you want to stay on working as a farm hand (provided you have a working holiday visa in your passport). A course at the Leconfield School of Jackarooing in New South Wales (www.leconfieldjackaroo.com) is longer and therefore costs more (AU$950 for 11 days, or AU$1,050 if booked through an agent). JJ Oz (+61 428 617 097; www.jjoz.com.au) offers a choice of five or 12 day courses at Bingara, north of Tamworth, NSW; the costs are AU$670 and AU$1,360.

The New Zealand government no longer imposes a quota on the number of working holiday visas available to Britons aged up to 30, who can work for up to 23 months. Private agencies are also involved in the working holiday market. New Zealand Job Search (www.stayatbase.com/work) is a specialist job search centre for travellers attached to BASE Auckland backpacker hostel (+64 800 462 396; info@nzjs.co.nz). Work starter packs, starting from NZ$345, include a 12-month registration with NZ Job Search, job placement service, and various perks (one-way airport transfer, orientation session, sim card, etc).

LIVING ABROAD

Finding a temporary home in Marrakech or Memphis, San José or Salamanca, is an idyllic dream for many. Once you have a base in a foreign country, you will begin to feel as though you are really living there, however briefly. This concept was completely romanticised by *Eat Pray Love*, the surprise bestseller by New Yorker Elizabeth Gilbert and turned into a movie starring Julia Roberts. This has prompted thousands of women to consider a spell of spending time in some dream destination – in particular Rome, an Indian ashram, and Bali.

Sometimes your travels will lead you into an unexpected episode of living abroad. On the road you may fall in love with a person or place and find a way to extend your stay for months. Travelling without any intention of working, **Rachel Pooley** and **Charlie Stanley-Evans** were driving through Africa when they were offered the lease on a backpacking hostel in Malawi for £1,000 – which they ran for six months, living contentedly by the shores of Lake Malawi. They even considered buying the hostel outright and settling down indefinitely, but they decided that the expatriate life was not for them in the long term. But they describe this period spent managing the lodge as the most worthwhile experience of the whole trip and enabled them for a time to live in a 'heavenly place'.

An alternative way of life on the other side of the world can be so appealing that some are tempted to make their gap year destination a permanent home. This may be trickier if you are a couple rather than a singleton, because often one partner (usually the female one) misses the social and family networks at home more than the other.

JOINING THE EXPAT COMMUNITY

In every major city of the world you'll find an international community of expat teachers, business people, medics, journalists, researchers, and hangers-on suspended between two cultures. So it is difficult to feel completely stranded abroad. You may particularly value the support and assistance of the expat community if you don't speak much of the local language, or if you need their help to find work.

Dan Boothby had read Arabic as an undergraduate and had lived in Syria as a student. Later he decided to leave his job as an awards coordinator with the British Academy of Film and Television Arts (BAFTA) to move to Cairo where a good friend lived, whom he hoped would introduce him to the local social scene. He was already in possession of a TEFL Certificate and planned to use teaching to support himself while he worked on a novel. He found it almost alarmingly easy to find one-to-one teaching work, which he did not enjoy all that much but it paid the bills. In retrospect he wishes that he had tried to break into local journalism as there were plenty of opportunities in local English-language magazines. Yet the time away from London allowed Dan to read incessantly and pursue his own literary endeavours.

Still, the constant round of expat parties meant that Dan wasn't short of company and he travelled extensively in his spare time. He lived very cheaply on a houseboat divided into flats.

Turning 30 in Egypt was a disturbing experience, and he began to wonder whether he had exhausted the pleasures of drinking beer on a boat. He felt he had to return to London to take up some professional challenges:

> *It was a very easy life in Cairo and it gave me time to think. I decided that I quite like the rat race, and I returned to London more mellow and confident. But I am a serial 'sabbaticalist' until I find out what I want to do long term ... After London, the chaos of Cairo was initially appealing but I finally decided that living there resembled an open prison because of the cultural divide. I had little contact with Egyptians and it's very difficult for European men to meet Egyptian women. It was rather frustrating for a single man.*

Of course you may try to function outside the expat scene and concentrate your energies on meeting and befriending the locals, as **Glen Williams** did in Madrid:

> *Madrid is a crazy place. During the gaps in my teaching timetable (10am to 2pm, and 4pm to 7pm) I pretend to study Spanish (I'm no natural) and just wander the back streets. I suppose I should try to be more cultural and learn to play an instrument, write poetry, or look at paintings, but I never get myself in gear. I think most people teach English here as a means to live in Spain and learn the Spanish language and culture, but there is a real problem that you end up living in an English enclave, teaching English all day and socialising with English teachers. You have to make a big effort to get out of this rut. I am lucky to live with Spanish people (who do not want to practise their English!).*

STAYING ON

Making the decision to take a career break abroad can be the prelude to an adventure that might take you in unexpected directions and last far longer than intended. Some people simply don't come home. The longer you stay away, the more difficult it will be to re-integrate (see section on Reverse Culture Shock on page 369).

Every individual will have to weigh up the gains and losses of staying or returning. The majority will have too many attachments and obligations back home to contemplate a permanent move. Sometimes the intention of eventually moving home disappears almost imperceptibly as it very gradually transpires that a career and the future are being built abroad. There's an irresistible attraction about living in a place you come to as an adult; you have more freedom to invent yourself and shed inhibitions. Away from family, school friends, college peers, and work colleagues, individuals can start afresh without the burdens of old baggage.

Living in the southern USA, **Kathy Hines Cooper** suddenly felt an imperative to unfurl a dream. With a 'Now or Never' attitude to the risks, she made the decision practically overnight to head across the Atlantic. After discovering how hard it is for Americans to get a visa to work in her first-choice countries of France and Italy, she turned her attention to Poland. Since her great-grandfather was born in Prussia in 1847 (he later returned to Poland), she soon transferred her enthusiasm, and within a week of doing a TEFL training course in the UK, had been offered a job:

> *Some years ago I got bored one evening, went to the bookstore and bought one of Susan Griffith's first books on a whim. I was hooked. I got a wild idea to go and do my own thing—*

what I really wanted was to live in Europe. I am now in Poland, experiencing this fabulous country, living in the small city of Raciborz, and teaching in international businesses.

'POLAND? You're kidding?' Such remarks from most, not all, family and friends only pushed me through this wild and crazy time of completely changing my life. A new country, culture, language, food, profession, no friends, and all faced alone, acquainted with nary a person – except for the typed signature of emails from the Director of Studies of the hiring language school in Opole.

And that was seven years ago. I never expected to stay this long. I was sure it was a path towards getting back west, to France or Italy, But I never tried. My heart is here; my life is here nine months a year. In the summers I return to America to my family.

Currently, my pay has quadrupled from when I arrived. I no longer have roommates, but a flat of my own. Living conditions run from comfortable (always warm in winter) to fabulous, as in my tastefully Tuscan marble-decorated flat that is freshly decorated; however, in a Stalinist 'cubist' building.

How gratifying it is to be so well respected as a teacher. Offer your expertise, background, and life. They will take it and accept you for who you are, as long as you are accepting of their cultures and lifestyle. Expect to be offered home-cooked dinner, theatre and opera outings, family holidays (don't eat for two days prior, please), weekend trips to the country or seaside. Would you like to experience castle hunting, Krakow, Warsaw, the surrounding mountains, snow skiing at its best, winter kulig (sleigh) pulled by horses and enjoying fresh kielbasa braised on your stick over an open fire pit in the depths of the snow? To me this is heaven on earth, and my destiny.

Some post-gap year changes of direction can be dramatic in the extreme. **Philippa Vernon-Powell** had been a very high-profile businesswoman and consultant in London earning up to £200,000 a year. In her late 30s, she decided to do an eight-month volunteer stint in Mexico with Outreach International at a shelter for street children in the resort of Puerta Vallarta, which turned her life around. She returned to London, and within a short time had raised £17,000 to buy beds, a washing machine, books, and sports equipment for the struggling shelter. She has now set up her own street children rehabilitation project in Puerta Vallarta called New Life Mexico, and is staying on to run it (www.newlifemexico.com).

Alienation from the materialistic values of the west often afflicts career gappers who have spent time in a developing country. Some find it impossible to slot easily back into what they have come to view as pleasure-seeking ways. **Kate Ledward** knew that accountancy was not her dream ticket to a happy life even before she went to Africa. Having become aware that her previous trips to Tanzania and Kenya had not satisfied her curiosity about Africa, she decided she needed to return. She stumbled across the charity SPW (now Restless Development) and was impressed with their methodology in partnering each overseas volunteer with a local volunteer and then sending the mixed-nationality group into rural villages. Not only were the Ugandans perhaps the most hospitable, happy, and friendly people Kate had ever met, the country was also breathtakingly beautiful:

When I returned to the UK, I was not able to settle. Having spent a further 18 long months back in the Financial Services sector, and indeed studying for Financial Planning exams, I kept my passion for the work I did in Uganda alive by volunteering on an organic farm at weekends and taking a short community course in organic growing. Now clear of the gloomy debts from university, I am free to return to one of my dreams come true, and am flying back to my beloved Africa to explore a path that I am now more certain than ever is the one I wish to follow.

TRAVEL AND ADVENTURE

THE ADVENTURE BEGINS

Traditionally, the gap year between school and higher education is associated with a period of travel, time spent working abroad, or a combination of the two. Many new graduates also head off travelling immediately after finishing their courses and before settling into a career. But why can't you have the same adventures at the age of 35 or 55? Perhaps a shortage of funds, a lack of confidence, or a reluctance to interrupt vocational training and career progression were factors that prevented you when you were younger. Some who were avid travellers in their youth may take the chance to rediscover the pleasures that had to be set aside when family and career commitments loomed large.

As a more mature traveller you might have a clearer idea about which countries and cultures you want to visit. Arguably, travel is wasted on the young. There is a tendency these days for very young students to travel rather indiscriminately to far-flung corners of the globe, to places they are not really interested in, just to meet up with other travellers, to eat, drink, and socialise in exactly the way they would at home but without as many inhibitions. At just 18, travellers are more likely to follow the crowd (and the party) than those who are 28, 38 or beyond.

Other travellers' blogs are a fertile source of travel ideas. You can hardly fail to feel inspired after perusing blogs with names like 'checkingoffeverywhere.com', 'livingthedreamrtw.com' or 'abandonthecube.com'. In fact, you could spend scores of envious hours absorbed in other people's travelogues on YouTube, or following adventures abroad on Facebook and Twitter. But at some point, you have to stop all this vicarious travelling and experience the joy of the open road for yourself. The sense of possibility, adventure, and even danger, can bring feelings of exhilaration unavailable in the workplace. When travelling in developing countries, you can shed – at least temporarily – the clutter and accoutrements of modern life in the western world, to live more simply.

Another of the less trumpeted pleasures of independent travel is the feeling of being free and unfettered. Anyone who has been working in a big organisation, or even operating within a family where the other members tend to dictate the rules (eg on holidays the man usually takes charge of the map), may have forgotten the unalloyed pleasure of exercising choice of activities and destinations from an infinite number of possibilities.

Almost anyone who has had some experience of independent travel catches the bug and longs to see more and spend a longer time abroad. It might stem from a personal passion like learning languages or saving the rainforest, or a fascination left over from childhood with an exotic destination like Madagascar or Patagonia. Cheap air travel has opened up parts of the globe once reserved for the seriously affluent. Today there's little surprise (but usually some envy) when you tell your colleagues that you are planning to go trekking in the hinterland of Rio de Janeiro or diving in the Philippines. Inside many an office worker lurks a secret Indiana Jones longing for a challenge.

Some people take time out from work to embark on a particular journey they have long set their hearts on following. This was the case with **Julie Fairweather**, an auxiliary nurse in Dundee:

My dream since I was little was always to go to Africa and get up close to wildlife (especially the cheetah). My 40th birthday was coming up and I thought it's now or never to do what I have always wanted to do.

Dream journeys range from solo backpacking, to expeditions using specially acquired equipment, to group adventure trips. Specialist companies can help with anything from mountain trekking to long distance motorbiking, as well as white water rafting, hot air ballooning, mountain climbing, off-road driving, scuba diving, and sailing.

Saga, the specialists in holidays for the over-50s, has noticed a four-fold increase in interest in more adventurous holidays from the over-50s with time and money on their hands. Older travellers taking a gap year may be in a position to travel in greater comfort than would have been possible in their student days, while others may choose to revert to their youth and go backpacking and hostelling. **David Moncur** had always felt a bit sniffy about backpackers' accommodation hostels, but since he wanted his redundancy money to last as long as possible, he used hostels in Australia and found that he absolutely loved them. He discovered it was very energising to be in the company of so many young people, though he also found people closer to his own age to chat to as well. Backpackers' hostels are far more convivial than hotels.

Maddie Kilgour from Scotland, who negotiated six months off from her administrative job, thoroughly enjoyed the non-volunteering phase of her trip booked with VentureCo when she travelled on her own:

I went off on my own on a journey of discovery. Most of this was in Peru – and I absolutely loved it. I travelled in buses, on boats, in cars, on foot. I clambered up mountains, walked through deserts, flew over the Nazca lines, followed Inca trails via graveyards and pyramids. It was the most fabulous journey of my life. Had I known that on my return I would be so quickly made redundant, I would have extended my time in Peru.

For many, travel represents escape and discovery. By immersing yourself in the unknown it is temporarily possible to disorient yourself, and undergo a process of detachment from banal and tedious routines and responsibilities that hem in the lives of all adults. Discomfort is almost inevitable, but enduring and even enjoying it is often the point. The author of *Eat Pray Love* vividly describes her addiction to travel:

I feel about travel the way a happy new mother feels about her impossible, colicky, restless newborn baby – I just don't care what it puts me through. Because I adore it. Because it's mine. Because it looks exactly like me. It can barf all over me if it wants to – I just don't care.

On 22nd November 2010, **Kath McGuire** blogged from Sri Lanka after an epic 16-week overland trip from the UK, and hers is a sentiment shared by many long-term travellers:

I have been travelling for 114 days now. I have been to a lot of places. I have eaten a lot of food. I have seen a lot of things. I have met a lot of people. And I have experienced a lot of emotions too. I have been alone, lonely, afraid, sad, happy, joyful, excited, deeply touched by the kindness of others, fed up, frustrated, exhausted, grossed out, dirty, cold, hot, sweaty, hungry, thirsty, awestruck, proud of myself, disappointed with myself, annoyed, bored, ill, tired, grumpy. But I have never, ever regretted making the leap and taking this trip.

An extended break gives an almost unique period (post-education) to explore in depth other regions and cultures of the world, as well as yourself. **Mike Bleazard** was lucky enough to become pair-bonded in his mid 30s with lawyer **Jane O'Beirne**, who shared his commitment to stepping out of the rat race. When Jane got together with Mike, she was discontented with the solicitor's office where she worked. After one particularly frustrating day at work, she blurted out, 'Shall we take off round the world?'. Mike nodded his assent and seven months later they did. They were both in the fortunate position of being able to save money quite handily in that period of planning – Jane by moving into the flat that Mike owned so that she saved everything she would have spent on rent, and Mike by getting a staggeringly well-paid contract (£50 an hour) turning techie-speak into human language. They were each able to budget £7,000 for the six-month trip on top of round-the-world airfares, plus they had the rent of £800 a month coming in from Mike's flat. Most of the African leg of their trip had been pre-arranged, whereas once they moved on to Australia they could improvise a bit more. Yet they realised that much of the time they spent driving the Great Ocean Road of Victoria (for example) was spent planning the next leg of their journey to New Zealand, and they decided to try to concentrate more on the present moment. Their most treasured possession that they never let out of their sight was a gadget capable of storing 12,000 digital pictures. In retrospect they were glad that they had done the trip in the order that they did: starting with the strangeness of Africa, relaxing into the familiarity of Anglo culture in Australia and New Zealand, and finally entering the most challenging phase: travelling around South America with minimal Spanish. They noticed that the average age of travellers they met in Chile, Argentina, and Brazil was higher than it had been earlier in their trip, and they came to the conclusion that adults on gap years are better equipped and more committed to leaving the beaten track than gap year students and other young backpackers, who congregate in Cape Town, Kathmandu, and Sydney.

Patagonia was firmly on their itinerary but because they were a little apprehensive about venturing into the tail end of the continent at the tail end of the season, they reckoned that they had better pre-arrange their trip. They tried to do this through a well-meaning agent in Santiago, though none of the arrangements they made with him came off. For instance, they arrived at a 10,000-strong penguin colony near Punta Arenas to find just four lonely penguins, since five days before the colony had decided to swim off. With hindsight, they would have done better making arrangements after arrival in Patagonia for visiting national parks, going trekking, and finding accommodation. It wasn't until near the end of their trip that they shared a zen moment in a bus station in southern Chile: they realised that they had absolutely no idea where they would end up that day. They opened their guidebook, liked the sound of a volcano in the vicinity, and proceeded to find out if any bus was going that way – but not until after they had retired for a coffee. They felt more free than they had in their whole lives. As the months had passed, so had their anxiety about mapping out what was to come.

More recently, another couple, **Christine and Mike Benson** from the USA, pursued a dream to travel the world that had been simmering (for Christine anyway) for ten years, ever since a school friend had referred in passing to something called a 'round-the-world ticket'. They saved feverishly until they reached a target of US$20,000 for spending, which they reckoned would last precisely 332 days if they stuck to a daily spend of $60. Interviewed by www.artofbackpacking.com, Christine itemised their outgoings:

A $60 a day budget seemed to be on the low end for two people, so we adjusted our list of countries to include more cheap countries and fewer expensive countries. Hello Cambodia; goodbye

Brazil. As we have travelled, we have chosen water over liquor and spaghetti over filet more times than I can count. We try to splurge (and only sometimes!) on experiences (safaris, snorkelling, yoga) instead of merchandise, and our only requirement is that our safety is preserved. We cannot deny the fact that this means we have woken up with cockroaches in our face, eaten peanut butter sandwiches for lunch one week straight, and chosen the free museums over the paid. But we have also hiked on a glacier in New Zealand, been charged by an elephant on a safari in South Africa, snorkelled the Great Barrier Reef in Australia, explored the jungle in Ecuador, hiked the Great Wall in China, and abseiled 100 metres down into a cave in New Zealand.

After nine months of travelling the world they had spent about $17,000, divided roughly equally among lodging, food, activities, and transport (on top of their RTW flights) — excluding miscellaneous expenses like souvenirs, internet access, and visas. Including all their pre-departure expenses (two six-continent RTW flights at $6,000 each, plus inoculations), their grand total was $33,605 which they admit is 'one huge hunk of change' but which is not much more than they would have spent at home in Chicago:

So there you have it. For nine months of travel, countless memories, and experiences we wouldn't give up for a million dollars, we have spent just over thirty grand. I'd say it's a fair trade.

COMBINING TRAVEL AND WORK

If, on an adult gap year, you wish to work or volunteer abroad (topics that are covered in other chapters), you will have more skills and maturity to bring to a foreign employer or project than younger gappers. Some older travellers consider it self-indulgent or shallow simply to travel. For London lawyer **Polly Botsford**, for example, it was important to work and not only travel. Because she thinks that, 'You can get jaded very quickly and then end up a mechanical tourist,' she decided to divide her six-month gap equally between travelling and working.

Likewise, **Daniel Smith** aspired to more than just travel in his four-month break from his job in publishing. He had long wanted to go to India but didn't just want to go backpacking or hang around in Goa. After looking at lots of different volunteer opportunities he ended up spending time in the publishing arm of an enterprising arts charity in Calcutta.

Interestingly, quite a few career gappers who have combined volunteering and travel end up enjoying the volunteering more. **Jackie Smith** and her husband **Peter** took a six-month sabbatical in India and Southeast Asia after many years of working, part volunteering through MondoChallenge and part travelling:

Since our return, we both agree that staying in a small rural village and living with the principal of a local school for two and a half months was the highlight of our six months away. It was fantastic being part of the community, if only for a short time. People got to know us and included us in local festivals such as Diwali, which included an impressively-run bingo competition on the field opposite our school, as well as lots of food, drink, and blessings. I do think that if we travelled again we might do a longer volunteer placement and perhaps even less time being a 'tourist' – maybe even something like VSO. While the world is a huge place and there is always something new to see, we felt that you really can't beat meeting local people, getting to know them and their way of life, and sharing stories. It is the only real way to get anywhere near understanding a place and making some sort of connection.

TRAVEL CHOICES

People travelling on a gap year later in life will be looking for a unique travel experience: one that is different from their annual holidays in Wales or Provence. Open-ended travel is considered to be distinct from tourism, which can be roughly defined as a trip abroad in which itinerary and accommodation are booked in advance. Yet a growing number of tour operators are now blurring the difference, by providing challenging adventure holidays on foot or vehicle over difficult terrain, or by catering to people who want to donate their time and labour to a specific cause like conservation or teaching (see page 151 for the Directory of Specialist Programmes). These packages attempt to introduce travellers to a more authentic experience of countries like Peru or Thailand. Such trips might include a variety of experiences like jungle trekking and cookery lessons, as well as free-time sightseeing.

ORGANISED TRAVEL

Heading into the wild blue yonder is a daunting prospect for most adults taking a break, unless they are hardened independent travellers from a way back. In many cases it will make sense for a solo traveller to consider joining some kind of structured programme, whether an organised trek in the Himalayas, an overland expedition through East Africa, or an adventure trip through South America – possibly combined with Spanish lessons and/or a volunteer placement. Environmentally- and culturally-sensitive tour operators design trips to introduce westerners to a region, country, or culture, by employing expert guides who can share their insights and knowledge. These trips address a growing market of people who want a trip that's organised for them without losing the experience of adventure and discovery that comes from independent travel. As this book tries to demonstrate, the choice of worthy small and large companies organising short and long trips is quite staggering. For someone in the early stages of thinking about a gap year, the range of possibilities can be overwhelming.

A possible starting place is one of the annual winter travel shows, like the Adventure Travel Live show (www.adventureshow.co.uk) held in London at the end of January, or Destinations (www.destinationsshow.com) at Earl's Court in London and the National Exhibition Centre in Birmingham, both of which feature companies and speakers relevant to someone planning a career break. When **Paul Carroll** reached his late 20s, he came to the conclusion that there was something seriously wrong with the work/life balance in his pressurised IT job. So he took himself off to the Destinations show in Earl's Court:

> There I saw lots of companies, but few offering specialist programmes for trekking, backpacking, and generally challenging itineraries. VentureCo was one, and White Peak Expeditions another. I took a VentureCo brochure that happened to be labelled 'Career Gap'. Later I sifted through all the brochures I had collected from the show and from the internet, and eventually chose VentureCo. I was very impressed, as they are very careful with their selection of individuals through a series of interviews.

Paul went on to book a four-month expedition to Patagonia with VentureCo (see their Directory entry). Afterwards he travelled independently for several more months in South America and experienced nature like he had never imagined: 'Glaciers, volcanoes, mountain ranges, condors, wild cats, rainforest, jungle, pampas, salt lakes, geysers, etc...' This proved a useful half-way house between going it alone and having a trip completely pre-arranged.

Another way of achieving this balance is to create an itinerary with the help of a specialist travel agent. An intriguing concept in travel is being pioneered by the online travel organisation Rickshaw Travel (01273 322399; www.rickshawtravel.co.uk), which offers pre-arranged independent travel. Their unique concept offers short travel programmes or 'modules', which last a few days each and are presented in a building block style. Clients can pick and mix from a wide selection of these modules (or pick a suggested itinerary) and the agency can join the dots by booking sleeper trains, ferries, and domestic flights. The accommodation used is mid-range, locally owned, authentic, and cosy. This kind of travel is perfect for people who don't want to join a group tour, but do want an independent and adventurous itinerary pre-arranged before they go – along with the security of booking in the UK with an ABTA/ATOL bonded tour operator. So far the countries covered are Thailand, Vietnam, China, India, Nepal, Malaysia, Indonesia, Laos, Cambodia, South Africa, Kenya, Tanzania, Egypt, Morocco, Mexico, Cuba, Peru, Argentina, and Brazil, with Namibia and Costa Rica in the pipeline.

For more conventional travel bookings, well-established agents like Trailfinders, STA Travel, and Flight Centre should be familiar with flight and tour options suited to the longer-term traveller. In 2010 STA launched a sister company called Bridge the World, with the slogan 'Aimed at getting the over 50s out to explore the planet', which proves how much they believe that market is expanding.

If solo travel does not appeal, as it often does not for novice travellers or women travelling alone, organised group travel offers many advantages. It can become an excellent way of meeting new people and sharing experiences, rather than facing the potential loneliness and anxiety of solitary, independent travel. Many appealing alternatives to the conventional coach tour for OAPs exist around the world; in the USA, consider the escorted trips aimed at people 18–38 offered by Trekamerica (0844 576 1400 or 020 8682 8920; www.trekamerica.co.uk) or by Green Tortoise in San Francisco (+1 800 867 8647 or 415 956 7500 within North America; www.greentortoise.com), which uses vehicles converted to sleep up to 36 people that make interesting detours and stopovers. On Green Tortoise trips, which place more emphasis on outdoor activities like hiking and canoeing than sightseeing, about a third of clients are aged 25–35 and 6% are older.

Overlanding by motorbike appeals to some: possibly more to midlife males than other groups. Specialist companies like Globebusters (www.globebusters.com) and Kudu Expeditions (www.kuduexpeditions.com) offer up to four-month motorcycle journeys through Africa and America, which are accessible to anyone who can afford them.

INDEPENDENT TRAVEL

The clear alternative is to travel completely independently in as basic or as luxurious a style as you choose. Students do not have the monopoly on backpacking. There is no reason why at an older age you shouldn't aim for something more than relaxation and predictability. If you decide to take the independent route, it's a good idea to map out a plan or itinerary in advance, because you will probably want to make at least some flight bookings while retaining the pleasure of following your nose. Many round-the-world tickets cost less than £1,000 (before tax), and allow you to hop through different countries and continents at your own pace.

So give yourself enough flexibility to act on impulse. You may meet locals who take you off the beaten track to visit their homes, or recommend a beach or waterfall overlooked by the guidebooks. Inspiration can come from someone met in the pub, from the travel section of your local bookshop, television documentaries, from the travel pages of papers like the *Independent*, or glossy travel magazines like *Wanderlust*. The worthy organisation Tourism Concern publishes a book called *The Ethical Travel Guide* (Tourism Concern, 2nd edition, 2009) describing 400 places in 70 countries which are guaranteed not to be tourist traps.

Americans might consult the links-laden website www.vagablogging.net, maintained by veteran travel writer and shoestring expeditioner Rolf Potts. Potts is the author of the classic *Vagabonding: An Uncommon Guide to the Art of Long-Term World Travel*, where 'Vagabonding' is defined much as this book defines an adult gap year, ie taking time off from your normal life to discover and experience the world on your own terms. The author argues persuasively that time is a more precious commodity for travellers than money, and liberates you from having to over-organise your itinerary in advance. Another title of interest is *The Practical Nomad: How to Travel Around the World* by Edward Hasbrouck (Avalon Travel, 2007) which is a 'How-to handbook of advice and tips for independent, on-your-own travel'. Many people are anxious about the language barrier when contemplating travel within or beyond Europe. With a phrase book and a lack of inhibition about playing charades, this perceived hindrance usually melts away.

The best source of information on what to see and how to get there is other travellers, met on the road or in internet forums such as the invaluable www.lonelyplanet.com/thorntree. Here members can post any query under the sun about border crossings, departure taxes, or tourist site rip-offs, and expect a prompt and illuminating answer. It also caters to potential adult gappers in its forum 'The Long Haul – Living and Working Abroad'.

PLANES, TRAINS, AND AUTOMOBILES

There follow some general guidelines for finding bargains in train, coach, car, ship, and air travel. More detailed information on specific destinations can be found in travel guides from Lonely Planet, Rough Guides, Footprints, and others, and the amount of travel information on the internet is staggering. There are websites on everything from sleeping in airports (the fabulous www.sleepinginairports.net) to sharing lifts across the USA and Canada (www.erideshare.com). Many sites have intriguing links; to name just one, try www.travelindependent.info, which provides useful snapshots of individual countries.

BOOKING FLIGHTS

Air travel has changed out of all recognition, with no-frills airlines forcing national carriers to drop their fares in order to be competitive. A few low-cost airlines have tried to break into the long-haul market, but it is a lion's den, with some falling by the wayside – like Canada's Zoom Airlines and the Hong Kong airline Oasis, which had been flying passengers between London and Hong Kong for £150. Meanwhile there has been a surge in regional discount carriers on the Ryanair model, including Kingfisher Red and SpiceJet in India; AirAsia in Southeast Asia (which now links Kuala Lumpur with Stansted, Australia, and other long-haul destinations), Jetstar, which links many Australian cities plus South and East Asia; Southwest in the USA; Taca in Central America; GOL in Brazil, and so on. All these airlines have their own websites and many allow online bookings, some at remarkably low prices, or you might go through an intermediate site such as www.alternativeairlines.com. Note that the British Air Passenger Duty increased in November 2010, so that the departure tax on a trip to Europe is £12, North America is £60, and Australia is now £85 (up from £55).

For long-haul flights, especially to Asia, Australasia, and more recently Latin America, discounted tickets are available in plenty. The following reliable agencies specialise in long-haul travel:

- **Trailfinders Ltd**, London W8 and other branches (0845 058 5858 worldwide; 0845 050 5940 Europe; www.trailfinders.com). There are 22 branches in UK cities, plus Ireland and Australia.
- **Bridge the World** (0871 221 3900; www.bridgetheworld.com). STA's sister company launched in 2010 for the over-50s market. Branches are opening in Bournemouth, Edinburgh, Manchester, Bristol, Leeds, and London. The company plans to take 50,000 on 'grey gap years' in 2011.
- **Flight Centre**, branches around the UK (0870 499 0040; www.flightcentre.co.uk).
- **Get Travelling**, Tunbridge Wells (0844 418 0002; www.get-lost.co.uk/Gap-Breaks). Markets flexible gap breaks to people of all ages.

- **Marco Polo Travel**, Bristol (0117 929 4123; www.marcopolotravel.co.uk). Discounted airfares worldwide.
- **North South Travel**, Chelmsford (01245 608291; www.northsouthtravel.co.uk). Discount travel agency that donates its profits to projects in the developing world.
- **Travelbag**, Alton, Hants. (0871 703 4700; www.travelbag.co.uk). Originally Australia and New Zealand specialist, owned by ebookers.
- **Travel Nation**, Hove (01273 320580; www.travel-nation.co.uk). Staffed by real experts who specialise in finding the best deals on round-the-world flights, discounted long-haul flights and multi-stop tickets.

Other discount agents advertise in the travel pages of newspapers like the Saturday *Independent*, such as Dial-a-Flight (0844 811 4444; www.dialaflight.com).

General websites like www.cheapflights.co.uk, www.travelocity.com, www.expedia.com and www.opodo.com are good starting points, though comparison shopping this way can be time-consuming and frustrating. Skyscanner.net is fast and efficient. Even after long hours of surfing, the lowest internet fares can often be undercut by a good agent, particularly if your proposed route is complicated. For example, an agent is more likely than the internet to come up with an offbeat route down under using Emirates, and SriLankan Airways to travel via Dubai to Mumbai, overland to Trivandrum in Kerala, on to Colombo, Singapore, Sydney (or Melbourne or Perth), then back to London via Dubai for less than £1,200.

When purchasing a discounted fare, you should be aware of whether or not the ticket is refundable, whether the date can be changed (and if so, at what cost), whether taxes are included, and so on. **Roger Blake** was pleased with the round-the-world ticket he bought from STA that took in Johannesburg, Australia, and South America, but once he embarked he wanted to stay in Africa longer than he had anticipated and wanted to alter the onward flight dates:

> *That is the biggest problem of having an air ticket. I had planned for six months in Africa but I've already spent five months in only three countries. I have been into the British Airways office here in Kampala to try my verbal skills, but have been told the 12-month period of validity is non-negotiable. How stupid I was to presume I would get a refund when it states clearly on the back of the ticket that they may be able to offer refunds/credit. A lesson for me and a warning to future world travellers: to check whether or not the ticket is refundable/extendable before they buy.*

Jen Moon is another adult gapper who found it difficult to predict how long she and her two young daughters would want to stay in any one place on their four-month adventure:

> *Dividing the time was the hardest bit as I didn't know what to expect. In fact, dates changed three times before I finally paid and three dates changed during the trip. Thank God for Trailfinders and unfixed dates.*

Almost everyone nowadays will give some thought to minimising their carbon footprint. Of course it is best for the planet if you don't fly at all, but if you do, consider offsetting your emissions with a donation to fund tree-planting or other mechanisms to reduce the impact of air travel on the environment, which is offered by many companies including Climate Care (www.climatecare.org) and Carbon Neutral (www.carbonneutral.com).

ROUND-THE-WORLD FLIGHTS

The most common RTW itineraries are ones that have been specially marketed by groups of airlines that co-operate and have formed various 'alliances'. A good travel agent will quickly tell you which alliance of airlines (if any) is best suited to your needs. Fare levels change according to how many stops and what distances you want to cover, so you will need to make some careful calculations about your route, and whether you want to travel 26,000 miles or up to 39,000 miles (which might mean a £700 difference in price). Note that if you don't particularly want to include North America on your itinerary, you may not really need a RTW ticket.

The price of RTW tickets has remained fairly consistent over the past few years, though taxes and fuel surcharges have leapt up. You shouldn't count on getting any change from £1,000, even for the most limited route. Check www.roundtheworldflights.com (020 7704 5700), Travel Nation (www.travel-nation.co.uk), or Travelmood (www.travelmood.com) for ideas. RTW fares inclusive of tax start at about £999 for four stops, departing London between April and June on Air New Zealand, with a maximum validity of one year. The cheapest fares involve one or more gaps, which you must cover overland or by separate domestic flights. A classic itinerary would include seven stops and cost from about £1,400.

Before contacting agents, spend some time poring over an atlas and deciding where you are sure you want to go and on what approximate dates. A specialist agent will quickly be able to tell you whether one of the alliance promotions is better than a DIY itinerary. It is possible to include almost anywhere on a RTW itinerary – at a price. For example, it is usually disproportionately expensive to zigzag between hemispheres, so flying London–Johannesburg–Bombay–Sydney–Tokyo–Santiago could end up being astronomically expensive. Be prepared to compromise on your wish list of destinations.

SHORT-HAUL FLIGHTS

No-frills flights have exploded over the last decade, opening up all corners of Europe. Fortunately new regulations mean that published fares must include compulsory extras, so that you no longer see £5 flights advertised (that really cost £79). Normally the earlier you book on off-peak no-frills flights out of Stansted, Luton, or regional airports, the cheaper the fare (though not invariably). Bookings should be made online because telephone bookings are more expensive.

Make sure that you factor in the cost – and time – of getting from the airport to your city of choice. Cheap airlines often use small airfields some way from the city (or indeed from anywhere). If France or Belgium is your first destination, it can be easier to take Eurostar – costing from as little as £59 return London St Pancras to Paris, if bought well in advance. Cheap airline websites include ryanair.com, easyjet.com, bmibaby.com, flybe.com, jet2.com (Leeds-based) and thomsonfly.com. This style of flying has spread to the continent and discount airlines have proliferated, including clickair.com (Spanish), airberlin.com, germanwings.com (both German), transavia.com (Dutch), wizzair.com (Polish), smartwings.com (Czech), SkyEurope.com (Central Europe), blue1.com (Finnish), norwegian.no (Norwegian) and so on. Central sources of information include flycheapo.com and whichbudget.com. Scheduled airlines like BA and Aer Lingus have had to drop fares to compete and are always worth comparing.

RAIL, COACH, AND SHIP

One of the classic gap year experiences is to InterRail around Europe (www.interrail.net): an experience which is readily available to people over 26, albeit at a higher price than it is to young travellers. It may sound a little tame compared to round-the-world flights or Himalayan treks, but it can provide an amazing taste of the delights of Europe. In the past, tickets were divided into zones, but this system has been simplified. Now one Global pass covers the whole of Europe for one calendar month, from £526 for those 26 and over. A shorter duration of 22 days is also available for £412. Small discounts are available to travellers 60 or over. If you plan to make a few long journeys in a certain number of days, investigate Flexipasses; they permit five days of travel within ten days, or ten days of travel within 22 days. Also, you can buy one-country passes that will cover three, four, six, or eight days of travel within one month. A number of specialised agencies sell InterRail products and add slightly different mark-ups. Passes can be bought online (in which case you will probably have to pay an extra £5 or £10 for Special Delivery) or in person at branches of STA Travel and similar outlets. Websites to check include www.trainseurope.co.uk (usually the cheapest), www.raileurope.co.uk, www.internationalrail.com, www.railpassshop.com, or the marvellous site for train travellers everywhere: www.seat61.com.

Eurolines (www.eurolines.com) is the group name for 32 independent coach operators serving 500 destinations in all European countries, from Ireland to Romania. Promotional prices start at £17.50 from London to Amsterdam if booked in advance. Bookings can be made by phoning 08717 818178 or online, where you might find a so-called 'fun fare' – meaning that some off-season fares booked ahead from the UK are even lower, eg £6 to Brussels or Paris. Eurolines also sells coach passes (www.eurolines-pass.com) valid for 15 or 30 days. Prices vary according to season, from €205 for 15 days in low season (January to March; November), to €455 for 30 days in the summer. Private coach operators still serve eastern Europe, such as Poltours (www.poltours.co.uk), which links London with various Polish cities and Prague for about £55 one way and £75/£85 return, though these fares can often be undercut by cheap airlines like Wizz Air.

Travelling by cargo ship has a romantic mystique that appeals mainly to retired people who can be completely flexible with their dates. Cargo ships have a limit of 12 paying passengers for insurance reasons. Cabins can be comfortable, but of course there is none of the holiday camp razzmatazz of a cruise. Prices start at about £100 a day and the specialist travel agency is Strand Travel (www.strandtravel.co.uk).

GREAT RAILWAY JOURNEYS

Undertaking one of the great rail journeys of the world is something that might easily appeal to people taking a gap year at any age. Anyone who has read any of the abundant literature of rail travel, like Paul Theroux's *Great Railway Bazaar* and Eric Newby's *The Big Red Train Ride* about the Trans-Siberian Railway, may have had their appetite whetted and want to take a longer-than-usual holiday to travel by train between Moscow and Beijing, or on Via Rail's *Canadian* from Toronto to Vancouver. Some lesser known routes might also appeal, such as the Blue Train of South Africa, the Eastern & Oriental Express of Malaysia, or the Sierra Madre Express of Mexico.

You can either plan a rail journey independently or via a specialist agency like Western Air Travel in Devon (0845 680 1298; www.westernair.co.uk) which, despite its name, is good at arranging rail and coach travel as well as long-haul flights. Specialist travel agents can arrange the Trans-Siberian trip for you: for instance, the excellent travel company Regent Holidays (0845 277 3317; www.regent-holidays.co.uk), which pioneered tourism in Cuba, Eastern Europe, and Central Asia. For lesser-known routes, such as the Silk Route Railway through Kazakhstan and China, you will have to put it together yourself – possibly with the help of the very useful website www.seat61.com, which has links to specialist booking agencies. It also provides a guide cost of £335 for travelling by train Moscow–Beijing via Irkutsk and Ulaanbaatar, excluding visa costs. If you are already in China, you can organise the ticket and visas yourself, as **Barry O'Leary** did:

I had discovered that if you book the Trans-Siberian on your own (and don't pay for an agency to rip you off) and organise everything yourself, it's actually really cheap. Sure you have some hassle getting visas for China, Mongolia, and Russia but isn't that all part of the fun?

Alternatively you can use a Chinese agency, such as Monkey Business located in Beijing's Red House Hotel (www.monkeyshrine.com). For detailed advice, see the *Trans-Siberian Handbook* by Bryn Thomas (Trailblazer, June 2011).

CARS

If you are considering taking your own vehicle, contact the AA or RAC for information about International Driving Permits, motor insurance, and so on. Members of motoring organisations should ask for free information on driving and services provided by affiliated organisations in other countries. Although plenty of sources (especially the motoring organisations that sell them) recommend obtaining an International Driving Permit (IDP) for £5.50, your national licence is sufficient for short stays in many countries. The relevant RAC web page provides a list of countries (like Albania and Japan) in which an IDP is required (www.rac.co.uk/idp/where-do-i-need-an-idp).

In some countries, like Australia and the USA, you might decide to buy a cheap car or camper van after arrival and hope that it lasts long enough for you to see the country. Buy a standard model for ease of finding spares. Some travellers have even managed to sell a vehicle at the end of their trip.

Adult gappers who remember the joys (and dangers) of hitch-hiking will have noticed that the practice has died out virtually everywhere. However, lift-sharing agencies do exist to pre-arrange shared rides across Europe. Ride-sharing can be fixed up via websites such as Allostop in France (www.allostop.net), Taxistop/Eurostop in Belgium (www.taxistop.be), and Citynetz-Mitzfahrzentrale in Germany (www.citynetz-mitfahrzentrale.de). The normal practice is that passengers make a contribution to the driver's expenses, eg €50 for Amsterdam to Warsaw. Most require you to register, which is free in some cases or costs €10–€20 in others. In most cases you will have to pay €0.30–€0.40 per kilometre you want to travel. Matches can seldom be made straightaway, so this system is of interest to those who can plan ahead.

Social networking has seen the invention of a new version of hitch-hiking. Last year journalist Paul Smith from Newcastle, aka the Twitchhiker, set off to test whether social networking could possibly get a person round the world on the good will of people contacted solely through Twitter. Amazingly, he got to New Zealand, close to his destination, but had to abandon his attempt to find a boat going to remote and uninhabited Campbell Island near Antarctica. If this idea inspires you, check out his book *Twitchhiker* (Summersdale, 2010).

DRIVING EXPEDITIONS

Anyone planning to take a vehicle off the beaten track will need to be pragmatic and able to rise to various challenges. Diesel is more easily obtained than petrol and, in general, a diesel engine is more reliable and requires less maintenance. Taking your own vehicle is an expensive way to travel, but the freedom it offers is appealing if you have the resources. In some parts of the world it is unwise to leave your car or van unattended, in which case you will usually receive local advice about how to hire a watchman. For example, in Egypt, 'boabs' or apartment building concierges/doormen often double as guards and charge a couple of dollars a night.

Crossing borders with your own vehicle is often fraught with difficulties and expense. For example, **Rachel Pooley** and **Charlie Stanley-Evans**, whose experiences of driving a Land Rover through Africa are recounted in this chapter, found themselves being charged extra 'costs' by border officials. This was particularly bad in Romania, Bulgaria, Turkey, Syria, and Egypt (but not Jordan). Crossing into Egypt by ferry from Jordan they were asked to pay a staggering £200 because the Land Rover had an engine over 2,000cc. Exercising some ingenuity, they claimed to constitute a 'group' because, as Rachel claimed, she was pregnant with twins; but this ploy did not succeed and their budget took a big hit. In your projected budget, allow for these unforeseen levies. Red tape in Egypt was especially onerous and they spent two weeks in Cairo organising the paperwork to ship the vehicle to Kenya.

Other problems included poor roads, difficulty interpreting road signs in a foreign script, and suicidal driving styles. Entering Cairo, a huge sprawling city choked with traffic, Rachel and Charlie were stumped by an inability to read the Arabic road signs or ask for directions. Sometimes it may also be difficult to buy fuel; it is crucial to carry plenty of spare supplies. Syria and Jordan are countries with almost no campsites, and they were once forced to pitch their tent on a roundabout in Aleppo, after asking permission from the local police. The discomfort of staying in the middle of a Syrian Piccadilly Circus was aggravated by the absence of public toilets for women.

Specialist companies can help you to arrange self-drive expeditions in hired vehicles. For example, the British company Safari Drive (www.safaridrive.com) undertakes the logistics and provides fully-equipped Land Rovers. A sample two-month itinerary starts in Windhoek, Namibia, and takes in Bushmanland, Botswana, Zambia, Malawi, and the Kalahari Desert. This and other relevant companies and organisations participate in the Explore seminar event hosted every November by the Royal Geographical Society (1 Kensington Gore, London SW7 2AR; 020 7591 3030; www.rgs.org). The RGS encourages and assists many British expeditions and its historic map room is open to the public daily, from 11am to 5pm.

DESERT DRIVING

Motorists must be sure to be suitably equipped for journeys across inhospitable terrain – modern folklore is laced with stories of skeletons being discovered a few miles from broken-down cars in desert regions. The first essential when planning a journey off the beaten track is to ensure your vehicle is fit for the task. It should be mechanically sound, and suitable for the roads you intend to use. Local advice can be sought from a motoring organisation or the police on whether your vehicle is fit for the journey you plan to make. You should notify a responsible person of your intended route and ensure that you let them know when you arrive safely at your destination.

At least two spare wheels are advisable; the heat on desert roads can melt the bitumen, which then sticks to tyres. Punctures are commonplace on unsealed roads, so make sure you know how to change a tyre (and that the wheel nuts are not jammed) before you leave civilisation. Fuel may not be easily accessible, so substantial supplies should be carried – as well as of water – not least in case you need to help out a less well-prepared motorist. The standard calculation of the amount of water needed is ten litres per person per day. A selection of spare parts such as a fan belt and electrical fittings is also advisable, as well as shovel, axe, and tow rope. If stranded, crawl under the vehicle for shade and drink the radiator water, provided it has no chemical additives. If possible, do not exert unnecessarily, reduce your salt intake, increase your sugar intake, and keep a fire going so that the smoke might be spotted. Never leave your vehicle in the event of a breakdown since you have a much better chance of being rescued.

One of the hazards on unsealed (or newly-surfaced) roads is of flying stones hitting the windscreen. Some drivers take the precaution of placing their fingers on the windscreen whenever they meet an oncoming vehicle, which absorbs the shock of the impact and reduces the risk of shattering. If the windscreen breaks, however, use gloves or a cloth to punch out a hole to see through. It is a good idea to carry a plastic windscreen for emergency use.

USEFUL CONTACTS FOR LAND ROVER DRIVERS

Many off-road driving centres can be found throughout the UK. Look for members of the British Off-Road Driving Association (www.borda.org.uk/members.html).

- **Keith Gott Land Rover Specialists**, Greenwood Farm, Old Odiham Road, Alton, Hampshire GU34 4BW (01420 544333; www.keithgott.co.uk). Specialist dealer that services and customises Land Rovers for a range of clients, including the Foreign & Commonwealth Office and the National Trust. The company can equip a vehicle for any journey: for example, by extending water and fuel tanks, and by providing roof racks, tents and showers.
- **Brownchurch Ltd**, Bickley Road, Leyton, London E10 7AQ (020 8556 0011; www. brownchurch.co.uk). Markets overland equipment and heavy-duty roof racks for Land Rovers. Full list of items with prices available is on their website, as well as info on Expedition Planning.
- **Land Rover** (www.landrover.com). The company website links to half- or full-day off-road training courses (normal price £175–£275+) at eight centres around the UK.

DESIGNING YOUR OWN ADVENTURE

Hitting the road can take many forms. At the most basic you can walk. Walking one of the world's best or lesser-known long-distance footpaths, whether the spine of Corsica or the Southern Alps of New Zealand, would be a worthy ambition for a gap year and a means of getting to grips with the landscapes and people of one region. Closer to home, many grown-ups take up the challenge of a long-distance path like the Pennine Way or the Pembrokeshire Coastal Path, and are amazed to have them virtually to themselves. Unless you plan to take a 'gap decade' you are unlikely to want to emulate the project of Briton Karl Bushby, who is attempting to walk 36,000 miles around the world – which he has dubbed the Goliath Expedition (www.odysseyxxi.com). He has been having endless headaches renewing visas and finding sponsors, but he is determined to prevail.

A 33-year-old Dutch woman called Manon Osseboort is at the moment continuing a journey from her home village to the South Pole in a tractor (www.tractortractor.org). She has made it to the southern tip of Africa and is now waiting for finance to make the rest possible. Others have made dramatic transcontinental trips in London cabs, double decker buses, and tandem bicycles. The drawback is that you become dependent on a piece of machinery that might prove difficult to protect and maintain in remote areas of the world. However, a vehicle offers autonomy and allows you to chart your own course.

Each of the tales from the road profiled in this chapter illustrates some of the choices available if you are contemplating a gap year to travel the world. These individuals chose different means of travel through different regions. Each has a unique story to recount, and each represents just one of the thousands of journeys that travellers take every year in which they hope to experience adventure and a measure of self-discovery too. Beyond the picket fence and the privet hedge lies the excitement and challenges of travel.

INTO THE HEART OF AFRICA

When **Rachel Pooley** and **Charlie Stanley-Evans** were in their late 20s, both decided to leave their jobs in London and drive to Cape Town. Rachel had been working for a mental health charity and Charlie had been employed in the wine trade. Together they felt an urge to travel and so planned a long-distance trip by road. Initially, Rachel's father felt she should be thinking about settling into a career, but neither had commitments and they wanted to see Africa. They were bored with London and wanted change. Charlie made a good profit from the sale of his flat, so he had capital to put into the expedition.

For £18,500, Rachel and Charlie bought an old MOD Defender TDI/long wheel chassis from a specialist dealer, Keith Gott (address above), who then built a new body and new engine to allow them to sleep in the vehicle and on the roof. Brownchurch Ltd supplied a roof rack with tent, which could be put up in half a minute on wooden boards and could be stored at the front of the rack. Other important supplies included jerry cans for water, which could be warmed in the sun during the day to supply water for a shower. Looking back on their hugely ambitious journey, one practical mistake they identified was not taking a fridge for food and drinks. But they do not regret their decision to take neither a phone nor a camcorder because it forced them to take a closer look at what they were seeing.

They spent three months planning what to take, and trying to anticipate all their requirements for day-to-day life in the tropics and for emergencies. To prepare themselves they took an off-road driving course and learnt motor maintenance: all about air and oil filters, and how to change tyres. They also took 500lbs of spare parts, including special air snorkel attachments to keep out dust and water.

Leaving in April, their trip took them through Europe and to Turkey, on the threshold of Asia and its more alien cultures. They travelled on through Syria and Jordan to Egypt, where they shipped the Land Rover to Kenya with P&O – which they had booked in advance because it was impossible (at that time) to travel through Sudan. Picking up the jeep in Kenya, they then took it through safari game parks and into neighbouring Tanzania.

Without the vehicle, their experience of Africa would have been wholly different. It enabled them to escape the well-worn routes covered by crowds of other tourists and to take their own safari into fascinating places like the Tsavo West National Park. They slept either in the Land Rover or on the roof. At other times they could use campsites with loos and showers.

In Malawi they accidentally fell into buying a six-month lease on a backpacker's hotel: the Mwaya Beach Lodge on the edge of Lake Malawi. This was the highlight of their journey through Africa but wholly unplanned. Despite the difficulties of supplying the lodge with food, dealing with difficult guests, and managing the staff of nine people, it taught them skills they could use back home in Britain. They built a house for themselves with brick and thatch for £200, together with a garden: 'We were tempted to stay long-term and buy the lodge, which had potential. It was a heavenly place and we enjoyed the work, but the life of expats in Africa is a little strange. We met too many who were stoned or drunk,' says Rachel.

From Malawi they headed south through Zimbabwe and into Kruger National Park in South Africa, Namibia, and on to Cape Town. In general their African adventure was hugely rewarding:

We learnt a lot about each other and other people. It makes us appreciate life more now. We are less concerned about work and fussier about the work we choose to do. The mentality in Africa is very different because there's no concept of planning ahead. Each day is a new challenge.

Of course other means of transport can be equally exciting in Africa, even public transport. **Mark Tanner** is a New Zealander in his late 20s who thinks that, 'It's a shame more people don't take time out from the job'. He aims to take off about every year in three from office life, where he works as a product marketing manager. Most recently, he took six months off to teach English in Khartoum through the Sudan Volunteer Programme (see Directory entry), followed by a very ambitious paddling expedition. Along with a Canadian friend, Mark became the first man to paddle from the source of the Blue Nile to the Mediterranean Sea: a journey that took just short of five months and covered 5,000 kilometres. An account of their epic journey, complete with descriptions of terrifying rapids, crocodile attacks, and hostile locals can be found at www.niletrip.com. For Mark, volunteering in Sudan was a useful precursor to the rafting adventure:

I guess you could say the time in Sudan was a gap year for grown-ups. Teaching was a breeze compared to the paddle, but it prepared me for many of the cultural challenges during the paddle. Also, having taught at the University of Khartoum helped give me creditability with officials during the paddle.

TRAVELLING BY BICYCLE

One of the most rewarding and accessible ways of travelling is by bicycle. You remain in control of your own route and can veer off the beaten track to take the back roads, while still maintaining a healthy mileage each day. Cycle touring represents freedom. It is a cheap and clean form of transport, and for improving physical fitness, you can't improve on a bike journey. A bicycle allows the rider to stop to appreciate the views or sights along the route. Due to their speed and relative quietness, cyclists have a much better chance than other road users of seeing animals and birds. It can often provide a peg for interacting with the local population, both in areas where cyclists abound and in areas where cyclists are a rarity and have novelty value. Enormous pleasure can be derived from the knowledge that you are crossing a landscape under your own steam. Walking achieves the same end, but cycling allows you to travel much further in the same time.

Provided you take the right equipment it's possible to be very versatile: either taking roads or mere tracks. You can also skip regions that hold no interest for you by putting your bike on a train or bus. It is not unknown for trucks to stop and offer a lift to a cyclist, especially one labouring up a mountain. Also, bear in mind that you don't need to be an experienced cyclist to use a bicycle for a long-distance journey. Everyone can obtain a bike and find a pace that is comfortable. An average target in relatively benign terrain might be 50 miles a day, which might seem daunting to a novice, but is manageable for most reasonably-fit people. By comparison, experienced and super-fit cyclists routinely cover twice that.

Let us imagine that in your youth you were a keen (not necessarily avid) cyclist. You remember with great fondness your cycling holidays in the Cotswolds, round the Ring of Kerry, or along the Loire Valley. Perhaps your dedication to cycling survived into your working life and you have used your trusty machine on and off for commuting to work. The arrival of children has inevitably cramped your cycling style and if you're lucky you have got your money's worth out of the bicycle rack you bought at Halfords in a fit of enthusiasm. Come to think of it, you haven't been on a decent long ride for a decade and certainly not taken your bicycle abroad. It is an astonishing statistic that the British own 21 million bicycles (more than they do cars) – the majority of which are gently rusting in garages and sheds.

A gap year might provide a chance to resurrect an interest in this most wholesome of pastimes. The National Cycle Network in the UK (www.sustrans.org.uk) covers more than 12,000 miles of designated cycle routes, many of them along disused railway lines and canal towpaths. But you needn't confine your aspirations to the UK. With a large-scale map and a comfortable bicycle with a good gear range, you can enjoy cycling almost anywhere.

Route-finding will be key to enjoyment. Many long-distance cyclists consider mastering GPS technology, so that a day's route can be worked out on a laptop and then uploaded to a GPS. But poring over a paper map is a pleasure that should not be discounted. Either way, daily routes on minor roads will maximise the cycling pleasure and minimise the risk of accident. Unless you are willing to free-camp, distances covered will often be determined by the availability of accommodation. Essential equipment includes waterproof panniers (Ortlieb panniers are recommended), tool kit, spare inner tubes, puncture repair kits, and spare brake cables.

Ambrose March and **Leah Norgrove**, together with their sons Griffin (13) and Simon (10) on the back of a tandem, cycled from Istanbul to Estonia between April and June 2009. Somewhere in rural Hungary, Ambrose described some of the pleasure:

> *When you are riding a bicycle the view is so important. It makes the ride interesting, it makes the ride pass, it makes you forget any aches or pains or leg fatigue ... Day by day we could see the botanical process unfold, until by the time we were in Central Bulgaria there was a daily progression and procession of flowering trees unfolding before us. Even our ignorance of which tree was which couldn't dampen the visual enjoyment.*

The good days usually outweigh the bad, though mechanical problems are almost inevitable. Unfortunately, the worst one this family experienced was on the very first day, when they discovered that the chain wheel of their tandem had been badly bent in transit from Canada. But the local spectators in a small Thracian town came to their aid, providing tea, arranging for the teeth to be straightened, and for them to be driven to three separate places to find a machinist who could straighten the 'wow' with an industrial metal press – all without any language in common. Many trouble-free weeks of cycling ensued, with daily distances gradually creeping up from the 53km they cycled on their first day (the younger son's comment: 'Let me tell you, my butt was sore. I felt like I was going to faint of tiredness but I didn't!'), to the 100km they ended up cycling on Griffin's 14th birthday. The very last day of their trip was one of the worst, cycling into a fierce Estonian headwind, working very hard for every metre along a road under construction: rutted, gravelly, and horribly dusty whenever a vehicle passed. They reached their destination with ten minutes to spare till their train departure, 'too stunned to realise we were done, because we were done in'.

In the remoter corners of your expedition, be prepared to shock and awe the locals. Leah reported from Bulgaria: 'We get waves, honks, curious stares and in smaller villages a look of absolute dumbfoundedness as three bikes (one a tandem) fly through.' That is nothing compared to the reaction that round-the-world 50-year-old Mark Perriton elicited in South America: *'The people of South America are still getting used to seeing this 6 foot 8 giant in their midst – often they stop me to get their photo taken with me.'*

Sometimes long-distance cyclists have to be almost as resourceful as the astronauts on Apollo 13. Extremes of climate and altitude can create problems never anticipated on the quiet lanes of home, as **Mark Perriton** discovered in Ecuador, on his classic round-the-world cycling gap year in 2010/11:

> *I woke the next morning to find a problem with my new tyre from Vancouver: the altitude had expanded the air in the tyre and pushed out a bubble in the side. I tried to sort out the problem from my hotel but I needed to find a bike shop. The nearest was Tena: 70 miles away and a drop*

of 3,000 meters. I hoped the tyre would hold as I went downhill – fast. I collected a couple of spare inner tubes which I had ordered from Quito. The repair work to the back wheel will be tested tomorrow. I have tried to repair the side wall of the tyre with a section of a plastic drinks bottle and duct tape, which I hope will hold for the next 1,500 miles.

Ambitious cycling journeys are often undertaken to raise funds for a good cause. To take two examples, a small group of cyclists from Cambridge calling themselves Downright Kenya chose as their destination Gilgil in Kenya, where a long-established charity HSK supports schools in rural Kenya. All the riders succeeded in their ambition to raise £3,000 each in sponsorship, and they had a hundred adventures en route: for example, they filmed themselves doing bicycle aerobics on the long flat stretches of highways through Egypt.

Not content to undertake the challenge of cycling the deserts of Africa, champion fund-raiser and self-described 'capitalist turned adventurer', **Reza Pakravan**, aims to get into the *Guinness Book of Records* in 2011 by crossing more than 1,000 miles of the Sahara in punishing heat in a record time. By raising corporate sponsorship, he hopes to donate £20,000 to the Malagasy charity Azafady (see Directory entry) with whom he volunteered last year.

MY GROWN-UP GAP YEAR: MARK PERRITON

Mark Perriton had long had a yearning to do an epic cycle trip. He got to a position where his commercial interiors business could look after itself, and his family was willing to release him for a year to fulfil his dream of cycling around the world: starting in Alaska in September 2010.

I wanted to have a break from my normal life at 50 (I celebrated my 50th birthday last week in Chile, November 2010), and I wanted to see countries that take too long to visit on a two-week holiday. I wanted to challenge myself from a physical perspective. I have a long-term interest in cycle tourism and I wanted to see if it could be done in more remote locations. I wanted a chance to meet new people and explore new business ideas, which should provide me with a fresh perspective on my next 15-20 years of work.

The process of arranging your life to allow a break for one year is a complicated one. You need to start as early as possible and work through all the issues. You need to accept that when you start the trip there will still be issues to resolve. I had to sort out my business activity to allow me to continue to receive an income from the business while away, but I also wanted to have a business to return to as I might pick it up and develop it in the future.

I had to get the support and understanding of my family, but this was not difficult in my case. I think the view taken was, if you need to do this trip then it is better to get on and do it, rather than sitting around at home being unhappy.

Starting in Alaska was a memorable moment. I had a great sense of excitement as I set off from Anchorage. The scale of the distances travelled is very frightening at times, but I take each day as a fresh challenge and do not plan too far ahead. I have had my son and my brother visit me on this trip, which has been very good to break the routine. The times that I have spent with locals from any country, learning about the culture and politics of an area, have been great.

When I booked my round-the-world flights I knew that I would need to supplement the cycling with buses, trains, and planes. I have spent six weeks cycling from Quito in Ecuador to Lima Peru, and have only seen a very small part of the area. You would need many months and years to properly explore this area. When you travel you need to make choices about what you want to visit, and accept that you will miss out on other places. I will have to come back to this area and spend some more time here.

It is great to have my brother with me to celebrate my 50th birthday. I am pleased to be spending it with good company and not in the office. I have been planning what to do to celebrate half a century for a long time, and this will do nicely.

BACKPACKING: TRAVELLING BY YOUR WITS

The purest form of travelling is by hitching rides, or on public transport cheek-by-jowl with the local people. Many dream of indulging their wanderlust, following their noses, crossing a country by any means possible. By creating your own route and using your wits to find your way, you'll find yourself obliged to interact with local people rather than being cocooned with other tourists.

Yet you will seldom be entirely isolated. Almost everywhere in the world, from Baluchistan to Patagonia, you'll encounter other travellers and expats. Often you will find yourself inside an informal community of travellers who stay in the same hostels, travel on the same ferries, and swap travellers' tales. This camaraderie of the road often provides a welcome grapevine and support system far from home. But sometimes it is a depressing reminder of how small the world has become for privileged westerners.

When engaging with local people, always follow the golden rule of trusting your instincts. It may be stating the obvious, but you should never accept an invitation to go somewhere or participate in an activity that makes you feel uncomfortable or threatened. Even if you run the risk of offending a 'host', you need to keep your internal compass functioning. Bear in mind that foreigners may be viewed as easy targets for some form of exploitation: principally financial. If you feel that an offer sounds too good to be true, then it is, full stop.

Don't lose sight of why you're travelling. Often, it will be hard work and occasionally gruelling. Travelling in reasonable comfort is exhausting enough. Sightseeing is often a pleasure but it is taxing too, so give yourself plenty of time out for relaxation: whether reading in cafés, writing entertaining emails to friends and family, strolling in foothills, or lounging on a sunny beach. Occasionally, it's a good idea to splash out on a comfortable hotel, particularly if you are feeling under the weather. Clean sheets, air-conditioning, and a laundry service are reviving treats after several weeks on the road, and are usually worth the extra expense.

While juggling bus or train timetables and the need to find suitable accommodation, try not to rush. The slow pace of life as a traveller, especially in the developing world, is something to be savoured – not bemoaned. Dawdling allows you to appreciate different experiences and sensations in places to which you may never have the chance to return. Dashing hither and yon should be left to the very young who, in the words of the veteran traveller and writer Dervla Murphy, 'Seem to cover too much ground too quickly, sampling everywhere and becoming familiar with nowhere … it would be good if the young became more discriminating, allowing themselves time to travel seriously in a limited area that they had chosen because of its particular appeal to them, as individuals.' This is something that more mature travellers on a gap year can aim to achieve. Remember that your sabbatical is designed precisely to give you the time you normally lack on a conventional holiday from work.

Once you have been carrying your pack for a couple of weeks, caught the right buses, and met a few other travellers, you will probably laugh at your pre-travelling misconceptions of danger and risk. Not that you can always count on dodging risk, as **Hannah Adcock** found during her travels in 2010. A freelance writer and events organiser from Edinburgh, she and her husband decided to do some serious travelling in Southeast Asia:

I've just got back from travelling, which was brilliant and even more adventurous than expected. We got caught up in the flash floods in Ladakh when we were out trekking and had to make a bolt to Delhi via Kargil and the Vale of Kashmir, with the help of some great guys from Canada, a damsel in distress (until she met us), and a taxi driver from Srinagar who just happened to be in the area. We'd left some luggage at a guest house in Leh but there were three bridges down (and another being eaten) between us and Leh, so we gave up the bags as lost and got down to the rather more important business of getting out of the region so we could catch our Indonesia flight. It was only later we learned that Leh had been so badly hit by mudslides, although of course Pakistan made the international news for suffering the same fate on a catastrophic scale. Anyway, the Vale of Kashmir was spectacular. I'm so glad I got to see the place, even if the FCO warns against it. Indonesia was also great fun. We did a bit of an overland volcano tour and then an openwater scuba course on Gili Trawangan, which is the kind of place you imagine when someone talks about a paradise island. Anyway, I have a picture of me with a shark, which is great, and I was a little pleased with myself because I've always had a bit of a phobia about deep water (possibly now laid to rest). It was so great to be travelling – I don't imagine it will be long until we leave Britain again, possibly to spend this winter in Dahab in Egypt.

The economy end of independent travel is a burgeoning market worldwide, especially in Australasia, Latin America, and Africa, and you will soon find a bewildering choice of destinations with suitable facilities. If you are trying to capture the essence of travel and want to make a distinctive break from your annual holiday, then open-ended backpacking guarantees a chance to find your own adventure.

At the same time that it offers the romance of travel, backpacking is undeniably arduous and uncertain. Sleeping on crowded trains or hiking through mosquito-infested jungles may hold little appeal. For some, pitching a tent on Dartmoor in a drizzling mist and bedding down in a soggy sleeping bag requires plenty of courage and daring. People past their thirties may decide that they don't want to rough it any more or to replicate student life, and will travel accordingly. They may have little interest in experiencing foreign cultures at a grassroots level and may prefer to concentrate on some other aspect, such as making a study of the art and architecture, history or language of a foreign culture. (See Part 9: New Skills and New Projects.)

MY GROWN-UP GAP YEAR:
LISA LUBIN

Lisa Lubin was an Emmy award-winning writer and TV producer at ABC in Chicago. She had worked there for nearly ten years, producing lifestyle and entertainment segments (travel, dining, fitness, etc). At some point earlier, her bosses had declined her request to take six months off. Years later when she was in her early 30s, she just quit because she knew she was ready to do something different.

I have always loved travelling. When I was little I would ride my bike down new streets, mesmerised by something I'd never seen before. A few years after college I went backpacking for a month across Europe. That was it. I got the bug. I fell in love with the world and a world traveller was born. I had never really planned on taking a year off before; the trip just kind of revealed itself to me and evolved over time. I've always come back from previous trips a bit sad and always wanting more. The year before I took a gap year (which turned into three years), certain things in my life just fell into place and I realised I was 'free'. I broke up with my boyfriend of five years, I was bored at work, and my sweet cat had died. Then I read a book called One Year Off and I realised if the author and his family could do it, I could do it! I was a little nervous about doing it solo, but I'm pretty independent at home and I realised I couldn't let that stop me. The opportunity was there and I needed to grab it! I think in fantasy this is a dream trip for many. But in reality, the packing, leaving everything, quitting, saying good-bye for a year, is way too much a risk for most. I had thought about doing this a while back, but even for me it was too much. But then my plan seemed to evolve slowly right before my eyes and before I realised it, I was going to do it. Kind of like most other big decisions in life, you never really know what the outcome will be until you do it and just take the leap?

Many people's first assumption is that travelling for a year must be very expensive, but this is just not so. It certainly will be if you stay at four- and five-star hotels, but it also can be very affordable if you stay in hostels and budget hotels and get all the discounts you can. For me, staying and living in Chicago would have cost me much more than this trip, when you take into account my mortgage payments, bills (gas, electric, cable, phone, cell phone), and other monthly costs such as grocery bills and random expenses that come up. I'd eliminated all of those and had even gotten rid of my cell phone (never liked it anyway!). Most hostels average around $20 per night, depending on the country you are in, but can be cheaper: in Costa Rica I stayed at one that was $6 a night and in Hanoi $10 for a single room. By saving money in cheaper countries you can make up for these costs. I cut corners where I could, but also didn't want to deprive myself of some special 'once-in-a-lifetime' opportunities like a trip to the Galapagos.

I saved a lot of money during my time working at ABC, and I sold my condo in Chicago that would more than pay for a trip around the world. My average spend was $2,000 a month, including everything: airfares, transport, food, lodging, tours, visas, thrill rides, and all my other random expenses. I spent time in some very inexpensive countries in Southeast Asia and South America that allowed me to stretch my budget and then, on the flip side, places like Australia, Dubai, and Europe, had been rather expensive and made it harder to cut corners. I worked while I travelled too. I got a job in Australia at a café, did some English tutoring in Istanbul, and ended up doing some PR work for an English Immersion programme in Spain for one year, which covered all my travel expenses. If I had remained in Chicago, where the overall cost of living is high, I would have definitely spent more. Not only did I work, but I also took classes along the way - Spanish immersion in Costa Rica, salsa dancing in Ecuador, surfing lessons in Costa Rica, cooking classes in Vietnam. In Vietnam, I also did a two-week cycle trip that was the most amazing way to see a country close-up. In London, I volunteered during Christmas week with homeless people. All these different activities ensured that I would meet new people, both travellers and locals. My adventures have been amazing, but the best part would have to be all the wonderful people I have met from all corners of the globe - good, kind people. I made good friends and had some romantic experiences as well. I have absolutely no regrets. I think I thought, 'What am I doing?' on my very first day when I landed in San Jose, Costa Rica. I was all by myself in my hotel and didn't know quite what to do next. Luckily those feelings were usually quite fleeting.

If you are organised everything kind of falls into place. I love the logistics, but it's just a matter of making a to-do list and prioritising. One of the best things I did was put a 'call out' to everyone I knew and ask for their friends or contacts anywhere around the world. I met some really cool people this way and had more local experiences by hooking up with friends of friends. I definitely felt much less stress on my trip than I had felt at home with a job and a million things to worry about and obsess over. Now I know, in the grand scheme of things, none of that really matters.

ADVENTURE TRAVEL

A gap year is an ideal time to indulge a taste for adventure. Some will consider one of the classic overland journeys across continents, or will want to pit themselves against the elements on the high seas (see section on Sailing, below). But staying put and going native can provide the backdrop for any number of adventures.

While staying in the town of Kratie in Cambodia for six months of her gap year, **Hannah Stevens** was more willing than most to experiment with new experiences:

> *I took a few days off work to travel with three friends up to Ratanakiri in the north east of Cambodia. We went trekking through the rubber plantations on an elephant to a hidden waterfall that was directly out of* The Jungle Book. *In fact, I'm pretty sure I heard Baloo singing in the distance! The whole thing was absolutely phenomenal, and I had to keep reminding myself that this is where I live! It certainly made me smile! Sometimes, I can't quite work out how I've ended up here in such a glorious place, with wonderful people and a rich culture.*
>
> *On one journey, I found myself volunteering to sample the local cuisine: fried tarantulas! The head was absolutely hideous and popped in my mouth, drowning my tastebuds in brain fluid; but the legs and body were fairly acceptable – somewhat crunchy, but certainly edible. I spent the following four hours of the journey picking leg hair out of my teeth, and doing fairly repulsive burps! I think I'll pass next time!*
>
> *With the rainy season come crickets. Swarms of noisy, ugly, flying cockroaches. But, unlike six months ago, I don't squeal and flap, but catch and eat them! Chop off their legs, rip out their guts, stick a peanut up their bum, and deep fry them. Genuinely delicious, and it keeps us occupied. Coming soon to a dinner party near you!*

Like tarantulas and crickets, risk-taking may be an acquired taste, but it is one that can bring enormous satisfaction. When long-time Religious Education teacher, **Nigel Hollington**, set off to join a conservation project in Zambia, he knew that he would be expected to handle rodents, and decided to confront his phobia head on. He packed an extra-strong pair of gardening gloves for the purpose and did not shirk when the moment came. His year off included a succession of minor triumphs such as this, which he found extraordinarily satisfying.

Pushing yourself to the edge of danger can hold a special appeal. More conventional challenges like bungee-jumping, white water rafting, parasailing and various other adrenaline sports are tempting to many independent travellers (but make sure your insurance policy will cover them).

OVERLAND JOURNEYS

Venturing across vast continents, dark or otherwise, can be a daunting prospect for an independent traveller. An alternative is to make the journey with one of the numerous established overland tour operators, most of which charge between £100 and £150 a week, plus a food kitty of about £50 a week. The longer the trip, the lower the weekly cost: for example, Oasis Overland (www.oasisoverland.co.uk) trips start at £95 per week, plus £37 a week local payment for food and camping fees on a 40-week trans-Africa trip, and go up to around £140 a week plus £70 kitty for shorter South American trips. Adventure tour operators follow a huge number of routes through all the continents of the world. Whereas some overland routes are fraught with difficulty, others are comfortable and almost routine.The old hippie overland route to India and Nepal has been problematical for many years, though not impossible if travelling from Iran to Pakistan and bypassing Afghanistan – which is completely off-limits. In 2010, 35-year-old maths teacher **Kath McGuire** saved up to return to Sri Lanka to resume volunteer teaching she had greatly enjoyed the year before, and decided to travel overland. Her route took her via Poland, Moscow, Kazakhstan, Urumqi in China, Tibet, Nepal, and India.

Even more than on ordinary group trips, personal dynamics are crucial to your enjoyment on an overland journey. **Carol Peden**, a doctor in her 40s who took six months off, joined two separate trips with Intrepid Travel and describes how they differed:

> *I did some travelling with an Australian-based company called Intrepid Travel. Their Southern India trip was fantastic: great food, wonderful Indian experiences, and fun travelling companions – a group of 12, and ten of us were singles and we all got on really well. On another Intrepid trip we travelled through China for three weeks by train, but this was not as successful as the first. This time my 11 travelling companions consisted of a family of four, including two disgusted teenagers who did not speak for the whole trip, a trio of birdwatchers, and two loved-up couples, which was very lonely for me. With hindsight I would have checked out small group travel more carefully, eg would I be the only single in the group?*

There is surely an element of luck in the composition of any group. Another woman career-breaker in her middle years had been travelling for months on her own in Canada, New Zealand, and Southeast Asia. She felt a bit daunted at the prospect of travelling in India, so she signed up with a Dragoman trip from Chennai to Mumbai. It so happened that one of her fellow travellers seemed to take against her, and she found that a small group purposely excluded her, which made her feel more lonely than if she had been on her own. Out of her nine-month trip, this proved to be the low point, though she still does not regret joining the trip and saw much to enjoy in India.

Petrol-heads might be tempted by the poor man's/woman's variation on the Paris–Dakar Rally. Teams that enter the Plymouth–Banjul Challenge (www.plymouth-banjul.co.uk) must travel to the capital of the Gambia in an old banger, and then auction their vehicle on arrival for good causes. A couple of years ago Tony Wheeler, founder of Lonely Planet Publications, and his wife Maureen, joined the race in a 1989 Mitsubishi they bought in Devon for £350 (although rules stipulate that the vehicle should cost no more than £100). New rally destinations keep being added: for example, Timbuktu and Murmansk.

If planning an independent overland trip through Africa, routes should be well researched, eg on Lonely Planet's Thorn Tree forum. At the present time, travellers are passing from Egypt through northern Sudan to Ethiopia and on to Kenya.

OVERLAND TOUR OPERATORS

A selection of overland companies is listed here, and others may be found on the Overland Expedition Resources website www.go-overland.com. Many overland companies also advertise in the glossy adventure travel magazine *Wanderlust*, available in large newsagents (www.wanderlust.co.uk). The average age on most of these would be 20–30, though older trekkers are usually welcome and find that they fit in. There is usually a higher ratio of women to men.

- **Absolute Africa** (020 8742 0226; www.absoluteafrica.com). Adventure camping safaris in Africa.
- **Acacia Adventure Holidays** (020 7706 4700; www.acacia-africa.com). Africa specialist, with 16 tours in Southwest Africa lasting from three to 70 days. A 116-page colour brochure can be viewed online.
- **Dragoman Overland Expeditions** (01728 861133; www.dragoman.co.uk). Expeditions to Africa, Asia, South and Central America. Travellers are carried in a specially-adapted vehicle, which is a cross between a Jeep, minibus and army truck.
- **Exodus** (0845 287 3753; www.exodus.co.uk). One of the leading adventure travel companies in the UK, organising adrenaline-fuelled activities graded according to difficulty to give you guidance about physical endurance. In addition to overland expeditions, Exodus offers trekking holidays, cycling holidays, multi-activity holidays, and trips in Europe lasting from one to 24 weeks. 500 tours in 90 countries, mostly for an older, civilised clientele.
- **Explore Worldwide Ltd** (0845 013 1537; www.explore.co.uk). Small group adventure and special interest tour operator worldwide, with similar range of destinations, clientele, and prices as Exodus.
- **Imaginative Traveller** (0845 287 7019; www.imaginative-traveller.com). Runs small group adventures around the globe. Ring them to request a brochure on your chosen continent or region. Trips last up to 11 weeks.
- **Intrepid/Guerba** (0203 147 7777 or 01373 826611; www.intrepidtravel.com). Leading operator of adventure holidays to Asia, Latin America, Africa, Australasia, Middle East, and Europe. The company runs more than 400 trips a year in 35 countries, at varying levels of comfort.
- **Journey Latin America** (020 8747 8315; www.JourneyLatinAmerica.co.uk). A fully-bonded agency which specialises in travel to and around all of Latin America. Runs dozens of escorted tours throughout the continent using private or public transport, and also offers some activity adventure trips such as cycling in Costa Rica and rafting in Peru.
- **KE Adventure Travel** (017687 73966; www.keadventure.com). Organises adventure trips on bike or by foot around the world, from the Himalayas to Brazil. Most trips last two to four weeks. Was recently voted the best trekking outfitter in the world by *National Geographic*.
- **Keystone Journeys**, New Zealand (www.keystonejourneys.com). Specialist tours to Africa, Middle East, South America, Central Asia, and New Zealand for the over-40s, as well as a programme of other tours open to all ages 18–60+.
- **Kumuka Expeditions** (020 7937 8855 or 0800 068 8855; www.kumuka.com). Itineraries through Africa and Latin America.
- **Oasis Overland Ltd** (01963 363400; www.oasisoverland.co.uk). Africa, the Middle East and South America.

- **Tucan Travel** (020 8896 1600; www.tucantravel.com). Open age group adventure tours and independent travel worldwide, including Antarctica. Budget Expeditions is their brand for the 18–35 age range.
- **Wagon Trails** (01524 419909; www.wagontrails.co.uk). Short tours of Southern Africa, and a 43-week London to Cape Town trip (costing £3,500 plus £2,150 kitty).
- **World Expeditions** (020 8545 9030; www.worldexpeditions.co.uk). Long-established adventure travel company with large choice of journeys on all continents, including the Arctic and Antarctic. Trips lasting up to 30 days for all ages and fitness levels, including dedicated trips for the over-55s.

Collectively these companies employ large numbers of competent expedition staff, including leaders and cooks, though most companies require a longer commitment than would be available on a career break. See Overland Tour Leaders on page 222.

OASIS OVERLAND
This is Africa – the best way

I was in a fortunate situation that I was able to take a few months off work to travel. I wanted to see Africa and identified that the best opportunity to experience as much as possible (and as cost-effectively as possible) would be to go with one of the specialist overland travel companies. This would mean sharing the trip with twenty or so like-minded individuals, in a purpose-built and adapted truck, managing catering and budgeting as a group and sleeping in the tents we carried on the truck or in hostels and lodges along the way. I'd travelled independently on short trips before, but this would be totally different and right on the edge of my comfort zone.

The company I travelled with (Oasis Overland) were experts in this field and having an experienced driver and tour leader allowed our group to make the most of our trip, experiencing extraordinary places that many people won't even consider travelling to. We dived in the crystal clear waters off Zanzibar, came face to face with elephants in Tanzania, swam in Lake Malawi and walked with lions in Zimbabwe. We bungee-jumped at Victoria Falls and quad-biked in Namibia, and by the time we said our farewells in South Africa to return to work or university or continue with gap-year travels, we knew that we had shared a very special few months together.

The friendships that were made while bouncing over African roads in the back of the truck remain the stand-out memories from the trip. We had a mix of ages and nationalities and a mixture of opinions and preferences, but we all shared a sense of humour and adventure, and that is what travelling overland through Africa is all about – a great adventure.

Alan Green

CHARITY CHALLENGES

A large and growing number of charities in the UK now offer adventurous group travel to individuals who are prepared to undertake some serious fundraising on their behalf. Household names like Oxfam, the Youth Hostels Association, and the Children's Society organise sponsored trips, as do many more obscure good causes. Specialist agents like Charity Challenge (www.charitychallenge.com) allow you to select your trip (most of which last no more than a fortnight) and the charity you want to support. Participants are asked to raise a certain minimum amount – for example, £2,500 – for the charity, and in return receive a 'free' trip. You are in a far stronger position to ask people for donations if you can say you are supporting the Children's Society/British Heart Fund/Whale Conservation Society or whatever, than if you say you are trying to raise money for a holiday to Morocco/Patagonia/Borneo.

Charity trips seldom last longer than a fortnight, so are perhaps not of central interest to people on a career break. But the chance to participate in a group activity which at the same time funds a good cause is welcomed by many, especially those who don't relish the prospect of taking an adventurous trip on their own. Cycling, trekking, canoeing, rafting, mountaineering: all are on offer in most corners of the world. These trips have proved particularly popular among women in middle life, who perhaps lack the confidence to undertake an adventurous trip on their own and who often find it easier to justify a trip abroad if it is for a good cause – as well as for their own pleasure.

Specialist companies organise 'open challenges' which allow you to nominate the charity you want to support. Companies that organise a range of overseas charity challenge events include:

- **Across the Divide** (01460 30456; www.acrossthedivide.co.uk)
- **Charity Challenge** (020 8557 0000; www.charitychallenge.com)
- **Classic Tours** (020 7619 0066; www.classictours.co.uk)
- **Different Travel** (07881 698623; www.different-travel.com)
- **Discover Adventure** (01722 718444; www.discoveradventure.com)
- **Kuoni Challenge for Charity** (01483 410085; www.challengeforcharity.co.uk)
- **Tall Stories Challenge Events** (020 8939 0413; www.tallstories.co.uk)

Note that experienced tour leaders and medics may be needed for these trips and may be eligible for subsidised or free places.

While these events have proved a popular way of raising money for a favourite charity, some critics have argued that it is an inefficient way of raising money for worthy causes. In fact, some key charities such as Cancer Research UK have been reducing their International Challenge programmes in the interests of cost effectiveness. As much as half of the money raised by each sponsored traveller goes towards paying for their holiday (flight, accommodation, etc) – something which family, friends, and colleagues who support the fundraising might come to resent. One solution is to simply pay that portion out of your pocket and fund-raise the rest. Charity challenges do appear to achieve the dual goals of raising money and raising awareness of the charity's purpose and achievements by engendering a sense of occasion. Of course, anyone undertaking a challenging trip independently can use it to raise money for a good cause.

SAILING

Sailing is a versatile sport that can form the basis of an adventurous gap year. Learning to sail the oceans is a perfect way to fill a gap in your career. It is possible for experienced sailors to charter a boat with or without crew, or act as crew for someone else with a boat, for short or long crossings. The pleasures of open-ended island hopping in the Aegean, Caribbean, or South Pacific are easily imagined, though difficult to realise. Sailing represents the ultimate freedom to chart your own course and, for some, a chance to stretch mental and physical limits by sailing around the world in a yacht race.

On a sailing adventure you are bound to see dolphins, whales, flying fish, and rare birds. You get in touch with nature by seeing and feeling the rhythms of the sea. You learn about sailing, meteorology, navigation. But there are also drawbacks. There is the claustrophobia of living in a confined space. The constant need to maintain the equipment may begin to feel burdensome; one experienced sailor's advice was that you have to love doing repairs to love cruising. You will probably suffer from seasickness at the beginning. You will have to deal with a panoply of adverse weather conditions and probably experience terror at least once, especially when you move into the path of a supertanker. You have to get up in the middle of the night to take the watch. Every little task is made more difficult by the constant movement of the boat. It may be that there will be no wind for days at a stretch. But, if you are prepared to cope with all this, a sailing trip can be exhilarating in the extreme.

In the context of a career break, sailing is a truly escapist activity. Out at sea you have no choice but to stop thinking about work and home because the daily tasks will require all your concentration. Long-distance sailing allows you to suspend your life while simultaneously demanding an intense and unique form of communal living. Having finished her accountancy exams, **Jennie Sanders** wasn't sure what she was aiming for next and suddenly felt as though all she had ahead was a lifetime of work:

I had often seen adverts for sailing courses in the back pages of sailing magazines and thought how much I would like to do one, but I also knew that my employer PricewaterhouseCoopers invest a great deal in training up new graduates and are understandably eager to hang on to them once they are qualified. The company is keen to promote flexible working policies though, and career breaks are one option they offer to staff who have worked for them for at least four years. So I followed up one of the ads and booked a three and a half-month course with Flying Fish in order to indulge my passion for sailing (I had been sailing with my family since the age of 10) and qualify as a professional skipper.

The first month in North Wales was fairly windy and wet, but with Australia to look forward to, no one seemed to mind too much. We spent most of the first month learning (or refreshing) the basics and doing classroom work, including chart work. No sailing experience was required; in fact, one participant hadn't even been on a ferry before. Whereas some of the grown-up train-ees found it strange going back to a classroom, living in shared accommodation (on the boats at very close quarters) and being told when to be where, I found it relaxing not to have to think about what to do next.

Soon we were all off to Sydney, where we were installed in an apartment right on the beachfront in Manly – amazing. Sailing consisted of day sailing on Sydney harbour and some longer passages – including night sailing up and down the east coast of Australia – as well as some racing. We took it in turns to be skipper, in order to get in the necessary practice to pass the Yachtmaster exams.

The course was expensive [the current price is £11,690], but by using my savings, working for a couple of months whilst I was away, and making the most of a six-month interest-free loan when I returned, I managed to do virtually everything I wanted to whilst I was away. Following the course I got a sailing job in a marina in Sydney (a far cry from sitting in front of a computer in an office in London!). Originally I had applied to my employer for a six-month unpaid break but decided to extend it to nine months since I was having such a good time. This allowed me to travel up the East Coast of Australia to Fiji for a couple of weeks, and then return to the UK to do some more sailing – including to the Scilly Isles and Ireland – as well as take my final Yachtmaster exam.

After passing the exam, I decided that I couldn't put off the return to work any longer. Price-waterhouseCoopers had agreed to keep my job open (although they didn't guarantee it would be in exactly the same department), but it was felt that my technical knowledge at work might get too out of date if I stayed away for a year or more. When I was quizzed by one of my bosses as to what I had got out of the course, I was able to stress that the forward planning, organisa-tion, and people-managing involved in being a skipper would be of potential benefit at work. In fact, a few months after my return, I was promoted to manager. The return to work was more difficult than I had anticipated: for instance, finding people who had previously been junior to me promoted ahead of me, and also working to tight deadlines didn't come easily again.

I never worried that my career break would harm my career. I am now a corporate tax man-ager with six people working under me. As well as having improved my work skills, I now race in a very competitive sports-boat class, which I do every Sunday nine months of the year. It gives me something to look forward to all week, and keeps me active and refreshed so that I am able to do my job better. I hope to take another career break when I can, but next time I'll use it to sail round the world.

The RYA Yachtmaster qualifies you to charter a yacht from almost anywhere in the world or enter the yachting industry. To judge whether sailing might be an idea to pursue for your own career break, dip into the wealth of sailing literature – including a classic like Joshua Slocum's *Sailing Alone*, or a light-hearted account of sailing with small children in *One Summer's Grace* by Libby Purves, about sailing around the British Isles with her husband Paul Heiney and their two children aged three and five.

Many sailors do not set aside their passion when they have children, and the oceans are liberally sprinkled with cruising families. Check out www.noonsite.com, 'The global site for cruising sailors', maintained by the World Cruising Club on the Isle of Wight, which has an active message board for cruising families who want to meet others in similar circumstances. Channel 4 documentary makers followed the Lawrence family on their sailing adventure for the series aired in 2010: *My Family's Crazy Gap Year*. It vividly illustrated the potential tensions between the fanatical sailor in a family (in this case, father Jason) and the others (mother Amanda and small boys Jean Jacques and Louis). But it also showed the pleasures and op-portunities for family bonding.

CREWING ON YACHTS

In every marina and harbour, people are planning and preparing for long trips. There may be requests for crew posted on harbour noticeboards, in yacht clubs, or chandlery shops, from Marina Bay in Gibraltar to Rushcutter's Bay in Sydney. The most straightforward (and usually the most successful) method is to head for the nearest yacht marina and ask captains directly. The harbour water supply or dinghy dock is usually a good place to meet yachties.

People who display a reasonable level of common sense, vigour, and amiability, and take the trouble to observe yachting etiquette, should find it possible to persuade a yachtsman that they will be an asset to his crew. As one skipper comments, 'A beginner ceases to be a passenger if he or she can tie half a dozen knots and hitches, knows how to read the lights of various kinds of ships and boats at night, and isn't permanently seasick'. Obviously, it is much easier to become a crew member if you have some experience, but there are opportunities for people who lack experience at sea and it is unwise to exaggerate your skills. Once you have worked on one yacht it will be much easier to get on the next one. The yachting world is a small one. It is a good idea to buy a log book in which you can enter all relevant experience and voyages, and be sure to ask the captains of boats you have been on for a letter of reference.

Inexperienced crew are never paid and most skippers will expect a contribution towards expenses; at least £15 a day is standard for food, drink, fuel, harbour fees, etc. Obviously airfares to join the yacht and visa fees will be in addition. The more experience you have, the more favourable arrangements you will be able to negotiate. Also, your chances are better of having a financial contribution reduced or even waived if you are prepared to crew on unpopular routes: for example, crossing the Atlantic west to east is much tougher than vice versa. If you demonstrate to a skipper that you take safety seriously enough to have learned a little about the procedures, and if you are clean and sober, sensible and polite, you are probably well on your way to filling a crewing vacancy. Offshore sailing is a risky business and you should be sure that the skipper to whom you have entrusted your life is a veteran sailor. A well-used but well-kept boat is a good sign. A good starting place for novice crew might be to get to grips with a good yachting book such as *RYA Competent Crew* (Royal Yachting Association, 2002), which contains invaluable information on technical sea terms and the basics of navigation.

Even better would be to sign up for a sailing course. The first level, Competent Crew, can be reached in a five-day course at any Royal Yachting Association-recognised centre for £400–£500. If you are planning your trip a long way in advance, scour the classified columns of *Yachting Monthly, Yachting World* or *Practical Boat Owner*, though advertisers are likely to require a substantial payment or contribution towards expenses on your part. Increasingly, skippers use the internet to find paying crew. Sites that promise to match crew with captains include www.floatplan.com/crew, which carries details of actual vacancies – quite often a male skipper looking for a female crew, eg 'I'm a 58-year-old Dutch/Canadian sailor looking for a 45+-year-old female sailing partner to join me in the Med on my 28' Bristol Channel Cutter. I'm physically in good shape and speak four languages. Share cost.' Captains who look for crew through agencies (see below) may be less likely to have a lonely hearts motive.

USEFUL CREWING CONTACTS

Crewing agencies in Britain, France, Denmark, West Indies, USA, and elsewhere match yacht captains and crew. These are mostly of use to experienced sailors. In the UK the Cruising Association (020 7537 2828; office@cruising.org.uk; www.cruising.org.uk/crewing/introduction) runs a crewing service to put skippers in touch with unpaid crew. Meetings are held on the first Thursday of the month at 7pm between February and May for this purpose. They claim to offer a variety of sailing (including two or three week cruises to the Mediterranean and transatlantic passages) to suit virtually every level of experience. The fee to non-members for this service is £20.

Some of the largest crewing registers in the UK:

- **Global Crew Network** (0870 910 1888; www.globalcrewnetwork.com). Specialises in crew recruitment for Tall Ships and traditional boats, as well as luxury yachts worldwide. Individual membership costs £35 for six months; £45 for 12.
- **Crewseekers Crew Introduction Agency** (01489 578319; www.crewseekers.net). Their membership charges are £60 for six months, and £85 for a year; joint members may be added for an extra £15.
- **Crew Network Worldwide** (www.crewnetwork.com). Crewing offices in Antibes, Viareggio, Fort Lauderdale, Auckland, and others.
- **Reliance Yacht Management** (www.reliance-yachts.com). One year registration fee of £38.
- **Crewfile.com** (www.crewfile.com). Crewing positions with visible email addresses. One advertiser estimates that crew members will need about $200 a month for food and expenses.
- **World Cruising Club** (www.worldcruising.com). Has a forum (in association with Noonsite.com, mentioned below) on Crewing Opportunities (though the majority of posts are from people looking for crew vacancies).

Concentrations of crewing agencies can be found in yachting honeypots, such as Antibes and Fort Lauderdale. The main crewing agencies in Antibes are housed in La Galerie du Port, 8 boulevard d'Aguillon, 06600 Antibes. For example, try contacting Peter Insull's Crew Agency at www.insull.com/crew.

RACING THE OCEANS

Sailors with the prospect of an extended career break might want to consider participating in one or more legs of a round-the-world race. This will require a huge commitment of time and money. A round-the-world race can be brutally demanding, where you live from watch to watch, with no more than three hours at any one stretch to sleep, eat, and wash. For all of the romance of sailing, it remains a dangerous and strenuous sport – wherein lies part of its enormous appeal. The lure of the sea draws many to try their luck and the boat becomes a sealed world of its own.

Whereas some yacht races like the Volvo Ocean Race are open only to professional sailors, others cater to novices as well as more experienced yachtsmen and women. However, if you're drawn to the notion of joining the crew of a racing boat, there are other opportunities such as the Clipper races described below. It is possible to join a crew for one leg of a race or for an entire race, though costs are colossal. **Humphrey Walters** lectures on inspirational leadership after deciding to join the BT Global Challenge (which no longer takes place): a notoriously gruelling round-the-world yacht race, which involved racing the 'wrong' way around the world (ie, against the prevailing winds, currents, and tides). His primary motivation was to increase his knowledge of team-building and leadership: 'I wanted to know what makes the difference between average and high-performance teams, and the critical actions needed in hostile and unpredictable conditions'. Such a learning experience, he hoped, could be applied to developing his business. Humphrey also wanted to learn how to step away from his responsibilities and to delegate to others in the company. It would be a chance to re-focus and re-energise himself. However, he wanted to do something dramatic during a career break; to embark on a project with a purpose. Sailing around the world proved to be as informative as he had hoped at the outset:

> *It was astonishing what I learned. Leadership is only one element in a successful organisation. I found that the most important thing is 'followership': how people follow a leader. Leaders can go through anything, provided they know they are supported. Great leadership is born from great followership. Otherwise the leader won't take the risk.*

The environment of a yacht produced uncertainty, instability, turbulence, and complexity, all features of the business world. What many have discovered before, the effectiveness of each team to work together, is what matters ultimately. Because the conditions of the race were particularly demanding, an outstanding level of co-operation was necessary. Crews lose track of the normal calendar in a perpetual rhythm of working on deck and attending to the body's most basic physical needs. It was a dangerous journey. Humphrey seriously believed that the boat would sink the night that it was hit six times in a row by huge waves and knocked down.

Humphrey Walters is now an energetic advocate of taking a career break to test yourself. He sees many people in their thirties avoiding the opportunity to take on a major challenge outside work:

> *People around 35 and up should go on a career break. They need to find experiences which will allow them to find out that they can do things they never realised they could do, and stretch themselves to limits they never thought possible. You are likely to come back notched up a gear in terms of your confidence, the way you operate, and your ability to handle difficulty. It doesn't need to be yachting. You've just got to keep yourself in a learning environment, especially nowadays in the competitive economy. It took me three times as long as a 25-year-old to learn new skills and I'm not stupid.*

More accessible sailing opportunities also exist: for example, the Jubilee Sailing Trust operates two tall ships – the *Lord Nelson* and the *Tenacious* – which are crewed by disabled and able-bodied volunteers, on short voyages costing from £425.

Ocean rowing is another way of pushing yourself to the limit. The progress of teams attempting this feat is recorded on the website of Woodvale Events (www.woodvale-events.com).

SAILING CONTACTS

- **Clipper Round the World Yacht Race** (www.clipperroundtheworld.com or www. clipper-ventures.com). Race starts August 2011. The company is looking for people of all ages and walks of life, including those without sailing experience, to sign up for legs of varying lengths. A berth for the whole 11 months costs well over an average annual salary, and a single leg costs from about £7,000: half of which is for the compulsory 19-day training.
- **Flying Fish** (See Directory entry).
- **Jubilee Sailing Trust**, Hazel Road, Woolston, Southampton, SO19 7GB (023 8044 9138; www.jst.org.uk). The JST was created in 1978 to provide an environment which promotes the integration of physically disabled and able-bodied people, on board two square-rigged tall ships the *Lord Nelson* and the *Tenacious*. Anyone can join the crew on voyages to the Continent, the Canaries, or even Antigua, at reasonable prices.
- **Plas Menai**, Caernarfon, Gwynedd, Wales LL55 1UE (01248 670964; www.plasmenai. co.uk). Important sailing and watersports training centre that runs a fast-track instructor training programme, which would suit career-breakers who are attracted by the worldwide employment opportunities for qualified yacht skippers and outdoor instructors. Plas Menai offers an 18-week Professional Yachtmaster course, as well as 12- and 18-week dinghy, windsurfing, kayaking, and mountain instructor courses.
- **Royal Yachting Association**, RYA House, Ensign Way, Hamble, Southampton, SO31 4YA (023 8060 4100; www.rya.org.uk). As the governing body for sailing and motor boating in the UK, the RYA is the best starting place for any information about courses at every level for sailing or power boating.
- **UK Sailing Academy**, West Cowes, Isle of Wight PO31 7PQ (01983 294941; www. uksa.org). A registered charity to promote maritime training and experiences: £7,800 for 12-week Yachtmaster course; £910 for Kick Start (two weeks in UK), and other options.

SPECIAL INTEREST HOLIDAYS

A survey in 2010 revealed that of the Top Ten Travel Adventures, four involved interaction with wildlife – topped by tiger tracking on elephants in India's Kanha National Park, followed by diving with hammerhead sharks in the Galapagos, encounters with mountain gorillas in Rwanda, and checking out the caimans, jaguars, and green iguanas of the Pantanal in Brazil. Swimming with dolphins always ranks highly on the list of 50 things to do before you die. Many wildlife charities and placement agencies listed in the Directory, in Part 5, such as The Great Projects, arrange for untrained volunteers to work with rangers and conservationists, and these are among the most popular ways to spend part of a grown-up gap year.

SKIING AND SNOWBOARDING

Just as life at sea or in the bush becomes an obsession for some, spending time on the snow slopes is the ambition of a whole community of initiates. Many were introduced to skiing or snowboarding at a young age and have returned to the mountains at every opportunity. But snatched holiday weeks do not satisfy the craving, and taking a whole season out to ski can constitute a fantastic gap year at any age.

A growing number of companies specialise in running intensive instructors' courses (see Part 9: New Skills and New Projects), or you and your partner might be suitable candidates to run a chalet for a season. Those who want to arrange to spend a whole season in a ski resort can book accommodation through an operator that specialises in long-stay ski and snowboard holidays. For example, Seasonaires (0870 068 4545; www.seasonaires.com) have properties in a large number of resorts, from Tignes in the French Alps to Breckenridge in Colorado. Be warned that most people who want to spend a whole season in a ski resort are young party animals. To offset the expense of skiing, it may be possible to pick up work in ski resorts (see Part 6: Working and Living Abroad).

ADVENTURE SPORTS

Sailing and skiing are only two sporting activities among many that can form the basis of an adventure trip. Many tour operators specialise in delivering extraordinary experiences: rafting, trekking, cycling, mountaineering, or diving, to name just a few. As well as checking adverts in the magazine *Wanderlust*, check the searchable listings of the Association of Independent Tour Operators (AITO, www.aito.co.uk).

The Travel-quest site (www.travel-quest.co.uk) is a free online directory of specialist tour operators, including activity and adventure holiday providers. It provides company profiles and gives information on activities from heli-skiing to hot air ballooning around the world. Also check Action-Outdoors (www.action-outdoors.co.uk), which links to hundreds of activity and sports holidays in a range of destinations.

Operators in the field of adventure sports holidays often make a pitch for older people fed up with everyday routines and conventional holidays. The following publicity from a rafting company is typical and hard to resist:

Take a break from your modern, hectic work schedule. All too often now we are so caught up in the hustle and bustle of life that we forget the important things: good friends, lots of fun, a bit of sunshine, and great food. A river journey for those who have yet to experience it offers complete escapism from your regular life – no hassles and no stress! If you need a real holiday, we have the perfect solution.

After his expedition with Raleigh in Sabah (Malaysia) came to an end, **Matt Heywood** relished the prospect of realising huge ambitions for the rest of his gap year, before returning to work as an engineer:

I intend to take my PADI Open Water diving course in Borneo, then do a six-day expedition up the East Ridge of Mount Kinabalu. I will then spend three weeks doing a lap of Sabah by bicycle. Following that I intend to get as many adrenaline fixes as possible as I mountain bike, climb, and raft my way around Canada, USA, Central America, and New Zealand. I may try to use my Raleigh experience to gain temporary employment as a mountain bike guide. The final part to my dream year is to use my Raleigh experience to gain managerial employment within Holden, Ford of Australia (however, my girlfriend still needs a little convincing).

Another ambition that some people have is to learn to fly, whether as a paraglider, hang glider, or Microlight pilot: for example, Verbier-Summits Paragliding in the Swiss Alps (see Directory entry), offers all types of paragliding holidays, from introductory courses to instructor courses specially designed for British career-breakers and gap year students. Closer to home you can join paragliding and microlight training courses at places like Airways Airsports in Derbyshire (01335 344308; www.airways-airsports.com), with a sister airpark in Ontur, Spain.

BIRDWATCHING HOLIDAYS

Anyone who pursues birdwatching as a hobby should be aware that trips organised by specialist ornithological tour operators are often over-subscribed. This has been attributed to the gathering anxiety in the developed world that unspoiled natural environments are being whittled away and species lost at an alarming rate. The media has in recent years made people in the developed world aware of all the threats to unspoiled natural environments, creating a feeling of urgency that these precious places should be visited before it is too late.

The Reverend **Brian Blackshaw** fitted in two birdwatching holidays during his 14-week sabbatical from his parish duties. He greatly enjoyed his trip with the eco-tourism operator Company of Whales (www.companyofwhales.co.uk) from England across the Bay of Biscay to the Picos Mountains of northern Spain, on which the group saw more than 104 species, including the exceedingly rare middle-spotted woodpecker. In the latter part of his sabbatical,

Brian went to Scotland with Speyside Wildlife (www.speysidewildlife.co.uk) and felt mentally and spiritually renewed by his time spent in wilderness landscapes, away from the telephone and the pressures of work in a busy Hertfordshire parish.

MY GROWN-UP GAP YEAR: HOWARD PETERS

Having just seen in an unwelcome 58th birthday, Howard thought it was a time for reflection 'when middle-age shows signs of losing its middle'. He had been running a small business importing fashion accessories from the Andean countries of South America, which involved lots of long journeys to remote places, but he had decided it was time to wind down. He had come across a Coral Cay Conservation project in Belize some years earlier and so thought it was time to investigate what they had on offer.

Around the world, coral reefs are under relentless pressure from overfishing, pollution, and other human impacts. My time around the Amazon and the primary forests of Central America had shown me first-hand the widescale destruction being inflicted on the terrestrial world. CCC were attempting to address issues of equal or even greater severity in the tropical marine environment. Supported by the government of the host country, their reef assessments were leading directly to the establishment of marine protected areas to conserve fish and protect their habitats. It was a cause with which I could relate.

And so it was I enrolled to join a small band of ten volunteers and a team of professionals - expedition leader, science officer, scuba instructor and medical officer - as the pioneer group in the inauguration of a new base in the Mamanuca group of islands in Fiji, in the western Pacific. It was an eclectic mix of individuals: mostly young and waiting to go on to university, but with a few mature volunteers in their 30s and 40s, and with me approaching 59 - soon to be celebrated on a remote and largely uninhabited island. Although I was a qualified diver, albeit with limited experience, the majority of volunteers were novices who first underwent on-site training to a level that would give them the capability to dive to the 30m survey depths. Dive certification out of the way, the next two weeks involved comprehensive education in species identification, held in the classroom and on practicals diving the reefs. Only then could the volunteers be formed into survey teams and return reliable statistics. Later, my dive training would be taken by CCC to divemaster level.

Almost all the volunteers had no previous experience in marine environmental sciences. The older members in particular had come from occupations as diverse as a furniture maker from Canada, to an oil driller from the North Sea. But it would be wrong to imply it would suit everyone. Volunteers need to have the time available, a reasonable level of fitness, and an affinity with the water. They must be prepared to leave behind many daily comforts and accept basic living conditions, and they should expect to work intensively - especially during the training period. Most importantly, they must enjoy being part of a team. But the rewards are substantial for those willing to accept the challenge, whatever the age.

PART 8

TAKING THE FAMILY

ADJUSTING THE WORK/LIFE BALANCE
TRAVELLING WITH YOUR KIDS
SCHOOLING

ADJUSTING THE WORK/ LIFE BALANCE

Taking a sabbatical to spend more time with family is one of the major reasons that people take time out from work. Paid maternity leave can be viewed as a statutory career break, and new family-friendly legislation ensures that either parent is allowed to take up to 13 weeks of leave (unpaid) to look after each pre-school child.

Once they return to full-time work, many parents harbour feelings of loss and guilt at the relatively small amount of time they can spend with their tiny children, and resent being forced to delegate too much of the responsibility for rearing a child to a nanny or nursery. Obviously childcare is essential for anyone who wants to maintain and pursue a career, but any parents in a position to step off the professional treadmill for a time to spend time with their children might be tempted to read this chapter. And when the children get a little older, parents who work long hours often feel as if they are missing out on much of their offspring's childhood. It is a motivating factor in some parents' decisions to take time out from work to participate in a collective family activity. It might mean experimenting with living in a foreign country for several months, or it can involve a family adventure like overlanding, sailing, or cycling.

Many parents decide to take a break from work to enjoy an expedition together or a family project. An extended family break allows the (increasingly rare) chance for a collection of individuals, sometimes with widely differing interests, to operate as a single unit. It affords a rare, unbroken, opportunity to experience unadulterated family life: undistracted by phones, meetings, deadlines, work, and the demands of a social calendar.

The producers of the TV series *My Family's Crazy Gap Year*, aired by Channel 4 in 2010, must have thought that the idea had such a broad appeal that viewers would tune in on four consecutive Mondays to follow different families around the world. A recent article in the *New York Times* entitled 'Making the Dream Trip a Reality', and an explosion of targeted websites like www.familiesontheroad.com, makes it clear that a growing number of families with school-age children are taking off on ambitious travels. A number of these families record their odysseys on blogs or even in newspaper columns – like the gap year of the Tims family, which lasted 17 months and was featured in a series in *The Times*. Anyone contemplating a gap year with their children might be a bit intimidated by the mind-boggling travels of the French Canadian family Dury-Leclerc with *nine* children, who cycled 2,000km across Canada, or the home-schooling Escampette Family (www.escampette.net), or the Andrus family (www.sixintheworld.com), who, with their four children ranging in age from high school to pre-school, spent 11 months visiting six continents. According to an NBC news report last year, a surprising number of families live and travel in motor homes (RVs): some because redundancy meant they were in danger of foreclosures on their home; others because they want to reclaim quality family time. (Many links can be found at homeschooling.gomilpitas.com/weblinks/traveling.)

One problem about watching on television or reading about these extraordinary family adventures is that in some cases the families must be fabulously wealthy. A comment added to the timesonline.com site expressed scepticism about the value of reading about the 'incredibly privileged lives of this, presumably, ultra-rich family', referring to the Tims. But plenty of more average families remove their children from the comfortable routines of home to create a memorable and bonding trip together, and these too will pop up in internet accounts.

Children will undoubtedly make a gap year more complicated, whatever their ages. In the first place, you will have more expenses and responsibilities than when you were childless (though if you are paying for full-time childcare or private school fees, the saving of taking them out will be colossal). Certain things like doing a round-the-world yacht race or spending time at a meditation centre in India will be out of the question, unless you have a long-suffering partner willing to hold the fort during your absence. Sometimes a break away from family life as well as a job can be to the benefit of everyone, though you must make it clear to the children (and your partner!) that they are not being abandoned permanently.

This chapter is for those who have decided to spend a large chunk of time *with* their families on the road. Do not underestimate the number of people who will raise objections to a sabbatical *en famille* on grounds of risk to career, risk to health, irresponsibility to children's education, expense, etc. Mostly they are just envious. **Jen Moon** courageously decided to follow a promise she had made to herself, that on her 40th birthday, she would be doing something completely different. As a single mother of two daughters then aged nine and eleven, she faced even more opposition and describes the school yard reaction: 'Although other parents at the girls' school kept saying how they wished they could do it, all the while they were looking at me as if I belonged in a mental home'. An account and assessment of her trip is included later in this chapter (see page 287), plus she maintains a website for family gappers (www. grownupgapyear.co.uk).

A sample objection is raised by someone on the www.bootsnall.com 'Travelling with Children' messageboard, in reply to several families planning round-the-world trips with small children – though it seems clear that the killjoy did not himself have children. In any case it is best to be prepared for such negative attitudes:

> *You do know the kids are not going to get much out of the experience. I always wonder about adults with small children who want to satisfy their travelling joneses [Americanism for 'desires'] without taking into consideration the comfort of the children. Just do a favor and don't put them in danger, like the Canadian woman I met while trekking in Nepal who had her six-month-old baby on her back at 5,000 meters because she always dreamed of seeing the Himalayas. Small children should be in their neighborhood playing with their friends, instead of being taken to museums, enduring long flights and car rides, and essentially being treated as an extra set of luggage when their parents have a travel agenda to satisfy. Sorry if this comes across as harsh and I am sure you will disagree, but I can't stand it when adults who have had children put their needs before the needs of their children.*

The broadcaster **Libby Purves** looks back in wonder at the summer a long time ago when she and her husband took their two children (aged 3 and 5) on an adventurous and sometimes dangerous cruise around the British Isles, recounted in her book *One Summer's Grace* (which could serve as a subtitle for any number of gap years *en famille*). Tragically the elder child, Nicholas, took his own life aged 23. Not long afterwards, Libby Purves wrote movingly of how important it is for families to spend time together on holiday:

Family holidays are great. Family holidays are indispensable. They are the stuff of life, they should go on as long as possible, and their blemishes do not matter ... While routine memories are all very well, the ones that sustain us best through the darkness are the dozens of journeys, expeditions, skives, weekends, ferries, trains, planes, boats, and adventures we somehow fitted in ... We do get asked if there is any lesson the tragedy has taught us, and there is. Take family holidays! Take them now. Splash out. Forget the new car, sofa, autumn wardrobe — do a Grand Tour instead, together. And if you've any money left over, send it to the Family Holiday Association, which organises trips for the poorest and most hard-pressed of our fellow citizens, because they need the break and the memories just as much, and lasting joy can flow from a week in a caravan at Rhyl.

Libby Purves is still an advocate for the Family Holiday Association, and her article is linked from their homepage at www.fhaonline.org.uk.

MATERNITY LEAVE

Maternity leave is the most common reason for female employees to take time out from work, and it is now an accepted feature of modern working life. New mothers in the UK who have been in employment for at least half a year are paid at least 90% of their salary for the first six weeks after a birth, and then £124.88 (as of April 2010) per week for the next 33 weeks. When that period is up, mothers are entitled to take a further 13 weeks of unpaid leave (making 52 weeks in total), while their jobs are guaranteed (provided they have worked for that employer for a continuous 26 weeks before taking maternity leave). Provision was substantially enhanced by the Labour government, and it looks as though the Coalition government is not planning to reverse any of these advances. However, the proposal to extend Statutory Maternity Pay from 39 to 52 weeks has been indefinitely postponed. For detailed advice, consult the admirably clear government website www.direct.gov.uk, or the national arbitration service ACAS (see below).

For working mothers, a career break is a physical necessity in the period shortly before birth and in the baby's young life afterwards. Now that maternity leave is a commonly-accepted feature of employment, companies have adopted strategies and set aside resources to cope with these temporary absences. The degree of generosity beyond the legal requirements varies among companies, depending on criteria such as how eager a company is to encourage a female employee to return to her old job, instead of remaining at home. The annual lists of the 50 or 100 best companies to work for, as produced by the *Financial Times* and the *Sunday Times*, invariably include companies that are the most family-friendly and allow flexible working hours. Many allow mothers to take career breaks for child-rearing, ranging from the statutory minimum to five years.

Information from the arbitration service ACAS on employment protection and rights is available via their searchable site www.acas.org.uk, by telephone 08457 474747, or from Jobcentre Plus (0800 0556688).

Other useful resources include:

- **Working Families** (0800 013 0313; www.workingfamilies.org.uk). Lobby group whose website carries some information about sabbaticals.
- **Work Foundation** (www.theworkfoundation.com). Carries some information about work/life balance issues. According to a 2010 report, workers' rights are being eroded during the recession and 40% of workers have encountered longer working hours and challenges to work/life balance.

PATERNITY AND PARENTAL LEAVE

Increasingly, fathers are taking time out to help cope with the arrival of a new baby, as Ed Miliband, leader of the Labour Party, did in November 2010. Paid paternity leave of up to two weeks following the birth of a baby is paid at the same rate as maternity leave, ie £124.88 per week or 90% of salary, whichever is greater. Naturally, a two-week absence from work hardly qualifies as a gap year, but it indicates a growing acceptance that many fathers want to take time off from work to help with children. On the other hand, many new dads do not take up the entitlement because of the relatively low wage, preferring to take time out of their annual leave after the birth of their babies.

Both mothers and fathers are permitted to take up to a total of 13 weeks' unpaid leave before a child turns 5 (or 18 if the child is disabled), though this is restricted to four weeks in any given year. To be entitled to this parental leave, a father (or mother) must have been employed continuously for at least a year. The government has announced that for babies born after 3 April 2011, mothers will be allowed to transfer to fathers up to six months of their 12 months' maternity leave to enable them to return to work, and for their partners to become the proverbial 'house husband' for a period of time, while their jobs are kept open for them.

GETTING EVERYBODY ON BOARD

In almost all cases, the idea of a gap year is the grand design of one person in a family who tends to be the prime mover, the one to initiate and orchestrate the break, and who is prepared to bear the responsibility for uprooting the rest of the family. Whereas one parent might be enthusiastic about putting their professional life on hold, this may not be so welcome or manageable for the other. As 'the Dad' wrote in the De Jager Family blog (blogs.bootsnall.com/Dejags), several months before he and his wife and children aged one and four set off on their round-the-world trip: 'Well my wife's enthusiasm, courage, and drive have finally paid off; she has drawn me out of the well called home renovating and into the world of travel, and I finally got down to the business of planning the first leg of our trip'.

According to a 2009 article in the *Daily Mail*, it isn't always the parents who push for a family gap year. Twelve-year-old Gerald Roseman from Worcestershire decided that he would like to see the world before starting secondary school – an exclusive public school to which he gained admittance when he was younger than his peers, hence the gap to fill. He talked his parents into joining him on an extravagant world trip from Bhutan to Canada. Sometimes the instigator's enthusiasm is sufficient to carry all before it, but it is essential that the followers should not bury their reservations since this can escalate quite quickly into resentment.

The Grant family embarked on a remarkable journey to become the first to encircle the globe in a horse-drawn caravan, described in sometimes painful detail in David Grant's book *The Seven Year Hitch: A Family Odyssey*. On the tenth page of his narrative, after the family has had a trial run with a caravan in Ireland and before the Big Trip begins in earnest, he writes:

> *Unnoticed by me, Kate was beginning to have reservations but she did not say anything. She did not want to be the wet blanket who spoiled the fun. She had enjoyed Ireland as much as anyone but I think she foresaw, even then, that a prolonged sojourn in the confines of a caravan might not suit her. In her words, 'I really did have doubts about David and me travelling in such close confinement. The children I didn't doubt at all. Children are very adaptable, curious about new ideas and concepts. But I thought it was a trifle unfair to expect them at ages 5, 7, and 9 to appreciate what our proposed wee doddle round the world would really mean.' I was in no mood or state to notice. Fired by all I had learned during our travels, I was as eager to go as a horse in a starting-stall.*

By page 39, Kate has found the trip unbearable and flies home to her father's house. She rejoins the family at intervals and is with them as they trudge to their final destination – Halifax in Canada – seven long years after setting off. The index is telling; of the several headings under David Grant, we can look up 'tensions of journey', not to mention 'horse collar accident' and 'sued for assault'.

Loved ones cannot always be expected to share our dreams, passions, and grand schemes. If there is a great discrepancy in what partners want out of a gap year, accommodations must be reached – perhaps dividing the allotted time into two phases: the first an overland trip to the Andes or a sojourn in a Hebridean bothy for her sake; the second a cycling tour or cookery course in Tuscany for his. The journalist **Mary Ann Seighart's** husband wanted to take his family sailing around the world, but his wife balked because, 'The sea makes me sick and our girls make each other sick, particularly at close quarters'. So they settled for a four-month gap with their daughters aged 12 and 14, split between sailing down through the Caribbean and backpacking in Central America.

Of course most differences occur at the micro-level. **Marie Purdy** and long-term partner Howard went round the world when she was made redundant at age 50. He particularly wanted to stop over in Dubai (which she was sure she wouldn't enjoy) and the South Pacific Islands of Fiji and Cook Islands, which she knew would be too hot for her. All trips on this scale involve daily concessions.

If children are part of the picture, further compromises will be necessary. Children seldom welcome change and upheaval, especially as they get older. Whatever their ages, the children should be included in the planning and preparations, and their preferences taken into account. They could be allowed to choose the odd treat destination like a theme park or a safari, or even be given a chunk of the itinerary to arrange.

Apart from the challenge of persuading the children, you will be faced with daunting logistical complexities depending on your plan. Take the ambitious plans of **Ambrose Marsh** and **Leah Norgrove**, two physicians in Victoria, Canada, who had long nurtured the dream of taking a year off with their sons aged 13 and 10. When struggling to rent out their house, Leah wrote: 'We are stuck at task number 46 (renting the house out) and there are moments of doubting the Great Adventure, because we will be so fried before we get there. It would be good to take two years off: one to prepare for the Great Adventure and one to do it!' Their family gap year was indeed remarkable: six months of volunteering in palliative medicine in Tanzania, a month or so of exploring Turkey, and then an epic cycling trip from Istanbul to Estonia, with Simon the younger boy on the back of a tandem.

Shorter stints of family volunteering present far fewer organisational problems. The Tubbs family joined a summer 'mini-leap' project in Kenya organised by The Leap, as first Rupert Tubbs and then his son Felix describe:

> *The four of us (two desk-bound parents, 10-year-old Felix and 8-year-old Minna) stayed in Shimoni, the southernmost point on the coast of Kenya and 15km from the nearest tarmac. Just getting there feels like an adventure. We went to help in some way towards conservation and communities in the area, to do something different, something that would broaden the children's horizons, and, it has to be said, for a holiday. In the forest, walking for up to five hours along narrow trails and through thick undergrowth, we jumped lines of soldier ants, removed animal snares, and logged the local fauna and flora. We were there to map the extent of deforestation and search for the endangered Colobus monkey. Every day a team also went to sea. This was the flag-ship project in Shimoni: recording the dolphin population in the Pemba Channel ... This, like the forest, was real work, whose results would add to the sum of human knowledge about the world, and would help protect our wildlife by presenting the locals with alternative livelihoods to the netting that decimates the dolphin population. From Shimoni, an hour's walk further into the forest is Mzizima ... This is the isolated and desperately poor village where we took part in the schools project: building, plastering and painting, teaching in the schoolroom, and on the undulating scrubland that passes for a games pitch. This is where we met coastal Africa at its most needy, and where we found the biggest smiles. If we learnt anything important on this trip, and I include the children, it was here: how to be happy when you have nothing.*

Eleven-year-old Felix Tubbs's take on the trip is a little more focused on his encounters with the local fauna:

> *On the first day of project work I was on the boat. We were looking for dolphins. In the first 20 minutes we saw two bottlenose dolphins, and that was it for the day! The next day we saw nothing, but I caught a King Mackerel which we all ate for supper (20 of us – it was huge!) And on the third day we saw three more bottlenose dolphins; five dolphins altogether in three days, when my sister saw 80 dolphins in three days (ugh!). At six o'clock every evening I went to play volleyball at the local school – I loved it. After the marine project, I went to a school and I helped teach them about triangles. After teaching, we plastered a wall because we were building a library, or we painted the nursery walls. I painted the numbers. On the last day we could choose what we wanted to do, and I went on the boat. That day I saw 61 dolphins; that included 33 spinner dolphins, two spinner babies, two indo-pacific dolphins and 24 bottlenose. And then we caught two fish!*

THE IDEAL AGE

After children reach school age, disrupting their education becomes an issue. Some families prefer to take off just before their children start school, declaring that this is the blessed age of innocence. In Matthew Collins' book *Across America with the Boys*, in which the ex-BBC Travel Show presenter describes his transAmerica drive with his two sons aged three and nearly-five, he concludes that ages three to four is a perfect period to take children away for a long trip. Before that you will have to contend with nappies and toddler problems; after they start school they begin to lose some of their innocence. Looking back at the American trip, Matthew Collins believes that it was one of the best things he has ever done:

> *A glorious experience; I'm so glad I did it. At the age of three and four, the boys were so fresh. They had a pre-school innocence. Here was an opportunity to spend a large chunk of time with the children, watching their personalities develop. It was a time to enjoy my kids and they enabled me to appreciate new places through their eyes.*

Matthew remembers that the children never got bored in the United States and there was no VCR for them in the motor home: 'One of the great things about travelling with kids is that you spend so much time talking. We talked about everything. The stimulation was so great for the children.' The other significant advantage of travelling with children was that they were fearless about talking to anyone and acted as an icebreaker between adults. Once they approached a Hell's Angel and asked why he had so many horrible tattoos. Instead of a hostile response, the tough biker was won over by their naïve charm.

Libby Purves' warts-and-all account of the coastal cruise in *One Summer's Grace* mentioned above, includes the low as well as the high points. She describes how the children's moods swung wildly and on occasions they were overcome with rage, or homesickness, or anxiety that they would never see their friends and family at home again. The parents patiently tried to explain that 14 weeks might seem like a very long time but they would all return to their normal lives afterwards. Libby Purves writes: 'As we set off northward from Puffin Island Sound, crew morale was low, pulled down by this insistent infant undercurrent of discontent … Alone of the crew, I was relishing the whole adventure. I felt rather guilty about this because I had originated the whole thing, set the dates, organised the finance and the empty house for it, and effectively dragged my whole family off to sea. I realised that, as the only happy human being on board, I had a duty to improve our lot.' And for the most part she was successful.

Other families argue that the ideal age for a big trip is the pre-adolescent years of 9 to 12. This is the age actress Emma Thompson chose when she announced in the summer of 2010 that she was going to take her ten-year-old daughter Gaia out of school for a year to see the world. Every family will have to choose its moments according to its own circumstances.

Another possibility is the inter-generational family gap, ie combining a school-leaver gap year with a grown-up one, as Sue Fenton and her daughter did in Nepal.

MY GROWN-UP GAP YEAR: SUE WRENN FENTON

Sue Wrenn Fenton is a self-employed editor and publisher of a monthly Scottish environmental magazine. She sounds like a sane pillar of her community near Inverness, but describes herself as a 'midlife crisis gapper'. In her late 50s she suddenly had a longing to join her daughter on part of her gap year.

I decided to take a break from the humdrum rut of home life just after the death of my mother, for whom I had been caring. My daughter, Mairi, was on a 'traditional' gap year before going to Glasgow University. I asked her if she would mind if I muscled in on her plans and she very kindly agreed to share the last part of her year out with me. I financed the trip myself, with some help from a venture grant from the windfarm community benefit fund - which was, until this time, exclusively awarded to youngsters.

Mairi and I met in Delhi, and we flew to Kathmandu. I had found a locally-run charity in Nepal, Hope and Home, on the internet, which didn't fleece foreign volunteers like some of the other organisations I had researched (and Mairi had experienced). The small charge covered a week's orientation (Nepali language lessons, sightseeing, and local cultural events) whilst staying in a guest house with other volunteers. Mairi and I were then placed in a girls' orphanage in Kathmandu and lived with a Hindu family close by, who provided all meals. We tried to help the girls, aged three to twenty, in all aspects of their daily life and education. I am also a trained teacher but I immediately enrolled on a TEFL course on my return to learn how it is done properly - I wish that I had done that before I left! We also trekked in the Annapurna area, flew to Everest in a light plane, and saw elephants in Chitwan.

The monsoon was bearable - it was warmer rain than at home in Scotland - but I hated the leeches! It was magic to spend time with Mairi, out of our comfort zones and away from home - not as mother and daughter with all those inherent parental trappings, but as colleagues. This has formed the basis of a solid, new grown-up relationship. She taught me a great deal, as did the girls in the home. I would love to have had more time, perhaps a full gap year, in order to feel that I was really making a difference, and not just indulging myself. Then I would have the dry season as well.

I slotted right back in to 'real life' right away. I had taken a rucksack full of gifts and clothes donated by folk in the village for the children, and brought back gorgeous Nepali paper goods to fundraise for them.

TAKING THE CHILDREN OUT OF SCHOOL

If the children are in school, you will have to obtain the permission of the Local Education Authority to take them out of school for more than ten days; the school office should have the form. Permission will be granted only if the authorities can be reassured that the child's education will not be damaged (see section below on Schooling). Try to avoid taking them away when they are scheduled to do special exams; in the UK, children sit Standard Assessment Tests (SATs) in the summer term of year six. Although an obvious time to take the children away is between finishing one school and starting another, it might make it harder for them to re-enter normal school life when all their peers have already made the transition.

An increasing number of parents are refusing to be deterred from taking the break they crave. They are finding ways that will be beneficial for their children, while at the same time allowing them to spend a substantial amount of time together during the formative years of childhood. If there's a guaranteed way of maximising that elusive 'quality time', a sabbatical expedition surely is one solution. Parents report that taking the kids away from television and videos teaches them to entertain themselves with reading, drawing, and writing.

Transplanting teenagers from their natural habitat can be more problematic, even if you are happy to interrupt their preparations for GCSEs or other exams. Most well-adjusted adolescents will resent being removed from their social network and forced to spend more time with their parents and siblings than they would at home. If possible, try to give adolescents as much freedom as possible. One way of placating them might be to make sure they are allowed to spend plenty of time in internet cafés or places with WiFi, so that they can maintain contact with their friends at home. You might consider arranging the exclusive use of a laptop for them.

Outsiders will often exclaim over the educational benefit of travel with children. But children have a way of subverting expectations and are more likely to remember the street urchin pestering them to buy a flower than the great Buddhist temple; or the time a wave knocked them over, rather than the sea creatures on the beach. A career break with children should be organised at a time when the parents will most appreciate it, not the children. It doesn't matter if you go when they are too young to remember anything. It does matter that you communicate enthusiasm and demonstrate a zeal for travel, for nature, for history, for whatever it is you are zealous about, which they will emulate and someday apply to their own interests (you hope).

TRAVELLING WITH YOUR KIDS

The best opportunity for a joint family enterprise is an adventurous expedition abroad. This may involve backpacking in a developing country, sailing, or off-road driving. For some parents a travel adventure is an ideal time for the family to spend a concentrated period of time together – finding ways to live harmoniously, while also discovering new cultures and seeing some of the great natural and constructed wonders of the world.

RESISTING THE DOOM MERCHANTS

As mentioned, taking children on an extended trip overseas is not universally admired. While a few friends and family may question the legitimacy and wisdom of taking a sabbatical as an individual or in a couple, taking children abroad can be a source of friction. It may be deemed irresponsible, selfish, risky, destabilising, or unfair to uproot the children. Questions will be asked, although perhaps with the best intentions. Will it be safe to take young children to extreme climates? How will their education suffer? Will they catch malaria or hepatitis? Won't it be very disruptive?

Every family sets its own priorities, rules, and patterns of behaviour, and they need not be dissuaded from a jointly-desired project by the criticisms of outsiders. While some parents believe that keeping to a routine in the familiar environment of home is the best policy for keeping kids contented and attentive at school, others – especially those who have done some serious travelling in the past – concentrate on the positive potential of a Big Trip together.

Steps can be taken to minimise the unsettling effects of travel on children. Obviously they should carry a couple of their most beloved objects. A small photograph album of their friends and favourite places at home can serve to remind them that their old life still exists, and can also be of interest to people met on the road. Whenever possible a routine should be established, so that certainties such as a bedtime story or a regular Skype chat with their grandparents are maintained. Encouraging each child to keep a diary, write a blog, or fill a scrapbook is a good idea. Ipods with their favourite music and stories are a godsend on long boring bus or train journeys. Playing cards and travel Scrabble are essential.

The key to minimising stress and fractiousness is to avoid constant movement. If possible, base yourself in one place long enough for the children to create a temporary network of familiar faces, if only the waiter or the greengrocer's son. And when you all need a break from each other, ask in your lodgings or contact a local student organisation about hiring a babysitter.

Cultural differences can result in incidents that can sometimes be upsetting, sometimes amusing. In many parts of Asia, children are considered almost public property. Local babies may be used to being prodded and cooed over and passed from hand to hand, but your western children may not be so keen on these little acts of idolatry. Older children may well enjoy the attention and like to be in the photographs of umpteen Oriental matrons, but may balk when they are squashed up beside the shy daughter to be in a photo. Be prepared to rescue your child from any situation that is making them uncomfortable.

Cultural clashes will be less apparent in Europe, though some parents have commented on the German penchant for intervention. While accompanying her children to a playground in Germany, **Alison Hobbs**, wife of a university physicist on sabbatical, was taken aback to be offered some money by a stranger in order to buy shoes for her (cheerfully shoeless) baby. Still on the subject of shoes, another mother was berated in German for wearing flip flops while balancing a 2 year old on her shoulders, on a popular climb to the Dikteon Cave on Crete – where Zeus was born.

THE INCALCULABLE BENEFITS

A family adventure can provide an educational stimulus that will exceed anything available in a classroom. Instead of merely looking at photographs of the Amazon or the Taj Mahal in a book from the school library, children can actually experience their beauty and scale, and glimpse the civilisation out of which they emerged. In terms of the geography field trip, driving across Europe or sailing round the Caribbean certainly outclasses a visit to the local wood. The world becomes a classroom for both parent and child – just don't harbour inflated ideas of how rapt your children will be by the Himalayas or the Pyramids. From the time an infant is 24 hours old, parents learn that generalisations and advice about childcare are sometimes helpful, sometimes useless, depending on their child's nature. So the experiences of other parents on gap years may be of very limited use. While some will enthuse wildly about how their children learned Swahili/took up birdwatching/wrote poetry, you may be stuck with kids for whom the highlight of a trip was the size of the billiard table in a faded old colonial hotel, or how they mastered the art of building card houses. Your moment to enthuse wildly might come unexpectedly when you realise what little trojans your sturdy, capable, and long-suffering children turned out to be, cheerfully wielding their chopsticks or stoically carrying their luggage through crowded and sweltering bus stations.

Single parents might be even more reluctant than other parents to contemplate a gap year with children. **Jen Moon** is an exception. Convinced that it would be a wonderful learning experience for the children, she was determined to take 9-year-old Sarah and 11-year-old Lisa on a big trip. She successfully negotiated with her employer for a four-month break (which she decided in the end was just long enough) and also with the school. After years of saving by working at two jobs and writing a book (about working on yachts), she decided that her dream was affordable. Such a trip is inevitably expensive but she begrudged none of it: 'Seeing how happy I feel having achieved the dream, and seeing how incredibly the children have come on, it would in my eyes be worth double what I paid. It's lovely to be home and I feel far more contented in my life having done what I did'. When asked about the high points, she says that out of 120 days, at least 108 had high points. That conclusion, with the benefit of hindsight, displays a more confident attitude than she felt in the planning stages:

> *One of the low points was the stress before actually going. It was incredibly tough, knowing that, as I was a single parent, the kids would have no-one should something happen to me. I found that very scary.*

The trip to Australia, New Zealand, and America was a resounding success for all three of them. However, Jen admits to odd moments of loneliness, especially when the young gappers headed off clubbing or wherever their fancy took them. She was surprised to encounter relatively few travellers in her age bracket, which is squarely between all the school and college-leavers and the retired folks. The kids would also have liked to have met more travelling kids.

With hindsight Jen would have stretched the budget to get a bigger camper van and two laptops. The children both did lots of homework during the trip and wrote journals, so that competition for laptop space was always intense and one or other was invariably behind. But the experience was overwhelmingly positive:

> *The rewards have been immense, not least of all spending concentrated quality time with the kids. Both of them have had their maths level improve significantly (Sarah by three grades), their geography means so much more to them, and both generally feel 'special' in that they have done something that most kids never even dream of doing. That makes them have a sort of inner confidence that many of my friends and family back home have noticed and approved of, as it is not a brash precociousness.*

An extended family trip can be educational in another sense for fathers, many of whom have had less contact with young children than their partners. Author **Helena Drysdale** says that travelling around Europe in a motor home while researching a book on tribal peoples, was instructive for her painter husband Richard: 'Having been working since their birth, he was aghast at how little time children left him to do his own thing. Like most men, he had no idea what bringing up children day in, day out, really means'. Be prepared to experience occasional feelings of loss when you recall your travels pre-children. Some of the old carefree magic may be missing, to be replaced by what might seem at times relentless domesticity. But parenthood at home or abroad encompasses highs and lows, and the lows always pass.

Until September 2010, the **Collins family** from Australia were among the community of families cruising the oceans. But after three years of sailing with their three children who were aged seven, six, and six when they set off, they are finally back on home soil, on the Sunshine Coast of Queensland. Mother Nicole reflects on their epic voyage:

> *We wanted the opportunity to spend time with the kids before they got into their teenage years, and school and outside commitments became too great for them. Our plan started out as a year around Australia in a caravan, and developed into a three-year break sailing from Sweden to New Zealand. So our 'caravan' lost its wheels and gained a keel. Our time together 24/7 over that long period has strengthened our family. We know we can tackle any task and probably succeed. You realise your partner's skills, traits, and strengths. Things that would go unnoticed in day-to-day life are right there in your face – like it or lump it! I really don't know how but the kids managed to fill every day of those three-week passages across the Atlantic and Pacific without much electronic assistance! You really miss family and friends and the arrival of an email can change and brighten your day immensely. You learn to 'not sweat the small stuff' and just get on with things. Life on a boat can be cosy but a short paddle on a kayak will soon give you some space. Sometimes a long paddle is required!*
>
> *I look back and think 'I can't believe we did it', and now we are home it certainly does not feel like we were gone for over three years. I don't regret a minute of it. The hardest decision of all was making the decision to go: after that it all just came together.*

For more details about their trip and practical advice about ocean cruising, see their blog www. slowtravelongrace.blogspot.com.

WORKING AND VOLUNTEERING ABROAD

Volunteering to work for a charity abroad is much trickier to organise for a family than an individual or couple. Companies that place volunteers in overseas conservation projects or as English teachers are simply not equipped to find housing for families. One organisation that does place families is VSO. However, VSO stresses that it can place families only in certain circumstances: for example, if there are more requests for assistance than there are volunteers. In this case VSO can provide additional support for partners and/or dependant children, which would include housing and insurance. It stresses that each case is considered on its own merits, and taking a partner and children may reduce the range of placement options. Sometimes it's possible for a parent to take children unsupported by VSO at additional cost to the family.

When **Bryony Close** and her husband turned 50, they decided they wanted to go on a special holiday with their two teenage daughters that would not only be fun and adventurous, but also allow them to take action to improve the world around them. They signed up for a six-week volunteer expedition with Blue Ventures, diving through unexplored coral reefs in Madagascar, collecting data on marine species, and helping conservation scientists develop plans to protect threatened coastal habitats. Blue Ventures' scientific research lab is located adjacent to the remote fishing village of Andavadoaka, population 1,200, where there is no electricity or running water and where people live on less than £1 a day. While Bryony and her husband went diving to collect data on marine health, their daughters (aged 14 and 16) spent their days snorkelling, tutoring village children how to speak English, and exploring local coastal areas and baobab forests:

> We're not into sitting on beaches and doing nothing. This was a holiday, but you're actually doing something; not just spending money. We felt we were really doing something great. It was good for the kids to learn about the Third World. I think what got us all was the fact that although they're poor, the people there are extremely happy. The kids learned that when you've got a strong community and a lot of support, you don't need money to be happy. We loved it. It was totally different from anything we've done before. I hope this trip will encourage our kids to do volunteer work in the future. This put it in their minds that it's something they can do. Meeting other volunteers on the trip from around the world and of all ages was also part of the fun. There were people who had just left university, people who were on career breaks, and one woman who was a little older than us. It was a complete cross-section of people but we all got along. It was quite eye-opening for us and the girls. You can make friends with all sorts.

You will have to do some intensive research to find volunteer projects that will accept children, but they do exist. To take just one example, Peru's Challenge (www.peruschallenge.com/families) welcomes families. Children under 16 are free with fee-paying adults. Like the adults, children will be given up to four hours per day of Spanish lessons too.

The **Battye Family** from New England, USA, were looking for a volunteer opportunity abroad that could incorporate their whole family for up to three months: a tall order with four children aged 3–13. After much research they chose Volunthai, a teaching programme in rural north-eastern Thailand (see Directory entry) that arranged a homestay and an opportunity to teach English in the local school. While the father (a teacher) and boys taught older children, the mother and two little girls aged three and seven worked with young children. The parents wrote on their blog of their motives before leaving (www.planetranger.com/battyefamily):

So why do all this? Why put our normal lives on hold, take the kids out of school, and travel so far from all that is familiar? Well, that's pretty much the point. It's so easy to stay in the same cycle for years at a time and we really wanted to take ourselves out of what we know and experience more of what is out there beyond our own small community. We also wanted the kids to see that there is more to the world than Portsmouth, New Hampshire, and to realize their own potential to do good things for others. We felt it would be an incredible education for them.

And later looking back on the experience, they felt that their hopes for the trip had been more than realised:

The most meaningful thing by quantum leaps has been the homestay and volunteer teaching experience. I can only say that it has been a turning point in our lives ... The experience in Thailand made an immense impact on our family and I would love to show others how easy and fulfilling that kind of travel can be ... The benefits of making such a trip far outweigh the fears that might hold you back. There were so many moments that made it all worthwhile: my daughter, only there a week, proclaiming with conviction that we have way too much 'stuff' at home and could get along just fine with just a couple of toys; watching my sons bargain (respectfully, artfully, and successfully) in Thai at the local market; having the chance to watch the stars in an ink black sky from the back of a pickup; being part of daily life in a rural Thai village populated with the most generous people on earth; and, most importantly, seeing all of my kids pick up the custom of local Thai children, who treat helping out and daily chores as an honor, not an obligation. Imagine that!

This kind of adventure is undoubtedly easier with two-parent families, who also have the option of letting one parent take a paid or voluntary job while the other looks after the children. But what about single parents who want a break from home routines? Having spent long periods of her life living in Barcelona, Orlando, and Australia, **Jacqueline Edwards** wanted to live abroad with her 2-year-old son Corey after studying aromatherapy and massage. Ingeniously, she inserted notices in vegetarian and vegan magazines throughout Europe and received a number of offers, including an offer of a free house in Austria in exchange for helping to look after rescued animals from an elderly couple near Paris, and a natural therapies retreat centre west of Madrid. She chose to accept a live-in position as a cook/cleaner in Spain, though she soon came to understand that her hyperactive son needed more of her attention than she was able to give, if trying to earn enough to keep them. They both needed the support network in England with grandparents, family, friends, etc, to help with childcare, so she cut short her gap year in Spain.

Living and working on an organic farm, as described in the section about the international organisation WWOOF in Part 4: Doing Something Worthwhile, is something that families can do. For example, one of the highlights of the **Whitlock Family's** one-year round-the-world tour was their short stay at an organic farm in Hungary, which they arranged through WWOOF (Worldwide Opportunities on Organic Farms). Because of his interest in habitats and conservation projects, Nick Whitlock was especially looking forward to living and working alongside local people and fellow travellers on WWOOF farms. The family arranged to stay on a goat farm in a remote area about 25km from Kaposvar, where they picked fruit and helped in the kitchen and where ten-year-old Tom helped look after the herd of goats, and stayed in an idyllic old farmhouse.

The most inspiring of the Channel 4 documentary series about 'crazy family gap years' was the one that featured Nikki McClements from Devon: single mother of nine-year-old Beth. After years of working long hours and delegating a lot of the childcare to her parents, Nikki wanted to reclaim the relationship with her daughter by travelling together for a year. She wanted Beth to be exposed to the less fortunate, and to lay down foundations for turning her into a caring adult. By dint of careful research, she found an orphanage in South Africa and a school in northern Thailand where she and Beth could spend time as volunteers. An interview can be read at www.channel4.com/programmes/my-familys-crazy-gap-year/articles/interview-with-nikki-and-beth-mcclements.

RED TAPE

Children of British nationals need their own passports. Always check that every member of the family has a current passport with enough validity to last for the whole trip, plus a safety margin of six months – which is demanded by some countries. All family members will require their own visas to countries that require them, which can add significantly to the expense. Note that some countries (like Canada) have signed up to the Hague Convention on International Child Abduction to discourage unauthorised removal of children across borders, and a lone parent travelling with children can be asked to show a letter of permission from the absent parent.

ACCOMMODATION

If travelling with young children, take it slowly, allowing plenty of fun and relaxing interludes between the days of travel and sightseeing. Try to find accommodation which is not only child-friendly, but where your children are likely to meet other children. Animals are always popular, so you might try to stay on a farm or a campsite in the bush. Self-catering accommodation means that you don't have to worry about your little tearaways terrorising other diners in the hotel restaurant or other eating establishments.

Campsites and youth hostels are venues where children often feel most at home. Nature Friends International (www.naturfreunde-haeuser.net), with headquarters in Vienna, run a network of 1,000 mountain, forest, and city hostels, mostly on the continent, which welcome parents and children. This would be one way of keeping costs down in an expensive country like Switzerland. Many have their own playgrounds and most are very inexpensive.

Agritourism is another appealing option, where you spend a week or more on a working farm. One possibility for finding addresses of farms which might welcome families is to obtain one of the guides from ECEAT (European Centre for Eco-Agro Tourism; www.eceat.nl). They publish separate English-language *Green Holiday Guides* for Bulgaria, Poland, and the Baltics, and many other countries in Dutch- or German-language versions, most for €10 or €15.

Renting or exchanging a house for a few months and staying in one place is often a better way to organise a long family break. Everyone enjoys the chance to get to know (and to become known in) a new community, but children especially like the security that familiarity imparts and the chance to develop relationships with local children or adults, and perhaps even go to school.

CHILDREN'S HEALTH AND SAFETY

Attention to hygiene and care about what children eat and drink in developing countries is critically important. Children tend to be conservative eaters, so may be more content than adults with safe foods like peanut butter and packet soups brought from home. But children also get thirsty, and care will have to be taken about purifying water in some countries. Purifying tablets and iodine make the water taste unpleasant, so you might want to invest in a piece of high-tech equipment which purifies water without changing the taste. General information on obtaining health advice can be found in Part 2: Nuts and Bolts. Most GPs nowadays have computer access to detailed information for patients heading for the tropics, and will be able to advise on the recommended and necessary immunisations (including the correct dosage for children) for specific destinations.

Malaria poses such a serious risk in some parts of the world that parents of young children will have to think very carefully about their route. Parents of children travelling through a malarial zone will soon come to dread the pill-taking ritual, since some, like chloroquine, have an exceedingly bitter taste and most children find it difficult to swallow pills whole. Practising on something more palatable before departure might help. Mechanical precautions against malaria are easier to manage (eg wrist and ankle bands soaked in DEET); younger children might enjoy the experience of sleeping under a tent of mosquito netting.

Among the items in your medical kit, carry a disinfectant to treat even minor cuts and scrapes. In tropical climates, even minor wounds attract flies and can easily go septic. And be very disciplined in applying high factor sunblock at frequent intervals.

If travelling with very young children, make sure your luggage does not encumber you so much that you don't have a hand free to hold your child's hand at stations, airports, and busy streets. One precaution is to obtain an ID wristband, eg from Chesterford Ltd (www.chesterford.co.uk) which could have your mobile phone number on it in case a child goes missing in a crowded place.

BOOKS AND RESOURCES

■ *Across America With The Boys* (MATCH Publishing, 1998) and *Across Canada With the Boys and Three Grannies* (MATCH Publishing, 2002) by Matthew Collins (www.matthewcollins.co.uk).

- *The Seven Year Hitch: A Family Odyssey* by David R. Grant (Simon & Schuster UK, 2002). Out of print but available second-hand from sites like www.abebooks.co.uk. The highlights of this epic journey by horse-drawn caravan seem few and far between, especially as the father and three children struggle to find enough to eat and keep warm as they cross Kazakhstan, and then get bogged down in Mongolia. Hard to imagine anyone wanting to emulate this trip.
- *The Rough Guide to Travel with Babies and Young Children* (Rough Guides Reference Titles, 2008) by Fawzia Rasheed de Francisco.
- *Are We Nearly There Yet?* by Sheila Hayman (Hodder & Stoughton, 2003). Amusing book about travelling with children.
- *Family Travel: The Farther You Go, the Closer You Get* edited by Laura Manske (Travelers' Tales, 1999). Collection of 45 tales narrating the joys and trials of families finding their way abroad. The contributors include well-known personalities like Michael Crichton and Tim Parks.
- *One Summer's Grace* by Libby Purves (Coronet Books, 1997). In the summer of 1988, Libby Purves and her husband Paul Heiney sailed with their children aged 3 and 5 on a voyage around the coastline of Britain.
- *Your Child Abroad: A Travel Health Guide* by Dr Jane Wilson-Howarth and others (Bradt Travel Guides, 2004). Aims to help adventurous parents travel confidently with their kids, and explains how to diagnose any health problems.
- *The Poisonwood Bible* by Barbara Kingsolver (Harper Perennial, 1999). A fictionalised account of an American missionary family's attempt to live in Africa during the Congolese struggle for independence.

As usual, the web contains a wealth of useful and useless information. Start with www. travelwithyourkids.com, which has advice and suggestions from longtime expats and real parents on how to travel internationally (or just long distances) with your children. Try also www. travelforkids.com, which lists kid-friendly sites worldwide. As mentioned earlier, family blogs on the internet can be both inspiring and instructive. Lonely Planet's Thorn Tree has an online forum called Kids to Go, and www.bootsnall.com includes a travel forum about travelling with children, which is worth surfing.

SCHOOLING

Most parents will feel anxious about removing their children from formal education for an extended period. Some lucky parents have managed to enroll their children in a school abroad, which can be very worthwhile even for a relatively short time. The usual problem is language, but most children would prefer to spend time interacting with children over a language barrier than being cooped up with their family. Sports, games, music, smiles, and many other pleasures are still accessible to them.

Leah Norgrove's description of the way her sons adapted to spending six months in Tanzania while their parents (both doctors) worked in the hospital is heartening. Griffin (13) and Simon (10) were the only non-Africans enrolled in the local primary school:

The boys are a joy to watch. Griff is now chief market bargainer and probably has the best Swahili of the family. He is super bored in school, but takes his home-schooling maths book that we brought with us and is working through his own maths. During their Swahili classes, he works on 'Teach yourself Swahili'. He came forward with the scary experience of seeing his classmates hit hard with a yardstick, to the point of tears.

Simon has been a wonder, especially when I think of how far he has come from his initial huge fears of being the only white kid at school, and of missing out on everything at home. He is making friends, and making thoughtful comments about what he is seeing around him. For a couple of weeks it was really hard for him to go to school, but he seems over the hump. He is with kids a year or two older and the maths work is actually about where he left off. Both boys are becoming voracious readers and finding the joy in curling up with a good book.

They are both learning important life lessons, such as how to navigate on a gearless bike at top speed the deep unpredictable ruts of the trails to school (especially after a rain when the slippery mud congeals between your tire and your fender), how to win at marbles on the playground (several different complex games), how to take enough showers and drink enough water to stay alive in 35 degrees, how to sleep through the call to prayer at 4am and the moaning cow across the road, how to avoid ugali and macheecha (Tanzanian staples), and squat toilets.

It has been unbelievable to watch the boys develop and blossom and adapt. Since returning to school in January, there is suddenly a young lad named Ally who rides with us to school, and a gaggle of boys have appeared at our house daily after school. Language is still a barrier, but what they have in common is a curiosity about each other. I am so glad we persevered with Holy Family Primary School and didn't bail to the international expat school in Tanga.

I look at my family in wonder and know I will look back at this time as an incredible gift; a rich and complex experience for us all, not the least of which is simply to have all this time together so intimately.

In countries where English is spoken, it can be a wonderful eye-opener for children to experience a different school environment for a few months. Even if the school is ghastly, the children will learn to appreciate their old school instead of taking it for granted. People travelling on a tourist visa will not usually be permitted to put their children in the state education system free of charge, but it is worth investigating the possibility both beforehand and locally. If one of the parents has a special visa (eg, work permit, academic visitor visa), it may well be possible. If the children's visas are to be added to a parental visa, make sure they go on the one that has the permission to work/reside.

Lindsay and Nick Whitlock decided to spend an inheritance of £25,000 on something that would change their lives as a family for the better. They were not unduly worried about the schooling that Thomas, aged 10, and Esther, aged 4, would miss. With the benefit of hindsight on their year-long travels, their confidence was justified. It turned out that the academic disruption was less an issue than the social disruption:

Although both our children missed a year of school, and Tom even missed his SATs, this, offset against the experience they had gained, does not seem to have had a long-term effect. In fact, we never sought official permission from the LA – although I wrote to Thomas' headmaster, who was happy to give his full support! As a teacher myself, I felt that I would be able to provide a 'skeleton' curriculum as we travelled. This was not possible as I had envisaged it, as the conditions during the trip meant that it was impossible, and, even when we did do 'travel school', it was generally met with resistance by the children. However, my children are resourceful and have developed an immense ability to overcome difficulties, and catching-up has posed no problem for either of them.

On our return, my son had grown unused to communicating with his peers. While he was brimming with enthusiasm and confidence talking to adults, and could happily entertain a hostel full of backpackers with eloquent travelling tales, he found it very hard to relate to others of his age group. He quickly gained a reputation at his new school, where he tried so hard to settle in, for being a bit freaky. Fortunately, in some ways, circumstances forced us to move again four months after returning to the UK, and he had adjusted enough to cope better second time around.

For our daughter Esther, aged 5 on return, the adjustment was easiest. She had missed her 'reception' year at school, and, having shown no interest in being taught formally by me, was therefore behind academically. However, she is a naturally sociable child, who had, if anything, developed quite exceptional social skills in play with children everywhere, language no obstacle, and she quickly fitted in and caught up. Now, at nearly seven, she's doing very well at school, and in all areas of her life.

HOME SCHOOLING

If you decide to take the children on a trip abroad, their formal education need not be completely suspended. Several sources of help are available from organisations that produce courses and reading material for parents who want to teach their children themselves. Not all children are receptive to being taught formal lessons by their parents, and the project may not succeed with stubborn, wilful, or rebellious children. But 'lessons' can be disguised: a child may be keen to keep a diary of the trip while being loathe to do an exercise from a textbook. Realistically, most children won't put up with more than a couple of hours of formal tuition every few days.

As mentioned earlier, **Jen Moon's** daughters did plenty of homework while they were on the road, mainly thanks to their mother's determination to keep them at it. Nine-year-old Sarah wrote in her journal after a 'really looonnnggg walk' to see giant redwoods in southern California: 'Although it was pouring with rain and it was really cold, Mum started to give me a geology lesson! It just goes to show we do homework whatever the weather! I was glad to get home and have my nice hot chocolate'. Writing a journal is of course an education in itself. Jen was fascinated to notice the progress they made from the rough efforts at the beginning, especially of 9-year-old Sarah when she could barely write, to the 'very accomplished, laugh-out-loud, work' at the end. Much of the daily accounts concerned food, but the educational benefits often shine through, as in this extract from 11-year-old Lisa's journal, written in their campervan in northern New South Wales:

> We walked down on to the beach where we splashed in the sea. Suddenly mum spotted something sparkly in the sand, it was called phosphorescence, it was so amazing. There were little sparks everywhere. It was so weird, like stars in the sand. It was really magical, almost fiction. We had a splash in the water, the sparkles were in the water too and it all got in my hair. Sadly we got cold so we had to go back. We had been there nearly two hours. It felt like 20 minutes! It had been a strange night that I will remember forever.

The value of ticking curriculum boxes palls in comparison.

Bonny Havenhand was 13 when her parents decided to leave their comfortable oceanside house in Newcastle, New South Wales, and spend a year in Siem Reap, Cambodia. Carrying on his publishing business remotely, her dad Bryan took on the role of home tutor which, he learned, requires serious commitment:

> Home schooling is hard work and takes a lot more time than originally anticipated! Everything seems to be done with minimum effort, but maybe that's all you get from a 13-year-old. Bonny's going OK with it, but needs a lot of help with maths, so I've had to relearn fractions, algebra, the Pythagorean Theorem, etc, etc. She is keeping up with her schoolwork and is half way through her second term's work. Not, I might fairly add, without a great deal of hassling and patience from me. I'm not wanting to take anything away from her though, as she has spurts where she does a lot by herself without being hassled.

Bonny's school in Australia sent material on a regular basis; as soon as it was returned it was marked and new work would be sent. This worked well until someone at home in charge of forwarding the post failed to do so, which caused problems. Bonny was not just on the receiving end of education. Despite her young age, she started teaching English to the local kids each afternoon for an hour and the numbers grew so much that her father had to step in to lend a hand.

The Education Act in the UK makes specific provision for home schooling, stating that parents are responsible for their children's education, 'Either by regular attendance at school or otherwise'. Children who are registered as being home schooled do not, by contrast with children who attend schools, need permission from the local education authority before departing. For information about the legal situation, see the Department for Education's site (www.education.gov.uk).

Most travelling families latch on to technology. A wealth of online courses and educational CDs are now available, though these materials can be expensive. Numerous options for online and open learning allow a child to study accredited courses. Usually, a child will be assigned to a teacher who monitors progress via email.

The Home Education Advisory Service (HEAS) and Education Otherwise have good reputations for helping parents take on the formidable task of creating their own school. The HEAS Advice line can put you in touch with other subscribers who live abroad, who might be able to offer practical advice. Some families may prefer to follow the British curriculum for Key Stages 1, 2, 3 and so on by taking the syllabuses and textbooks with them. If you know what school your child will be attending on your return, make an appointment to discuss with the relevant teachers the syllabus they follow. HEAS publishes a leaflet called *Examinations and Qualifications*, giving information about the different options available for taking formal qualifications.

MY GROWN-UP GAP YEAR: BRYAN HAVENHAND

Bryan Havenhand from Australia spent one whole year in Cambodia with his wife Anna and 13-year-old daughter Bonny. Anna found work as a language teacher after arrival in Siem Reap, and her wages covered all local living expenses including the rent of a comfortable house. They had a fascinating year, though not without its challenges.

My wife Anna wanted to teach English overseas and had completed a CELTA to this end. (A native German speaker, she ended up mostly teaching German instead to tour guides at Angkor Wat in Cambodia.) Our daughter was in the early years of high school so if we were to go, this was the time. I took the idea on as a bit of an adventure. The family (siblings and parents) were not overwhelmed by the idea, and both sets of parents were opposed to it. They did not say this outright, but constantly stressed the negative side of things. It was seen as dangerous, more so because of the spread of bird flu in Cambodia and nearby countries. It was seen as somewhat irresponsible, taking our 13-year-old daughter as well. Our friends thought it was a great idea and especially encouraged our daughter, who was not looking forward to it as she thought she would miss her friends badly.

The year out was self-funded, although my wife earned up to US$700 per month - which well and truly covered our basic costs in Cambodia, including the rental of our house. We did not travel much (our daughter didn't want to travel around the country at all) though we went once to Thailand, once to Laos just before we left, and two short trips around northern Cambodia. I also did some English teaching that came along, plus I taught quite a few local kids (as did our daughter for a while). Otherwise I was still working on my business (a small publishing company called Global Exchange), attempting to help home school our daughter, running the household (we did have a housekeeper), and generally keeping things on an even keel.

The highlights were the people who lived around us (we had much more contact with the locals than with other expats), the Angkor temple complex, people we met in villages, and locals we befriended. We were also lucky to have quite a number of friends from both Australia and Germany visit us during the year. For me the hardest part was the constant heat (for much of the year it would be 35 degrees Celsius at 6.30am and it would only get hotter from there). I also had problems with the monotony, the barking dogs at night, and the early morning (4.30am) chanting from nearby wats. Sometimes I got little sleep.

It was definitely worth the effort, and I think it has given our daughter a useful perspective on life that she wouldn't have otherwise got from simply travelling to a place. She dropped her Paris Hilton look-a-like friends not long after she came back, and took up with some new friends who have a healthier outlook on life. When our daughter has finished high school we might just do it again.

HOME SCHOOLING RESOURCES

The two principal organisations in the field are Education Otherwise and HEAS:

■ **Education Otherwise**, 125 Queen Street, Sheffield, S1 2DU (0845 478 6345; www. education-otherwise.org). UK-based membership organisation which provides support and information for families whose children are being educated outside school, and for those who wish to uphold the freedom of families to take responsibility for the education of their children. Membership costs £25 and includes a membership forum, online bulletins, etc.

■ **Home Education Advisory Service (HEAS)**, PO Box 98, Welwyn Garden, Herts AL8 6AN (01707 371854; enquiries@heas.org.uk; www.heas.org.uk). National organisation providing information, advice and support for home educating families. Annual subscription is £16 (£22 overseas) and includes a quarterly bulletin, access to the Advice Line for curriculum information, and a regional list of subscribers. The service produces several publications like the *Introductory Pack*, the *Home Education Handbook*, and the *Big Book* *of Resource Ideas* for information on books, CDs, websites, and clubs for most school subjects. Leaflets are available too, covering exams, special educational needs, and home education overseas.

■ The specialist website homeschooling.gomilpitas.com/weblinks/traveling also has a good selection of links to resources for travelling families.

■ Exam revision sites proliferate on the web; for example, the BBC has very good 'Bitesize' sites for Key Stages 2, 3, and GCSE (www.bbc.co.uk/schools/gcsebitesize).

■ *National Curriculum* (curriculum.qca.org.uk). Information about the National Curriculum for England, subject by subject. For the Scottish curriculum visit www.ltscotland.com; for Northern Ireland visit www.ccea.org.uk.

■ Singapore Math scheme (www.singaporemath.com) is popular with travelling families since it is user-friendly, portable, and lively.

RESOURCES FOR DISTANCE LEARNING

■ **Cambridge International Exams (CIE)**, Cambridge (01223 553554; www.cie.org.uk). This examination board sets the International GCSE (IGCSE), among many other exams. You can contact them for information about the syllabus, the location of examination centres abroad, past exam papers, and suggested book lists to accompany the relevant syllabuses.

■ **International Centre for Distance Learning (ICDL)**, (http://icdl.open.ac.uk). Database of 5,000 UK courses and programmes taught by distance learning – mainly post-secondary.

■ **National Extension College (NEC)**, Cambridge (01223 400200; www.nec.ac.uk). E-learning primarily for learners in the UK, who have missed out doing GCSEs and A-Levels in the conventional classroom.

■ **Worldwide Education Service (WES)**, Carlisle (01228 577123; www.weshome.com). WES supplies tutorial-based courses for children aged four to 14. All courses are based on the National Curriculum of England and Wales. WES Home School families live in more than 100 countries on every continent, or are travelling between them.

■ **Schoolfriend**, (0871 871 2018; www.schoolfriend.com). This website (accessible by subscription only) was set up to help children aged four to 13 practise online what they have learned at school. While not directly intended as a resource for distance learning, it can be used as an additional tool by parents teaching their children while they travel. Subscription charges are from £2 a week.

PART 9

NEW SKILLS AND
NEW PROJECTS

CHANGING GEAR
CREATING YOUR OWN PROJECT
ADULT EDUCATION
OPEN LEARNING
LEARNING FOR PLEASURE
LEARNING A LANGUAGE
SPORT AND LEADERSHIP COURSES

CHANGING GEAR

Stepping back from the daily responsibilities of a career offers the unrivalled luxury of being able to enjoy time to pursue personal interests. Time is a precious commodity in the developed world, and in short supply. Away from the hurly-burly of professional obligations, individuals can take stock of their lives and re-evaluate their personal ambitions. At least that's what they hope.

Having time for yourself allows you to define yourself as an individual, rather than as a worker. Anyone who takes time off can use it – as many of the interviewees for this book have done – to develop new or under-used skills. Literally and figuratively, it's a time to climb mountains, to set yourself challenges, and learn how to accomplish them beyond the confining arena of the conventional workplace. All those avenues and byways for which a working schedule does not normally leave time can be explored, and opportunities grasped to participate in an activity for the sheer pleasure of it. Pursuing a new activity also expands your social horizons. It can prove remarkably stimulating to link up with a group of people totally unconnected with your professional experiences.

Those whose working lives began immediately after finishing their education may never have deviated from the pre-ordained path of working life. A career break can change all that, giving people a chance to take up further education, retrain, or expand their skills. Studies may be wholly for pleasure, or they may be chosen to advance your professional profile – such as learning a foreign language (which often satisfies both requirements), or gaining a further qualification in business, catering, or whatever your employment field. Qualifying in TEFL (Teaching English as a Foreign Language) as a means to earning while travelling is popular and is discussed in Part 6: Working and Living Abroad.

The choices for further education are immense, ranging from weekly courses run by the local authority to a full-time university degree course. The Open University, described later in this chapter (see page 309), is one of the most successful institutions to come out of the 1960s, enabling students to take degrees without having to become residential students.

Exploration of an entirely new field expands horizons and sometimes even prompts an unplanned-for career change. If you've only known one area of work, then taking a career break might allow you to glimpse other professional worlds.

CREATING YOUR OWN PROJECT

A career break for study or leisure involves a serious commitment of money and time, so it should be used well. It deserves careful planning so that the time doesn't leak away. You might have a generalised desire to see the world, as described in Part 7: Travel and Adventure. On the other hand, you may want to take the chance to fulfil a specific ambition – such as perfect your watercolour or guitar-playing technique, learn to parachute, join an archeological dig, trace your family roots, row across the Atlantic, write a novel, make a pilgrimage, study circus skills, or help to protect an endangered species. In those moments of disgruntlement at work, each person is likely to have a private fantasy of an alternative life, even if it involves just a couple of months away.

It is not essential to go abroad to satisfy one's curiosity about different worlds or fulfil long-held ambitions outside one's sphere of employment. Among the favourite alternatives to the pressures of the corporate world are working on the land or in the country, eg gardening and animal care. For example, Hadlow College in Kent offers a range of courses suitable for people who want a complete change; horticulture, equestrian studies, animal management, etc, can be studied full- or part-time (0500 551434; www.hadlow.ac.uk). The Royal Horticultural Society offers a range of gardening courses for interest and career advancement (www.rhs.org.uk), and the English Gardening School, which is run by the Chelsea Physic Garden in west London (020 7352 4347; www.englishgardeningschool.co.uk), is a good place to turn a hobby into a job. One-year diploma courses are available in Garden Design (£7,850; three days a week) and Practical Horticulture, Plants and Plantsmanship, and Botanical Painting (all for £4,850, one day a week). They also offer courses by distance learning.

Domestic circumstances may make leaving home impossible or undesirable, but that need not rule out a gap year. **Mike Bleazard** wanted to see how much fun he could have by staying in his home environment of Cambridge, pursuing a personal project that he would never have had the time to pursue while working. As a self-employed computer geek, he had saved up enough pennies to take three months away from work to pursue a new idea which he had developed with a friend. They wanted to design and self-publish a series of themed walking tours of Cambridge, and distribute them in pamphlet form through local shops and online. It proved to be great fun to research and design the short guides; one on the old colleges, two on modern architecture, another on churches, with the possibility of adding one on punting. His aim was to break even, though of course it would not be unwelcome if his venture ended up making a profit.

He ended up working harder than he did when he was in employment, but found that he enjoyed the experience intensely. Through the project he met people from many different worlds, from architects to publicans. Not everyone was wildly enthusiastic about his take on the sights: for instance, a senior member of St John's College strenuously objected to his description of the statue of King John in the gatehouse as 'effeminate'.

USING A GAP YEAR TO DEVELOP YOUR CAREER

One practical way of taking a gap year without creating too much distance between yourself and your work, is to create a project that enhances your professional skills. Some bodies have established schemes whereby employees are temporarily assigned to another organisation to learn from a different environment, but you could also initiate such an exchange.

Often, individuals will take a career break to pursue a particular goal within their own field. This is well-established among university academics who (in theory, if not always in practice) are given a break from their teaching duties one term in seven (the meaning of the word sabbatical), in order to engage in full-time research. This time enables specialists to concentrate on their field and be productive – often resulting in an article or book. Some other employers have taken over the idea of sabbatical: for example, newspapers like the *Financial Times* sometimes bestow paid or unpaid leave on their columnists who want to write a book. School teachers, lawyers, doctors, and other professionals occasionally organise an attachment to a different institution to work on a particular academic project.

After working in the same London law firm for five years, **Sara Ellis-Owen** was a valued member of staff. She came to a point where she felt she needed time out from work and from London, and so asked for unpaid leave for three months. She also asked the *pro bono* department (meaning working for the public good) whether they would be able to support her once she had found a short-term legal placement abroad in a developing country. They generously agreed to pay for her flight to Belize and her placement fees to the Edinburgh-based charity Challenges Worldwide, with whom she had fixed up a legal placement in Belize City. Challenges Worldwide is experienced at placing volunteers in professionally-relevant positions abroad, from which they can gain new skills and different areas of expertise. Similarly, Outreach International aims to match skills to placement. For example, **Helen Balazs**, an orthotic technician in her early 30s, went to Cambodia for three months to train landmine victims and disabled young people to become commercial artists. It is often true that a change is as good as a rest.

Some career-breakers who join volunteer projects in the developing world without much thought come back fired up to pursue international development more seriously. The Charities Advisory Trust (www.charitiesadvisorytrust.co.uk/development/index.html) runs a two- or four-week residential summer course called Development from the Inside in Mysore, India, which can serve as a taster of career-level work in development. It includes sessions led by Indian activists, and visits and two work placements with local NGOs. The full course fee of £1,250 covers accommodation, food, and transport within India. (For more information about a career change to the field of international development, see Part 11: Back to Normal or a Change for Life?)

ADULT EDUCATION

Lifelong education has been one of the buzzwords of our era and can provide an exciting chance to move in a different direction, whether purely for pleasure, self-improvement, or a combination. The choices available in adult or continuing education are vast, despite the scaling back of courses in the wake of savage budget cuts in 2010. It is possible to study subjects from Mandarin to massage, or computing to archaeology. Are you interested in a part-time or full-time course? Do you want a vocational degree? Or are you keen to study a subject for pleasure? Think about what it is you want to achieve by further study during a career break. You might want to take your undergraduate studies a stage further by gaining an MA, MSc, or even a PhD. After taking early retirement at age 58 from a small importing business, **Howard Peters** signed up with Coral Cay Conservation to do a volunteering stint helping to set up a marine environmental base in Fiji, and went on to do other CCC expeditions in Malaysia and the Philippines:

As for me, my years at CCC so motivated me that I went on to complete a full-time MSc university course in Marine Environmental Management at York University, and will progress on to a PhD in the hope of adding the fruits of my research to the benefit of marine conservation.

During the past ten years the numbers attending postgraduate courses in the UK has quadrupled (including students from overseas). Most mature students prefer to study at their local university or college, although some elite institutions cater particularly for the needs of mature students. For example, Birkbeck College is a member of London University and specialises in teaching mature students, although its funding has been badly hit recently too. While it is possible to take a full-time postgraduate degree, most teaching takes place in the evenings so that mature students can continue working during the day. It is possible to enroll in first or higher degrees in the arts, sciences, or social sciences. Most course details can be found on the college website (www.bbk.ac.uk) or you can write to the Registry, Birkbeck College, University of London, Malet St, Bloomsbury, London WC1E 7HX (enquiries at 0845 601 0174).

Ruskin College in Oxford specialises in providing educational opportunities for adults who want a second chance in education. For a variety of financial, personal, or social reasons, some adults have never had access to higher education. Ruskin seeks to redress this shortfall and has established a strong reputation for the quality of its adult education. The age range of students is from 22 to 74. Interestingly, dyslexic students make up a significant proportion of the total student body of 300. Courses are residential, although it's possible to take shorter courses too. For information call 01865 554331, or check the website www.ruskin.ac.uk. A fully-funded residential programme at Ruskin called Ransackers is aimed at people over 55 who have never benefitted from higher education, and who have a topic that they want to explore for a ten-week term.

At Cambridge University, Lucy Cavendish College (www.lucy-cav.cam.ac.uk) admits only women aged 21 and over, and encourages applications from women of all ages and backgrounds, including those with few or no academic qualifications. **Myra Fonseca** left school with an impressive list of O-Levels 50 years ago, but she didn't go to university. She married young, and happily, had two children, and travelled all over the world. She ran a small-holding and became president of her local Women's Institute in Devon. In 2009, she became the oldest person to get a history degree from Lucy Cavendish College, Cambridge. Her first step was to quietly sign up for an access course at Exeter Further Education College, and then to pursue her studies as long as they interested her – which turned out to be all the way to degree level. Many students at the college, where the average age is about 30, have returned to full-time study after a spell in the workplace or bringing up children, or are making career changes. Every July the University of Cambridge puts on a free long weekend called 'Going Further', aimed at encouraging mature candidates thinking seriously of returning to university to gain a degree (see www.cam.ac.uk/admissions/undergraduate/mature/events).

According to UCAS (Universities and Colleges Admissions Service), the number of applicants over 25 years of age who applied to universities and colleges for 2010 rose by 23.3% over the previous year. This means that with many more mature students at university, you are quite likely to find a peer group wherever you enroll. The first step would be to look at www.access-tohe.ac.uk, which links to courses in England and Wales, or www.scottishwideraccess.org for Scotland. A lack of confidence inhibits many older potential students, not to mention the normal requirement of a GCSE in Maths. Many mature students feel an extra burden of stress because often they have given up a lot to return to education, and stand to lose more than a 19-year-old who drifts on from school. Most institutes of higher education have a mature student guidance officer who will be able to offer reassurance and practical advice on funding (see page 311 for more on Financial Support).

LIFELONG LEARNING

Those who turned their backs on further or higher education at an earlier stage are now being encouraged to go back to college to acquire new skills and knowledge, and an analytical training. A gap year might be the time, whatever your age, to pick up qualifications you never had the chance to study before, or which you fluffed while being distracted by more entertaining youthful pursuits.

Formal adult education courses that award certificates and degrees can be roughly divided between further education, which takes place in local further education and tertiary colleges mainly offering vocational courses; and higher education, which encompasses undergraduate and postgraduate study leading to a degree. Higher education includes degrees, Higher National Diplomas (HNDs) and Certificates, and Diplomas of Higher Education. Increasingly, universities run recreational courses for adults through departments variously called Continuing Education, Extra Mural departments, or Short Course Units. These courses do not offer the same academic challenges as the degree programmes, but they do give adult learners access to the same academic resources, like tutors and libraries, without subjecting the students to the same pressure or commitments in terms of time and cost. If you already have a degree and professional qualifications you may not want to study towards another degree. If you want to study for pleasure, there may be little justification in putting yourself through another round of exams. Studying during an adult gap year should be pleasurable, as well as enlightening.

USEFUL CONTACTS FOR ADULT EDUCATION

- *Adult Residential Colleges Association (ARCA)*, Felixstowe (01394 278761; www.arca.uk.net). A group of 20 colleges specialising in short-stay residential adult education courses for the general public.
- *City & Guilds*, London EC1 (0844 543 0033; www.cityandguilds.com). Set up in the 19th century to provide technical training for a variety of trades, C&G is now a leading provider in the UK of vocational qualifications such as NVQs, Certificates, and Diplomas suitable for anyone wishing to improve their skills or to retrain before returning to work. Subjects for study include agriculture, catering, textiles, construction, education, electronics, upholstery, healthcare, IT, retail and distribution, sport, and tourism.
- *Floodlight* (www.london.floodlight.co.uk). The official guide to part-time and full-time courses across London.
- *National Institute of Adult Continuing Education (NIACE)*, Leicester (0116 204 4200; www.niace.org.uk). Leading organisation for adult learning; publishes a range of booklets on topics related to lifelong learning and co-ordinates Adult Learners' Week each May (www.alw.org.uk).
- *UCAS (Universities & Colleges Admissions Service)* (0871 468 0468; www.ucas.com/students/wheretostart/maturestudents). The national organisation that manages applications to UK universities.
- *University of the Third Age* (www.u3a.org.uk). Promotes lifelong learning among retired people.

BUSINESS STUDIES AND THE MBA

Mature students often consider embarking on a business degree to facilitate a career change or improve their prospects. Using a gap year to obtain a Master of Business Administration (MBA) is not uncommon among employees working in any form of financial or commercial administration. In recent years it has become almost *de rigueur* for advancement in certain professions, like management consultancy. It's a trend that has taken its lead from the United States, where this field of study was pioneered. Some of the major American business schools like Harvard, Columbia, and Wharton in Philadelphia are prestigious and expensive, but European business schools are catching up: the London Business School was ranked first and INSEAD in Paris fifth by the *Financial Times* in their 2010 survey of global MBA programmes.

The MBA is an ideal degree for individuals who have spent some years in work following graduation. It offers the chance to study abroad in the USA or France, for example, while gaining a degree that is highly valued in business. Effectively, it almost guarantees a significant lift in professional salary and opportunities. Students tend to be aged between 26 and 35. Holders of MBAs are some of the best-paid employees in the workforce, which is just as well since fees for one year's MBA study can easily rise to £27,000.

The Association of MBAs (www.mbaworld.com) is the internationally-recognised authority on postgraduate business and management education. In the crowded and complex market, the Association provides impartial advice to potential MBA students. It also runs a loan scheme with NatWest, for financial assistance at preferential interest rates to prospective MBA candidates with a Bachelor's degree or suitable professional qualification, plus two years' relevant work experience. (Non-graduates must have five years' experience.)

OPEN LEARNING

Distance learning is now often referred to as open learning, replacing the old description of 'correspondence course'. It is a concept of keen interest to individuals who want to embark on adult education without leaving home. By definition, the concept allows any student to study from home with the assistance of the internet, supplemented by text and audio-visual materials. Tutorial help is provided by email, post, telephone, Skype, and occasionally in face-to-face meetings. One-week residential courses are usually built in to the programme.

Many of the same qualifications are available through open learning as by attending courses on college campuses. Realistically, most adults in their 30s, 40s or 50s do not have the freedom (nor the inclination) to leave their comfortable homes to live in student digs or residential halls for extended periods. Parents at home caring for children also often find this a valuable option.

Flexibility is at the heart of open and distance learning, giving students the ability to learn at their own pace, and in their own time, from anywhere in the country – or indeed the world. Course materials can be quite expensive, although this can be mitigated by access to a good local library and the huge resources now available online. Generally speaking, distance courses are much cheaper than full-time residential ones. Learning any subject, especially practical ones, from books can be a challenge, as can disciplining yourself to stick to a self-imposed timetable. Be wary of extravagant claims by distance learning course providers, since an element of practice may be considered essential for certain areas of endeavour, eg learning to teach English.

THE OPEN UNIVERSITY AND OTHER PROVIDERS

The Open University was established with charitable status to teach mature students, including those individuals without any formal qualifications. Now considered a great success, the OU has established a reputation for the quality of its teaching and research. All of this is a tremendous resource for aspirational adult students.

The large range of courses vary from short modules to PhDs. It is possible to construct your own degree programme by choosing from the 160 single nine-month courses, or signing up for one of the 30 two-year diplomas listed in the *Undergraduate Prospectus*. Courses can be spread over many years with breaks, and students can begin studying at any level appropriate for them. Most work is undertaken by distance learning, using interactive learning, audio-visual and printed materials, CDs, television and radio programmes on the BBC, and personal contact with tutors. Open2.net is the online learning portal from the Open University and the BBC.

Aside from first and higher degrees, Open University students can study a variety of non-degree courses like computing, health and social welfare, management, the history of ideas, and art history, among many others; log on to www3.open.ac.uk/study to conduct a search. Most courses from the undergraduate programmes are available too, without proceeding to a full degree. For further detailed information contact your nearest OU regional centre. To find the nearest centre call the Course Information and Advice Centre on 0845 300 6090.

Alternatives to the Open University take the form of specialist distance learning colleges, such as the Open College of the Arts and the National Extension College. For information on accredited colleges, contact the Open and Distance Learning Quality Council (all listed below).

People considering doing a distance course with a private institute should try to ascertain how widely recognised the qualification or 'diploma' will be. Certain fields attract the occasional cowboy operators: for example in the booming field of Teaching English as a Foreign Language (TEFL), a few companies have a definite credibility gap (often operating from a Post Office Box). Try to find out if there is an accreditation council in the field and, if so, whether the institute is a member. Ask to be put in touch with past students and seek the opinion of respectable organisations or prospective employers in the field.

OPEN LEARNING CONTACTS

■ *The Open University*, Student Enquiry Service, PO Box 197, Milton Keynes MK7 6BJ (0845 300 6090; www3.open.ac.uk).

■ *Association of British Correspondence Colleges (ABCC)* (020 8544 9559; www.homestudy.org.uk). A trade association representing distance learning providers, offering advice and information for prospective students. Standards are regulated and a common code of ethics applied.

■ *Learndirect* (0800 101 901; www.learndirect.co.uk). Government information service on education at all levels, including Distance, Open, and Flexible Learning.

■ *National Extension College*, Cambridge (0800 389 2839; www.nec.ac.uk). Offers 150 home-study courses.

■ *Open College of the Arts (OCA)*, Barnsley, Yorkshire (0800 731 2116; www.oca-uk. com). OCA offers home-study courses in art and design, supported by tutors who are practising artists. Courses are offered in painting, sculpture, textiles, interior design, photography, garden design, dance, creative writing, and music composition. Students can begin their course at any time of the year. Most courses cost £595 or £695 and include either distance tuition or (for £50 extra) face-to-face feedback.

■ *Open and Distance Learning Quality Council (ODLQC)*, London (020 7447 254; www.odlqc.org.uk). Grants accreditation to private colleges offering distance learning. Accredited colleges range from Music for the Media, to the Horticultural Correspondence College.

■ *RDI (Resource Development International)*, Coventry (024 765 15700; www.rdi. co.uk). Distance learning in Accounting, Finance, Management, Marketing, IT, Business Administration, and Law, via partners such as the Universities of Sunderland, Bradford, and East London.

■ *University of London International Programme* (020 7862 8360; www.london international.ac.uk). One hundred different degrees and diplomas are delivered externally to students in more than 140 countries.

FINANCIAL SUPPORT FOR RETURNING TO EDUCATION

Finding financial support for further education is undeniably difficult. At a time when the government has increased student fees in England and expects undergraduates to take out huge loans to fund themselves through college, it will be difficult to find financial aid as a mature or postgraduate student. The 1960s, 70s, and 80s, can now be viewed as a golden age for higher education in which studying was seen as an entitlement rather than a privilege.

Mature students over 21 and under 60 are eligible to apply for the means-tested student loan, like any other student. People over 19 who missed out on education when young and want to study full-time for GCSEs, NVQs, or A-Levels, may be eligible for the means-test Adult Learning Grant of up to £30 a week. Full-time students who have dependent children may be eligible for a Childcare Grant and, depending on the household income, a Parents' Learning Allowance. Further information is available on the website www.direct.gov.uk, which includes information about routes into higher education for mature students.

If you need help funding a training course, in anything from feng shui or TEFL teaching, to ski instructing abroad, you may be eligible for a Professional & Career Development Loan. PCDLs are bank loans from £300 to £10,000, to help cover the cost of a vocational course. The Department for Education pays the interest until a month after your course finishes, whereupon you must begin repayments at a favourable rate of interest. Details are available as always on www.direct.gov.uk or by ringing 0800 100 900.

Sometimes access bursaries are made available to eligible students. Colleges can make discretionary child care grants to help parents pay for care while they study. Similarly, colleges also run hardship funds from their respective social service departments.

When applying to a college or a university, enquire about the availability of financial support. Many educational institutions award scholarships and bursaries, so it is always worth asking how to qualify for additional support. Sometimes paid research or teaching assistant positions are available in higher education, which can partially offset the costs of your own study.

LEARNING FOR PLEASURE

It is never too late to revive an old interest or introduce yourself to a new one. Everyone has interests over the course of their lives that go into hibernation. Sometimes interests move on and change, but more often a shortage of time is to blame. Perhaps while at school or college, or before you had children, you had a passion for football, art, photography, an allotment garden, chess, human rights campaigning, Thai cookery, mountaineering, creative writing, playing in an orchestra, pigeon racing, or singing in a choir. Gradually this may have dwindled as work and family commitments have taken up more time and energy. A gap year can provide the leisure time to pursue an interest at a recreational level. Perhaps you have discovered an activity while on holiday like riding, diving, art, or cookery, which you want to explore in more depth. A career break presents an ideal opportunity to immerse yourself for several months in a new interest.

Fiona Carroll felt she had been neglecting her own life in favour of her job as a project manager for a software company in Switzerland, and decided finally to take a full year's break to spend time with her family in Ireland, and also to take painting courses in Switzerland. She believes her old company would have kept the job open for her, but she wanted a change to decrease the amount of time she spent at work and obtain a better balance between her job and her private life: 'I didn't want to travel. I just wanted to be'. Remaining at home gave her the opportunity to pursue her love of art. She started taking lessons in painting near her home, which she is able to continue by working a four-day week. **Brian Blackshaw** had been Vicar of Cheshunt in Hertfordshire for eight years, working in a very large and challenging parish, when he investigated the possibility of a sabbatical.

The Church of England is an employer that allows its hard-working staff to take occasional sabbaticals, and Brian's application for a three-month sabbatical was accepted when he was aged about 60. Such sabbaticals are not uncommon in the Church, though only after at least ten years of service. In the past, when C of E sabbaticals tended to be longer, recipients were expected to pursue formal studies or do some writing. But three months is too short a time for that and, although it is necessary to demonstrate that one's time off will be spent in something worthwhile, a degree of latitude is given for pursuing personal interests.

Brian had been studying Italian on and off, and one of his ambitions was to deepen his knowledge of the Italian language and culture. He had visited Florence before and had been encouraged to return by a Polish friend who loved the city. Like almost everybody else, he began his search on the internet and his Google search for the British Council led him to the British Institute of Florence (see Directory entry), whose programmes sounded ideal. So he rented an apartment in Florence and attended intensive Italian language classes for four hours a day. On arrival he noticed that the Institute also had places on a Baroque and Mannerist art course, so he enrolled in that as well. This involved a one-hour lecture a day with some eminent art historians, both British and Italian, and visits to the Uffizi Gallery and other Florentine galleries, as well as to Rome. He considered the standard of teaching to be superb and describes his art course as a joy. He felt that this intensive and enlightened exposure to some of the most magnificent examples of Renaissance art allowed him to break into a circle of knowledge which he had long found intimidating, and from which he had felt excluded. He feels that many people are deterred by a perception of how difficult something will be, but that given the right circumstances it is possible to prick the bubble and enter the charmed circle.

He enjoyed the company of the 15 or 20 other people on his courses, although most were much younger, including several post-A-Level students, some interested in pursuing art history at university, and a sprinkling of more mature people including a couple of Americans temporarily resident in Florence. He was delighted with the facilities at the British Institute and now feels that he could make it a base for any future sojourns in Florence.

Altogether Brian was off work for 14 weeks and three days, and felt that he made good use of his time. In addition to his month in Italy, he joined two birdwatching trips – one to the Picos Mountains of northern Spain and the other to Speyside – visited friends in Switzerland, and his eldest daughter in America. He also luxuriated in having enough leisure time to read an average of two books a week. But the highlight remained his time in Florence, when he felt in some ways he rediscovered his humanity. In his busy parish, 180 funerals must be conducted a year plus hospitals and prisons visited, and countless other duties fulfilled. With the Church of England financially stretched, the vicar's workload can be gruelling, and time off all the more necessary.

RECREATIONAL COURSES ABROAD

A gap year allows you to contemplate studying something that interests you in a foreign country, like African drumming, flamenco dancing, or skiing. Specialist travel companies can arrange special interest courses: for example, the Association of Independent Tour Operators or AITO (020 8744 9280; www.aito.co.uk) lists a number of upmarket tour operators that can arrange watercolour courses in Italy, wine appreciation tours of Chile and Argentina, birdwatching in China, and so on.

The American counterpart is the Specialty Travel Index (305 San Anselmo Ave, San Anselmo, CA 94960; www.specialtytravel.com), which is a useful source of information about 400 specialist tour operators. Their website is searchable by destination and activity. Cultural tours and special interest programmes tend to be fairly upmarket, and it is usually much cheaper to sign up with a local organisation abroad – something which is becoming easier with the help of the internet.

The American journalist and author Alice Steinbach seems to have made something of a career as a career-breaker. After leaving her high-powered job as a journalist in Baltimore to spend six months in Europe, recorded in the book *Without Reservations*, she went on to further travels – but in this case to sign up for courses that appealed to her. In her follow-up book *Educating Alice: Adventures of a Curious Woman*, she records her impressions and encounters while studying dog training in Scotland, writing in Prague, gardening in Provence, calligraphy and flower arranging in Kyoto, music in Cuba, cooking in Paris, and Jane Austen in Exeter.

Others will want to focus on one or two interests on a career break. For example, inveterate traveller **Dave Sands** and his wife have become fascinated with tango:

The tango gives us an additional opportunity to travel to interesting places. Since we started tango we have travelled to Switzerland, France, Italy, and Croatia just to attend classes in tango. The Cuba trip, if we go, is entirely for tango instruction, while the trip to China is mainly for a week of tango classes in Shanghai, but we will also travel around China whilst we are there.

Tango enthusiasts might want to look at www.festivals.tango.info for a calendar of forthcoming tango events worldwide, or the organisation which (bizarrely) combines tango with Zen Buddhism (www.tangozen.com/workshopsUpcoming_new_en).

MY GROWN-UP GAP YEAR: CAROL PEDEN

Finding herself a widow in her mid 40s, Carol Peden knew that she wanted to get away, and obtained six months' unpaid leave – which was granted once she found someone to cover for her post as a consultant in Anaesthesia and Intensive Care Medicine in Bristol. Partly by making use of an earlier edition of this book, she pieced together a remarkable variety of experiences.

I started with two months in India, with the aim of relaxing but also of experiencing some alternative medicine and yoga practice. Next the plan was to spend one month in SE Asia, followed by two months in China: the first in Xian arranged by Cross Cultural Solutions - again I wanted to experience some traditional Chinese Medicine; the second on a small group tour with Intrepid Travel. Finally I booked one month in Florence at the British Institute, studying Italian and Art History.

One of the highlights was living in the centre of a Chinese city, going to the park in the morning to do Tai Chi, wandering through the streets on my own with my camera, making friends with the Chinese doctors - wonderful. I did some travelling with an Australian-based company called Intrepid. Their Southern India trip was fantastic: great food, wonderful Indian experiences, and fun travelling companions (a group of 12 and ten of us were singles and we all got on really well).

The low point probably should have been breaking my foot (à la Wayne Rooney) six weeks into the trip in India, and having to spend six weeks in plaster and another four on crutches. It did force me to change my plans - I had to abandon Laos. The worst part however was that it made me travel very expensively because I could not manage on my own. I stayed in the Raffles hotel in Siem Reap at Angkor Wat in Cambodia, and was studiously ignored by the rich package tourists as otherwise they might have to speak to the mad woman travelling on her own on crutches! That was a very lonely time.

In Florence I was advised to rent a room in a widowed lady's apartment. Perhaps someone younger without my personal experience would have found it easier, but I was acutely aware I was invading her space and wished I'd rented my own place or even shared with some of the younger students.

The time away was fantastic - a great life experience. I spent too much money and was quite lonely at times, but the good bits were some of the best experiences of my life.

COOKERY COURSES

Eating good food was a high priority on Elizabeth Gilbert's agenda when she plunked herself down in Italy for the first part of her 'eating, praying, and loving' career break. More recently another author's midlife crisis took the form of giving up his lucrative job in the London publishing business to embark on a round-the-world gourmandising tour, which also resulted in a book: *Eat My Globe: One Man's Search for the Best Food in the World* by Simon Majumdar (John Murray, 2009). Meanwhile 30-something **Steve Gale** was working as an e-commerce manager when he decided to travel around the world, and then turned his experiences into a website with recipes (www.gapyeargourmet.com).

A more constructive gap year could incorporate a cookery course, either to pursue as a hobby or a way of opening up appealing employment options in ski resorts, private villas or private yachts for those who are looking for a change of direction. A course in the Alps that attracts ski-loving career breakers is the Ultimate Chalet Host Cookery course: a one-week course that aims to teach everything about running a successful chalet. Quick easy recipes that work for large numbers at altitude are taught, plus tips on menu planning, shopping, budget control, health and safety, living in the Alps, the life of a chalet host, language skills, and tricks of the trade to maximise ski time, are all covered. The company offering it is Snowcrazy, which is based in a luxury chalet in La Rosière in the French Alps. The couple who run it, **Mike and Laura Kew**, themselves met on a career break from busy London jobs; contact Snowcrazy on 01342 302 910 or email laura@snowcrazy.co.uk (www.chaletcookerycourse.co.uk).

Private certificate and diploma courses are expensive, especially if you splash out on one of the household names like Cordon Bleu or Tante Marie. Here is a selection of courses in the UK and Europe:

315

■ **Ashburton Cookery School & Wine School**, Old Exeter Road, Ashburton, Devon TQ13 7LG (01364 652784; www.ashburtoncookeryschool.co.uk). Average age mid 30s. From £149 for one-day course to £3,180 for four-week Cookery Diploma course, including five-day intermediate course (£795) recommended for people looking to work in a catered chalet or yacht.

■ **Ballymaloe Cookery School**, Shanagarry, Midelton, Co. Cork, Ireland (+353 21 46 46 785; www.cookingisfun.ie). Situated on organic farm by the coast with access to excellent ingredients, and affiliated to www.jobsforcooks.com. A 12-week Certificate in Cookery course plus range of short courses. €9,975 for certificate course, excluding accommodation.

■ **The Cook Academy**, The Station Mill, Station Road, Alresford, Hampshire SO24 9JQ (01962 734850; www.cookacademy.co.uk). £1,600 for four-week course.

■ **Cookery at the Grange**, The Grange, Whatley, Frome, Somerset BA11 3JU (01373 836579; www.cookeryatthegrange.co.uk). A four-week Essential Cookery course costs £3,090–£3,690.

■ **Le Cordon Bleu Culinary Institute**, 114 Marylebone Lane, London W1V 2HH (020 7935 3503; www.cordonbleu.net). Also branches in Paris and many other cities.

■ **Edinburgh School of Food & Wine**, The Coach House, Newliston, Edinburgh EH29 9EB (0131 333 5001; www.esfw.com). A four-week intensive course costs £2,450; six-month January to June Diploma in Food and Wine course costs £9,500.

■ **Food of Course Cookery School**, Middle Farm House, Sutton, Shepton Mallet, Somerset BA4 6QF (01749 860116; www.foodofcourse.co.uk). Four-week Foundation Cookery Course (£3,350), among others.

■ **Gables School of Cookery**, Bristol Road, Falfield, Gloustershire GL12 8DF (01454 260444; www.thegablesschoolofcookery.com). Specialists in training chalet hosts and yacht cooks. £3,450 inclusive, for four-week course.

■ **Leiths School of Food and Wine**, 16-20 Wendell Road, London W12 9RT (www.leiths. com). Basic Certificate course lasts four weeks full-time in August/September (£2,650). Beginners' Certificate is ten weeks between October and December (£6,000).

■ **Orchards Cookery**, The Orchards, Salford Priors, Nr Evesham, Worcestershire WR11 8UU (01789 490259; www.orchardscookery.co.uk). Five days to two weeks, year round.

■ **Rosie Davies Course for Cooks**, Penny's Mill, Nunney, Frome, Somerset BA11 4NP (01373 836210; www.rosiedavies.co.uk). Four-week Certificate course for £3,350, including shared accommodation.

■ **Tante Marie School of Cookery**, Woodham House, Carlton Road, Woking, Surrey GU21 4HF (01483 726957; www.tantemarie.co.uk). UK's largest independent cookery school.

THE EDINBURGH SCHOOL OF FOOD & WINE (EST. 1987)

The Edinburgh School of Food & Wine (ESFW) has built an enviable reputation since opening in 1987 with students aged 7–70 participating in a wide variety of leisure and professional courses. Based in an 18th century coach house in the grounds of the Newliston Country Estate, 12 miles from the centre of Edinburgh and just ten minutes from the airport, ESFW is registered as a learning provider with the British Accreditation Council – the only cookery school in Scotland to hold such status.

ESFW is an inspiring place to study and develop cookery skills; its beautiful rural setting provides the perfect backdrop to immerse oneself in the craft of cookery. Single day master classes allow participants to focus on a skill-set or cuisine of their choice; from Thai and Indian to Scotland's own seasonal larder. Both the enthusiastic novice and the budding professional delight in the creative recipes & professional tips to create faultless dishes.

For career-minded students our professional courses provide an individual approach to student learning coupled with practical hands-on teaching. This ensures students leave with confidence in their core culinary skills allowing them to build a platform for continuous professional development for life. ESFW has been a time-established springboard for literally hundreds of culinary careers for the past 20 years and has created a rich tradition of success amongst graduating students.

Inspiring Cooks in Scotland for over 20 years

For Your Career:
Professional Diploma and Certificate
    Courses
Chalet and Gap Year Courses
Specialist Masterclasses
Business Courses – Build your own
    business and explore your creativity

For Your Business:
Corporate Events
Team Building
Food Hygiene Training
Wine & Spirit Education

For Your Enjoyment:
One Day Leisure Classes
Glenfiddich Gourmet Cookery
    School for Men
Veuve Clicquot Champagne
    Cookery School for Women
Cocktail Masterclasses
Wine Tasting Dinners

The Coach House, Newliston, Edinburgh, EH29 9EB
0131 333 5001 www.esfw.com info@esfw.com

NEW SKILLS AND NEW PROJECTS

LEARNING FOR PLEASURE

CREATIVE WRITING AND ARTS

The working world is full of aspiring writers of fiction, poetry, travel journalism, plays, and so on. A career break allows the leisure time to pursue this aspiration a little more seriously, and a course in creative writing might provide a useful fillip in this direction. You can't learn to write well without practice, and without bouncing your attempts off a critical audience. Evening classes are available in most centres of population.

The Arvon Foundation (www.arvonfoundation.org) runs five-day residential creative writing courses at its several locations in rural Britain (West Yorkshire, Devon, Inverness-shire, and Shropshire). Courses are open to anyone keen to try their hand at writing poetry, fiction, stage drama, or TV and radio scripts. The course tutors are professional writers, some of whom are well known from newspapers and bookstands, such as Posy Simmonds (whose *Tamara Drewe* represents a writers' retreat in a satirical light). The current cost is £545–£595, inclusive of accommodation, food, and tuition. Grants are available to teachers, students, unemployed, and those on low incomes (see their website).

Other courses, some abroad, are advertised in the literary pages of the quality press. For example, writing courses are offered in the Writers' Lab between May and September on the Greek island of Skyros, at the holistic holiday centre mentioned below in the section on Spiritual Tourism (see page 336). Past courses have been tutored by extremely well-known authors like Margaret Drabble and Sue Townsend, author of the *Adrian Mole* series.

Serious writers may want to take a longer career break to pursue a Masters in creative writing. Lawyer **Matt Cox** took what he described himself as a 'grown-up gap year' to do a

Professional Writing MA at University College Falmouth, which paid off when he won a prestigious prize for his idea and research for a biography of a little-known West Indian prince-turned-racing tipster in the 1920s.

The dream of becoming a published travel writer is one that is chased by some career breakers. Because so many people are now blogging about their travels, some of them extremely entertainingly, it is becoming even harder for publishers to find a market for that kind of thing in print form. The cheapest way to acquire some practical wisdom is to look at *Lonely Planet's Guide to Travel Writing* (Lonely Planet, 2009). The American Tim Leffel (publisher of the well regarded online travel journal Perceptivetravel.com) has just brought out a new book *Travel Writing 2.0: Earning Money from Your Travels in the New Media Landscape* (Splinter Press, 2010).

Two companies in London offer short courses in travel writing: Travellers' Tales (www.travellerstales.org) and Travel Writing Workshops (www.travelworkshops.co.uk) are both taught by working journalists and well-known writers. As well as teaching participants ways to focus their observations, these courses also cover the essential topic of how to sell your work. A three-day Travellers' Tales course in London costs about £400, while their occasional courses held abroad in Istanbul or Marrakesh cost twice as much, including accommodation. You will have to be prepared to expose your writing to group criticism. Radio 4's travel programme *Excess Baggage* featured one of these travel writing courses in Marrakesh, attended by **Tessa Mills**, who now runs the Career Break Guru. Naturally it is possible to study a travel writing course online, for example, at the San Francisco-based www.matadoru.com.

Travel inevitably inspires artists. To take one example of a special interest holiday, Art Safari, based in Suffolk (www.artsafari.co.uk), leads tutored painting holidays worldwide, suitable for artists of all standards and experience. Destinations include Namibia, Malawi, Kenya, Zambia, Antarctica, and India. Although the majority of clients treat such a trip as a one-off special interest holiday, some join as part of longer travels, for instance, if they are doing voluntary work in the destination country and want a break, or if they are about to start travelling and want to start their journey learning a new skill which they can develop throughout the rest of their trip. The director Mary-Anne Bartlett says that she can also help her guests who want to stay on to do placements with creative industries in the country.

Music is another of the arts that might be rediscovered in a career break, whether singing, playing an instrument, or even joining a band. In the USA, there is a growing trend for professional adults to join a residential summer camp that specialises in their interest. A searchable database can be found at www.grownupcamps.com. The *New York Times* drew this resource to its readers' attention under the headline 'Taking a Break from Life to Live the Fantasy', which included interviews with stressed doctors and lawyers who become utterly absorbed in playing jazz or perfecting their cello technique or whatever else, and were therefore rejuvenated.

LEARNING A LANGUAGE

A gap year is an ideal opportunity to brush up on a barely-remembered GCSE (or perhaps even O-Level) language, or start from scratch with a new language. Most current and future employers will view this as a commendably constructive allocation of time, and anyone with competence in another language has an advantage in many job hunts. Many older people might have in the back of their minds the possibility of buying property abroad or even retiring permanently, and therefore have a straightforward motive in mastering a language.

British professionals are often put to shame by the linguistic superiority of their counterparts on the continent, and feel that they were poorly taught at school with too much emphasis placed on grammar and literature. Even with a GCSE and A-Level in a language, many Britons arrive in France, Germany, or Italy still tongue-tied through lack of confidence and a serious linguistic deficiency.

LANGUAGE LEARNING IN THE UK

Britons are notoriously slow to learn foreign languages. Yet the spirit is willing if a recent statistic is true, claiming that 7% of the UK population are studying a language at any one time. Evening language classes offered by local authorities usually follow the academic year and are aimed at hobby learners. Intensive courses offered privately are much more expensive.

After stepping down from the post of Director General of the CBI, and long before becoming Chairman of the Financial Services Authority, **Adair Turner** (now Lord Turner) spent many months writing a book about the future of capitalism from his home in London. But he also exploited the time he took away from formal employment to improve his meagre French, which he felt was a serious gap in his education. Each week a tutor would visit him at home to develop his conversational ability:

> I suspect that most people 15 years after leaving full-time education are aware that there are some things that they could have done, but the choices they made or the education they were given didn't develop that. In my case it was languages. I made the right choices in education except that I wasn't taught languages very well. I wanted to fill that in.

If you are really dedicated, consider using a self-study programme with distance learning courses online, or books and CDs: for example, the *Take Off In...* series from OUP (www.askoxford.com/languages), for £25 including mp3 downloads; the BBC (bbc.co.uk/languages); Linguaphone (0800 136973; linguaphone.co.uk); and Audioforum (audioforum.com). Linguaphone recommends half an hour of study a day for three months to master the basics of a language, which will require iron discipline.

Polly Botsford, a lawyer in her early 30s, thinks that learning the language is the key to understanding a foreign country, because that is the only way to communicate with the people. Although she made some progress in learning Khmer after joining her volunteer project in Cambodia, she regrets that she didn't study the language more seriously before leaving home:

> *It is arrogant to arrive somewhere and expect to hear and speak only English. I read quite a few books and talked to a lot of people, which is part of the fun and the build-up. For me the low point in Cambodia was a constant sense of frustration that I could not properly understand people. Often I felt like a complete uncultured idiot for not conversing with people in their native tongue. It has been the bane of my life that I cannot traverse linguistic borders.*

Hold out a carrot to yourself of a trip to a country where your target language is spoken. Even if you don't make much headway with the course at home, download some material on to your iPod and take books, including a good dictionary, with you since you will have more incentive to learn once you are immersed in a language.

Useful contacts include:

- **Alliance Française** (www.alliancefrancaise.org.uk). Sponsored by the French government, the Alliance manages 1,000 teaching centres worldwide, including 13 in the UK. Sample cost would be £285 for 30 hours of tuition in French over two weeks.
- **Instituto Cervantes (Spanish Cultural Institute)**, 102 Eaton Square, London SW1W 9AN (020 7235 0353; www.cervantes.es or www.cervantes.org.uk). The non-profit Instituto Cervantes is the largest worldwide Spanish-teaching organisation, with headquarters in Madrid and a network of centres around the world, including London and Manchester.
- **Italian Cultural Institute**, 39 Belgrave Square, London SW1X 8NX (020 7823 1887; www.icilondon.esteri.it).
- **CILT (Centre for Information on Language Teaching)**, 3rd Floor, 111 Westminster Bridge Road, London SE1 7HR (0845 612 5885; www.cilt.org.uk). National Centre for Languages.
- **Goethe-Institut**, 50 Princes Gate, London SW7 2PH (020 7596 4004; german@london.goethe.org; www.goethe.de). German language courses at all levels in institutes around the world. UK branches in London, Glasgow, and Manchester.

LEARNING A LANGUAGE ABROAD

A more enjoyable and successful way of learning a language is by doing it on location. While studying French or German at secondary school, you normally have two hours of classes a week – which works out at about 80 hours a year. While doing an eight-week intensive course, you might have 240 hours – the equivalent of three years of school instruction – plus you will be speaking the language outside the classroom, so progress is normally much quicker. To give a very rough idea of the cost, a typical intensive German language course in a major German city might cost from €800 for four weeks of 20 lessons per week, including accommodation.

Numerous British and international agencies represent a range of language schools abroad offering in-country language courses. The agents are very familiar with differences between schools, qualifications, locations, etc, and what is most suitable for clients. CESA Languages Abroad, Caledonia, Cactus Language, and Language Courses Abroad (see Directory entries), among some others listed below, all have wide-ranging programmes abroad in Europe and beyond. These agencies also provide a useful back-up service if the course does not fulfil your requirements in any way.

CESA LANGUAGES ABROAD

Amy Kuan
12 weeks (May/July 2010) in Madrid learning Spanish

Linguistically I really wasn't sure what to expect, I assumed it would be hard at first and I hoped I would improve over the three months there.

My expectations were met and exceeded. The course was lots of fun and what made it so enjoyable was the fact I was learning with students from a variety of backgrounds. Linguistically, by the end of the 12 weeks I had moved up three levels, so I was pleased with my improvement. There was always a good balance between the speaking, listening, writing and reading elements and at all times good student/teacher interaction. The teachers were also flexible enough to let the students dictate the nature of classes at times, if they thought it would be beneficial to all of us – which made some classes very interesting.

One of the best parts of the experience was being able to learn and talk Spanish every day, and it literally was every day, which was fantastic to really get to grips with the language.

After spending three months in Madrid I have absolutely fallen in love with the city and cannot think of anything negative to say about it. It is a brilliant city to learn Spanish; there are lots of students from all over the world which makes it vibrant and cosmopolitan and therefore very fun! It is also a great place to practise your Spanish with the locals, since many of them are happy to let you talk in Spanish.

CESA have been absolutely brilliant! When I was planning my trip to Spain I had so many questions (hundreds!) and I was so impressed with how happy and willing Katherine was to answer every single one of them! I have already and will continue to recommend CESA Languages to anyone considering learning a language abroad.

In her late middle years **Pamela Tincknell** began to toy with the idea of spending more time in Spain. Like so many others, Pamela has always hated the dark and gloomy British winter and fancied the idea of the Costa del Sol. She had been taking the regulation holidays in Spain since the 1960s and had dabbled in beginner Spanish evening classes, but decided that the time had come to extend her linguistic aspirations. A chronic hoarder, Pamela fished out a cutting from a Sunday supplement she had squirreled away as many as 20 years earlier, which was about language courses abroad. To her surprise she found that the company she featured, CESA, was still going strong, and so she requested their brochure.

She knew that she wanted to be on the coast rather than inland, and chose the civilised resort town of Nerja. She joined a fortnight-long course at the Escuela de Idiomas Nerja (www. cesalanguages.com/over-50s-language-courses/spanish) designed for the over-50s, consisting of three hours of language tuition a day plus plenty of excursions. That experience hooked her and she began to consider spending an entire year learning Spanish. She is thoroughly convinced that going off-season was a good move, not only because of the lovely weather, but because the winter attracts older people – including what Pamela calls 'lifers'. Pamela recommends a small resort for an initial language course, but now feels that she has outgrown living near an expat enclave and has grown tired of waiters who reply in English to questions in Spanish.

David Storey is another satisfied CESA customer. Because his job as a long-distance lorry driver takes him frequently to France, he wanted to improve his French – so he signed up for a three-month course in Bordeaux one September:

I obviously improved my French, but also I found the whole experience of meeting new people and noting the cultural differences to be very rewarding. I had taken up the course out of a desire to improve my French, which since A-Level had not been practised and just barely remembered. In my work for an international freight company I had travelled extensively throughout Europe, working with many colleagues for whom English was not their first language. As I was reliant on people speaking my language I began to regret my inability to speak a second language myself, so I decided to pick up again with my long-neglected French.

I found that many of the French people I met were very welcoming and friendly, and were generally impressed that I was trying to speak their language. Whilst in Bordeaux I played at two small squash clubs and was welcomed, which was a great opportunity to chat and mingle. Also there was some good dressing room banter on the subject of football, and I found myself on more than one occasion having to defend the football merits of Peter Crouch. I recommend going to watch the local football team in Bordeaux as well. The Saturday evening kick-off times really foster a family atmosphere.

I stayed in the home of a local man and found the experience to be delightful and informative in itself. For one thing his apartment was very near the school in a very beautiful part of the Centreville, and he even invited me to spend time at his coastal home at Lacanau –which is a surfers' paradise, and in winter a wonderfully peaceful retreat from the madness of the city. It was a great introduction to the French 'esprit', as he would share his philosophies and outlook on life. As for Bordeaux it's a fantastic city, with the Centreville being just the right size to retain a friendly and intimate atmosphere. I certainly plan to go back there next winter and settle a few squash match grudges.

Of course it is not necessary to book a language course via a mediating agency, as **Hannah Adcock** from Edinburgh reported at the end of 2010, just before setting off to Egypt to study Arabic out of interest:

> *I know Arabic is fiendishly difficult, but I always prefer to have some idea of the language of a country if I'm staying around for a while. Even being able to haggle with taxi drivers and tell importunate men that I'm married, makes a difference to day-to-day life. It's not that you'll ever blend in, but at least you'll be able to differentiate yourself from the lumpen 'tourist' groups that tend to bring hassle and occasionally contempt in their wake. We chose a course by browsing the web – there was still a 'Transitions Abroad' web page up about language schools in Egypt that was extremely helpful. After that it was a case of seeing what looked to be good value and suitable for casual learners, rather than diplomats. We chose a language school in downtown Cairo that looked to have some personality and a certain degree of dynamism (ie, they are on Twitter!).*

Literally thousands of language schools around the world would like your business, so care needs to be taken in choosing one that suits individual needs. Possible sources of language school addresses on the web are language.studyabroad.com, languagestudy.goabroad.com, and language.shawguides.com. After considering the obvious factors like price and location when choosing a language school, also try to find out the average age and likely nationalities of your fellow learners, how experienced and qualified the staff are, whether there will be any one-to-one tuition, whether the course concentrates on oral or written skills, whether extracurricular activities and excursions are included in the fee, and generally as much as you can. One key factor is whether or not a school prepares its students for exams. If they do and you are there only for the fun of it, you may find that lessons are not suitable. **Yolande Blanchette** from Canada was very pleased with the German course she did with Horizonte (affiliated to IALC in the Directory), located in the southern German city of Regensburg:

(translated from the French original)
The activities programme was interesting and relevant to the course, and was suitable for all age groups. I felt easily integrated, despite the difference in age ... Usually, when my courses in a school come to an end, I feel delighted – but not this time. In fact, I regret not having registered for a full three months. The language courses I do abroad always have two objectives: to learn the language and to visit the country. I wanted to spend long enough to feel comfortable.

Whereas some language schools run purely recreational courses, others offer some kind of qualification. Some schools, such as the Alliance Française and the Goethe Institute offer qualifications that are instantly recognised. At the other end of the spectrum, some schools offer nothing more than a certificate outlining the period of study and perhaps the level of language reached or work covered in the course, which may be of limited value if you ever need to show proof of language attainment.

However, the majority of adult learners are there not to gain a diploma, but to have fun and learn more about a foreign culture to which they have been attracted. Recreational language courses are offered by virtually every school. Some programmes are more structured than others, so students need to look for flexible courses which allow them to progress at their own rate.

A recent innovation is language lessons on the street; instead of simulating a shopping situation in the classroom, instructors take their clients to the shops so that the language can be used in real situations. For instance, Español Andando in Buenos Aires (www.espanol-andando.com.ar) offers Spanish tuition in this 'fun, budget, and different way'.

Many people agree that the fastest way to improve fluency is to have one-to-one lessons, though of course these are more expensive than group classes. Usually a combination of the two works best. Retirement can provide the perfect catalyst for planning new language learning departures, as was the case for **Ed McFadd** from southern California:

Retirement was to be a new adventure. In preparation for a vacation we had taken in France a couple of years previously, I had bought some language-learning tapes, which I listened to on my suburban commute. Turned out I rather enjoyed my re-acquaintance with the language after three and a half decades. Even though I retained only a few rudimentary lessons from back then, the attraction was still there.

A highlight of my studies has been a three-week sojourn at a private language school in Montreal. I chose the winter, in part because it was less expensive, and also because I enjoy the change in seasons. Further, I stayed in a host family setting, which was a treasured experience and I continue to correspond with the host as well as some other students from the school.

Studying with the younger generation as well as a few more mature students, walking about one of North America's premier cities in mid winter, making new friends, and learning to speak French, all combined to reaffirm my decision to stick with this hobby.

Staying with a host family is obviously much better for language progress. Another possibility is to forgo structured lessons and simply live with a family. Several agencies arrange paying guest stays which are designed for people wishing to learn or improve language skills in the context of family life. Try En Famille Overseas (www.enfamilleoverseas.co.uk), which specialises in France but also arranges homestays with or without language tuition in Germany, Italy, and Spain. EIL, a non-profit cultural and educational organisation, offers short-term language exchange homestay programmes in a range of countries (0800 018 4015 or 01684 562577; www.eiluk.org). Of course you may prefer the most informal route of all, which is simply to use a phrasebook and interact with the locals. Round-the-world travellers **Stefan and Vanessa Aalten-Voogd** always made an effort, but with varying degrees of success:

Stefan had grown up in a multilingual environment in Brussels and with his natural interest in languages and ability to pick them up, he rapidly outstripped my attempts to learn Spanish before we left. A few words in the local language, no matter how poorly executed, were always well-received and often opened up the chance to make contact with local people, rather than just other tourists. With English spoken widely in all but the most rural areas, our fudged linguistic attempts definitely gave us a richer experience than those who did not make the effort. Sign language, facial expressions, a bit of acting, and a handy little book with pictures of everything from a chicken to a clothes peg, created entertainment as well as aiding conversation.

Several years ago, 30-something **Mike Bleazard** and his partner **Jane** took six months off to travel around the world. They were especially looking forward to the last leg of their travels since South America was the first completely non-English speaking region they visited. In preparation they had bought some 'Learn Spanish in no time at all' tapes and struggled through the first 90 minutes of lessons in six weeks. Once they landed of course they noticed a decided improvement, if only in motivation:

After seven weeks in Chile, we can now order a beer, a bus ticket, and ask for a double room with private bathroom – fluently. We still can't understand a word that anyone says back to us, so we've taken to just nodding sagely and saying 'si' when anyone replies – which has got us into all kinds of trouble.

USEFUL ADDRESSES FOR LEARNING A LANGUAGE ABROAD

The following companies represent language schools worldwide. Note that other key players (CESA, Caledonia, Cactus, IALC, and Language Courses Abroad) all have more detailed entries in the 'Directory of Specialist Programmes'.

- **Don Quijote** (020 8786 8081; www.donquijote.org). Spanish specialist, with courses in Spain (including Tenerife) and Latin America. £2,000+ for 12 weeks, including student flat accommodation. Good feedback on www.abroadreviews.com.
- **EF International Language Schools** (020 7341 8777; eflanguages@ef.com; www.ef.com/ils). Foreign language courses at privately-owned and EF schools in France, Germany, Italy, Spain, Ecuador, China, and Costa Rica.
- **Eurointerns**, Madrid, Spain (+34 667 838 136; www.eurointerns.com). Finds internships for about 100 candidates (average age 25) in Spanish, Belgian, and Italian firms, for practical language enhancement and work experience. Basic internship placement lasting two to six months costs €1,100.
- **Gap Year for Grown-ups**, Tunbridge Wells (01892 701881; www.gapyearforgrownups.co.uk/Learn-a-Language). Spanish language courses in Ecuador, Bolivia, Argentina, Peru, Guatemala, and Costa Rica.
- **Journey Latin America**, London W4 (020 8747 8315; www.JourneyLatinAmerica.co.uk). Specialist travel agency and tour operator, which arranges Spanish and Portuguese courses throughout South and Central America. All programmes offer the opportunity to stay with a family for one to four weeks.
- **Lanacos**, Sevenoaks, Kent (01732 456543; www.lanacos.com). Language agency run by linguists, offering courses in 200 destinations. From about £520 for a fortnight in Granada, to £1,650 for 12 weeks in Cologne or Berlin.
- **OISE Intensive Language Schools**, Oxford (01865 258333; info@oise.com; www.oise.com). Primarily an English language-teaching organisation, OISE offers expensive small class tuition of French in Paris, German in Heidelberg, and Spanish in Madrid.
- **S.I.B.S. Ltd**, Devon (01884 841330; www.sibs.co.uk). Language consultancy which arranges language courses abroad for clients. From £300 per week, including accommodation.
- **Vis-à-vis**, Epsom, Surrey (020 8786 8021; www.visavis.org). French courses for all levels, at schools in France, Belgium, and Canada.

LANGUAGE COURSES FOR NORTH AMERICANS

At a time when broad-minded Americans may find themselves wanting to try to dispel accusations of insularity and supremacy, going abroad in a gap year to learn or improve a foreign language may have special appeal. Programmes that combine structured study of a language or culture with volunteering, are arguably a paradigm of the kind of foreign travel experience that can more than justify taking time out from work. Many organisations, both international and local, can arrange such placements, often in conjunction with a homestay to maximise exposure to the language. One of the cheapest options for Americans who want to study French is to head for Québec in Canada: for instance, Language Studies Canada in Montréal (www.lsc-canada.com).

As in the UK, agents in the USA and Canada make it easier for North Americans to find and book a suitable language course. An effective search engine for locating courses is provided by the Institute of International Education on www.iiepassport.org, which makes it easy to search by country and programme. Other recommended sites include www.worldwide.edu, www.languagesabroad.com, and www.studyabroad.com.

SPORT AND LEADERSHIP COURSES

Few better ways exist of shaking out the cobwebs than to learn to sail, climb, or lead trekkers, during a gap year later in life. It is often difficult to master a sport or make significant improvements if you can only dabble in it during your free time and brief holidays. Concentrating over an extended period may allow you to gain useful qualifications for future use, such as a PADI diving certificate, a Yachtmaster sailing qualification, or a Mountain Leadership course. Longer courses leading to a National Vocational Qualification (NVQ) are available in adventure sports and expedition leadership, which might be of interest if you are considering changing professional direction.

If you would like to do a sports course with a view to working abroad, you might be interested in courses offered by Flying Fish (www.flyingfishonline.com; see Directory entry), or one of the other training specialists. A gap year with Flying Fish starts with a course, leading to a qualification as a sail, surf or windsurf instructor, yacht skipper, divemaster or dive instructor, or ski or snowboard instructor. A typical three-month course involves three or four weeks of sports training in Cowes on the Isle of Wight, followed by a work experience placement (eight weeks on average) in the UK, Australia, or Greece. Trainees can seek advice from a Flying Fish careers adviser to find paid work too. The topic of sailing, including crewing on yachts, is covered in Part 7: Travel and Adventure.

SAIL AND DIVE TRAINING

Several training organisations specialise in preparing people for undertaking some serious sailing or watersports. A leader in the field is the UK Sailing Academy, whose range of watersports courses extends to three and four months, and which offers an on-site careers service used by more than 700 companies looking to recruit instructors. Course details are available from UKSA, also based in Cowes on the Isle of Wight (01983 294941; www.uksa.org). Qualifying as a Yachtmaster does not come cheap: the UKSA fee for the 12-week course is £7,800.

Diving in an exotic location is another option that may appeal. Check www.divesitedirectory. co.uk for links to diving sites worldwide. A random sampling of possibilities includes:

- **Dive Indeep Co. Ltd**, Koh Samui, Thailand (+66 772 30155; www.diveindeep.com). PADI Scuba Diving Courses from beginner to divemaster, which is taught as an apprenticeship.
- **PJ Scuba**, Mermaids Group, Jomtien, Pattaya, Thailand (www.learn-in-asia.com). Internship programme for Learn in Asia Dive Internships Co Ltd.
- **Sportforce**, London SW6 (020 7384 3028; www.sportforce.org). Fast-track divemaster training in Dahab, Egypt, for PADI divers. £1,455 for four weeks to £2,215 for six weeks.
- **Rich Coast Diving**, Playas del Coco, Costa Rica (www.richcoastdiving.com). Dive training at all levels on the Pacific coast.

- **Scuba World Philippines** (www.scubaworld.com.ph). Dive centres throughout the Philippines, with scuba career training programmes.
- **Subway Watersports**, Turquoise Bay Resort, Roatan, Bay Islands, Honduras, Central America (www.subwaywatersports.com/Courses/internship). Internship working in a dive shop while training towards a professional PADI Divemaster. Cost is approximately $1,350 for four weeks; $1,950 for six weeks; $2,490 for eight weeks.
- **Ticket to Ride Ltd** (020 8788 8668; www.ttride.com). Surfing gap years, including for career breakers in South Africa, Mozambique, and Costa Rica, plus kitesurfing courses in Kenya. A ten-week programme includes some volunteering in community projects; cost is $8,475.

Many dive shops operate an internship programme whereby dive trainees receive subsidised or free accommodation and/or instruction, in exchange for general help in the shop, filling tanks, and so on. This is an excellent scheme for people who have obtained their PADI Open Water Certificate (which can be done in a week) and are aiming for the Divemaster qualification. **Helen Tirebuck** took advantage of such a scheme at one of the dive shops in Playas del Coco, on the west coast of Costa Rica:

Leaving a good, secure office job in the UK for a vague plan of becoming a dive master in Costa Rica certainly raised some eyebrows! I was determined to go to a Spanish-speaking country and wanted somewhere hot! I first started diving in 1998, but was basically a once-a-year holiday diver. I already had my qualification as an advanced open water diver but needed to gain my rescue qualification, which I did within two weeks of arriving, then started my internship to get my Divemaster straight afterwards. The deal is I work for free for them for three months, and in exchange I receive training and a scuba diving qualification – which will allow me to work guiding scuba dives and assisting in courses.

SNOW SPORTS

A surprising number of UK companies specialise in running intensive courses for aspiring ski and snowboard instructors, many of them for pre- and post-university gap year students. As in the case of many of the gap year agencies, some have recently started to target older clients: for example, the Basecamp Group offers a course geared towards 'sabbatical' clients, which is going strong and attracts dozens of career-break clients – mostly from the IT, financial, legal and medical professions. Nonstop Ski & Snowboard markets to career breakers more than the gap year market, and claims that half of their clients are on sabbatical breaks or looking for a career change or time out.

Among the other companies listed in the Directory offering snow sports training for recreation or for qualifications, see Flying Fish, International Academy, Peak Leaders, and the Warren Smith Ski Academy. As for the British Association of Snowsport Instructors, BASI runs training and grading courses throughout the year in alpine skiing, snowboarding, Telemark, Nordic and Adaptive; details from the office in Inverness-shire (01479 861717; www.basi.org.uk). The most junior instructor's qualification is a Level 1, which is awarded by BASI after a five-day foundation course. Courses take place throughout the season and also on glaciers in the Alps in the summer. At age 34, **Wayne Beba** thought he was a bit young for a midlife crisis but knew that he needed a new challenge:

After researching various companies, NONSTOP came out as a clear winner for me, particularly as they were happy to accommodate my wife as well and they were the only one using all three Banff ski areas. As well as making great new friends, I gained my CSIA Level 1 and 2 qualifications. Highlights were the snowmobiling trips and the many other extra activities enjoyed. Thanks to the course I'm now back in Banff working as an instructor.

Peakleaders also attracts older clients. For example, **Diane Freer** had worked in the insurance and re-insurance industry for 25 years before deciding to take six months off – the first three months of which were with Peakleaders in the Canadian resort of Whistler. She chose Whistler because it is consistently ranked in the top ten ski resorts in the world, and after comparing hours of instruction, standard of accommodation, etc, she chose Peakleaders (at her age she definitely wanted her own room). She passed her Level 1, although when she arrived she had only about two weeks of experience on skis.

ADVENTURE TRAINING

Experience or training in adventure sports can open many doors. Even if a career change is not on the agenda, leadership training can be put to good use during vacation time. The website www.bluedome.co.uk has information about useful outdoor qualifications, including the Walking Group Leader and Mountain Leader Awards, as overseen by Mountain Leader Training (www.mlte.org). An all-round adventure instructor course lasting ten weeks has been developed by Dunolly Adventure Outdoors in Aberfeldy, Scotland (www.dunollyadventures.co.uk), which costs £4,495 inclusive of board and lodging.

World Challenge Expeditions (01494 427600; leaderinfo@world-challenge.co.uk) is a long-established schools expedition company, taking on several hundred overseas expedition leaders for at least a month of the summer to lead groups of young people to places like Bolivia, Zambia and Borneo. Leaders, who must be over 24 and have a Mountain Leader or Walking Group Leader (WGL) award, have their expenses covered for the duration of the expedition plus a fee. Training courses are organised through WCE's Leadership and Development Centre in the Peak District.

Opportunities exist closer to home as well. For example, PGL Travel (www.pgl.co.uk/recruitment) offers training and work opportunities to people who want to work in the outdoors either in the UK or France, especially as kayak, canoeing, and sailing instructors. The long-established charity HF Holidays (www.hfholidays.co.uk) owns 19 country house hotels in scenic locations around the British Isles, where guests enjoy a walking and social programme. Voluntary walks leaders are chosen after an assessment course held in the Lake District in the spring; ring 01768 899988 for details.

MY GROWN-UP GAP YEAR: GEMMA WHITEHOUSE

Gemma had been working for KPMG, managing graduate re-cruitment marketing for the southern region for a few years, and had just completed a part-time Masters degree in market-ing. Despite these achievements she felt that something was missing, and thought it was time to use her skills in a totally different way and take time out to reflect.

When I told KPMG that I wanted to take some months to do volunteer work in Africa they offered to keep my job open for me. Although I decided not to take them up on this offer I was pleasantly surprised that they had a policy that supported staff taking career breaks. My friends, parents, and husband were all supportive and this made all the difference. I spent three months working with an African organisation, which is responsible for the world's first lion breeding/release project in Zimbabwe. The project aims to address the massively decreasing number of lions on that continent and offer a solution to re-populate the National Parks and Game Reserves all over Africa. I offered to help them market this project in order to generate funds. I also got involved in looking at the marketing for other volunteer programmes they had initiated, to help deprived communities throughout Africa.

As I was offering my marketing skills and not joining the programme for paying volunteers to work with the lions, all I had to pay for was my flight and personal expenses. I had the most amazing experience and feel it was one of the best decisions I have ever made. Working in a marketing capac-ity for something I felt passionately about was very motivating, and I came home with some incredible memories. The highlight was meeting Amanzi: a lion cub born during the time I was there, who was rejected by his mother and would have certainly died if he had not been removed and hand-reared. I was fortunate enough to be one of the people there to care for Amanzi. When I returned to the UK I set up an organisation offering other peo-ple incredible volunteer experiences in Africa, helping on wildlife conservation projects throughout the continent, as well as teaching and medical place-ments. This company is named Amanzi Travel.

PART 10

SPIRITUAL DEVELOPMENT

MOTIVATION
RETREATS
COMMUNITIES
RELIGIOUS PILGRIMAGES
SPIRITUAL TOURISM

MOTIVATION

Stress may not kill you, but it can stifle your inner life and shorten your actual life. Unfortunately, modern lifestyles don't allow much time for harmonising our minds and bodies, or listening to our inner voices. The usual remedy of a relaxing holiday in the sun is often insufficient to recharge the batteries for the increasing strains to which people in full-time employment are constantly subjected.

Small wonder then, that there is a growing trend among people of all types to take time out from their careers to 'find themselves'. Some prefer to be guided in the ways of self improvement, while others just seek the opportunity for the time and space to do their own thing. The growing demand for soul therapy, spiritual growth, personal development, or whatever you want to call it, has created a bewildering variety of options for the path to nirvana. As a measure of the rising demand, an increasing number of commercial travel companies are offering alternative holidays and spiritual enlightenment packages. The options given here are intended to represent the more traditional and less commercialised possibilities, many of which you can arrange independently.

RETREATS

The main point about a retreat is that it springs from a conscious decision to step out of your normal daily life, away from ego and daily responsibilities, to go on an inner spiritual journey. This does not necessarily mean having spiritual experiences (though many people do), but it is about refreshing yourself, re-ordering your priorities, and making contact with your deeper self. It might be worth quoting here an iconoclastic view of retreats as expressed by *The Times* journalist **Matthew Parris**:

> *A vicar who came to stay told me he was shortly to go on a 'retreat'. I suggested he try an 'advance'. Why do people go on retreats? What is there to retreat from? Many of one's friends would benefit more from a rocket under them, than from moping dreamily around in a meditation centre for a week.*

WHAT KINDS OF RETREAT ARE THERE?

The range of options that might once have been limited to convents, monasteries, or ashrams, is now much wider and can take you as near or as far from home as you wish. Retreats can involve anything from Buddhism to gardening, and from communing with nature to timetabled lectures and seminars in a French convent, or American religious foundation.

Many people's idea of a retreat is probably one where you stay in a convent or monastery for a period of reflection and meditation. This has long been practised by Christians, especially Roman Catholics, as well as Buddhists and other religious groups. But you don't have to be a devout adherent of the particular religion to take part. Ignatian retreats, based on the spiritual exercises of the founder of the Jesuits, can last 30 days (though shorter durations are also common). These are directed retreats on a one-to-one basis, during which passages from the Gospels are chosen for daily contemplation and discussion. Seekers are led to review their lives in the light of the Gospels. Despite their religious origins, Ignatian spiritual retreats are available to anyone, religious or not. For further information contact The Retreat Association (see end of this chapter for contact details).

Among the best-known Christian retreat communities in the UK is Ampleforth Abbey, home to Benedictine monks (www.ampleforth-hpo.org.uk), which runs a programme of retreats throughout the year on different themes such as Art and Spirituality. Other well-known destinations are the Iona Community mentioned below and Mirfield, an Anglican monastic community in West Yorkshire (www.mirfield.org.uk). In France, the Taizé Community (www.taize.fr/en) invites adults over 30 and families with children to make Sunday-to-Sunday visits between March and October. Visitors may camp or stay in Taizé accommodation (prices €13–€25 a day), and participate in the three daily services plus Bible study.

Short retreats can be joined in countless places. To take just one example, *L'Ermitage Sainte Thérèse* is a convent in Lisieux, France, where pilgrims are welcome to book in. Mass is said daily and the teachings of St Theresa form the focus of the retreat. A retreat does not have to be bound to the belief system of a particular religion like Buddhism or Catholicism; it can be totally secular, as in mind-body-spirit retreats which deal with awareness and self-discovery. A considerable revival of interest in Celtic spirituality has taken place in recent years. Celtic retreats tend to focus on a sense of God present everywhere in the natural world.

The price of spiritual therapy can be very reasonable, but then a monastery or convent offers no frills or distractions. A typical charge for a week's full board is £200–£250; commercially-organised alternative holidays start at around £350 per week. Some organisations make no specified charge at all, but expect a voluntary contribution and help with the domestic chores. The time you can spend in such an arrangement should be negotiated with individual establishments. If you stay for several weeks and work for your keep, you will still normally be expected to make a token contribution of, say, £30–£50 per week.

BUDDHIST CENTRES

Buddhism has wide appeal to westerners, and many Buddhist centres in Europe welcome individuals interested in learning the fundamentals. The Throssel Hole Buddhist Abbey in Northumberland offers introductory weekend retreats once a month, as well as longer guided Zen retreats. Guests make a voluntary contribution towards their keep, which includes vegetarian meals. The association Buddhafield organises camping retreats in beautiful locations that cost about £200 for a week.

Other Buddhist centres in the UK that welcome guests include the Losang Dragpa Buddhist Centre in West Yorkshire; the Madhyamaka Centre, also in Yorkshire, which accepts visitors for a week or longer; and the Manjushri Mahayana Buddhist Centre in Cumbria, with no limit on length of stay. Most retreat centres operate a working guest programme whereby people can stay at reduced prices if they help with domestic and maintenance chores.

Sunnier climes can be even more life-enhancing, and the Guhyaloka Buddhist Centre in the mountains near Alicante in Spain is a peaceful place for a break. This full-time community dedicated to study, meditation, and work welcomes male visitors who want to spend a summer or winter retreat. Guests choose between a solitary retreat in one of the small chalets dotted around the nearby valley, or a working retreat.

With the dramatic rise in tourism to Thailand, Sri Lanka, and other Buddhist countries over the past decade, more and more Buddhist centres welcome western seekers for short or longer stays. Some offer very challenging experiences, such as the Vipassana meditation courses: typically ten days long, offered worldwide, and especially throughout India. Followers follow a strict regimen of silence and focus on nothing but the physical sensations of remaining still. For a vivid, and at times hilarious, account of a westerner who subjects herself to this discipline for ten days, see Sarah Macdonald's (rather shallow) book *Holy Cow: An Indian Adventure* (Broadway, 2004).

ASHRAMS

The trend for foreigners to stay in ashrams or Gandhian communities in India and Nepal has probably been given a huge boost by the 'Pray' part of *Eat Pray Love*; both book and movie. Needless to say, the depiction isn't very realistic. For a more accurate account of what it is like for a westerner visiting various ashrams, see the memoir *Yoga School Drop Out* by Lucy Edge (Ebury Press, 2005), who, as a burned out city professional, went in quest of healing in India. Her book balances descriptions of the scams and the committed.

Ashrams, gurus, and yoga schools offer teaching in every conceivable Hindu discipline, including *hatha* yoga, mantra, meditation, study of the scriptures, or a combination. Ashrams vary greatly: rich and poor, modern and urbanised, humble and rustic. A few are even located in caves. Each ashram has a guru (leader) or ashram-in-charge, whose personal style is crucial in determining the atmosphere of the ashram and whether or not you will find it sympathetic. Some have a fixed price for a stay; others request donations.

YOGA

Yoga can give you a whole new outlook on life as it works equally on the mind, body, and spirit. Although many people use yoga simply as a way of staying fit instead of reaping its metaphysical benefits, others get interested in the spiritual aspect and want to explore more deeply. The obvious answer is to take a career break and book a place on a spiritual retreat at an ashram in India. Others get interested after they have travelled in a country where it is practised. Since discovering Sri Lanka on a turtle conservation project, **Sarah Spiller** became very interested in Buddhism and yoga. Practising both in Sri Lanka and London, she (almost) mastered standing on her head and will have plenty of opportunities to develop her practice since she has bought a holiday house in Sri Lanka.

Yoga teacher Ruth White of the Ruth White Yoga Centre has been running an annual yoga retreat (one to three weeks) in spring, on the Aegean island of Lesbos for many years. The syllabus is validated by the yoga governing body in the UK, the British Wheel of Yoga.

COMMUNITIES

Many communities (previously referred to as communes) welcome foreign visitors who share their values. Sometimes a small charge is made for a short stay, or the opportunity given to work in exchange for hospitality. The details and possible fees must be established on a case-by-case basis.

Rob Abblett from Leicester is someone who has over the years taken dozens of breaks in communities around the world:

> *I've visited, worked, and had many varied experiences on over 30 communes around the world. I like them because they are so varied and full of interesting people, usually with alternative ideas and beliefs, but also because I almost always find someone that I can really connect with – for sometimes I need to be with like-minded folk.*

Before arranging a longish stay in a community, consider whether or not you will find such an environment congenial. Some are very radical or esoteric in their practices, so find out as much as you can before planning to stay for any period of time. Most communards are non-smoking vegetarians and living conditions may be primitive by some people's standards.

Shorter stays in more distant places can be readily arranged. Many communities are engaged in special projects, which may coincide with your interests. For example, the long-established Christian Corrymeela Community in County Antrim (www.corrymeela.org) works for reconciliation between Protestants and Catholics in Northern Ireland.

Many well-known communes in the world welcome visitors: for example, *Stifelsen Stjärnsund* is located amongst the forests, lakes, and hills of central Sweden. Founded in 1984, the community is working towards an holistic view of life, with the aim of encouraging personal, social, and spiritual development in an ecologically-sustainable environment. It operates an international working guest programme (which is quite restricted as of late 2010). Carpenters, builders, trained gardeners, and cooks are welcome to enquire. In Denmark the Svanholm Community consists of 120 people, including lots of children. Numbers are swelled in the summer, when more volunteers (EU nationals only) arrive to help for at least a month with the harvest of the organic produce and other tasks. Guests work 30–40 hours a week for food and simple lodging.

One of the most famous utopian communities is Auroville (www.auroville.org) near Pondicherry in the South Indian state of Tamil Nadu, whose ambition is nothing less than 'to realise human unity'. Unfortunately it became the subject of allegations of child abuse a couple of years ago, and its Volunteering, Internships & Study (AVIS) Programme has been suspended, possibly to resume in 2011. Participants in the scheme in the past have worked to reclaim land and produce food, and are charged up to $20+ a day for board and lodging.

An excellent way of networking with like-minded people interested in communal living is to attend a Rainbow Gathering, which are temporary outdoor intentional communities promoting peace and harmony.

CONTACTS AND RESOURCES

■ *Diggers and Dreamers: The Guide to Communal Living* published by Edge of Time, BCM Edge, London WC1N 3XX (029 8133 1451; www.edgeoftime.co.uk). The 2008/9 edition contains a listing of communities in the UK.

■ *Eurotopia: Directory of Intentional Communities and Ecovillages in Europe*, (Utopian Studies, 2009 edition in German only).

■ *Fellowship for Intentional Community*, Main Office (at Sandhill Farm in Missouri), RR 1 Box 156-W, Rutledge MO 63563-9720 (+1 660 883 5545; www.directory.ic.org). Publishes *Communities Directory: A Comprehensive Guide to Intentional Communities and Co-operative Living* (2010). It lists about 1,000 communities in the US and 250 abroad, including 'eco-villages, rural land trusts, co-housing groups, kibbutzim, student co-ops, organic farms, monasteries, urban artist collectives, rural communes, and Catholic Worker houses'. Much of the information is available on their website.

■ *Global Ecovillage Network (GEN)*, (info@gen-europe.org; www.gen-europe.org). GEN functions as the umbrella organisation for a wide range of intentional communities and eco-villages all over the world, many of whom welcome guests and volunteers.

■ *Stifelsen Stjärnsund*, Bruksallén 16, 77071 Stjärnsund, Sweden (+46 225 80001; www.frid.nu/english.htm). Community that occasionally welcomes working guests, who must make a small contribution to their keep.

■ *Svanholm Community*, Visitors/Guest Group, Svanholm Gods, 4050 Skibby, Denmark (+45 4756 6670; www.svanholm.dk).

RELIGIOUS PILGRIMAGES

There are as many kinds of pilgrimages as there are faiths. Catholics, Protestants, Muslims, Hindus, and others all have their sacred shrines to which their followers make pilgrimages. Whether it is to Lourdes, Knock, or Mecca (the latter strictly only for Muslims on the Haj), Canterbury, or Varanasi, the experience of being a pilgrim may clear a path to God or constitute a voyage of the inner self towards some kind of healing integration.

SANTIAGO DE COMPOSTELA

Probably the most-publicised pilgrimage in western Europe takes place along a 500-mile route (*El Camino de Santiago*) through France and northern Spain, to the purported grave of St James the Apostle (Sant Iago to the Spanish). The name 'Compostela' comes from *campus stellae* (field of stars), named after a hermit who was attracted to the site of Sant Iago's resting place by starry visions, which reputedly preceded the rediscovery of his bones. A popular place of pilgrimage since the 9th century, it fell out of favour in recent, more secular times, but was revived and was given a spectacular boost in 1994 when the pope visited.

Pilgrims to Santiago are not all Catholic and many are not even religious, as the experience is individual and meaningful for those of all faiths or none. About a third of pilgrims are Spanish and the rest are foreigners. The true pilgrim covers the entire route on foot, which is a gruelling lesson in humility and blisters and takes at least three weeks. But many people content themselves with doing just a section of the route, or cover some of it by car or public transport which serves some of the towns en route.

Pilgrims can sleep out under the stars or stay in pilgrim hostels, many of which are in historic old buildings where cheap or even free simple accommodation is provided in dormitories. If you walk the route in autumn you may be able to sustain yourself in authentic pilgrim style on the bounty of nature garnered en route: walnuts, figs, chestnuts, apples, and mushrooms are just part of the fare that can be picked wild. A classic modern account of the pilgrimage from Paris to Santiago, *The Pilgrimage to Santiago* by Edwin Mullins (Readers Union, 1975), is essential reading, as is a guide to the walk and *refugios* such as *Walking the Camino de Santiago* by Davies and Cole (Pili Pala Press, 2009).

The account of a Canadian (Anglican, bureaucrat, obscurantist) who walked 756km of the Camino is worth exploring on the site of a UK-based Christian webzine www.ship-of-fools.com/mystery/specials/camino/intro. Some of the conclusions he draws from the experience were that, 'Time spent watching the sky is well spent', whereas 'Staff meetings are blasphemous wastes of time'. He identified what was perhaps the greatest change from everyday life: that you enter a world of few choices. He was intrigued by the range of people he met on the route:

Everyone on this ancient trail has their own reasons: in mediaeval times, walking to the tomb of the Apostle James was often prescribed as a penance. Of the 100 or so pilgrims I spoke with, I heard everything possible: thanksgiving for recovery from cancer, an exploration or pause for a new life following a divorce or a spouse's death, fulfillment of a vow, a respite from a period of stress. And I met those who had heard of it, quite by happenstance, and started walking.

INDIA

Many westerners are attracted by Eastern faiths, particularly in India where the Hindu religion dominates. Among the most sacred Hindu shrines are the cave at Amarnath in (terrorist-affected) Kashmir, the all-year shrines at Ayodhya, Gaya, and Varanasi in Uttar Pradesh, and the summer-only shrine at Badrinath. You can also visit Dwarka in Gujarat all year round. Kurukshe-tra in Haryana is a popular destination for viewing eclipses of the sun or moon, and Gangasagar Mela in West Bengal can be visited in January or February. In Sri Lanka, April is the favourite time of year for climbing Adam's Peak (Sri Pada), which can easily be done in a day. The biggest spiritual festival on earth is said to be the Kumbh Mela, which takes place every three years on the banks of the Ganges, attracting up to 60 million pilgrims.

Although these sites are sacred mainly to Hindus, westerners are seldom prohibited from making a pilgrimage alongside believers just for the spectacle and sense of occasion. The more serious seeker after enlightenment may want to find a teacher (guru) or holy man (sad-dhu) in the vicinity of a temple or shrine. Saddhus are often rather alarming in appearance: unwashed, ash-smeared, unshaven, with matted dreadlocked hair, wearing only a loincloth and with coloured markings on their forehead and bodies. However, there are plenty of bogus ones, so if they seem too keen to get their hands on your money or even your body, you should make excuses and leave. Genuine saddhus normally seek solitude and should be approached with respect and courtesy. Don't touch them under any circumstances, as you will defile their purity.

SPIRITUAL TOURISM

Travel companies are never slow to exploit a demand, and the hunger for spiritual enlightenment has already produced packaged products. One route to self-improvement might be with Skyros. Skyros offers a variety of holistic holidays and courses for a self-improvement sabbatical. People over 21, preferably with experience of nursing, catering, or maintenance, may be eligible to become 'work scholars' at the holistic holiday centre on the Greek island of Skyros in the northern Aegean. In exchange for basic duties, work scholars are given full board and accommodation and a weekly allowance of £50. The minimum stay is three months, from April or July. The main perk is that workers are allowed to participate in one of the 250 courses and workshops on offer, including windsurfing, music, ikon painting, feng shui, and yoga. Skyros also has centres in Havana (Cuba) for salsa and the island of Koh Chang (Thailand) where the courses include an introduction to Thai culture, meditation and pilates. Details are available from Skyros (www.skyros.com). One past work scholar, **Sinead**, is quoted on their website:

I wanted to take some time out, career-wise, to do something different, and being a work scholar has facilitated this. I have met incredible people, both colleagues and participants, and been able to participate on a daily basis on a variety of self-development courses. A truly wonderful experience.

Religious organisations have often been canny when it comes to free enterprise. In the Middle Ages this usually took the form of selling indulgences. Nowadays you can go on a religious holiday, which may or may not contribute to remission of your sins. The ecumenical Christian Iona Community maintains a resident community on the Isle of Iona in the Hebrides. Visitors can share in the common life, at the Abbey or in the more modern MacLeod Centre, with a week's programme costing £286 per person in the summer season. There is an access fund for those on low incomes. The Iona community also accepts volunteers to help with many different duties, normally for periods of at least six weeks. The season runs from March to October. Details of all the above are available on their website: www.iona.org.uk.

If your requirements are for something older than Christianity, then you can search for enlightenment amongst the oldest sciences of ancient civilisations, which are mainly of the holistic and herbal medicine variety. These include *Ayurveda* from India, *reiki*, and *tui na* (a healing art of Chinese massage). Many other healing techniques can be used to minister to the mind-body-spirit. Neal's Yard Agency distributes a free quarterly *Holiday & Events Guide*, listing green and holistic holidays.

Among the reasons that 54-year-old **Madeleine Wheare** from the Cotswolds decided to spend December to March 2010 mainly in Kerala, was that she had a strong feeling that she could not continue her personal journey without going to India. One of her main ambitions was to find out exactly what Ayurveda is all about, and whether it would solve some of her deep-seated health issues. Alongside the volunteer placement she had arranged, working with a charity that carries out social work among fishing villages, she undertook a 21-day course of Ayurvedic treatment, without really knowing all that it would entail. She discovered that in one given week, she would undergo three different sorts of treatment: Nasyam, Abyangham, and Kizhi every day for seven days. She hadn't appreciated that not all aspects are particularly pleasant: for example having boluses (muslin bags of brown rice boiled in a herbal decoction) and milk rubbed all over the body, to improve both skin and muscle condition. Nor did she realise the full extent of the time commitment (four hours a day):

The treatment hampered me in several ways. During this time I couldn't travel on weekends, so missed several outings with the other volunteers. I couldn't swim. I couldn't wash my hair for one whole week (yuck!) and I felt unwell for at least a week. I managed to work throughout, but struggled to put up with the discomfort levels and the other stresses of life. I wouldn't repeat this part of the experience.

Cortijo Romero has been organising year-round, personal development holistic and creative holidays in Spain for more than a dozen years, and offers a choice from holistic massage to the joy of communal singing. Many courses revolve around unlocking your hidden potential and finding your true self.

Emotional and even physical healing can come from sources other than retreats and holistic treatment. You could take a leaf out of St Francis of Assisi's book and find your ideal retreat communing with creatures. There are many who swear that swimming with dolphins or walking cheetahs in order to rehabilitate them to the African wild is a cure-all, especially for the emotionally dysfunctional and those suffering from depression. Living and working among less privileged people often has a spiritual dimension. Those who think that this might be their route to inner harmony should consider some of the voluntary opportunities canvassed throughout this book. **Nicholas Carbis**, a potter and deacon of the Russian Orthodox Church in Devon, spent six weeks at the Kitezh Community for orphans in western Russia through the Ecologia Youth Trust (see Directory entry), and describes how the experience fed his inner self:

When I first arrived at Kitezh it was like a beautiful painting, peaceful under a blanket of snow. I walked through the frost-hard compacted snow to share in the meditation exercises as the red sun crept through the silhouetted forest. Together, connecting with natural energy that warmed the circle of figures, flying without leaving the ground. Afterwards I would jog to the church to say some prayers, and I would pass the children in their circle preparing for the day. I have a picture of the Church alive with angels, waiting for the Easter procession lit by candles under paper wigwams. I would like to render down my thoughts of my time at Kitezh by giving two illustrations: while standing in the church of the monastery of Optina Pustyn, looking up at the beautiful icons and listening to the most lovely voices singing, I had a deep feeling of reverence. Later I had the same feeling of reverence standing in the middle of Kitezh, looking up at the most beautiful starlit night, listening to the nightingales sing. Life in Russia is hard, and the Community of Kitezh is burdened with many pressures. However, I believe it is the way Kitezh incorporates beauty and reverence into everyday life that enables people to have hope.

RELIGIOUS RETREATS

- **Buddhafield Retreats**, Trevince House, Hittisleigh, Exeter, Devon EX6 6LP (01647 24539; www.buddhafield.com). Meditation and Buddhism taught at festivals, fairs, and other events, as well as retreats in Devon and Somerset.
- **Guhyaloka Buddhist Retreat Centre**, Finca El Morer, Sella, Alicante 03579, Spain (+34 647 240791; www.guhyaloka.com). Summer or winter retreats for men only, at a centre in a remote valley of Spain.
- **Iona Community**, Iona Abbey or MacLeod Centre, Isle of Iona, Argyll PA76 6SN (01681 700404; ionacomm@iona.org.uk; www.iona.org.uk). £286 per person for a one-week stay, but 130 volunteer positions available between March and October for a minimum of six weeks.
- **Kadampa Buddhist Centres** (www.kadampa.org/en/centers). Links to meditation and retreat centres worldwide.
- **Kagyu Samye Ling Tibetan Centre** (01387 373232; admin@samyeling.org; www. samyeling.org). Tibetan monastery retreat near the River Esk in the Scottish borders. Weekend workshops cost £63. Volunteers with maintenance skills sometimes needed.
- **Krishnamurti Retreat**, Brockwood Park, Bramdean, Hampshire SO24 0LQ (01962 771 748; www.krishnamurticentre.org.uk). Study centre in peaceful countryside, with vegetarian cooking.
- **Losang Dragpa Buddhist Centre**, Dobroyd Castle, Pexwood Road, Todmorden, West Yorks. OL14 7JJ (01706 812247; www.losangdragpa.com). Working volunteers pay £40 per week.
- **Madhyamaka Buddhist Centre**, Kilnwick Percy Hall, Pocklington, York YO42 1UF (01759 304832; www.madhyamaka.org). Free meditation classes, three vegetarian meals a day, and dormitory accommodation, given in return for 35 hours of gardening, decorating, etc, per week alongside community residents. Retreats cost from £112 for a week; all meals included.
- **Manjushri Mahayana Buddhist Centre**, Conishead Priory, Ulverston, Cumbria LA12 9QQ (01229 584029; www.manjushri.org.uk). Free dormitory accommodation and meals in exchange for 35 hours of work a week.
- **Tara Buddhist Centre**, Ashe Hall, Ash Lane, Etwall, Derbyshire DE65 6HT (01283 732338; www.taracentre.org.uk). Working visitors get free board and lodging.
- **Throssel Hole Buddhist Abbey**, Carrshield, Hexham, Northumberland NE47 8AL (01434 345204; www.throssel.org.uk). Another Buddhist centre that welcomes visitors.

ALTERNATIVE HOLIDAYS AND TRAVEL COMPANIES

- **Bonhays Meditation and Retreats**, Bonhays Farm, Whitchurch Canonicorum, Dorset DT6 6RF (01297 489615; www.bonhays.co.uk). Non-religious retreats with spiritual guidance and support.
- **Spiritual Holidays & Retreats**, PO Box 96, Kingsbridge, Devon TQ8 8WR (0845 456 1007; www.spiritualholidays.com). Organises spiritual journeys to Bhutan, Nepal, India, Peru, etc. Also organises Wellbeing Weekend Retreats in the UK (www.wellbeingretreats. com).

SPIRITUAL DEVELOPMENT

SPIRITUAL TOURISM

■ **Cortijo Romero** (01494 765775; www.cortijo-romero.co.uk). Centre located in southern Spain, offering interesting range of alternative and personal development courses; typical cost is £580 per week.

■ **Neal's Yard Agency**. See below for contact details.

■ **Journeying**, 1 Westfields, Saffron Walden, Essex CB11 3DZ (01799 513750; www. journeying.co.uk). Ecumenical Christian walking pilgrimages around the British Isles, eg to the Hebrides, etc. Walking through mountains, island hopping, traditional music, and seashore worship.

■ **Retreats Beyond Dover**, c/o St Etheldreda's Church, 14 Ely Place, London EC1N 6RY (02476 315520; www.retreats.dircon.co.uk). Organises annual time-out-with-God retreat in Spain or Italy. Sample price £1,400 for ten days in Andalusia (October 2011).

■ **Pax Travel Ltd**, 152–156 Kentish Town Road, London NW1 9QB (020 7485 3003; www. paxtravel.co.uk). Organises pilgrimages for individuals to Rome, Santiago, Romania, etc.

■ **Skyros**, 9 Eastcliff Road, Shanklin, Isle of Wight PO37 6AA (01983 865566; www.skyros. com). UK office of Skyros Holistic Holidays.

■ **Soul Projects** (www.soulprojects.org). Spiritual volunteer expeditions in Guatemala for five, seven, or ten weeks.

■ **Tangney Tours**, Pilgrim House, Station Court, Borough Green, Kent TN15 8AF (01732 886666; www.tangney-tours.com). Office also in Lourdes. Organises retreats and stays at shrines, convents and monasteries.

CONTACTS AND PUBLICATIONS

■ **Body & Soul Escapes** by Caroline Sylge (Footprint Handbooks, 2007) has info on 450 spas, healing retreats, and yoga centres worldwide.

■ **The Good Retreat Guide** by Stafford Whiteaker (Rider Press, 2010). Over 500 secular and religious places are listed, ranging from cottages to castles, in Britain, Ireland, Spain, France, and further afield.

■ **The Retreat Association**, Kerridge House, 42 Woodside Close, Amersham Bucks HP6 5EF (01494 433004; www.retreats.org.uk). Group of Christian retreat centres which publishes *Retreats*, an annual guide to 200 retreats mostly in England, Scotland, and Ireland. You do not have to be a committed Christian, but must respect the rules.

■ **The Retreat Company** (www.theretreatcompany.com). One-stop resource and searchable database for all those seeking to take a retreat of any kind at home or abroad.

■ **Neal's Yard Agency**, BCM Neal's Yard, London WC1N 3XX (0844 888 5050; www. nealsyardagency.com). Gives independent advice on holistic, yoga, and alternative holidays in the UK and worldwide. Agency operates a booking service.

■ **British Wheel of Yoga**, 25 Jermyn St, Sleaford, Lincolnshire NG34 7RU (01529 306851; www.bwy.org.uk). Primarily deals with Yoga Centres in the UK, but can help provide contacts for studying at yoga centres in India. Membership (£25) includes a subscription to the quarterly magazine *Spectrum*, which deals with yoga issues worldwide.

■ **Ruth White Yoga Centre**, Lane House Farm, Milton Road, Shipton-under-Wychwood, Oxfordshire OX7 6BD (01993 831032; www.ruthwhiteyoga.com). Weekend yoga retreats around the UK, plus three-week yoga holiday in Greece every May.

PART 11

BACK TO NORMAL OR A CHANGE FOR LIFE?

COMING HOME
JOB-HUNTING AFTER A GAP YEAR
CHANGING DIRECTION
REVERSE CULTURE SHOCK

COMING HOME

The thrill of a grand project or adventure during a gap year will ultimately run its course and eventually the time off that has been negotiated will come to an end. With luck you will be anticipating many pleasures on re-entry. If you have been abroad for an extended period, you may have escaped homesickness but you might still be longing to be reunited with your family and friends, to visit your local pub for a pint and a bacon sandwich, to switch on Radio 4's *Today* programme or walk through a woodland in a gentle rain. These and many other compensations should help to alleviate the post-travel blues. In some cases the prospect of returning to a former career is too dismal to contemplate. There is nothing shameful in changing direction in midlife if you have discovered that your heart lies elsewhere. By the same token there is nothing shameful about returning to your old employer if that is what you choose to do. After all, that is what the majority of teachers, nurses, managers, computer geeks, etc, who take a gap year do.

Changing direction can take many forms. For four years **Helen Tirebuck** had enjoyed working for an Edinburgh charity before deciding to move south, where she quickly realised that London was not for her:

> *At the ripe old age of 29 I decided it was now or never, so handed in my notice and started looking for my next challenge – but this time somewhere overseas ... Following completion of my divemaster qualification, the whole experience in Costa Rica has overall been extremely positive for me. Having never considered diving as a career before, I am now contemplating going on to complete my instructor qualification. It's tempting to look at a job in the diving industry as a 'gap year' or beach bum lifestyle, but having now worked in the industry for the last three months it has shown me that it is indeed a thriving industry to be a part of.*
>
> *The experience so far has definitely spurred me on to not go back to the life I had before. I have always had itchy feet and loved travelling; now I have a real opportunity to combine that with gainful employment in some of the most incredible places in the world. Even if I don't work in scuba diving in the future, the experience I have had taking a break from my life in the UK has inspired me beyond belief. Having successfully completed my internship and had a great time in the process, I now feel even more passionate about staying true to that decision to make a shift in my life. I feel now, more than ever, that the world truly is my oyster.*

Returning to your old life can bring about a roller coaster of emotions. You are delighted to be reunited with your friends and family, but you are all at sea. They are all rooted in their busy workaday and social worlds, and you are the outsider. You don't want to turn into the Ancient Mariner, boring everyone to distraction with your tales of having seen the biggest albatross ever, or the funny little man who invited you back to his house on a Greek island. The longer you have been away, the more alienated you might feel from your past life. After three years on the road, **Lisa Lubin** was not thrilled about 'coming back home to this other reality, to boredom, to being on auto-pilot just coasting through life, to constant marketing and materialism'. On the other hand, **Christine and Mike Benson** were ready to come home after ten months of adventure. They were still in the honeymoon phase when they described their homecoming in November 2010:

> We arrived back into the States recently and can only comment on how salty the food is, how big the cars are, and how huge the portion sizes. We returned according to our own priorities, without anyone knowing. We surprised our friends and families for the Thanksgiving holiday, and they all freaked. Needless to say, that weekend was a whirlwind of events and emotions, and only after the holiday weekend have we had an opportunity to feel what it's like to really be back. And it feels normal. Sometimes it feels like we never left. Other times we wish we were still gone. But there is so much to do right now. Find jobs in a career that we want to pursue, move out of our family's house, and become the people we have decided we want to be while we were on our trip.

Everybody's experience of the post-gap year phase is different. **Lynne Earley** and her husband **Michael** had spent time volunteering at neighbouring schools in South Africa, arranged by people and places:

> Nothing could prepare me for all the emotions I felt when I returned home. Usually after a holiday I am ready to return, to get back to my bed and my comfort food. I didn't feel this when leaving Port Elizabeth after a month of volunteering. Of course I was pleased to be seeing my family and friends, but I felt different! It's all too easy to say the experience was 'life changing' – but it is more than that. To fit into life in a South African township seemed easy, and within days everything from wandering dogs to children playing with tyres seemed normal. Coming back to the UK and returning to my comfortable life was not so easy. Why not? I guess there is the comparison of my lifestyle to that of someone in the township, and everything seeming so inane. Why are people moaning about the weather and why do children say they don't like peas? I really wanted to get on my 'high horse' and say, 'you have no idea do you?' I think I may quickly lose friends using that method.
>
> Instead it was easier to name my feeling – grief. I felt numb and was looking for the friend-ly faces of the children and carers, but really knowing that they were not there. Remembering all the lovely memories is a good process, but the yearning of wanting to have them again is painful. I know that grief is a process – I am grieving for the loss of leaving the Emmanuel Care Centre, their spirit, the children. I can't look at photos easily or watch videos without becoming a bit emotional. I can't listen to the CD of local songs without a huge smile coming on my face. It is getting easier and my energies are now being channelled into raising money for Emmanuel.

RETURNING TO WORK

Returning to work after a lengthy career break is bound to be challenging. Your time away should have energised you and given you inspiration to make changes in your personal life and in the way you work. Ideally, the experiences you had while your career was on hold will not only have enhanced your appreciation of life and added to your professional versatility, but also equipped you with new skills.

These skills may not seem to have an obvious application in your department or office, but your experiences are bound to have boosted your self-confidence, improved your ability to think on your feet, handle a crisis, or persevere in the face of setbacks. If you have helped to build a medical centre in the Andes, taught English as a foreign language, trekked in the Himalayas, or made a temporary home in a foreign city, you will have pushed yourself in difficult circumstances beyond the safety of your daily routine. It is your job to sell this positive angle to your current and prospective employers.

Some people use a career break to sample alternative lifestyles, particularly if they aren't happy with the direction their professional lives are taking. In some cases people discover a new or better vocation. In others, the fantasy idly entertained while commuting to work may prove impractical or unsuitable. Their gap year may have brought about a process of disillusionment, which is not a bad thing in itself, since no one wants to build a future on illusions. It is always worth getting such things out of your system if you can. The result might be that an unrealistic ambition can now be put aside, leaving you to move on and rededicate yourself to your profession. After six months of travelling round-the-world, **Jane O'Beirne** and her partner **Mike Bleazard** flew home from Rio, mildly dreading the prospect of re-establishing themselves.

Jane had wrestled with the idea of making her career break into a career change. While on the road she had considered many alternatives to the law, from care work to opening a pasta restaurant. After a couple of months of combing the ads in the newspaper it became clear that without going back to do extensive retraining (eg, in physiotherapy), she would be eligible to apply only for relatively lowly administrative or care jobs, paying a third of what she had earned as a solicitor. So she enlisted with a legal temp agency near Cambridge and enjoyed a series of locums of short duration, which is an efficient way of sampling the working environments of potential permanent employers. Jane soon found full-time employment in the probate department of a small laid-back law firm, where hours were civilised, pressures few, and where 'billable hours' were not the motive force.

Mike was also faced with having to find another job on his return. He had kept in touch with various potential employers by email. However, while he was away, many high-level IT businesses had been forced to batten down the hatches in the current economic climate, and he could see no way in. He could have walked into a contract in London but was determined to find a job within cycling distance of home. After a few months he did so, and was content to be once again earning a steady income since he and Jane have now got a young son.

At a more private level, a gap year can act simply as a time for personal development. Priorities change with age. The successful career that seemed such a glittering prize in your youth may not seem so important in later life. Some careers begin to feel insatiable in their demands, in which case returning to work may require careful deliberation. How are you going to avoid the problems that plagued you before the gap? It may be a question of working fewer hours to spend more time with family. You may now want more time to enjoy interests outside work, or it may simply be a desire to take on less managerial responsibility to alleviate levels of stress. Before you return to work, evaluate the aspects of your working life that you might like to change. Have your career goals shifted?

The **Battye family** spent a marvellous six months volunteer teaching in a Thai village and exploring New Zealand together (see Part 8: Taking the Family). Re-integrating into life at home in the USA was not so easy:

The truth is our heads are still really whirling. Life will be different for us now as the result of our experiences during these travels. Part of the reason for this trip was to get out of the fishbowl, as it were, and think expansively about what we want our lives to be about. We explored the idea of John getting a teaching job overseas, Susan pursuing a career in writing (perhaps something relative to family travel), and moving our family to a community that we feel really great about. When I reflect on the impact of Thailand on our lives, I know that it was an important stepping stone; one that is continuing to propel us as we look at discovering who we are and how we can help.

On returning they moved to a progressive school in Virginia for a year, but decided New Hampshire was home after all and moved back at the end of the school year.

RETURNING TO YOUR OLD JOB

It is advisable to keep up some contact with a workplace during a career break and to demonstrate your ongoing commitment to return, to allay understandable doubts on the part of your employer that you will actually return from your adventure. Keeping yourself informed of staff and organisational changes will also prove beneficial on your return. Particularly in fields where change occurs at a rapid pace, efforts to remain abreast of changes will assist the process of returning to work. After cramming in a whole series of African and European adventures in the year off that **Ambrose Marsh** took with his family, he and his wife Leah returned to their medical jobs in British Columbia. As Chief of Staff at a busy hospital, Ambrose came home in July 2009 to looming cuts in the healthcare budget and much stress. His wife Leah writes:

All is settling, and we are back to work. It is strange, almost like that year never happened – which is not such a nice feeling. All the layers of work are still there, just as if we had never left. Hoping that once we organise our photos, we will get reconnected with the experience and begin to show our pics and tell our stories.

Some organisations that offer formal career breaks stress the importance for absent staff of keeping informed of any changes at work and their old department. Employees will probably want to stay in touch by email with colleagues or other freelancers in the field. Lots of companies and organisations produce staff newsletters, which you should make an effort to obtain so that a connection to the workplace is maintained during the absence – which will help the process of readjustment.

Some professions make provision for people who have taken a break for whatever reason (often maternity). For example, the Training & Development Agency for Schools (www.tda.gov.uk/Recruit) publishes lots of information on returning to teaching, and puts on a Return to Teaching Programme (0845 6000 993 or by emailing info@return2teach.tda.gov.uk).

Returning to work is bound to be a shock to the system, even if you have been away for only a few months. Rarely do absentees return to find that their bosses or colleagues harbour any resentment, though your return to work may unsettle new working relationships or fiefdoms that have developed during the break. In your absence, you may have gained a new line manager or managing director who has made significant changes to a corporate culture. Old colleagues may have left and new technology introduced. Adapting to change is the principal challenge to returning to the workplace. Former travelling routines like commuting by train will have to be revived and tolerated. Freelancers will have to re-learn the discipline of organising their time according to the requirements of clients.

Sometimes individuals expect to be treated like conquering heroes, but are in fact given a rather matter-of-fact or even frosty reception. A jocular 'you lucky bastard' can disguise a modicum of resentment and jealousy. These feelings are not inevitable but they may surface, as they did when **Ceri Evans** returned from a spell of living in Barcelona to take up her old job as a senior counsellor in a sexual health clinic. She hadn't expected to encounter hostility, but that is what she sensed among some colleagues in her department.

The period of adjustment may be painful at first, though it is bound to get easier. In all likelihood, the office or department has continued to function smoothly without you, as any organisation must. On your return you may even be a little irritated to see how well others have coped in your absence.

People who have enjoyed life-changing gap years find ways of staying connected to the communities that have taken root in their hearts. They may carry on fundraising, join a campaigning group, or simply stay in touch with friends made during a gap year.

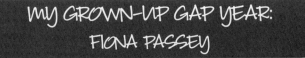

MY GROWN-UP GAP YEAR: FIONA PASSEY

Fiona describes herself as a young-at-heart 38-year-old (married, no kids, two cats, lives in Derbyshire) who is the sort of person who needs something to strive for. As soon as she obtained an MBA and completed a major project in the building society where she had risen to become Director of Offshore Banking, she turned to the internet to consider volunteering opportunities. She wrote from a rural village in Andhra Pradesh, India, part way through her four-month placement (and had to retype it on the computer three times because of the frequent power cuts).

In hindsight, many separate threads came together and culminated in my volunteering experience in India. Work-wise, I had just completed the sale of the business division that I managed for a regional building society. The sale process was exciting and incredibly hard work, but created a natural end to my nine-year career with the organisation. On a personal level, I sensed a change of direction. At 38, I had achieved many of the earlier goals I had set myself with regards to my career, most recently graduating from Warwick Business School with an MBA. I have a lovely home and a great marriage. I knew as soon as I took redundancy that I did not want to go straight back into the corporate world and the job market. It was a rare opportunity to refresh myself and take stock. My husband was amazing; he knew instinctively why I wanted to volunteer, and has supported me all the way. I think the hardship of volunteer life in a developing country is not as challenging as being the one left behind at home. We have promised each other that next time (yes there will be a next time), we will go together.

I decided to volunteer for four months during the summer of 2008. I found VESL on the web and liked what I read about them. The VESL selection day in London helped me make up my mind as Tom and Ian, VESL's co-founders, strike the right balance between the serious issues that volunteers face (poverty, AIDS, disease) with an acknowledgement that you are a volunteer who wants a great experience. When the offer came through, I cancelled all other applications and committed to the VESL teaching project.

For the first month, my volunteer partner Avni and I ran a summer school for local children, teaching spoken English and arts and crafts. For the next three months we taught English in local primary and secondary schools. We taught at four schools in the village which are desperately poor and short of teachers, so we were much in demand (you could send a busload of volunteers here). There have been so many great moments, but if I had to pick one it would be seeing the children's faces light up as they grasp something new for the first time, and the knowledge that in a small way you helped with their transformation. Teaching was a revelation in many ways. Firstly, it was a shock to learn how long it takes to prepare a good hour's lesson of spoken English when you have no props or blackboard. Secondly, I rediscovered my love for English literature - particularly creative writing and poetry. I think this came through in my teaching. Also I have come to understand how tiring teaching is, since to teach a good lesson demands a lot of you every minute. My respect for UK teachers has increased immensely, given they have the additional challenges of dealing with unmotivated and unruly children.

I am sure I will look back on this time in years to come as a special time in my life, when status and possessions were irrelevant; when kindness and being able to give to others made you richer than you ever felt possible. I have discovered new things about myself, as well as shedding some old doubts and fears. I think I will benefit for the rest of my life from this experience.

Then in November 2010 she added a post-script about the lingering effects of her gap year:

Before I left Andhra Pradesh, I had the chance to make a difference to some of the local women. Widowhood, particularly at an early age, is still stigmatised in rural India, with few women re-marrying - particularly those with children to raise. Many work in the rice fields all day for the equivalent of £1, and have no way out of this poverty trap. With the help of family, friends, and the parish church back in Derbyshire, I was able to set up Calves for Widows: a simple project that identified local women who wanted to raise a baby calf and create a second income stream from milk. Each calf cost £67, and once grown would produce £1's worth of milk a day. We also arranged insurance and free insemination. The day when the nine women came to the village with their new calves was one of the most inspiring of my whole experience. We all laughed and hugged whilst photos were taken, and even though we did not speak the same language, we communicated all the same.

I came back to the UK and the reality of job-hunting, but kept my India experience alive in two ways. I missed the children so I volunteered at our parish primary school. I had great fun doing things with the kids that I would never have done if I'd not been to India, such as teaching them some yoga. I also took classes in smallholding and horticulture at the local agricultural college, inspired by Indian village life.

I'm back in the corporate world now, but I keep a snow-dome that my India pupils gave me on my desk as a constant reminder of a very special trip.

JOB-HUNTING AFTER A GAP YEAR

If you need to look for a new job after a gap year, the technique will be the same as for any job search. The difference is that a career break means an interlude from formal work and therefore a gap on your CV, which will not necessarily be viewed in a positive light. However, if you can demonstrate that you have developed and acquired new skills as a result of the experience, a gap year can be seen as a strength and an advantage.

If you have volunteered in a relevant field, you may find your employability much improved. For example, **Phillip Elcombe** from Folkestone had finished a media degree, but had not been able to find the kind of work he wanted in the UK. With the help of the volunteer travel agency i-to-i, he joined a privately-owned and funded radio station in Accra, Ghana, which airs a variety of programmes including news, talk shows, music, and interviews with celebrities and politicians. Volunteers were expected to take a lot of initiative: bringing new ideas, styles of reporting, and giving a fresh perspective on local issues. He concluded at the end of his stint as a volunteer that his future career prospects had definitely been improved. In the aftermath of a bitter divorce 52-year-old **Anna Bisson** had fled to work in an orphanage in Mexico. She enjoyed the 15-week experience so much, and had gained enough confidence, to land a new job once she was back home, looking after children with disabilities.

Leaving a chronological gap on your CV will inevitably attract attention, so don't try to hide the fact that you've taken a gap year. There is no need to apologise or feel defensive about it. The time spent away will almost certainly have recharged your batteries and enhanced your employment prospects (unless you just sat at home and watched television). It might have also provided the impetus to attempt a step change.

After more than five years working as an engineer for Jaguar in the Midlands, **Matt Heywood** was ready for a long break. He also wanted to figure out whether to pursue a career in management on his return to normal paid life. Having chickened out of joining a Raleigh expedition before university, he now was impressed with what he learned from their website and thought that becoming a staff member on a three-month Raleigh expedition to build a school in Borneo would give him a competitive edge on his CV:

Whilst on expedition I have realised that there is a lot of satisfaction to be gained from developing people: not just products. As a result, I will be applying for managerial positions when I return to employment.

Career advisers and human resources people often say that a good CV can include some life experiences that may not relate directly to a job application. Often these unrelated activities demonstrate social skills, initiative, and breadth of interests. This is partly why students are urged to fill their time at college with a range of activities outside their formal degree studies.

THE OLDER JOB-SEEKER

With the recent proposals to raise the state pension age to 66 in 2020, we can all expect to work longer than our parents' generation did, mainly because we are living longer. Since the Employment Equality (Age) Regulations came into force in 2006, it has been illegal for employers to discriminate on the basis of age, in line with EU legislation, which reinforces the idea that the average working life will be extended. Rachel Krys of the Employers Forum on Age (www.efa.org.uk), which campaigns for diversity of ages in the workforce, teased out a relevant implication of these changes:

> *Given our ageing population, raising the pension age should come as no surprise. It does mean that flexible working practices, career breaks, part-time working, and job sharing can no longer be the preserve of the most enlightened employer – they have to become a reality for everyone in order to make working for longer palatable.*

If our working lives are being extended, why should a career break in our 40s or 50s present a problem for employers – particularly when skills are in short supply? Furthermore, a longer working life will save businesses millions in training and recruitment costs.

A return to work for women after raising a family may necessitate retraining or learning new skills. The major issues are childcare costs, loss of confidence, and lack of skills. By going back to work part-time, many women lose out on training opportunities open to full-time staff.

Specialist recruitment agencies in the Home Counties target older job-seekers or those returning to work after a break. For example, 40+ Recruitment Agency in Bicester, Oxfordshire (www.40plusrecruitment.co.uk), is geared to placing more mature candidates in positions at all levels, as is Forties People (020 7329 4044; www.fortiespeople.com), which specialises in admin and secretarial work for more mature candidates in London and Watford. Wiseowls in East London (www.wiseowls.co.uk) is a non-profit organisation providing an employment agency, educational website, and Business Start Up Initiative assistance for people over 45. Grey4gold.com is a free recruitment search service for executives with industry experience, looking for paid work in enterprises of all kinds.

Changing Direction (www.changingdirection.com) is a company dedicated to helping people to approach the workplace after a career break, especially women. As well as exploiting the resources of Job Centre Plus (the government job-finding service), you might be able to benefit from returning to the careers service of your old university. Institutions have different policies, but they are usually happy for an alumnus to make use of their resources. An increasingly-popular source of help is to consult a private career counsellor or life coach.

USEFUL WEBSITES

The ease with which recruitment websites can be updated and personalised makes them invaluable tools in providing up-to-date information, which can be quickly sorted according to preference. In these times of high unemployment and low growth in the economy, these sites carry fewer appealing vacancies than they did, though this situation should improve over the next few years. National newspapers like the *Guardian* and *The Times* have made a pitch for the jobs market, with entire sub-sections of their websites dedicated to this area. Note that you must now pay to access *The Times* website: £1 for a day; £2 for a week.

The internet offers a bewildering array of job-finding resources. Everywhere you look on the internet, potentially useful links can be found. Be aware that many seem to offer more than they can deliver and you may find that the number and range of jobs posted are disappointing. A surprising number of company home pages feature an icon you can click to find out about jobs with that company. Here is a brief selection of potentially useful sites.

- ■ ***www.rec.uk.com***. The Recruitment & Employment Confederation is the professional body representing recruitment agencies in the UK. Search the website for agencies in your field.

- ■ ***www.brookstreet.co.uk***. Brook Street is a UK-wide employment agency. Type in your postcode and the site will point you to the nearest office. There's also advice on compiling a CV, interview techniques, etc.

- ■ ***www.cityjobs.com***. Contains thousands of jobs, on behalf of clients who specialise in the finance, accountancy, and banking sectors.

- ■ ***jobs.guardian.co.uk***. Guardian Unlimited runs impressive job listings online. Particularly strong on public service, charity, and media jobs, the site also incorporates a special section for graduates.

- ■ ***www.JobsGoPublic.com***. A site aimed at public sector workers looking for employment in a range of fields, from museums and libraries, to nursing and midwifery.

- ■ ***www.manpower.co.uk***. Manpower is one of the UK's largest recruitment chains. On the site you can find current job listings, online training courses, and office addresses. The address of the international site is www.manpower.com.

- ■ ***www.monster.co.uk***. Lists thousands of jobs worldwide, and publishes advice on job hunting and preparing a CV.

- ■ ***www.prospects.ac.uk***. UK's official career site for graduates, maintained by the Higher Education Careers Services Unit in Manchester. Publishes huge amount of information for graduates and students in the UK.

- ■ ***www.realworldmagazine.com***. Mainly aimed at new graduates, though there is information of use to 'mature graduates'. It carries articles about various professional fields, including interviews with employees and advice on how to get hired.

- ■ ***www.workthing.com***. A free job site providing a searchable database of vacancies, editorial advice, information on training courses, and employment news.

MY GROWN-UP GAP YEAR: KATH MCGUIRE

Kath McGuire left her native Australia after university and ended up settling down in Cambridge, where she has lived for the past 11 years. While enjoying making a living from IT training and maths teaching, she had for years toyed with the idea of going off to seek adventure. Eventually the day arrived when she decided to go for it.

On Sunday the 11th of May I decided that now was the time for me to look at going overseas to do some volunteering. It's something I've wanted to do for a number of years, but every other time I've thought about it I've been more terrified than excited. This time was different. And while I still had moments of being terrified, I was so very, very excited and convinced that the right time had come to go for it. I did some internet research and found VESL, which looked like a fabulous organisation with some really fabulous projects, and Sri Lanka seemed like a really fabulous place to go.

I figured that doing a TEFL course could be quite a useful thing: brush up on my grammar and learn some techniques for teaching English. So I signed up for an online course with teflcorp.com. I had about six months to complete the units before going away.

Because I was headed for a project with a UK registered charity, I did fundraising for that part of it. My three-month teaching project cost £1,250, which included food and accommodation, insurance, training in the UK and in Sri Lanka – but not airfares. In order to help raise some money for my trip, and to reduce the amount of stuff to take with me or leave behind, I decided to sell most of my books and my other stuff. Anything that didn't get sold to kind family, friends, and readers of my website (www.kathmcguire.co.uk) went on eBay. Anything left after that went to Freecycle, or to a local charity shop.

The initial plan was to spend three months on a voluntary teaching placement, followed by six weeks of travelling. But I loved it so much that I did a further two three-month projects with more travelling in between. I stayed away for a year in total. Travelling and seeing the world is addictive, and it has changed the way I look at my own society and culture. For these reasons, when my first year ended I worked hard from January to July 2010 to earn enough money to do it all again – this time going overland from Cambridge to southern India, before flying to Sri Lanka.

There are too many highlights to mention. But the teaching has been so rewarding and so much fun, the people have been so loving and interesting and wonderful, and I have seen some wonderful places: Mt Everest base camp, sunrise over the Annapurna mountain range in Nepal, climbing Sri Pada in Sri Lanka. The list does go on.

There have been very few low points, though getting bitten by a dog last week that necessitated a course of rabies shots was no fun. Having my train ticket from Lanzhou in China to Lhasa Tibet fall through at the last moment was the most stressful thing that has happened. The travel sickness, dealing with tedious bureaucracy, the cultural exhaustion, the occasional loneliness, the scary traffic, being ripped off because I am white, etc, are things that are just part and parcel of travel, and throughout almost all of them I've kept a smile on my face. I have never regretted my choice to travel.

I don't think of my year abroad as a 'gap year'. For me, it was the start of my new life. I can't, I won't, and I don't want to go back to who I was before I went to Sri Lanka the first time. I have developed as a person. I have developed as a teacher. I have developed as a global citizen. Most importantly for me, I have had a lot of fun. I have had a smile on my face constantly for the past two years. I am happy. I am enjoying life. I am helping others. I am living life. I have never felt better.

CHANGING DIRECTION

A year spent away from professional life may be the prelude to larger, more permanent changes. You may have had an inkling that your old job was going nowhere or was causing dissatisfaction. A gap year may act as a stepping stone to leaving for good, even if that was not the original plan. Another scenario is that a break spent in another activity may have been so rewarding that it compels a re-evaluation of one's career path, which had once been taken for granted.

The charms of office life may have palled with distance. A career breaker met by the *Daily Telegraph* journalist Rosemary Behan (who took a gap year herself to travel the world) reported her motives for taking off to rough it in China:

> *I had bosses who made David Brent look competent. This has taught me that I have many options in life, and my time could be better used. I am going back to work as a freelance consultant, because I'm sick of working around people who sit behind a desk for eight hours a day, eat Mars bars for lunch, and don't even have time to look in the mirror to see how ill they look.*

Some career breaks are consciously taken at the outset as a way of forcing the pace; as a springboard for changing career. You may literally be returning to the first rung of a ladder. Of course skills learned in a former occupation will never leave you, even though you may be starting afresh in a new field. In some cases, it will mean modifying a previous experience, for example, applying a medical or legal qualification to a manufacturing, business, or commercial service.

Changing direction in life is often fraught with anxiety. However, taking a risk is sometimes necessary before reaching a certain goal. Cultural commentator Michael Bracewell, writing in the *Guardian* of a widely-held sense of entrapment in office life, puts it well: 'Whatever might lie beyond the office, from goat farming in Snowdonia to having that one idea which will make you worth more than Ikea, there is always that membrane of fear which keeps the bulk of us at our desks.' In an article in *Wanderlust* magazine of May 2009, **Catriona Carr** celebrates the new direction that volunteering with African Conservation Experience made possible subsequently:

> *I've always been interested in animal care, so I jumped at the chance to get hands-on experience in Africa. I spent a month at the Tuli Reserve in Botswana learning to track leopards and elephant. I'd sit in the tracker's seat on night drives, using a spotlight to look for eye reflections. Then on to Moholoholo Rehabilitation Centre in South Africa, which involved helping sick animals and drawing up plans to reintroduce them to the wild. I even gave physio to a vulture. Lastly to Shimongwe project, where I was working with the Big Five. I got to collar leopards, blood-test buffalo, and dart rhinos. The key thing throughout was being able to adapt. The projects reinforced my interest in animal welfare and spurred me on to apply for a job at Longleat Safari Park. I now work as a keeper, helping to educate the public about the animals there.*

A NEW CAREER IN DEVELOPMENT?

Some career breakers return from their travels or volunteer work in far-flung impoverished countries all fired up to carry on working in the field of international aid and development. They dream of living in exotic places, helping disadvantaged people to improve their lives, and getting paid for it. Working in development aid or disaster relief offers all these things. However, while many dream of such a career, only a chosen few actually manage to get a foothold in what has become a highly competitive and increasingly professional business.

A logical next step could be formal studies in international development. Some of the most well-established courses in the field are taught at the International Development Department of the University of Birmingham (IDD; 0121 414 5009; www.idd.bham.ac.uk), where several MSc programmes in development are on offer, which include overseas study visits.

After a six-month stint as a volunteer with Outreach International in Cambodia, **Dale Hurd** had made so many contacts that she intended to return in a private capacity, having used the agency placement as a stepping stone into the world of international development and longer-term humanitarian work. She says, 'Little did I know that my whole life would change in the most radical way'.

Till Bruckner has a great deal of experience in pursuing this trail, having travelled the world after university, funded by working in a bread factory in Wales, picking flowers in Cornwall, and so on. Over the past few years, he has gradually gained enough relevant experience with NGOs – for example, in Sudan – to land contracts with aid agencies that have seen him managing huge budgets, as he did on a contract to design a project for refugees in Georgia. Here he debunks some of the myths:

To understand why a few succeed where so many fail, it is best to look at what kind of people agencies like CARE, Oxfam, and Save the Children do not need. These fall into three categories: heroes, unskilled idealists, and people with skills that are available locally.

To take the first one, agencies do not need heroes. Many people believe that development work is in some way heroic, with western aid workers battling desert storms to get medicine to a relief camp in the nick of time. The truth is far more prosaic. The vast majority of relief and development work done by foreigners involves answering emails, writing reports, and attending boring meetings. The last thing a truck driver in a sandstorm needs is a foreigner giving smart advice, and the nightmare of every agency boss is an employee who jeopardises a whole programme by disregarding tight security restrictions. If you want to do heroic stuff, become a freelance journalist instead.

Secondly, agencies do not need unskilled idealists. Posters of aid agencies sometimes show good white people spoon-feeding starving African babies. In the real world, this never happens. Even if you offer to work for free, it makes much more sense for an agency to create much-needed employment by paying a local to do unskilled work. If you are an idealist and want to help poor people, get in touch with an agency in your home country and offer your services as a fundraising volunteer there. Alternatively, if you are in a poor country, just walk into an orphanage or nature park and ask if they can use some unpaid help.

The third group that agencies do not need, is people with skills that are available locally. Aid agencies exist to help poor people. Therefore, they will always hire car mechanics, forklift drivers, secretaries, and translators from inside the poor countries where they operate. Taking on a foreigner – even without any pay – to drive a truck in an African country makes no sense. It is far better to lift one more local person out of unemployment and poverty by giving him or her a job.

So what sort of people *are* aid agencies looking for? The best way to find out is to look at some of the websites listed below and see what skills are in demand. Generally speaking, agencies hire people with considerable technical skills and a few years of professional experience, including doctors, logisticians, accountants, and microfinance specialists. Most advertised vacancies will draw dozens, if not hundreds, of applications from qualified and experienced people. With no prior experience, unless you are a doctor and willing to work for free, it is nearly impossible to find a job this way. Most people working in development today originally started off far more informally. For example, many are former US Peace Corps volunteers, or hardcore travellers who somehow got a foot in the door while they were in a developing country. The majority began their careers as unpaid interns or volunteers, proved that they were capable of doing a good job, and then after some time started moving up the ladder and into administrative or managerial positions. However, even becoming an unpaid volunteer can be difficult. Volunteers create costs by taking up the time of their supervisors, and by requiring office space and computer access.

TILL BRUCKNER GOES ON TO SHARE HIS INSIGHTS INTO THE JOB HUNT.
So how do you find an international development organisation that suits you and convince it to give you a chance? Here's a step-by-step guide:

- **Think about what you can offer.** *One skill that is severely in demand in most countries is the ability to write coherent texts in flawless English. Development organisations produce an amazing amount of paperwork, much of which is produced by local staff with shaky English, and then has to be corrected or re-written by a native speaker. If you have good writing and editing skills, and you volunteer to subject yourself to the tedium of proofreading documents for half a year, there should be demand for your services. Alternatively, you could offer to teach English for free for a few hours a week, or give a course in writing skills. Also, think about special skills that you can offer. Maybe you could revamp an agency's computer system or layout publicity materials for free? If you are unsure about what agencies are looking for, just drop in on one, or take part in a training course for relief and development workers.*

- **Identify organisations you want to work for.** *In every poor country, there is some website directory listing most of the agencies working there with their activities in detail. If you cannot find this website, just ring the local office of any agency and ask them where to find the directory. Look for organisations whose work interests you. Do they work with children, farmers, refugees, or with the environment? Make a shortlist and then get the email address of the 'country director'. If necessary, phone the organisation to get it. An email to a general address is likely to get lost.*

- **Write a short email** *to the country director of each organisation you have chosen. State that you are interested in helping his/her work, and write precisely, identifying which problem you are proposing to solve for him/her, eg proofreading, training staff in specific software skills, language lessons, etc. If you have a professional-looking CV, attach it to your email.*

Make it clear that you expect little or no pay, but that in return, you would appreciate being able to learn about how international development works. Ask for a chance to meet and discuss your possible contribution. If you are already in your target country, you have a huge advantage. If not, state in your email that you will be visiting the country during a certain week in the future, and ask for an interview date then. Once you get a couple of positive replies, pack your bags and go! People are unlikely to take you on without having met you in person. Without a lot of initiative, you will never get a foot in the door.

■ **Be professional at the interview.** *If you get an interview, treat it like any job interview. Dress smart-casual (no tie). Have a copy of your CV with you. Make sure that you know in detail what the organisation does. Also remember that development aid has become big business. The person interviewing you is probably on a very good salary. If you save him/her time and money, it is perfectly acceptable to ask for what you will get in return, eg participation in training and workshops, remuneration for transport expenses, or even free accommodation. If the country director seems hesitant to commit to taking you on for a long time, offer to start by doing a week of free work with no strings attached. Once you have a foot in the door, it becomes easy to walk in. As elsewhere, most people are hired through word of mouth, and if you are good at getting things done, word will spread. Working part-time for two or three organisations at once can accelerate this process.*

Welcome to one of the most exhilarating, frustrating and challenging careers in the world!

People returning from conservation projects abroad often have the same impulse to change direction, as happened to **Richard Nimmo** in his early 30s:

For over ten years I had been working in London in sales and marketing for television and radio. I needed a break from a hectic and pressurised work life, and I also had a strong desire to take some time to see and work in a new environment, challenge myself, and make a positive contribution through a conservation project. My friends, family, and partner were all hugely supportive of the idea and my plans. This helped me make the decision to take a three-month break and join Blue Ventures' conservation expedition in Madagascar. Originally the break was intended to be two months – it turned into 16 months. My experiences as a volunteer in Andavadoaka with Blue Ventures and my travels in the rest of Madagascar were extraordinary. I decided that Madagascar was a place that I wanted to spend more time in. On returning to the UK in late May I applied for the position of Expedition Leader in Madagascar and was back working there in July, and since then I have been General Manager and now Managing Director of Blue Ventures in London. Living and working in a remote community with volunteers from many countries and local people gave me a huge sense of achievement, as we all contributed to a successful and award-winning marine project. Working and living in Madagascar was a wonderful experience that has given me a new focus and an impetus to work in a new sector. Seeing and travelling in another culture is always interesting, but to live in a different culture and work there gives you a deeper insight and understanding.

Blue Ventures has been built up into such an effective organisation that in November 2010 it won the top award in the volunteer tourism category at the Responsible Tourism Awards. The judges praised its efforts as an 'example of how social initiatives can … support community resilience in the face of upheaval'.

USEFUL WEBSITES FOR DEVELOPMENT WORK

Till Bruckner has provided this annotated list of resources on the web:

- **www.aidworkers.net**. Info for relief and aid workers.
- **www.bioforce.asso.fr**. French organisation that provides relief training and short courses with humanitarian experts.
- **www.bond.org.uk/jobs**. BOND stands for British Overseas NGOs for Development.
- **www.charityjob.co.uk**. Strong on administrative, fundraising, and finance jobs.
- **www.comminit.com/en/vacancy_listings**. The Communication Initiative Network, based in Victoria, Canada. Also information on relief training courses.
- **www.dotorgjobs.com**. Vacancies mainly in the US, so primarily of interest to Americans.
- **www.eldis.org/news/jobs.htm**. Based at the Institute of Development Studies (IDS) in Brighton; has useful links.
- **www.idealist.org**. Good for beginners. Idealist is an interactive site where organisations can post volunteer vacancies.
- **www.jobsincharities.co.uk**. Jobs in the UK.
- **www.reliefweb.int**. Lots of vacancies for professionals; good for checking out what is in demand.
- **www.sussex.ac.uk/careers**. Search for 'International Development' on the careers site of the University of Sussex. Other university careers websites can also be useful.
- **www.wse.org.uk**. World Service Enquiry of Christians Abroad offers one-to-one consultations for people of any faith or none, who are thinking of working overseas; consultation fees range from £80 to £240.

UNEXPECTEDLY DETAINED

A gap year may have an unavoidably life-changing effect, especially if it has involved exposure to new cultures, lifestyles, ways of working, and a different set of values. According to the 19th century aphorist and Harvard professor, Oliver Wendell Holmes, 'A mind that is stretched by a new experience can never go back to its old dimensions'.

In some cases the changes which a gap have brought about may be more than just psychological. Bachelors may have found partners, women may have found motherhood, and so on. Or the reverse may have happened: an earlier relationship may not have survived a separation or diverging goals, and you now find yourself free to form new attachments whether to new lovers, new cultures, or new pursuits. Perhaps you have fallen under the spell of Paris, Sydney, Rio, or the African veld, and have lost the urge to return to your roots.

The downside of an open-ended career break is the absence of security. Venturing through the game parks of Africa or learning to scuba dive on the Great Barrier Reef, is certainly more appealing to some if they know that they can return to normality by having a job to return to. For others, a clean break is the goal and any commitments back home would negate the mystique and catharsis of leaving old responsibilities behind.

MY GROWN-UP GAP YEAR:
KATE NELSON

Among the many strings to her business bow, Kate Nelson was a career break coach. After realising that she needed to make some changes to her hectic and stressful world, she took her own advice and organised a three-month 'gap' in southern Africa. That was four years ago and she is still there.

At the time of my self-analysis, I had just come through a difficult marriage break-up and was burned out after 20 years of 'hard labour' in the corporate IT market. Having reached my dream job of Sales and Marketing Director, I realised that whilst I was rich financially, I was poor in love, laughter, health, and spirit. A reminder that you must be careful what you wish for, in case it happens! I have always loved travelling, particularly in Africa, but my career meant that I had never had the opportunity for a gap year as so many students are fortunate enough to do today. Some 'me time' was well overdue.

I justified my own travels as a 'research trip' for my career-break business and left for a solo adventure around southern Africa. At the end of three months my return tickets and my watch were thrown into the braai fire with gay abandon, and on I stayed. After eight months I had fallen in love with the South African landscapes, wildlife, culture, and people, so made the decision that I wanted to live here for good.

I spent a fabulous month indulging my love of wildlife to qualify as a safari guide, before returning back to the UK to sell up my house and all my worldly possessions. Having just spent the best part of a year travelling through some very poor countries and surviving on just what would fit into my backpack, it really was a shock to come back to the materialistic world that I had previously lived in. I was appalled at how much clutter I had managed to accumulate over the years - eBay and car boot sales became a full-time occupation for four months whilst I awaited the sale of my house.

I returned to South Africa with the intention of working as a field guide on a game reserve, but fate intervened. I ended up meeting up with friends to watch the Rugby World Cup Final - and finally got together with a wonderful South African guy, with whom I had worked during my previous travels as a 'grown-up gapper'. Shortly thereafter Phil and I moved to a remote part of the Drakensberg Mountains and after 18 months here have established three guest farms, a bar/restaurant, and busy adventure trails business. You can take the girl out of corporate UK, but you can't take the ambition out of the girl!

We really do have the most idyllic life here in the mountains, and are so proud of the business that we have created from scratch. Life has come full circle and we are now in the position where we can offer others a career break of their own to assist us with the growth of our exciting adventure holiday business. If you love outdoor life and would like to help us out during summer months (and thereby escape the British winter), then we'd love to hear from you. Our holiday business focuses on hiking, horse riding, mountain biking, and river rafting (see www.wildmountainadventures.co.za). If there's one thing that I've learned over the last three years, it is that life is an adventure.

BECOMING SELF-EMPLOYED

For some people, being an employee suits their lifestyle and aspirations. They enjoy being part of a team in which the major decisions are taken by the boss. They feel that their contribution is sufficiently valued and financially rewarded, and they appreciate being able to leave professional worries in the office at 5.30pm every day and during four weeks of paid holiday. Whereas many employees feel that this leaves enough free time to pursue outside interests, others feel constrained by this regimen.

One means of taking greater control of your working life is to become self-employed which, in the eyes of the tax office, is the same thing as setting up a business, even though you simply want to deliver a service or product yourself without the worry and hassle of employing other people. Being a self-employed freelancer or consultant can be an economically efficient way of working because many expenses, like office equipment and business travel, can be set against tax.

Before deciding, it is advisable to speak to an accountant who specialises in working with the self-employed. Assess how your income is likely to change and whether you can expect to meet all your financial obligations. Above all, you will have maximum freedom to set your own working hours and holidays. The obvious drawback is that your income will be unreliable, and you will have to give up the company car, paid holidays, and pension contributions. A useful reference book here is *Go It Alone: The Streetwise Secrets of Self-Employment* by Geoff Burch (Capstone, 2003), or there are other more recent books which canvas all kinds of economic activity that can be conducted from home – many of which are concerned with self-employed activities like running a playgroup or bed and breakfast, through to practising complementary therapies. These guides provides you with all the hints and tips you might need if you are to make a success of it.

Some grown-up gap years are so inspiring that they spur the returning travellers to start a business based on their experiences. To take a couple of examples, **Laura Clarke** left a very successful job in London working for a top restaurant company to take a career break on the slopes and now, with her husband, met while skiing, runs a ski chalet business in the French Alps. **Tara Leaver** gave up being a Montessori teacher to travel in Central America, and came home with the idea of selling ethically-produced handicrafts online. The round-the-world travels of **Tessa Mills** taken at a crossroads in her life persuaded her that too many people are held back by fear and diffidence. She felt that if they could turn to someone like her to advise on how to construct a gap year, their reluctance could be overcome and their lives enhanced. So she set up her advisory business The Career Break Guru (www.careerbreakguru.com) to fill that hole in the market. When she set off, her main ambition had been simply to see the Taj Mahal. She could never have foreseen that nine months later she would return, itching to start her own business on the back of her adventures.

In April 2010 **Ricky Grice** left a lucrative job as a self-employed consultant in London to help develop the IT capabilities of a charity in Kenya, which led his life in an unexpected direction:

> I volunteered for a charity called SAFE (Sponsored Arts For Education) in Mombasa, which was arranged through 2Way Development in London. Although the three-month placement finished a few months back, I am still in Kenya starting a few businesses. I did look into jobs out here, but they were not that interesting, or well paid. So I've decided to go down the independent route, where I'll invest and assist in helping Kenyans start their own businesses. So far one company has started and produced a profit, while several others are in the research stage. The ideas range from equipment and marketing for a wannabe DJ, to raising pigs and mushrooms in a slum, to marketing and furnishing apartments to rent. My only requirements are that it will make money for both the Kenyans and myself, and that it is self-sustaining. I feel that this will allow me to stay in Mombasa and, almost accidentally, be more worthwhile than volunteering as it creates jobs. For example, the first project has created ten part-time jobs.

REVERSE CULTURE SHOCK

Before worrying about readjusting to the working world, you should be prepared for a certain level of disorientation on a personal level. Not everybody can be as upbeat as **Barbara Schick**, an Austrian photographer whose gap year was spent in Brazil travelling and volunteering: 'It was beautiful to be away for half a year, but just as beautiful to come back home to friends and work', though she goes on to confess that a year on, she was ready to leave again for a while.

Coming home from a stay away can engender reverse culture shock, especially if your gap year has included extended travels in the developing world. This can sometimes be worse than acclimatising to a different place because you are not prepared to feel differently about your old life. You may feel suffocated by the commercialism all around. Life at home may seem dull and routine at first, while the outlook of your colleagues, friends, and family can strike you as limited and parochial. You may find it difficult to bridge the gulf between you and your stay-at-home colleagues who (understandably) may feel a little threatened or belittled by your experiences.

Lisa Lubin describes her unease with American culture after returning from travelling and working her way around the world:

> More than ever, I now see how much we are bombarded with advertising and how wasteful we are as a society in general. We buy and throw away without a second thought. From paper towels to computers . . . we consume and throw away, fill up our landfills, rinse and repeat. I had felt all these aspects of the reverse culture shock – perhaps not all at once because I tried to 'stay away' or kept 'going away', even when I returned. In fact I am still living out of a bag, what's left of my belongings are still in storage pods, and I have not completely settled down yet. Perhaps this is my way of slowly coming back to reality or never really coming back to the same reality ever again. And I am just fine with that. Life is too short to do the same thing and then die. No thanks. I was lucky to 'slowly' integrate back into 'real life' and started working for myself. So since my life is a bit different, and I am more in control, the culture shock isn't so bad. Plus I fell in love upon return, which overshadowed a lot!

The process of shaking up your life is undoubtedly risky. The experience may leave you out of step with your social and professional circle at home. Even if you know that you are perfectly capable of settling back into your old life, you may not be willing, because too many of your views and values have changed to be comfortable. On the other hand you don't really have a choice, and will simply have to stop looking agog at your Starbuck's bill and telling everyone that this would pay for a week's travelling in India or a fortnight in Laos.

Joni Hillman vividly recalls her case of reverse culture shock after returning from being a volunteer in India:

I think being aware of how potentially difficult it will be to return home is the key. Give yourself time, or throw yourself into something. I moved house and started my Masters within ten days of arriving home. If you have seen horrific poverty or had conflict experiences, it can sometimes be really difficult to engage in a conversation with your oldest friends about seemingly trivial things like Eastenders! It can also be difficult to sum up your experiences in a couple of sentences, which is generally all people have got time for when they ask 'How was it?'. Keeping a diary is a good idea, because it can help you digest your experiences into manageable chunks for other people. And remember that they are invariably jealous of the wonderful experiences you have been gutsy enough to go out and find, while they waste their lives in offices.

This telling extract describes re-entry to normal life. It is taken from the final chapter 'An English Alien' of **Nigel Barley's** *The Innocent Anthropologist*, a superbly amusing account of the author's time spent researching the Dowayo tribe of the Cameroons (alas now out of print):

It is positively insulting how well the world functions without one. While the traveller has been away questioning his most basic assumptions, life has continued sweetly unruffled. Friends continue to collect matching French saucepans. The acacia at the foot of the lawn continues to come along nicely. The returning anthropologist does not expect a hero's welcome, but the casualness of some friends seems excessive. An hour after my arrival, I was phoned by one friend who merely remarked tersely, 'Look, I don't know where you've been but you left a pullover at my place nearly two years ago. When are you coming to collect it?' In vain one feels that such questions are beneath the concern of a returning prophet.

As Nigel Barley sees it, the sight of groaning supermarket shelves induces either revulsion or crippling indecisiveness. Polite conversation may seem temporarily impossible, but most returnees end up feeling overwhelming gratitude for having been born a westerner. Generally, the feelings of displacement and restlessness pass soon enough when the reverse culture shock wears off and you begin to feel reintegrated.

While at times it will seem that time has stood still during your absence, at others you may feel that you have missed important events while away: children are born, friends get married, couples part, neighbours move away, governments are voted out, radio presenters retire. Despite modern telecommunications making it much easier to keep abreast of these changes, there may be a feeling of alienation from your past.

One aspect that **Marcelle Salerno** found most difficult after one of her many adventures during her gap years, was the naïve generalisations some of her fellow Americans were prone to make:

Already I find it difficult to speak to people when they discuss 'world news' if I know they haven't seen anything of the world first-hand. After living with Muslims for a month in Morocco, I see the current political issues differently. After living with tribal Africans for six months, I see race in a whole different light.

Apart from social unease, you might have more immediate practical worries, such as where you will live. If you have a house or flat to return to, that should be no trouble, assuming the tenants or housesitters have looked after it adequately. But if you gave up your rented property or sold your house to take a career break, finding a place to live will be of primary concern. You can only camp out with friends for so long, though you will probably be welcome to stay longer with parents or siblings, at least to provide a base while you're house hunting. Casting yourself at the mercy of your parents again can be viewed in a positive light, as 30-something **Lucy Bailey** did after four wonderful months working at two different game lodges in Kenya with The Leap, though finding a stimulating job proved much more challenging in the short term:

> *I ended up going to live with my parents in Derbyshire for a few months (whom I get on with fantastically and which was actually a really lovely opportunity to be with them for a little while and get to know them again!), and did some temping to keep the wolf from the door before moving back down to London. I was a secretary for a company that made bespoke generators, located on an industrial estate on the outskirts of a really grim ex-mining town in rural Derbyshire! There was nothing to do at lunchtime apart from drive to the local gravel pit, where I'd sit in my car eating my ham butties, smoking cigarettes, and watching the giant rats scuttle in and out of the piles of burnt-out clothes and abandoned broken toilets. It was easily one of the worst jobs I've ever had, but certainly had comedy value, which is fortunate seeing as I do some comedy writing and performing and it's provided a great deal of material!*

If you have been away for a long time, consider throwing a party to let everyone know that you're home and available for a continuation of your former social life. But don't expect to slot back seamlessly. Be patient and gradually you will find common ground with friends and family. The physical trappings of your life may have changed too. The well-loved garden of a home you rented to strangers may have declined beyond recognition and years of hard work lost.

On the other hand, you may find that nothing much has changed at all, which can be equally alienating in its way. From having returned to her job in the law after six months spent in Cambodia, Japan and South America, **Polly Botsford** passes on what she learned about re-entry:

> *You just have to be realistic. If you think things are going to be different, then you are going to get very depressed. Time stands still – or so it seems. Your flat will look the same, your wardrobe will not have been revamped, and the tube strikes will still be going on. But in fact, much will have changed and happened without you; it just takes a bit longer to see the subtleties. If possible, plan to come back in the summer (always a little kinder). Get every photo into an album (or onto a web page, if that is how you are doing it) within a month or you'll never do it. Don't rely on staying in touch with fellow travellers as a way of keeping the experience alive. You have to move on. If you do develop fantastic new friendships then that's great but you can't force them.*

MY GROWN-UP GAP YEAR:
TESSA MILLS

After 26 years of marriage and a successful business partnership, 52-year-old Tessa Mills felt sure there was another world waiting for her, and so left the comforts of a sensible life for a journey that took her on the road less travelled.

I had been going to buy a house but I ended up going round the world instead, which came about through the most innocuous of sentences. When seeking advice about the possible purchase of a property, I was asked 'Do you like this house?' 'It's sensible and practical,' I replied; but as I said it I realised that buying a house wasn't REALLY what I wanted to do. Live a little, throw caution to the wind, do something adventurous, my family urged me.

I had recently waved off and welcomed back two children on their gap years. Why not me? I was at a gap and a new juncture in life. So many places to see, things I wanted to do. This really did seem a much more exciting, life-changing, and inspiring option. Then a thousand reasons suddenly occurred as to why I couldn't or shouldn't pack it all in and set off. But from somewhere a voice urged me on and encouraged me to continue to pursue this dream and opportunity.

Where would I go, what would I do? Explore India, do some conservation work in the rainforests of South America or Australia, spend time in Southeast Asia – all these appealed. And so I began to plan, and, as with anything big, I ate the elephant one bite at a time. Trips to travel agents, voluntary projects to research, luggage to buy, travel books to read: lots of little things to keep me focused and believing that I really was going.

As I now wasn't buying a house, I decided to stop renting my present flat and to use that money, along with some other savings from selling my business, to fund the adventure. It gave me an allowance of about £30 a day, which didn't quite cover everything but gave me a budget to work on. Obviously I spent more in Australia and New Zealand, but the dong, baht, and rupees went much further in Asia. Like anyone else, I succumbed to the occasional and very enjoyable extravagance. Jet boating in NZ, the occasional luxury accommodation, and one or a few 'souvenirs' that I couldn't resist.

Waved off by my daughters on a cold and snowy November morning, I settled a little apprehensively into my seat. There is something so thrilling about a plane as it hurtles down the runway, forcing you back in your seat. I knew I truly was off and away. The experience had begun.

I had hoped to do some work or a project on this trip and tried to find out about teaching, environmental projects, and voluntary work. In the event I didn't do any. During my nine months away I came to feel that this journey was not about saving others, or even the planet, but about saving me. And in more ways than one this journey certainly did rescue me. It was indeed a wonderful, inspiring, mesmerising adventure. It's not only the different and unique cultures that you become immersed in that are so rewarding, but the people and friends you meet along the way that are the memories you retain. Smells and sounds so different from those that are familiar, initially jar the senses but then become like comfortable companions.

I saw brown bears and Alaskan jade on remote islands off Vancouver where life is simple, real, and peaceful. I stayed with the grandchildren of some of the early European settlers, who now check their gold reserves on a computer whose batteries are charged by their own generators. I unexpectedly loved my time in Waikiki, where I 'hung loose' and exercised by joining a young Italian as he trained for the Hawaiian half marathon. Re-visiting Australia and New Zealand and catching up with old school friends was a time full of nostalgia and reminiscences. I had spent a year hitch-hiking in NZ as I left my teenage years behind. Despite the many changes and developments that I noticed, the rural idyll still remained even as the 21st century crept up around this gentle land. And a New Year celebration with old school friends beside the Sydney Harbour Bridge with a steak on the barbecue and a glass of champagne in your hand takes some beating.

I fell in love with Southeast Asia: the smiling faces of the Cambodians as I got lost amongst the ruins of Angkor Wat, and I loved the food of Vietnam so much I took cookery lessons. The love affair continued on into India, despite the fascination and frustrations as I travelled throughout its length. My two months there gave me a great depth and dimension in understanding this colourful and unique country. The dark-skinned southern

Indians with their highly colourful and decorated temples, and the buzzing night life in Mumbai where our evening's entertainment was paid for by two admiring Indians who were so impressed by our attempts at karaoke, and then north to the infinitely colourful and bewitching Rajasthan, a sunrise over the sublimely beautiful Taj Mahal, and even further north to the foothills of the snowy Himalayas.

Istanbul at the crossroads with Europe and Asia seemed surprisingly un-European, as I danced with the whirling dervishes there and headed west and homeward. It was only in Austria and Holland that I became aware of the effects of the European Union.

After such experiences, I knew life back in England would seem dull. Although inspired, invigorated, and empowered by my travels, I feared slipping back into the sensible, safe comfort zone of old. Fortunately a chance encounter with an inspirational businessman changed everything. He reminded me to continue to do in life only what I felt passionate about, and to make a Life and not a Living.

My nine months of travelling had given me a desire to keep pursuing my dream, and I was now thirsty to live life to the full. I began to see for myself a career and a life that I could be excited about. And so I started my new business in the travel industry, offering grown-ups a mentoring service to help them keep their dream alive as they plan their own grown-up gap year. For me it's a chance to give back and share with others my knowledge, enthusiasm, and passion for the world and all that it offers us.

And I still haven't bought a house - life is busy, inspiring and fulfilled.

INDEX OF ADVERTISERS

GAP YEARS FOR GROWN-UPS

INDEX OF ADVERTISERS

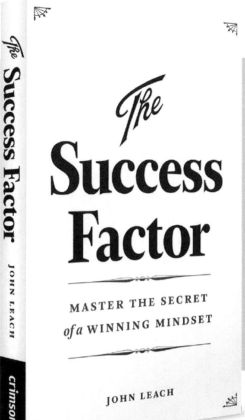